MATRIA REDUX

CARIBBEAN
STUDIES
SERIES

Anton L. Allahar and Natasha Barnes
Series Editors

MATRIA REDUX

CARIBBEAN WOMEN NOVELIZE THE PAST

TEGAN ZIMMERMAN

UNIVERSITY PRESS OF MISSISSIPPI / JACKSON

The University Press of Mississippi is the scholarly publishing agency of
the Mississippi Institutions of Higher Learning: Alcorn State University,
Delta State University, Jackson State University, Mississippi State University,
Mississippi University for Women, Mississippi Valley State University,
University of Mississippi, and University of Southern Mississippi.

www.upress.state.ms.us

The University Press of Mississippi is a member
of the Association of University Presses.

Any discriminatory or derogatory language or hate speech regarding race,
ethnicity, religion, sex, gender, class, national origin, age, or disability
that has been retained or appears in elided form is in no way an
endorsement of the use of such language outside a scholarly context.

Copyright © 2023 by University Press of Mississippi
All rights reserved
Manufactured in the United States of America

First printing 2023
∞

Library of Congress Cataloging-in-Publication Data

Names: Zimmerman, Tegan, author.
Title: Matria redux : Caribbean women novelize the past / Tegan Zimmerman.
Other titles: Caribbean studies series (Jackson, Miss.)
Description: Jackson : University Press of Mississippi, 2023. | Series:
Caribbean studies series | Includes bibliographical references and index.
Identifiers: LCCN 2023010353 (print) | LCCN 2023010354 (ebook) | ISBN
9781496846341 (hardback) | ISBN 9781496846358 (trade paperback) | ISBN
9781496846365 (epub) | ISBN 9781496846372 (epub) |
ISBN 9781496846389 (pdf) | ISBN 9781496846396 (pdf)
Subjects: LCSH: Caribbean literature—Women authors—History and criticism.
| Women authors, Caribbean. | Women and literature—Caribbean
Area—History. | Caribbean fiction—Women authors.
Classification: LCC PN849.C3 Z566 2023 (print) | LCC PN849.C3 (ebook) |
DDC 809.3/9928709729—dc23/eng/20230419
LC record available at https://lccn.loc.gov/2023010353
LC ebook record available at https://lccn.loc.gov/2023010354

British Library Cataloging-in-Publication Data available

CONTENTS

Acknowledgments vii

Introduction: Ex Matria 3

PART I: MYTHOLOGIZING MATRIA

Africa's Daughters: The Neo-Slavery Novel's
Caribbean Maternal Genealogy. 33

1 Maternal Genealogies and the Legacy of Nonhistory
in Dionne Brand's *At the Full and Change of the Moon* 43

2 Voice, Violence, and Masculine Suffocation
in Andrea Levy's *The Long Song* 65

PART II: DECOLONIZING MATRIA

Dispossessed Daughters: Searching for
Caribbean Mother-Land/Tongue 89

3 Maternal Conflicts, Coolitude, and Colonialism
in Jan Lowe Shinebourne's *The Last English Plantation* 103

4   *Matriz*, Transgressive Sexuality, and National Ambiguity
    in Judith Ortiz Cofer's *The Meaning of Consuelo* 123

PART III: REVOLUTIONIZING MATRIA

Politicized Mothers: Dreaming the Matria. 147

5   "Mother of the Rivers": Maternal Tropes
    in Edwidge Danticat's *The Farming of Bones*. 161

6   Revolutionary Herstory and Martial/Marital Law
    in Andrea O'Reilly Herrera's *The Pearl of the Antilles*. 179

PART IV: RETURNING MATRIA

Ancestral Mothers: The Caribbean Daughter's Homecoming 199

7   The Return of Daughterly Reincar(nation) and Rituals
    in Paule Marshall's *Praisesong for the Widow* 211

8   Cartography, *Hystérie*, and Matrilineage
    in Marie-Elena John's *Unburnable* 229

Conclusion: Matria Redux. 251

Notes. 257

Works Cited 263

Index. 277

ACKNOWLEDGMENTS

I would like to sincerely thank my family, friends, colleagues, and students for their encouragement, enthusiasm, and critical discussions. Our conversations were not only enriching but also fundamental in helping me realize this project. Specifically, I would like to thank Jairan Gahan, Peter Sabo, Alison Turner, Lori Hall-Araujo, Marta Heckel, Irina Sadovina, and David Buchanan for your feedback on drafts of various chapters. I am grateful to Lisa McMurtray for her support and guidance throughout the editorial process. I am also fortunate to have received advice and support from Claudy Op Den Kamp, Silvia Schultermandl, Alexandra Ganser, Pamela McCallum, Lorraine Markotic, Gertrude Postl, Tina Parke-Sutherland, Odile Ferly, Catherine Davies, Gill Rye, Kate Averis, Carrie Dawson, Marie Carrière, Ann McKinnon, Nora Bowman, Novella Nicchitta, Charlotte Hammond Matthews, Jocelyn Cullity, and Tatjana Takševa. I would also like to acknowledge the following institutions and organizations: the English Department at Dalhousie University and the Canadian Literature Centre at the University of Alberta for providing me with visiting scholar positions; the Centre for the Study of Contemporary Women's Writing at the University of London and the Northeast Modern Language Association for granting me research fellowships; the University of Vienna for awarding me the Visiting Käthe Leichter Professorship in Women's and Gender Studies (2018); and Okanagan College, Stephens College, and Saint Mary's University for additional funding to pursue my research.

MATRIA REDUX

INTRODUCTION

Ex Matria

This book formulates the postcolonial-psychoanalytic feminist theory of matria, an imagined maternal space and time, through reading fictions of history written by and about Caribbean women. Tracing the trajectory of the Caribbean woman's historical novel in four periods—slavery, colonialism, revolution, and decolonization—*Matria Redux* evidences the formation of a pan-Caribbean generation of women writers, of varying discursive racial(ized) realities, depicting similar matria constructs and maternal motifs such as mother-daughter bonds, genealogies, nonhistory, voice(lessness), herstory, trauma, return, and ritual. Put briefly, I read the Caribbean woman's historical novel as Dorrit Cohn does in the sense that first and foremost, the noun "novel" is that to which the adjective "historical" applies; this means that while history unequivocally informs or foregrounds the work, the text nevertheless maintains its status as fiction (162). Thus, to mark the rise of the Caribbean woman's historical novel, this comparative study applies the postcolonial-psychoanalytic feminist concept of matria to works from across the region, published in English between 1980 and 2010.

Although pairing postcolonial feminism with Caribbean women's writing is conventional, using psychoanalysis is not.[1] As Ranjana Khanna in *Dark Continents: Psychoanalysis and Colonialism* convincingly argues, "psychoanalysis is a colonial discipline" (6) with serious political implications.[2] Operating as a "civilizing mission ... [i]t brought into the world an idea of being that was dependent on colonial political and ontological relations, and through its disciplinary practices, formalized and perpetuated an idea of uncivilized, primitive, concealed, and timeless colonized peoples" (6). European colonialism, Khanna maintains, "situated itself, with fascination, in opposition to its repressed, concealed, and mysterious, 'dark continents': colonial Africa, women, and the primitive" (6). *Matria Redux* does not defend traditional psychoanalytic theories of either race and gender or the family but rather shows how radical mother-daughter countertexts can speak back to Freudian concepts and thus provoke new possibilities for psychoanalysis, Caribbean literary studies, and postcolonial feminist theory. Like Whitney Bly Edwards, I suggest that psychoanalysis "provides a fruitful area of possibility for reading Caribbean literature" and that certain texts, especially those exploring maternal themes, are "well-suited to [such] applications" (314). My work therefore advances matria as a distinct postcolonial-psychoanalytic feminist theory capable of rearticulating the Caribbean daughter's symbolic and/or literal break with the mother "not [just] in some utopian future or mythical . . . past but in a present . . . reality" (Davies 173) that encompasses different diasporas and (is)lands of the archipelago.

Matria Redux also acknowledges that using American-European scholarship on gender, which often assumes that "Caribbean feminist theory and action" derives from it (McDonald 52), warrants clarification. A significant part of postcolonial feminist intervention after all entails challenging Western ideology, for instance the notion of universal womanhood (Paravisini-Gebert, "Decolonizing Feminism" 7; Baksh-Soodeen 75). My approach to matria, however, shows that assessing and reevaluating the specific historical and material heterogeneities of Caribbean women's lives expands "the narrow, Western limits/terms of feminist discourse" (Boyce Davies and Savory Fido 17). As Patricia Mohammed argues, feminist perspectives, from both within and outside of the region, are critical in "interrogat[ing] the past" and in expressing "new challenges and opportunities to establish boundaries of identity and difference" ("Towards Indigenous Feminist Theorizing" 28). Thus, my work brings canonical conceptualizations of the region (e.g., Édouard Glissant) and psychoanalytic theories (Sigmund Freud, Luce Irigaray, and Julia Kristeva) into conversation with recent postcolonial feminist criticism—Simone A. James Alexander, Carol Bailey, Vivian Nun Halloran, Kelli Lyon Johnson, Brinda Mehta, Marisel C. Moreno, Sofía Muñoz-Valdivieso, and April Shemak—on the specific literary texts and historical periods under study.

Matria Redux reveals the (post)colonial and psychoanalytic assumptions underpinning previous feminist literary criticism on matria (Sandra Gilbert, Shari Benstock, Madeline Cámara Betancourt, Kelli Lyon Johnson) so as to decolonize the term, by reconceptualizing matria as an imagined maternal space and time that (re)unites Caribbean mothers with daughters. The tripartite introduction that follows therefore opens with the section, "Matri(a)lineage," which revisits Freud's theory of mothers and daughters in the Oedipal complex and traces matria's feminist psychoanalytic and (post)colonial feminist literary roots. The following section, "Mother-(Is)lands: Daughters Fictionalize the Past," explicates matria as a Caribbean maternal space and time, in relation to historical fiction and history. Lastly, "Volcanic Daughters: Matria Redux" provides an overview of the book's structure and the pre- and postmillennium novels selected for close reading.

MATRI(A)LINEAGE

According to traditional Freudian psychoanalysis, a daughter's first object of love and desire is her mother (Freud, "Female Sexuality" 21). She must, however, symbolically leave her "'Oedipal prime'... an attachment to the mother that leads to both an identification with the mother and a desire for her" (Oliver 2) and transition into "'Oedipal two'... [which] changes the girl's love object to the father and to the law" (Oliver 2). In "Female Sexuality," Freud notes that a daughter's initial attachment to her mother is "intense and passionate" and that this attachment lasts much longer than he originally thought (21). The shift from the mother (matria) to the Father (patria) depends on the castration complex, which entails two things: "that the girl has the task of giving up what was originally her leading genital zone—the clitoris—in favour of a new zone—the vagina" ("Female Sexuality" 21), and that the daughter, realizing her mother does not possess a penis, breaks her maternal bond in favor of the Father.[3] Unlike with the Oedipus complex, however, the mother does not strictly become the daughter's rival, although hostility between mother and daughter occurs (Freud, "Female Sexuality" 24, 27).

If the daughter wants to enter into the symbolic patriarchal order, the law of the Father, she must reject the mother: "The analytic situation indeed shows that it is the penis which, becoming the major referent in this operation of separation, gives full meaning to the *lack* or to the *desire* which constitutes the subject during his or her insertion into the order of language" (Kristeva 23). In short, the daughter experiences the castration complex as a realization that she and her mother lack a penis and that power resides in the penis-Father. The girl "acknowledges . . . the superiority of the male and her own inferiority," writes Freud ("Female Sexuality" 24). He adds that the realization that "the mother did not give her a proper penis—that is to say, brought her into the world as female," leads the daughter to resent, reproach, and turn away from her mother ("Female Sexuality" 27). As Luce Irigaray rightfully observes, Freud defines female sexuality only in relation and in opposition to the masculine: "[T]he female Oedipus complex is woman's entry into a system of values that is not hers, and in which she can 'appear' and circulate only when enveloped in the needs/desires/fantasies of others, namely, men" (*The Irigaray Reader* 136). Lack or silence defines the feminine, not the masculine, yet "how can we accept the idea that woman's entire sexual development is governed by her lack of, and thus by her longing for, jealousy of, and demand for, the male organ?" asks Irigaray (*The Irigaray Reader* 119). One of the only ways for a daughter to successfully reconcile with the alleged "absent female phallus" (Freud, "Fetishism" 155) and to rejoin her mother, according to Freud's theory, is to become a mother, ideally to a son (Kristeva 29).

Although Freud lists other reasons for why the daughter rejects her mother beyond not possessing the "only proper genital"—not enough milk during the period of breastfeeding, that she had "to share her mother's love with others," that the mother never fulfilled the "girl's expectations of love," and/ or lastly, that the mother aroused her sexually but then "forbade it" ("Female Sexuality" 27)—he also notes that they are inexhaustive and insufficient. He concedes that not all women give up their pre-Oedipus phase, that is their attachment to their mother, not completely anyway ("Female Sexuality" 22), and it is the postcolonial, feminist potential of this relation that *Matria Redux* takes up. As a theoretical concept, matria is both anti-Oedipal and anticolonial. The daughter's return to the maternal past can, to a degree, be likened to a return to the pre-Oedipal, prepatriarchal mother: both constitute searches for an alternative feminist relation between mothers and daughters. Caribbean women's writing therefore echoes Irigaray's critique of not only "the submission, subordination, and exploitation of the 'feminine'" (127) in the patriarchal world but also the expressed need to replace the Freudian penis and the daughter's so-called penis envy with the desire for the mother.

A rejection of the mother-daughter split, defined in Freudian terms, therefore contributes substantially to the Caribbean matrias discussed in this work.

Notably, the earliest references to matria can be found in Western feminist literary theory influenced by psychoanalysis. The publication of Sandra M. Gilbert's article in *PMLA* (1984) on the nineteenth-century English poet Elizabeth Barrett Browning is the leading example. Focusing on Barrett Browning's poetic engagement with and commitment to Italy's political unification, Gilbert writes that she "longs for a mother country or 'sister-land to Paradise,' in which women and men can live together free of the rigid interventions and interdictions of the father" (205). Barrett Browning imagines Italy as a particular matria with the potential to be "a land of free women, a female aesthetic utopia" (Gilbert 197). Defined as a psychic, imaginative maternal space, matria first reveals and then challenges the patria, the Fatherland.

Gilbert concretizes the psychoanalytic aspects of matria in her references to Freud. She writes: "In resurrecting the *matria*, moreover, these women fantasized resurrecting and restoring both the *madre*, the forgotten impossible dead mother, and the *matrice*, the originary womb or matrix, the mother-matter whose very memory, says Freud, is 'lost in a past so dim ... so hard to resuscitate that it [seems to have] undergone some specially inexorable repression'" (195). Matria relies on a palimpsest and a paradox: recollecting a forgotten and repressed matrilineage to create an alternative feminist society. In his late works, Freud admits that the mother-daughter relationship and woman's sexuality, and by corollary woman's history, have been neither adequately understood nor recognized. He writes: "Our insight into this early, pre-Oedipus phase in girls comes to us as a surprise, like the discovery, in another field, of the Minoan-Mycenaean civilization behind the civilization of Greece" ("Female Sexuality" 22). The possibility for reimagining mother-daughter relations creates a distinct connection between the maternal, history, and psychoanalysis and creates an opportunity for the Caribbean woman's historical novel to undermine patriarchal family/history from a postcolonial feminist perspective; the genre signals that a dialectical shift from patria to matria can and must occur for the female subject to emerge.

Importantly, for my work, Gilbert marks matria's connection to the Caribbean, albeit tangentially. She alludes that Barrett Browning's heroines, as allegories for Italy, resemble Bertha Mason Rochester—the infamously rebellious Creole woman in Charlotte Brontë's novel *Jane Eyre* (1847)—"large, heated, dark, [and] passionate" (Gilbert 197). Allegedly suffering from madness, Bertha is forcibly brought from Jamaica to England by her husband, Rochester. Rochester imprisons Bertha in his attic. The novel's climax occurs when Bertha maims and blinds Rochester in one eye before she sets fire to his estate and then dies by suicide. In her early seminal work *The Madwoman in the Attic*, cowritten with Susan Gubar, Gilbert argues that Bertha is Jane Eyre's—the poor, orphan English heroine's—alter ego, her "dark double" (360). They also suggest that Bertha symbolically castrates her husband (368), making the sightless Rochester an Oedipal figure. Curiously, however, Gilbert and Gubar do not mention that shortly after his marriage to Jane Eyre, Rochester's sight returns, and Jane fulfills her Freudian psycho-sexual promise, ostensibly avoiding penis envy, by giving birth to a son (Brontë 421).

Meanwhile, Gilbert's later work on matria develops the similarities between Barrett Browning's titular protagonist Aurora Leigh and Brontë's Bertha (206). Both, according to Gilbert, share a desire for the destruction of patriarchy (207). Problematically, the historical context of slavery and colonialism is overlooked by Gilbert (and Gubar) in both comparisons. For instance, Gilbert refers neither to the fact that in Brontë's novel Bertha is the daughter of slaveowners (272) nor to Barrett Browning's personal connection to slavery—being the daughter of a Jamaican plantation owner and an abolitionist penning such poems as "The Runaway Slave at Pilgrim's Point" (1846). Relevant to this discussion of a postcolonial feminist matria, however, is that Bertha is appropriated as the Caribbean woman, defined as the defiant "dark continent" of female sexuality, to quote Freud (*The Question of Lay Analysis* 43), a "clothed hyena" (Brontë 298) and the madly creative side to, or the fantasy of, the repressed white English/Creole woman/writer.

Matria Redux addresses the racial politics that have been largely absent in previous theoretical discussions of matria. Hence, postcolonial feminist rewrites of *Jane Eyre* such as Jean Rhys's historical novel *Wide Sargasso Sea* are critical. Published in 1966, *Wide Sargasso Sea*'s setting is Jamaica, shortly after emancipation in 1834. The Creole Bertha, not the Englishwoman Jane Eyre, is the main protagonist: Bertha has a backstory, a Caribbean home, and a mother prior to her marriage to and confinement by the unnamed husband, i.e., Rochester. The reader thus reperceives Bertha's "fragmented, alienated and victimized" (O'Callaghan 103) psyche/body in both Brontë's and Rhys's novels as a result of colonization *and* patriarchy. Bertha's incendiary act at the end of the novel solidifies her defiance. As Gilbert claims, the destruction of the patriarchy and "a daughter's desire to resurrect the lost and wounded mother" are necessary for envisioning matria (207). While Rhys's text reinforces the appropriateness of a postcolonial-psychoanalytic feminist perspective when analyzing the loss of the mother and mother-land in the Caribbean women's writing studied here, her work still omits much of the slave past and the enslaved female's perspective.

As if she were describing Bertha Mason's literal imprisonment at Thornfield Hall, Shari Benstock—referencing Gilbert's work to contextualize the expatriation and exile of American modernist women artists and writers in Paris—concludes "that *matria* is not the underside of *patria* or a shadowy lost civilization, but rather an 'internal exclusion' by and through which *patria* is defined. *Patria* can exist only by excluding, banishing *matria*; *matria* is always ex*patriated*" (25). Indeed, matria is not only "that which is repressed, rejected, colonized, written over, subjected, erased, silenced" (Benstock 25) but also "the excluded other within the law that ensures the law's operation" (26). Such thinking resonates with Irigaray's critique of psychoanalysis because in it, "the/a woman fulfills a twofold function—as the mute outside that sustains all systematicity; as a maternal and still silent ground that nourishes all foundations" (*Speculum* 365). Collectively, these thoughts indicate that matria is that which is both prior to and excluded from *patria*rchal language and law.

The matrias that Gilbert identified in Englishwomen's depictions of Italy and that Benstock noted in American women's writing from Paris are also recognizable in Caribbean women's historical fiction from the 1980s onward. This decade ushered in postcolonial feminist responses to the region's histories of slavery and indentureship, colonialism and independence movements, dictatorships and revolutions, and globalization and migrations. Influenced by and influencing this intellectual tradition, the post-1980 Caribbean author is not necessarily imagining another space as her matria, for instance another nation like Italy or France; the Caribbean woman writer, especially in the diaspora, is primarily concerned with actively reimagining the Caribbean mother-land. For instance, in Michelle Cliff's novels *Abeng* (1984) and *No Telephone to Heaven* (1987)—in which the mixed-race protagonist, Clare Savage, evokes Bertha in both *Jane Eyre* and *Wide Sargasso Sea*—the landscape of her island, Jamaica, is female ("Caliban's Daughter" 45). Since so many historical novels engender the nation, psychoanalytic considerations of the family—given the primacy of the mother—must also be taken into account.

In his postcolonial-psychoanalytic work on the Caribbean family *Black Skin, White Masks* (1952), Frantz Fanon, for instance, not only infamously mocks Mayotte Capécia's early novel *Je suis Martiniquaise* (1948) (*I Am a Martinican Woman*) for encouraging anti-Blackness, but he also keeps the patriarchal Freudian family more or less intact. For this reason, in her study on French Caribbean literature, *The Imaginary Caribbean and Caribbean Imaginary* (2003), Michèle Praeger persuasively argues that the filial must be read in relation to gender and race politics. Praeger problematizes the fact that in Fanon's work, "the traditional actors are in place: the Father, the Mother, and the Son. For good measure, the Father is white and the Mother and Son are black. To this triad the analysts add the black father, only to withdraw him immediately, along with the black daughter" (20).[4] In this scenario, the Mother castrates the Black father and favors her Black son. The Mother, meanwhile, grooms her daughter to be "a future m/Mother" (Praeger 20). Although the mother-daughter dyad receives little scholarly attention, the mother nevertheless trains her daughter to mimic her (so that the "daughter has become what her mother used to be" [Praeger 27]). In such literature, the Black Mother (doubly associated with lack and silence) becomes a scapegoat for both familial difficulties and sociopolitical ones (Praeger 28). As an allegory for the region, the traitorous Black Mother—and by corollary her daughter-becoming-Mother—must be rejected. The corrective power of the woman writer's imagination (Dash, "In Search of the Lost Body" 334) therefore exposes the problematic logic of such patriarchal-colonial thinking, and instead of relegating the familial and symbolic m/Mother, seeks to redefine her.

Desires "to be one again with the mother" (Hall 236) thus often manifest in a mother-island fusion. "The land and one's mothers . . . are co-joined," write Ann R. Morris and Margaret M. Dunn (219). "[T]he land . . . [is] redolent of my grandmother(s) and mother," observes Cliff ("Caliban's Daughter" 46). Or, as the eponymous protagonist waxes romantic in Jamaica Kincaid's novel *Annie John*, "I took her to an island, where we lived together" (58). Emphasizing a spiritual dimension in the quest for mother-land, Edwidge Danticat's *Breath, Eyes, Memory* (1994) sees the daughter returning to Haiti to bury her mother; standing in a cane-field, Granmè Ifé reassures Sophie that if she listens, she will hear her deceased "mother telling a story," and "at the end of the tale" when her mother asks, "'*Ou libere?*' Are you free, my daughter? . . . Now . . . you will know how to answer" (163). The postcolonial feminist novel proposes matria by bringing the spiritual, the land, and the ancestral mother together. Here, matria manifests as Ginen, an Afra-Caribbean mythic place, "where all the women in my family hoped to eventually meet one another, at the very end of each of our journeys" (Danticat, *Breath, Eyes, Memory* 121). As a postcolonial-psychoanalytic feminist theory, matria complicates Stuart Hall's description of the Caribbean writer's connection to the past, which he likens to "the child's relation to the mother . . . always-already 'after the break'" (226). Caribbean women's historical fictions fully realize, echoed by Hall's later concession, that "the same violent 'break' that subjects Caribbean writers to an 'endless desire to return to "lost origins"' also blesses them with an 'infinitely renewable source of desire, memory, myth, search, [and] discovery'" (Rody 110) that is directly tied to the mother. Such maternal loss and/or recovery can also, however, be read in terms of Freud's conception of melancholia.

Freud's identification of the psychic experiences caused by loss in "Mourning and Melancholia" resonates with both the maternal and the colonial past, thus proving productive for reconceiving matria. Khanna explains that colonial melancholy "[is] an affective state caused by the inability to assimilate a loss, and the consequent nagging return of the thing lost into psychic life" (16–17). The parallels with the maternal are striking. For one, the inability to assimilate the lost object, which we can call the mother, results in silence, a "phantom that haunts speech" (24), much like the pre-Oedipal maternal. In *Speculum of the Other Woman*, Irigaray makes a similar argument but fails to read the maternal as melancholia in relation to colonialism. Khanna, not making the maternal connection, notes that an inability to assimilate loss has political implications for colonialism; it points to the failure of any nationalism/colonialism to absorb the other—Indigenous person, slave, indentured servant, woman—entirely.

The remainder of melancholia that Khanna describes as "inaccessible[,] . . . unknown, inassimilable, interruptive, and present" might rightly be labeled the maternal (24). The fact that the maternal cannot be entirely absorbed, however, attests to its subversive power. In a literary context, this translates to daughters who cannot or will not let go of the mother or their mothers' histories: "Somewhere in the shadows of her own psyche her mother country endures, despite the pseudo-oedipal wrenching she has undergone," Gilbert contends (201). *Matria Redux*, however, acknowledges that "*matria* need not leave home to be exiled and expatriated; indeed, the effects of this outsidership within the definitional confines are most painfully felt at home, when the separation from language, body, identity, creativity, passion, and love . . . [has] been so thoroughly internalized" (Benstock 26). Perhaps, precisely because many authors, like Cliff, live(d) in the diaspora, the unknown or repressed Caribbean maternal past preoccupies this literature; thus, the region remains the primary matria, despite variances and ambivalences.

The discussion so far has shown both the shortcomings and strengths of earlier references to women writing matria, including its link to psychoanalysis and the region, which now leads me to examine the more recent application of matria to works set in the Spanish-speaking Caribbean. For instance, writing on Julia Alvarez's historical novel *In the Name of Salomé* (2000), Kelli Lyon Johnson articulates that the exiled daughter-protagonist Camila has spent her life searching for her mother, Salomé, and her homeland, the Dominican Republic. "The home she has constructed in her mind is what we might call a *matria*—not a patria—a mother/land in the territory of her memory" (Johnson, *Julia Alvarez* 33–34). Madeline Cámara Betancourt, in *Cuban Women Writers: Imagining a Matria* (2008), likewise illustrates that the concept suits both Cuban women's writing and feminist psychoanalytic perspectives, such as those of Julia Kristeva and Luce Irigaray. She argues that only "*a subversive women's discourse* can rewrite the Matria. Its *liberating* aspect creates a different *ordering* from that of the *Law of the Father* that applies in the male imaginary of the Patria" (9). Although both studies only partially explore matria as a theoretical concept, they do underscore the importance of language in constructing different Caribbean realities.

Both feminist psychoanalysts and postcolonial thinkers contend that language plays a crucial role in countering (M)aster discourses. In fact, matria as a postcolonial feminist alternative to the Latin word *patria*, can, as Gilbert suggests, revive the mother tongue (209). Resonating with Freud's belief about the pre-Oedipal, within matria "speech constitutes a different, mystically potent language, a mother tongue" (Gilbert 198). Benstock elaborates that "the dream of *matria*" is realizable through "motherland and mother *langue*" (26). Cámara Betancourt, however, reminds the reader that matria does not always entail a literal revival of the "mother's tongue on the writer's part" (144). For example, the Cuban woman writer can render "what remains in her of Cuban identity into the English language" (144). Within this study, bearing in mind colonial history, reader expectations, and current publishing practices—American publishers finding writing in English more profitable than translations (Paravisini-Gebert, "Caribbean Literature in Spanish" 700), and Caribbean writers having more opportunities in terms of audience and financial gain with American presses (Maes-Jelinek and Ledent 185)[5]—English functions as a mother tongue and/or as the dominant vehicle in which to express one's Caribbean identity. Caribbean women's writing proposes an alternative language when the maternal past is recuperated, however, and as such constitutes a "mode of resistance to dominant power structures," as Edwards suggests (321). The genre further "seek[s] to give a language to the intrasubjective and corporeal experiences left mute by culture in the past" (Kristeva 19), for example, Freud's incomplete view of women.

As a literary concept, matria indicates a relation not only to psychoanalysis and feminist theory but also to regional movements that have historically downplayed women's textual and political contributions such as Négritude, Antillanité, and Créolité. For example, Glissant's pioneering work *Le discours antillais* (1981) (*Caribbean Discourse*) fails to consider gender; yet, his theorization of "nonhistory," which addresses "peoples once reputed to be without history" (64), is particularly meaningful for Caribbean women's lives. *Matria Redux* therefore argues that because, generally speaking, racial politics are a blind spot in psychoanalytic studies and gender politics are a blind spot in postcolonial studies, it is necessary to refashion and combine these theories. Caribbean women's fictions of history further alert us to the disparaging of the mother in both postcolonial and psychoanalytic discourses: literal and symbolic matricides, as well as the daughter's separation from the mother, her mother-land, and her mother-tongue, all loom as moments of crisis throughout Caribbean women's historical fiction, thus making a vision for matria vital.

Women's postcolonial fictions envisioning matria therefore emphasize the region's shared maternal histories, claim the importance of the maternal to any theory of the Caribbean, and restructure the mother-daughter relation. Such acts also shift the emphasis away from a traditional colonial, patriarchal psychoanalytic reading of the family/History. Irigaray elaborates:

> If we are not to be accomplices in the murder of the mother . . . [we must] assert that there is a genealogy of women. There is a genealogy of women within our family: on our mothers' side we have mothers, grandmothers and great-grandmothers, and daughters. Given our exile in the family of the father-husband, we tend to forget this genealogy of women, and we are often

persuaded to deny it. Let us try to situate ourselves within this female genealogy so as to conquer and keep our identity. Nor let us forget that we already have a history, that certain women have, even if it was culturally difficult, left their mark on history and that all too often we do not know them. (*The Irigaray Reader* 44)

Hence, a tradition of postcolonial women writers, crafting nuanced responses or counternarratives to canonical colonial and Caribbean scholarship in the form of mother-daughter plots and matria constructs, emerged in the 1980s.[6] Analyzing women's historical novels from a postcolonial-psychoanalytic feminist perspective that is attentive to materiality and historicity thus discloses the Caribbean woman writer's desire to create a matri(a)lineage through novelizing her complex and pluralistic maternal past.

MOTHER-(IS)LANDS: DAUGHTERS FICTIONALIZE THE PAST

Matria Redux argues that although the post-1980 Caribbean woman's historical novel has roots in early Afra-Caribbean writing—Marie Vieux-Chauvet's *La danse sur le volcan* (1957) (*Dance on the Volcano*), Sylvia Wynter's *The Hills of Hebron* (1962), Merle Hodge's *Crick Crack, Monkey* (1970), and Simone Schwarz-Bart's *Pluie et vent sur Télumée Miracle* (1972) (*The Bridge of Beyond*)—Jean Rhys's *Wide Sargasso Sea* (1966) has influenced scholarship the most; see, for example, Caroline Rody's *The Daughter's Return: African-American and Caribbean Women's Fictions of History* (2001) or Véronique Maisier's *Violence in Caribbean Literature: Stories of Stones and Blood* (2015). While recognizing Rhys's contribution to the genre is necessary, this book demonstrates that it only partially relays the maternal literary heritage of the Caribbean woman's historical novel. This section therefore outlines the challenges, such as restrictive genre parameters, male-dominated notions of history, and the exclusion of memory and mothering, that Caribbean women historical novelists and scholars have faced and sought to overcome.

My scholarship therefore belongs to and builds on the body of twenty-first-century literary criticism (e.g., Francis, Halloran, Harford Vargas, King, Machado Sáez, Mehta, Rody) on Caribbean women's historical fiction. Rody's focus on mother-daughter plots in African American and Caribbean women's fictions of history (1970–1990) and her argument that a certain "Caribbean romance with maternal history" (10) characterizes the genre critically inform this study's concept of matria. The centrality of gender and sexuality, as noted by Donette Francis, Rosamond S. King, and Elena Machado Sáez, likewise influences my consideration of mother-daughter bonds and matria. Meanwhile, the book's organizational structure—slavery, colonialism, revolution, and decolonization—is guided by Vivian Nun Halloran's nuanced exploration of the slave past through the lens of postmodernism, Brinda Mehta's examinations of indentured servitude and colonialism, Jennifer Harford Vargas's insightful work on dictatorships, and Elena Machado Sáez's complex study of anticolonial dictatorship and revolutionary novels as shaping diasporic identity in the context of globalization/multiculturalism—a context that delocalizes and dehistoricizes the region and its writers; King's and Francis's consideration of how phallocentric histories of slavery, colonialism, and empire configure the postcolonial subject/citizen further elucidates the timeframes and texts under study. A distinct resistance to upholding "a teleological march from slavery to independence marked by epochal moments of revolution and resistance embodied . . . by the male heroic figure" (Francis 3) can also be detected when women's lives and voices are taken into account.

My inclusion of both island and diasporic writers-texts also echoes recent comparative approaches to the region (Francis, Harford Vargas, King, Moreno) that seek to map the dialogic relation between these literatures and locations, without privileging one over another. For instance, King's examination of the Cariglobal seeks to dispel the common belief that the island home represents a more authentic version of Caribbeanness while the diaspora offers more intellectual-creative-political freedom (6), or, as Machado Sáez puts it, seeing "diaspora as offering a utopic alternative to the nation-state" (192). Harford Vargas, meanwhile, articulates how the violence of US imperialism affects Caribbean women's lives in strikingly similar ways, both abroad and domestically. She uses the term "'Greater Cuba' to move beyond the Cold War rhetoric that ossifies a strict binary between Cubans on the island and Cubans in exile, instead foregrounding . . . Cuban cultural production on and off the island" (*Forms of Dictatorship* 150). Marisel Moreno's comparison of Puerto Rican women's writing from the island and from the diaspora (*Family Matters*) breaks new ground, while Donette Francis convincingly shows how analyzing "[s]exual citizenship disrupts the boundaries between the public and the private while also unsettling the borders between nation and diaspora. Connecting female citizenship both inside and outside the region challenges the dichotomy that posits diaspora as an empowering 'elsewhere' of sexual liberation versus home as a space of sexual oppression" (4). I am, however, mindful of Machado Sáez's concern that "the focus on mobility and hybridity as endemic aspects of Caribbeanness often leads to the conflation of the diaspora with the Caribbean island nation. The localities and contexts differentiating writing from the diaspora versus writing from the islands are suppressed, ignored, or elided"; the risk is that diasporic writing comes to "stand in for local island writing" (14). *Matria Redux*'s analysis of contiguous and contingent, "intimately linked . . . and mutually constitutive" (Francis 4) mother-daughter plots in Caribbean women's historical fiction thus aims to add another layer or dimension to the relation between island and diaspora.

For this reason, genre studies citing European (M)aster narratives, preoccupied with men's experiences of sweeping historical events as well as a desire "to create a national consciousness" (Watson 69) that by and large excludes women, prove inappropriate. For example, analyses such as Georg Lukács's 1937 study of Walter Scott's *Waverley* (1814)[7] do not accurately reflect Caribbean women's historical novels, which employ fantastical elements, counter the official historical record, and/or include the author's lifetime (Halloran 16). Similarly, an exclusive focus on men's novels, such as in Paschal B. Kyiiripuo Kyoore's *The African and Caribbean Historical Novel in French: A Quest for Identity* (1999), neglects women's contributions and perpetuates a false notion that male authors—H. G. de Lisser, Edgar Mittelholzer, V. S. Naipaul, and Wilson Harris—are the genre's "pioneers" (Wilson-Tagoe 285).[8] Although Caribbean men's historical novels decolonize authority and often centralize "the ex-centrics, the marginalized, the peripheral figures" (Hutcheon 114) of history, these works nonetheless rarely challenge patriarchal traditions. Often, female characters remain outliers, stereotypes, and/or incompletely realized.

The persistence of a male-dominated discourse that believes writing about "'His/story' is 'a male prerogative'" (Ferly 53) further suggests that "political independence ha[s] not restored speech to the Caribbean female subject" (Gikandi 13). Political autonomy for the nation, a founding principle in postcolonial Caribbean theory and literature, not to mention historical fiction, is therefore radically and strategically questioned in postcolonial women's writing within the purview of women's autonomy. Critics frequently draw attention to how the heroic-male "narrative of anticolonial history often relegate[s] women to the roles of silent witnesses or objects of history"

(Machado Sáez 120). Rosamond King, for one, identifies how "the historical narratives of Great Men who fought or defeated slavery (for example, Toussaint L'Ouverture and Cuffy), colonialism (Eric Williams, Frantz Fanon, and José Martí), or imperialism (Che Guevara and Maurice Bishop)" (161) keep exclusionary patriarchal-hero frameworks in place while simultaneously drawing attention to "a spectacular failure of male leadership, if not of Caribbean masculinity" (162). Harford Vargas echoes this thinking in her work on revolutions, while Machado Sáez concludes that the tragic romances found in many diasporic women's novels directly challenge the heteropatriarchal hypermasculinity championed within these various historical periods and movements.

Contemporary feminist scholarship further addresses the shift from "the romantic anticolonial hope for a utopian future," aligned with the 1960s, to "the tragic postcolonial nightmare of the present" (Machado Sáez 36). Machado Sáez, like Francis, expresses a discomfort, however, with demarcations that "occlude women and others not invested in a story that charts a linear anticolonial progression culminating in disappointment with the failed promises of romance" (144). Focusing on how being subjected to violence shapes the subjectivities of women and girls, Francis argues that the postcolonial period of women's writing constitutes what she calls "antiromance" (4). Considering the gendered associations with each genre, Machado Sáez contends that women's fictions propose a more nuanced approach that oscillates between tragedy and romance (36) while still "recognizing how nationalist discourses about history and progress exclude and marginalize certain knowledges and bodies" (37).[9] The historical novelists studied in this work thus participate in confronting he(te)ro-patriarchal narratives and historiographies that depend on and perpetuate woman's voicelessness.

In their canonical work *Out of the Kumbla*, Carole Boyce Davies and Elaine Savory Fido explain: "By voicelessness, we mean the historical absence of the woman writer's text: the absence of a specifically female position on major issues such as slavery, colonialism, decolonization, women's rights and more direct social and cultural issues. By voicelessness we also mean silence: the inability to express a position in the language of the 'master' as well as the textual construction of woman as silent" (1). Attesting to the noticeable absence of women writers from the early Caribbean canon (Gikandi 13), for example, is Ada Quayle's little-known historical novel *The Mistress* (1957). The text chronicles a violent Creole mother-daughter duo, both of whom are named Laura Pettigrew and lay claim to the title of "Mistress" on a Jamaican plantation circa 1917. Despite Sylvia Wynter's 1958 endorsement of her as "the first West Indian woman novelist," and calling the work "a competent historical piece" (qtd. in Campbell 82), Quayle and her novel have received little scholarly attention.

That the recent past, as a legitimate historical period, has been dismissed by traditional historical novel scholars, namely Lukács, might explain Quayle's omission from genre studies, but one also wonders if *The Mistress*'s exclusion might be explained otherwise, for instance the author "not adequately displaying" a "knowledge of Jamaican culture" (Campbell 82), the work's stereotyping of Afro-Caribbean figures, and/or the author's background as a Creole woman. Works like Quayle's nevertheless underscore that as a corrective to history is the woman writer's desire to express a new voice. If "the mother's identity is merged with her daughter's, creating a double-voiced" narrative (S. A. J. Alexander, "M/Otherly Guise" 211), then we might read the Caribbean woman's historical novel as always "told in two voices" (Boyce Davies, "Some Where" 26). This again signals a unique position and status in a genre formerly dominated by the singular male protagonist's perspective. The contemporary Caribbean historical novels analyzed in *Matria Redux* are therefore exactly the kinds of feminist interventions that defy voicelessness.

My work shows that Caribbean women writers have repurposed the genre to suit their creative and political visions. Literary scholar Diana Wallace persuasively argues that "the historical novel has allowed [writers] to invent or 're-imagine' . . . the unrecorded lives of marginalized and subordinated people, especially women, but also the working classes, Black people, slaves and colonized peoples, and to shape narratives, which are more appropriate to their experiences than those of conventional history" (2). Similarly, Sabine Von Dirke explains that the "historical novel achieves transparency and self-reflexivity in its portrayal of the past as a specific gendered and political reconstruction situated between the historical record and imagination. Therefore, this genre has the potential to explode the closed text of history, i.e., the dominant historical narratives, from a variety of perspectives. Why not from a feminist one?" (426). Indeed, exploding "the closed text of history" is exactly what Caribbean women's historical fictions do, and as such they open up multiple sites for postcolonial-psychoanalytic feminist textual and theoretical inquiries such as those undertaken in this book.

For instance, in Wynter's plurivocal *The Hills of Hebron*, set in 1930s Jamaica, Miss Gatha's voice shares equal textual space with the male protagonists, and sexual politics are at the heart of this narrative depicting the Church of New Believers. In a poignant metafictional moment, Wynter, writing from a male character's view, asks: "What was that woman rambling on about? Why didn't she say what he had told her to?" (55). Indeed, this early Caribbean woman's historical novel defiantly and unapologetically goes off script, telling *her*story, not regurgitating and ventriloquizing *hi*story. Merle Hodge's *Crick Crack, Monkey* also engages a herstory of the recent past (1950s Trinidad) but in doing so draws loosely on autobiographical elements, a strategy echoed in many post-1980s texts. Unlike Wynter's work, Hodge's Trinidadian novel is a Caribbean bildungsroman whereby Tee, having lost her mother at an early age, is shuttled back and forth between two aunties—each aunt serves as an allegory for the competing maternal/national allegiances between which Tee will have to choose. Tee's decision, at the end of the novel, to reunite with her father in England, however, not only adheres to the traditional Oedipus complex but also establishes the trope of the young Caribbean woman leaving her mother-land. Nevertheless, the burgeoning Afra-Caribbean "maternal subjectivity" (Hirsch 197) found in both *The Hills of Hebron* and *Crick Crack, Monkey* sets the stage for the postcolonial feminist perspectives found in the contemporary texts discussed in this work. Repositioning the Afra-Caribbean woman, her oral tradition, and her matrilineage as these narratives do alerts us to an alternative literary genealogy of the genre that emerged not only in relation to and alongside but prior to Rhys's *Wide Sargasso Sea*.

Since the genre's formative years, Caribbean women writers have transformed it in several notable ways. They have rewritten women into mainstream historiography such as rebellions and revolutions (e.g., Edwidge Danticat's *The Farming of Bones* [1998]); reclaimed women's images from the dominant masculine imaginary and, in turn, constructed their own narratives (e.g., Marie-Elena John's *Unburnable* [2006]); recuperated women's lives deemed by patriarchal, colonial History as unworthy of recording (e.g., Paule Marshall's *Praisesong for the Widow* [1983]); and/or broken with Western or masculine definitions of time and History (e.g., Andrea O'Reilly Herrera's *The Pearl of the Antilles* [2001]). Women's definitive turn toward historical fiction signals that literature, specifically that which novelizes history, not historiography, can more effectively rewrite the maternal past. Prioritizing

Caribbean "women's lives and loves, their families and their feelings," can also "give the concerns of the so-called private sphere the status and interest of history" (Light 59), while emphasizing its "importance to understandings of colonial and postcolonial subjectivity and citizenship" (Francis 1–2). The collective result is the undoing of many long-held misconceptions or fictions about women and the past.

Furthermore, that early Caribbean women's historical novels (such as those authored by Phyllis Shand Allfrey, Vieux-Chauvet, Quayle, Wynter, Rhys, Hodge, and others) concretized the indelible link between fiction and history has had a direct effect on Caribbean discursive practices, including contributing to women's history gaining legitimacy as an academic field in the 1970s—for instance, Lucille Mathurin Mair's pioneering work (Brereton, "Gender" 129)—authorizing creative writing to convey women's history (Brereton, "Gender" 131), and repositioning Caribbean feminism as essential (R. King 161). Patricia Mohammed, for instance, outlines the "unfolding history of Caribbean feminism[s]" to emphasize "the value of recording the stories of our own struggles" ("Stories in Caribbean Feminism" 122, 120). These stories, according to Mohammed, are routinely found in women's narratives: "Such stories become popular memory in the history of our societies, and they are inextricably linked to the way we see and define ourselves. Most crucially, the stories we record are legacies and lessons of struggle that we leave to future generations and these are then taken up and retold with their own flavour" ("Stories in Caribbean Feminism" 121). Women's historical novels complement the desire to bring "older stories into dialogue with the newer narratives" (Mohammed, "Stories in Caribbean Feminism" 123) and add not only complexity to the history of feminism but also visibility to the diversity of women's history across the region.

Matria, the dream of a symbiotic connection-separation between mothers and daughters, contributes to the maternal motifs that have been used repeatedly to depict Caribbean realities and to recast history in feminist terms which de-/mythi-fy space and time. Drawing on Kristeva's work, Rody shows that Caribbean women historical novelists routinely exploit their medium to "open up and liberate time in order to reach and release enslaved foremothers" (8). Favoring a women's time conceived as "exploded, plural, fluid, in a certain way nonidentical" (Kristeva 19) means rejecting "project, teleology, linear and prospective unfolding; time as departure, progression, and arrival—in other words, the time of history" (Kristeva 17).

Collectively, women's historical novels expose the absurdity of a logic that suggests Caribbean women be excluded from traditional History—defined by a phallic, colonial order—because they constitute lack or envy. Instead, these Caribbean texts redefine race, gender, sexuality, and history in terms that are more appropriate to women's lived experiences.

Caribbean women's novels therefore often propose alternative modes of history associated with the maternal such as cyclical (repetition) and monumental (eternity) time (Kristeva 17). For instance, in retelling Belize's slave past, Zee Edgell's novel *Time and the River* (2007) juxtaposes patriarchal, colonial time with maternal, cyclical time symbolized by the river: one is constructed, linear, the other natural, fluid, seemingly timeless, evidenced by Edgell's strategic title, which uses the grammatical conjunction to indicate difference. As if he were describing a fetus in the mother's womb, in *Faulkner, Mississippi*, Édouard Glissant alludes to how the river, "with its turns and bends" (203) and "haunting circularity" (203), "challenge[s] the certitudes of linear" (202) thinking. Consider also Dionne Brand's description of several Afra-Caribbean women's lives as synchronized with tidal and lunar patterns in *At the Full and Change of the Moon* (1999), or that Ryhaan Shah's novel *A Silent Life* (2005) draws on reincarnation and Kali, the Hindu goddess of time and death, by connecting her with the black waters or Kala Pani, crossed by Indian women immigrating to the region. Similarly, chapter delineations illustrated by a concentric circle challenge the notion of History as progress in Andrea O'Reilly Herrera's *The Pearl of the Antilles* (2001); moreover, the novel begins with an ancestral woman's vision of Cuba, likened to a pearl in the sea, being colonized: "[S]he lost all sense of time—confusing the past with the present and the future with the past. To her, time seemed to be moving in a restless circle" (n.p.). For postcolonial authors, writing maternal time and women's lives functions to critique or break the chain of past patriarchal and/or colonial violence carried out in the name of progress, that is, History.

Rody suggests that "[i]n these time-stopped moments, these restored maternal spaces, repressed herstory erupts, revealing a chain of births one from within the other, in an unwritten chronology spiraling from the depths of female time" (9). Cuban and Latin American scholar Catherine Davies concurs that women's writing can offer alternative "versions of historical time and time-consciousness which counter . . . the 'single, historical' view of modernity" (7). The depiction of maternal time signals a strategic postcolonial-psychoanalytic feminist position taken by Caribbean women authors to refuse the patriarchal-colonial concept of time, that is, History, which "makes the rupture from the mother explicit" (Rody 8). Rody elaborates:

> In psychological terms, the allegory of daughterly return to the body of the mother suggests a feminist privileging of the maternal-infant bond, as theorized by Freud, Lacan, Kristeva, and others.... Kristeva writes that to refuse separation from the maternal body would be to refuse "*the founding separation of the sociosymbolic contract.*"....[10] A narrative of *historical* return to the mother, then, might be a feminist rejection of the separations enforced by... "the time of history." (7–8)

Bringing feminist psychoanalytic approaches into conversation with Caribbean women's writing therefore reveals the effects of patriarchy, colonialism, and History on women's psyches and bodies.

Caribbean texts envisioning matria boldly ask: what might history/society look like if we embraced the myth of the divine "archaic mother"—"full, total, engbobing mother with no frustration, no separation, with no break-producing symbolism (with no castration, in other words)" (Kristeva 29). Reimagining the mother's role differently from that prescribed in the patriarchal Oedipus complex–symbolic system proposes an alternative familial-sexual dynamic for Caribbean mothers and daughters. As such, the genre firmly resists Kristeva's advisement against a radical "female society" that constitutes "a sort of alter ego of the official society, in which all real or fantasized possibilities for *jouissance* take refuge. Against the sociosymbolic contract, both sacrificial and frustrating, this countersociety is imagined as harmonious, without prohibitions, free and fulfilling" (27). Through revisiting and reclaiming mother-daughter relationships, Caribbean women's historical novels definitively imagine the possibility of matria as a postcolonial feminist future and homeland.

A commitment to sociopolitical change for women in the region, however, also materializes in the genre's reconfiguration of history and memory as they intersect with gender. The pairing of collective memory and popular memory—both of which Glissant reminds us were "erased" by nonhistory (*Caribbean Discourse* 62)—highlights why many women writers like Wynter and Hodge retrieve the recent past and/or present in their historical novels. They feel, as Glissant claims, a "duty" to explore the not-yet history of the past by insisting on its relevance to the contemporary moment (*Caribbean*

Discourse 64). The historical novel therefore becomes a tool invested with "the political use of memory . . . to right a wrong, make visible the invisible, or give knowledge where ignorance has reigned" (Khanna 13). Maryse Condé's canonical neo-slavery novel *Moi, Tituba sorcière . . . noire de Salem* (1986) (*I, Tituba, Black Witch of Salem*), poignantly echoes this thinking. Set in the late seventeenth century, the story reimagines Tituba, a historical Caribbean woman, forcibly brought as a slave to Salem, Massachusetts, where she was charged with and imprisoned for witchcraft. In Condé's version, powerful maternal figures guide Tituba, including when she returns to Barbados to join the maroons; yet, like her mother before her, she is hanged. With birth-like imagery, Condé writes: "Our memory will have to be covered in blood. Our memories will have to float to the surface like water lilies" (165). Condé stresses the need, no matter how difficult or painful, to recollect and express a maternal past that has passed, but that has not been forgotten. In these fictions, remembered and remembering mothers-daughters remind the slavers-colonizers that they cannot hide indefinitely from the wrongs of History.

As a postcolonial-psychoanalytic feminist term, matria recognizes the interplay between mothers and daughters, between history and memory featured in these texts. Gil Zehava Hochberg explains: "By assigning mother (or the maternal ancestor) the role of a 'medium' through which an alternative narrative emerges as a direct confrontation with history, 'woman' (as mother) is aligned with memory as an alternative to *history*. This promising role of the mother is promoted through a gendered mobilization of the radical division between 'history' and 'memory'" (2). The Caribbean woman's historical novel thus capitalizes on and constructs memory as/and history. Tellingly, the mother's personal and communal memories often (in)form the historical in the Caribbean novel. Matria thus concretizes a connection between nonhistory, memory, and the maternal as that which remain repressed, peripheral to, or unabsorbable by the patriarchal-colonial system (History), but as such, escape the very logic that tries to but inevitably cannot contain them. The radical potential of matria lies in its ability to offer another memory, another vision of the archipelago. The commitment of the Caribbean woman to tell her stories and to provide, through a gendered lens, "an imaginative reconstruction of the past in the void left by History" (Dash, "Introduction" xxxii) cannot be underestimated. Accordingly, images like Condé's rhizomatic water lilies, which evoke mother-islands with long aquatic umbilical cords, become a fitting symbol for the Caribbean writer's connection to her maternal history.

Despite the prominence of maternal history and mother-daughter imagery in this writing, Paula Sanmartín and Christina Herrera contend that motherhood "is still vastly overlooked in recent scholarship" (3). Meanwhile, in *Feminist and Critical Perspectives on Caribbean Mothering*, Dorsía Smith Silva and Simone A. James Alexander argue that criticism has failed to articulate the multidimensionality of mothering across race, class, or cultural and social differences, or to record the impact of slavery, colonialism, migration, and exile on the institution of motherhood in the region (ix). The historical novels studied in this book are thus concerned with recurring maternal motifs and "with representing mothers, othermothers, and maternal figures that challenge narrow conceptualizations of Caribbean women" (Sanmartín and Herrera 10).[11] Maternal identities and mother-daughter relationships are multifaceted: "(dis)empowering, problematic, violent, silenced, prejudiced, loving, nurturing, or ambivalent" (Sanmartín and Herrera 5). Take, for example, that Kincaid's *The Autobiography of My Mother* (1996) also makes use of the water lily to signal the maternal, but this time, young Xuela (the namesake of her mother, who died in childbirth) describes its "sweet, sickening smell" to express her ambivalent feelings for the absent mother (46). After all, the traditional Freudian drama requires that the daughter leave her mother, not the other way around. As a suitable term for defining the postcolonial-psychoanalytic feminist positions adopted by Caribbean historical novelists, matria therefore contributes not only to the fields of history and literature but also to studies on Caribbean motherhood.

In *Daughters of Caliban: Caribbean Women in the Twentieth Century*, Consuelo López Springfield reflects that "women writers of the Caribbean remind us consistently: that we are daughters, reweaving our mothers' stories into our own as we challenge convention" (xii). Dahlma Llanos-Figueroa's prologue to her historical novel *Daughters of the Stone* (2009) echoes this sentiment, for she relays "the stories ... told to [her] mother and her mother and hers ... the stories of a time lost to flesh and bones, a time that lives only in dreams and memory" (n.p.). In their recovery of "submerged mothers" (Brathwaite, *ConVERSations* 17), Caribbean women tell "the multiple stories ... of women rooted in the ... precarious past and troublesome present, stories that have been shrouded in silence and eras[ures]" (Theile and Drews viii). Storytelling, imagination, and memory in the Caribbean woman's historical novel show that the traditional masculine, colonial plot/genre can be intervened in and disrupted; and, matria redux, a return to the mother's past (factual/fictional, biological/symbolic), can serve as inspiration for writers and readers alike.

Redux, "the move of return and reworking, of going back in order to go forward" (Haigh 62), plays a critical role in imagining a Caribbean matria. For feminist critic Samantha Haigh, redux is "emblematic of the necessity for all women under patriarchy of going back specifically to explore their relationship with their mother" (62). The return to maternal history and the disruption of "'totalizing' and hierarchal master texts" (Dash, "Introduction" xxx) in Caribbean women's historical novels support this prescriptive. Clarisse Zimra asserts, "In short, the obsessive 'looking behind' is a pre-condition, if not a conditioning, of contemporary writing.... Th[e] Caribbean text, therefore, erects its ontological base oppositionally against origins defined by a dominant, territorializing, (once) metropolitan, (once) phallocratic discourse that it wishes to reterritorialize" ("What's in a Name" 98–99). She continues to emphasize: "The past is that which can, and must, be shared collectively. . . . [I]t can be reproduced, i.e., 'passed down' to the next generations; and, by the same token of its mythic dimension . . . passed 'up' because it enables the next generation, who is listening, to go 'back'" ("What's in a Name" 112). Hence the reason why so many Caribbean women are novelizing the past.

Matria Redux therefore argues that revisiting and reinventing mother-daughter figures constitutes a radical form of postcolonial-psychoanalytic feminist recollection and expression. And, "[r]ather than dismissing the past as inaccessible and textually dependent chimera," these multivalent, postcolonial feminist texts "insist on the political urgency of rewriting history [largely] from the perspective of the disempowered" (K. C. Davis 728). Invaluable for its ability to put forth a counterhistory, matria discloses, via various aesthetic modes, representations of Caribbean women from a plurality of cultures, nations, and historical locations/periods. To be sure, Gilbert was disappointed when she wrote that "inevitably the reality of patriarchal history, with its successes and successions, obliterated Barrett Browning's implicit but impossible dream of a matria" (209), but such cannot be said of the Caribbean woman's historical novel. Strategically imagined mother-islands floating on the sea like water lilies signal that the dream of other possible worlds, an alternative feminist Caribbean, is in full bloom.

VOLCANIC DAUGHTERS: MATRIA REDUX

To conceive the genre broadly and to emphasize the diversity of maternal histories in Caribbean women's fiction, I have selected conventional and non-conventional, canonical and lesser-known, diasporic, island, and continental works.[12] The quadripartite structure of this book mirrors the region's history as reflected in the creative texts: part I: Mythologizing Matria (slavery), part II: Decolonizing Matria (colonialism), part III: Revolutionizing Matria (revolution), and part IV: Returning Matria (recent past).[13] Each part offers a robust introduction to the genre and the specific postcolonial-psychoanalytic feminist theoretical framework adopted for analysis. The main comparative elements in the book, the introductory sections, not only set up the following two chapters as case studies of matria in the premillennium and postmillennium novel but also share specific island histories. The result is a deeper, more relational understanding of matria as a postcolonial-psychoanalytic feminist concept in these texts specifically and the genre more generally. Following Davies's lead in her examination of twentieth-century Cuban women writers, my analysis refuses a reductivist concept of matria; it aims to "show the plurality of women's voices, without resolving conflicting interpretations or reducing textual complexities to a synthesis" for the sake of "systematic coherence" (7). As the following overview indicates, the reimagined Caribbean in women's historical fiction evidences matria as a strategic and unique postcolonial-psychoanalytic feminist concept.

PART I: MYTHOLOGIZING MATRIA

Originating in and from the Afra-Caribbean enslaved woman, this genre's maternal imaginary and matrilineage counter literary and historical discursive absence. The introductory section, "Africa's Daughters: The Neo-Slavery Novel's Caribbean Maternal Genealogy," tracks the literary origins of an alternative maternal genealogy and then compares the history of slavery in Trinidad and Jamaica before turning to the two novels chosen as case studies: Dionne Brand's *At the Full and Change of the Moon* (1999) and Andrea Levy's *The Long Song* (2010). The period of slavery has minimal archival material from the enslaved woman's point of view, yet it serves as the backdrop for these writers. The neo-slavery novel suggests that social change in the present cannot be implemented if the maternal past remains unknown and/or told from the (M)aster's perspective. Reclaiming the rebellious African mother reorients the daughter's genealogy and challenges hegemonic patriarchal, colonial family arrangements such as those proposed by traditional psychoanalysis. A desire to realize a Caribbean matria that integrates the African past therefore emerges.

Chapter 1 argues that in *At the Full and Change of the Moon*, Brand's concept of matria innovatively repositions the Trinidadian enslaved mother's and her descendants' genealogy to show the traumatic effects of slavery and colonialism over several centuries and geographic locations. Proposing a combination of arbolic and rhizomatic root theory to express the enslaved woman's family, the novel challenges traditional patriarchal family trees and the laws of filiation. Chapter 2 argues that in Levy's *The Long Song*, the enslaved Jamaican woman's voice is centralized, but even after emancipation, she remains problematically enclosed in, figured through, and contained by the name of the Father and violent, colonizing, masculine parameters. Thus, the novel imagines matria as a space that reunites mothers and daughters and as a time that restores subjectivity and speech to Caribbean women.

PART II: DECOLONIZING MATRIA

Blending history with the bildungsroman, the novels studied in this section feature young women rewriting the Caribbean mother-land/tongue. Set in the mid-twentieth century colonial past (postemancipation, pre-independence), these works definitively establish the girl's maturation as developing alongside and in tandem with a historical and national consciousness. The introduction, "Dispossessed Daughters: Searching for Caribbean Mother-Land/Tongue," explains how a daughter's postcolonial feminist awakening is intertwined with her relationship to her maternal family: the mother, an antagonistic character, and her grandmother, a revered and trusted figure. The clever Caribbean girl consciously questioning her identity (familial and national) and her place in a colonial world thus defines the matrias in the two pioneering bildungsromane closely analyzed: Jan Lowe Shinebourne's premillennium novel *The Last English Plantation* (1988), set in Guyana, and Judith Ortiz Cofer's postmillennium novel *The Meaning of Consuelo* (2003), set in Puerto Rico. Brief histories of each land provide further contextualization of the genre.

Within this genre, the daughter's Freudian break from her mother in psychoanalysis plays an essential role and manifests in two diverging ways: either she reconciles with her Caribbean mother (as does June in *The English Plantation*), or she crosses the sea to the colonial mother (Consuelo moves to the United States in *The Meaning of Consuelo*). Chapter 3 argues that the Indo-Chinese girl's struggle against her mother and Guyana's growing demand for independence from Britain correlates to June's increasingly postcolonial feminist attitude of coolitude. Chapter 4 demonstrates that *The Meaning of Consuelo* recounts an awakening of a gendered and sexual consciousness that rejects traditional, patriarchal-heteronormative Puerto Rican society and family; Consuelo determines that if young Puerto Rican women want to attain freedom, they must do so by leaving the island and relocating to the US mainland.

PART III: REVOLUTIONIZING MATRIA

Contemporary historical novels concerned with public spaces and political revolution expand upon the volatile domestic settings such as plantations and villages studied in the first half of this book. This section's introduction, "Politicized Mothers: Dreaming the Matria," demonstrates how a political cause, the greater good, and a future feminist matria motivate many of the women in these narratives to endanger their own lives. Exploring the intersection of the familial and the national, the personal and the public, the exile and the refugee, these works are set in the mid-twentieth century during the time of dictatorships, national independence, and communist revolution. By focalizing wars, violence, and women, the novels offer a unique postcolonial feminist perspective on a subject typically told by men about men. Chapter 5 offers a close reading of Edwidge Danticat's premillennium Haitian novel *The Farming of Bones* (1998) and proposes that the main protagonist, Amabelle, after being militarily forced to return to her mother country, Haiti, becomes an allegory for the Massacre River, which flows between the two nations of Hispaniola. Chapter 6 focuses on Andrea O'Reilly Herrera's postmillennium Cuban American novel *The Pearl of the Antilles* (2001) and argues that this revolutionary family romance highlights that Margarita, the exiled female protagonist, privileges the mother-daughter bond over both the wife-husband and the daughter-father connection as well as any allegiance to either her birth nation, Cuba, or her adopted country, the United States. A postcolonial feminist approach to psychoanalytical terms like "uncanny," "trauma," and "taboo" are thus paramount to my discussion of matria.

PART IV: RETURNING MATRIA

The Caribbean women's historical fictions discussed in this section all take place in the recent past, indeed coinciding with the authors' lifetimes and challenging the limits of the genre. The introductory section, "Ancestral Mothers: The Caribbean Daughter's Homecoming," argues that these novels use myth and the distant past to confirm a direct impact on female protagonists in the present. African-derived familial-community narratives like songs and stories are reinvented in these works. Likewise, references to spirituality including non-Western and African-derived religions play considerable roles. A rich, subversive oral tradition rejoins heroines, feeling homesick, nostalgic, or disconnected while living outside the Caribbean, with their maternal heritage. This rejoining entails a return to the mother's Caribbean roots, as shown in my two close readings: chapter 7 concentrates on Paule Marshall's *Praisesong for the Widow* (1983), set in Grenada and Carriacou. *Praisesong for the Widow* emphasizes the spiritual importance of knowing one's ancestral past and ends with Avey, the protagonist, after a cathartic moment, reconnecting with her maternal history. For this reason, the importance of ritual as outlined in psychoanalysis is studied from a postcolonial feminist perspective. Chapter 8, however, offers a close reading of a postmillennial text in which the heroine, Lillian, cannot restore her maternal genealogy: Marie-Elena John's *Unburnable* (2006), set in Dominica. *Unburnable* reveals what Freud calls hysteria, which is reinterpreted here as *hystérie*, history as erupting through/as female madness and suicide. Together, these postcolonial feminist texts suggest that the daughter, having been born in or having lived in the United States for most of her life, does not know her maternal familial/communal history, her matria, and until she does, she will not be at home, psychically or physically.

CONCLUSION

Since the likes of Marie Vieux-Chauvet's *Dance on the Volcano* and Sylvia Wynter's *The Hills of Hebron*, Caribbean women historical novelists have indeed proven volcanic daughters. Fictions of Caribbean maternal history confront the unresolved traumas of the past such as slavery, colonialism, revolution, and imperialism while sparking critical feminist dialogues about reparative and transformative action in the future. The application of postcolonial, feminist, and psychoanalytic approaches further reveals the alternative realities Caribbean women are constructing for factual and fictional lives, both past and present. *Matria Redux* thus recognizes the literary and historical significance of novelizing the maternal past, for such narratives have not only "survived against the modes of silence engendered by the master class" (Gikandi 14) but have also radically transformed a previously male-dominated genre. Pre- and postmillennium Caribbean historical novels therefore stand as powerful symbolic reminders that the maternal past, as well as the (M)aster texts that have attempted to discredit and discard mothers and daughters, can be reimagined. Hence, the genre of women's historical fiction now manifests as the literary realization of a Caribbean matria.

PART I

MYTHOLOGIZING MATRIA

AFRICA'S DAUGHTERS

The Neo-Slavery Novel's Caribbean Maternal Genealogy

The Afra-Caribbean matrias in women's late twentieth and early twenty-first-century neo-slavery novels are indebted to a rich lineage of historical fiction that consists of works like Simone Schwarz-Bart's *Pluie et vent sur Télumée Miracle* (1972) (*The Bridge of Beyond*). Schwarz-Bart's indomitable heroine, Télumée, recounts her Guadeloupean matrilineage starting with her formerly enslaved foremother, Minerva. As if speaking about all the Lougandor women, Télumée's daughter states matter-of-factly, "She is steel grass, my mother, for she bends before no man" (244). Unbending in its postcolonial feminist reconfigurations of the genre, Caribbean women's writing has vehemently opposed (M)aster discourses. The recent proliferation of women's neo-slavery novels conceiving matria by centralizing Afra-Caribbean heroines like Minerva and Télumée—such as Maryse Condé's *Moi, Tituba sorcière . . . noire de Salem* (1986) (*I, Tituba, Black Witch of Salem*), Zee Edgell's Belizean novel *Time and the River* (2007),[1] and Dahlma Llanos-Figueroa's Puerto Rican–American novel *Daughters of the Stone* (2009)—therefore warrants a reevaluation of the Caribbean literary canon. This section considers two extraordinary novels that through their Afra-Caribbean mother-daughter plots and conceptions of matria have actively contributed to the neo-slavery boom, critically shaped the historical novel genre, and revised patriarchal-colonial conceptions of family: Dionne Brand's *At the Full and Change of the Moon* (1999) and Andrea Levy's *The Long Song* (2010).

Both Brand and Levy have stressed the importance of the intersection of race, gender, and history in their award-winning works—Brand's *In Another Place, Not Here* (1996) and Levy's *Small Island* (2004)—but these two novels constitute the authors' most explicit and direct treatment of the slave past. Writing from the Canadian diaspora, Brand addresses the slave history of her birthplace, Trinidad. *At the Full and Change of the Moon* is the first historical fiction to link an enslaved woman's past in Trinidad with her descendants in Canada (a British colony until 1867). This text highlights how the legacy of the slave past persists on the island and in the diaspora. Meanwhile, British-born Levy reimagines the slave history of Jamaica, where her Windrush generation parents were born. *The Long Song* is the first British historical novel written by a British woman with Jamaican roots to retell Jamaica's slave past from an enslaved woman's point of view. Brand and Levy both establish a concrete connection between the past and the present, slavery and migration, and the Caribbean and its diaspora, Canada and Britain, respectively. This literature brings to the forefront the often fraught and neglected history of the slave trade, especially the Afra-Caribbean slave past; it also explicitly links Britain's and Canada's refusal to fully acknowledge their involvement in the slave trade with the ubiquitous racism and sexism experienced by those with Caribbean heritage in the twenty-first-century diaspora.

Typical of premillennium neo-slavery novels, Brand's *At the Full and Change of the Moon* reimagines a historical enslaved figure. Thisbe's insurrections inspired Brand's character Marie Ursule, the mother figure who organizes the mass suicide of her fellow Trinidadian plantation slaves in 1824. After Marie Ursule sends her daughter Bola to live as a maroon with Kamena, another slave and possibly Bola's father, the novel progresses chronologically from the time of Bola's emancipation to young Bola's life in the late twentieth century. Brand captures the suffering and violence Marie Ursule and her descendants endure both on and off the island over the course of nearly 175 years, culminating when the story comes full circle, as Marie Ursule's ghost visits young Bola in the former-maroon-camp-turned-destitute-town of Terre Bouillante. Postmillennium novels like *The Long Song*, meanwhile, have tended to shift away from fictionalized historical figures to historicized fictional ones. *The Long Song* tells the story of July, a slave born to a woman named Kitty on a Jamaican plantation in the early nineteenth century: the narrative is written by July but ostensibly edited and published by her son, Thomas Kinsman, in 1898. July gives Thomas away when he is an infant (his father is a former slave called Nimrod who is falsely accused of murdering the master and is then murdered in turn). A British family adopts Thomas, raising and educating the child in England. July, meanwhile, has a daughter named Emily, with Robert Goodwin, the plantation's Irish overseer. Amid tensions between the slavers and the slaves, Robert marries the mistress, and soon after the pair kidnap and flee with Emily. Many decades later, postemancipation, Thomas, who has returned to the island, discovers that his mother is living in poverty, and he takes her in. He encourages July to write her story of enslavement and emancipation.

At the Full and Change of the Moon and *The Long Song* are both set on nineteenth-century British plantocracies. It is worth pausing to reflect on this colonial phenomenon as it pertains to the two novels. For both Trinidad and Jamaica, the advent of European colonization in the fifteenth century led to many Indigenous people dying from disease, war, or forced labor (Brereton, *An Introduction* 3). Survivors were often coerced to convert to Christianity. Before Britain's seizure of Trinidad from Spain, however, the Spanish Empire had begun serious land reforms to make the island a viable plantation colony. As Valerie Belgrave's neo-slavery novel *Ti Marie* (1988) recounts, prior to 1780 Trinidad's demographic consisted of "Spanish settlers, Amerindians in villages or in the forests, a few African slaves, and some people of mixed race" (Brereton, *An Introduction* 9). Land tenure became fundamental to Trinidad's success, and thus the island emerged as a hub for British merchants and French planters (Böttcher 165). By 1796, "Trinidad possessed 130 mills and 150 plantations. The result was a massive increase of the population: . . . 2,151 white inhabitants, 4,474 free coloured, and more than 10,000 slaves" (Böttcher 166). Although largely settled by French colonists, Trinidad remained in Spanish hands until 1797 when, with little military opposition, Britain conquered the island. Officially ceded to Britain in 1802 (Brereton, "Resistance" 158; Gott 492), "freedom of religion was proclaimed and the right of private property was guaranteed to those who would remain and declare their loyalty to King George III" (Böttcher 168). Despite being a British colony populated with English merchants, most of the island's inhabitants were Roman Catholic planters, and Spanish laws remained in place.

Noteworthy for Brand's setting is that though no major revolts occurred during the slavery period (1780s to 1830s) (Brereton, "Resistance" 157), several events greatly influenced Trinidad's political position and the slaves' mindset: the Napoleonic Wars (1803–1815), which included Haiti's defeat of the French and the abolition of slavery in Haiti in 1804, and the War of 1812—a conflict fought between the United States and the United Kingdom. Brand's novel evidences that resistance to slavery took many forms, including that "many of those enslaved in Trinidad did seek to escape from bondage. Marronage was endemic, and there were many small Maroon camps scattered throughout the island right up to the early 1830s" (Brereton, "Resistance" 157). In fact, Trinidad had the greatest number of maroons within the British Caribbean colonies (Higman 387). Even after the "slave trade . . . [became] illegal within the British Empire after the Abolition Act in 1808" (Böttcher 180), fears of uprisings or mass poisonings like those depicted in *At the Full and Change of the Moon* continued until slavery was abolished in 1838.

In Levy's *The Long Song*, the focus hinges on a fictional heroine during the Great Jamaican Slave Revolt of 1831–1832 (the Baptist War), prior to full emancipation. The third-person enslaved woman's voice is short-lived in Brand's text—Marie Ursule is hanged by her white master—yet in *The Long Song* the first-person enslaved woman's voice dominates the narrative and all the events. Even the mother's, Kitty's, hanging is told from July's point of view—although, in chapter 2, I argue that there are limits to the enslaved woman's voice. A Jamaican government website claims that in 1655 the English seized control, resulting in "the Spaniards surrender[ing] to the English, free[ing] their slaves and then fle[eing] to Cuba. It was this set of freed slaves and their descendants who became known as the Maroons" (Jamaica Information Service). During this time, the island became important to buccaneers, making it both a wealthy and dangerous location. With respect to plantations, "[t]he English settlers concerned themselves with growing crops that could easily be sold in England. Tobacco, indigo and cocoa soon gave way to sugar which became the main crop for the island" (Jamaica Information Service). As recounted in *The Long Song*, the British systemized slavery. Africans and their descendants were forced to work the plantations, and then the products of their labor were shipped back to Britain.

Nevertheless, historians note several slave rebellions in Jamaica's history, "for example, the Easter Rebellion of 1760 led by Tacky; and the Christmas Rebellion of 1831 which began on the Kensington Estate in St. James, led by Sam Sharpe. He [Sharpe] has since been named a National Hero" (Jamaica Information Service). The Christmas Rebellion occurs during the events of Levy's novel and plays a critical role in shaping July's life, as I discuss in chapter 2. In addition to slave rebellions, the maroons continued to wage wars with the English to the extent that after "two major Maroon Wars, treaties were signed with the British. In the treaty of 1740, they were given land and rights as free men" (Jamaica Information Service). These slave rebellions and maroon wars contributed to the eventual abolishment of slavery and the slave trade in 1838. Indeed, Levy's novel spans July's pre-emancipation and postemancipation life, from roughly the 1830s to the 1890s. It narrates a time in which former slaves like July faced socioeconomic difficulties, leading to another notable revolt in 1865—the same year the Civil War ended and slavery was abolished in the United States—called the Morant Bay Rebellion, led by Paul Bogle. These kinds of rebellions, as *The Long Song* contends, spearheaded social reform and the implementation of infrastructure such as roads, railways, and communication links over the next few decades (Jamaica Information Service). Jamaica and Trinidad both achieved their independence in 1962. The mythologizing of Afra-Caribbean mothers' and daughters' direct involvement in rebellions, marronage, and other modes of resistance actively rewrites the dominant accounts of slavery, which, historically, denied the slave her own account or voice.

Characteristic of Caribbean women's writing in this genre, Brand and Levy "draw on the slave narrative tradition, but they revise it to serve the needs of a new community of readers who can see that emancipation was not sufficient to change the experiences" of Afra-Caribbean women (Vint 245). These postcolonial feminist works also necessitate revisiting the neo-slavery novel's parameters (e.g., Muñoz-Valdivieso; Vint). For instance, a distinction is often made between a slavery novel and a neo-slave one (Muñoz-Valdivieso 43). Brand's third-person multivoiced text constitutes the former, while Levy's first-person single-voiced narrative constitutes the latter. Whereas Brand's settings branch out from Trinidad into several diasporas in different time periods, Levy's text stays more or less in one setting and time period—nineteenth-century Jamaica. I use the term "neo-slavery" in this book to reject this differentiation and to allow for a more expansive postcolonial feminist approach to the genre and to historiography.

For example, the envisioning of the maternal figure found in neo-slavery novels such as Brand's and Levy's "critiques the limitations of realist forms and 'objective' history to convey" Afra-Caribbean experiences (Vint 241). Sherryl Vint's consideration of earlier African American neo-slavery novels that strongly utilize the fantastic—such as Octavia Butler's *Kindred* (1979) and Toni Morrison's *Beloved* (1987)—resonates with the neo-slavery Caribbean novels studied here. Brand's and Levy's neo-slavery works employ similar postmodern techniques, including supernatural and spiritual elements, to reclaim the female slave's history and subjectivity. The mythologizing of the mother is indispensable in each, for instance Brand's resurrection of maternal ghosts and Levy's competing versions of July's birth. As such, both texts "can be considered examples of . . . the postmodern slave narrative, a form that 'force[s] us to question the ideologies embedded within "realistic" representation[s] of slavery in traditional history and historical fiction"' (Vint 241).[2] July speaking directly to the reader further mirrors and subverts traditional slave narratives, which were often written or dictated in the first person by slaves to editors, both of whom wished to convey authenticity to and garner support from pro-abolitionist readers.

Postmodern fictions of women's history intervene in the myth that subjectivity is reserved for (white) men; they also complicate the Afro-Caribbean "male story of resistance" found in fictional and factual slave narratives (M. Henderson 288) such as Alejo Carpentier's *El reino de este mundo* (1949) (*The Kingdom of This World*). Giving serious consideration to Caribbean women's contributions to the postmodern historical novel, Vivian Nun Halloran's *Exhibiting Slavery: The Caribbean Postmodern Novel as Museum* (2009) argues that these fictions of history compel contemporary readers to confront the atrocities of the historical slave past of which they "have no direct experience" (19). Depicting the everyday heroism of the known, the anonymous, or the invented female victims of slavery, women's postmodern novels "urge us to look at history from the point of view of a non-elite" (Praeger 10), and to question "just how much . . . [readers] actually know about the specific history of the trade in human beings" (Halloran 15). These texts strongly suggest that when the history of slavery is put into literary form, it can disrupt official, hegemonic historiographic narratives, which have attempted to forget or to suppress the emotional, psychological, and socioeconomic impact of slavery on the lives of mothers and daughters, both past and present.

Brand's and Levy's texts likewise evidence that Caribbean women authors are "mak[ing] the act of reading about fictional slaves' lives entertaining" (Halloran 15) without shying away from the brutality of plantation life. Graphic depictions of death, rape, abuse, and murder impress upon the reader the physical and psychical implications of slavery on all slaves but especially mothers and daughters. For this reason, Brand's matrilineal family tree employs both arborescent and rhizomatic root systems to challenge patriarchy and colonialism. In Levy's work, competing textual voices undermine (M)aster narratives of slavery including by those presently or formerly enslaved. The result is that both novels directly confront and question the limits of the Caribbean woman's voice in a patriarchal, colonial society. The adoption of postmodern, postcolonial feminist methods to not only critique History and familial formations but also reclaim their female ancestors and descendants, marks an unmistakable maternal redux in Caribbean women's fictions of slavery.

Though taking different approaches to rewriting the Afra-Caribbean woman back into (literary) history—the family tree for Brand and the female slave's voice for Levy—both novels revise familial dynamics. Referencing the pioneering work of Henry Louis Gates Jr., critical race scholar Gwen Bergner argues, "Family ties are more than a metaphor" in these texts; "'laws' of kinship structure human society on symbolic and sociolegal levels . . . [and] in the case of slavery . . . [the] 'patrilinear succession of the planter has been forcibly replaced by a matrilinear succession for the slave'" (258). Granted that masters could legally manumit slaves, Bergner's point, that on the plantation matrilineage bestowed slave status, holds. The master could do what he liked with *his* slaves, for instance take a child away from her mother, as seen in Levy's novel. Therefore, a slave's status can be traced back to the mother, though it is the slaver's colonial-patriarchal society that imposes this inheritance. The biological father's freed status is arguably irrelevant so long as the symbolic white/European (F)ather-(M)aster remains present.

Brand's polyphonic novel *At the Full and Change of the Moon* also strategically revises the traditional patriarchal, colonial family. She begins with the Afra-Caribbean family tree and the Trinidadian enslaved mother. Although Brand's rendering of Marie Ursule is fragmented, mirroring the historical record, the novel, occurring over several decades, aims to piece together the mother's life and the lives of her descendants within circum-Caribbean and diasporic regions. As in Schwarz-Bart's and Condé's earlier Francophone novels, Brand re-presents the African mother and her roots, and yet the maternal voice is short-lived: the rebellious enslaved African mother dies within the first few pages of the novel. Brand's heroic Marie Ursule—the origin of the family tree in the novel's paratext—despite being hanged, nevertheless literally and figuratively haunts the entire work. Reclaiming the defiant Afra-Caribbean slave-mother reorients the protagonists' genealogies and subverts traditional patriarchal, colonial family trees, which ostensibly and paradoxically exclude enslaved women.

In chapter 1 I demonstrate that in *At the Full and Change of the Moon* Brand's concept of matria innovatively repositions the historical Trinidadian enslaved mother's genealogy and that of her imagined descendants over several centuries and geographic locations to show the continuing impact of slavery on Black women. Brand's conception of the facile overlap between the past and the present, island and diaspora, speaks to that which Marlene Goldman refers to as "a specific form of haunting—possession" (186). In neo-slavery novels like Brand's, possession refers to the slave deemed the master's property, such as Marie Ursule, but also her many descendants who have broken, troubled lives, like young Bola. *At the Full and Change of the Moon* suggests that possession is "the principal link between slavery and capitalism owing to their mutual emphasis on dispossession and possession" (194). Referencing Brand's autobiographical text, *A Map to the Door of No Return* (2001), Goldman elaborates that both the logic of capitalism and the slave trade produce "a 'psychological arrangement' that, in keeping with the dynamics of possession, entails being physically and mentally 'emptied and occupied.'... 'The Black body is signed as physically and psychically open space ... not simply owned but *constructed and occupied by other embodiments*.... [T]he Black body is a common *possession*, a consumer item'" (193). *At the Full and Change of the Moon*'s return to Trinidad, as its ultimate setting and the place where Marie Ursule's ghost, disfigured by slavery, and her mentally unstable great-great-granddaughter meet in the 1990s, substantiates this claim. In Caribbean women's neo-slavery novels, women's minds and bodies bear the marks of possession and dispossession precipitated by slavery and global capitalism.

Caribbean women's novels therefore support Barbara Fletchman Smith's assertion in *Transcending the Legacies of Slavery: A Psychoanalytic View* that "[s]lavery's longest-lasting legacy is the dominant family structure that it shaped.... [S]lavery determined how the family formed in the Caribbean, and its repercussions are still with us today" (xii). For instance, Levy's novel, as with many neo-slavery narratives, painfully begins with the rape of the enslaved mother, the daughter being violently ripped away from her mother, and then shortly thereafter, the mother's death. Reflecting a pervasive "anxiety about . . . origins" (Lane 17), Caribbean women's neo-slavery novels speculate that not knowing one's mother, a kind of familial absence, corresponds with historical absence. Hence, the Caribbean woman writer's desire to not only recuperate the Afra-Caribbean slave mother and her genealogy but also reconceptualize the transatlantic slave trade. The daughter's break with the mother, described in traditional Freudian psychoanalysis, still occurs within these novels, but the impact of slavery on mothers and daughters dramatically influences this transition. The involuntary separation is not only psychical but also physical, which has serious implications for mother-daughter relations. Rejecting the moment as final—that the maternal past is irretrievably lost—however, daughters, like Levy's protagonist July, continue to search for and mythologize the mother and her history. Similarly, Kitty never gives up on seeing July again.

Race and literature scholar Helene Moglen argues that in such novels the primal "omnipotent and yet powerless mother" is brought "into history in the figure of the black woman whose children are born into the alienated relations of slavery" (210). Often the mother, like Kitty, "attempts to fill this absence by providing as mother what she could not be provided as daughter" (210), knowing that both mother-daughter are (re)produced through the violent matrix of slavery. Brand's and Levy's texts also negotiate the risk that the daughter's narrative subjectivity comes at the expense of the mother's. Marianne Hirsch cautions that "to speak for the mother, as many of the daughters . . . do, is at once to give voice to her discourse and to silence and marginalize her" (16). The marginalization of the mother's voice explains in part her spectral roles in Caribbean women's neo-slavery novels. Maternal haunting manifests psychically as the unknown maternal past. The presence of enslaved mothers as ghost-like figures further reminds one that the maternal slave past, including the matricides that occur, has not been appropriately confronted and acknowledged in scholarship—postcolonial, psychoanalytical, historical, or otherwise. The postcolonial feminist dimension to neo-slavery novels works to "open up a space for the black female" that is neither "marginalized" nor "subsumed under the categories of 'slave' and 'woman'" (M. Henderson 296). The specter of the mother serves as a potent reminder that the maternal past is neither fully absent nor present.

By featuring the death of the mother, Brand's and Levy's novels refute Freud's understanding of the path toward subjectivity, which overemphasizes the role of the son and patricide. Indeed, it is matricide that causes psychical and physical anguish for the Afra-Caribbean daughter. Such ambivalent endings question whether slavery's inherited traumas can be ever fully overcome. The mother-daughter duos remain unknown to each other and live geographically apart: Marie Ursule is murdered while young Bola's estranged mother lives in Canada; July's mother is murdered and her daughter is stolen and taken to England. Marie Ursule's daughter Bola never sees her mother executed by the master, but, in Levy's work, July witnesses Kitty's hanging. The daughter remembers the physical loss of the mother, which leads to the daughter experiencing "a kind of psychic death" (Moglen 211). Thus, as Rody argues, neo-slavery novels "mythify both the history-generating power of the female body and the birth of a female imaginative power from a traumatic historical matrix" (16). The inability to find narrative closure also supports Halloran's belief that open-endedness defines this postmodern writing (16) and in turn underscores that this genre "invent[s], rather than merely revise[s], the historical record, thus creating a new version of the past as it never was" (17). Hence, a mother-daughter reunion, the fantasy of matria, dominates these texts.

The African mother's death signals that in Caribbean women's historical fiction the search for matria shifts from the African mother-land to the Caribbean mother-land. In neither Brand's nor Levy's texts is an African mother the main protagonist, and with the rare exception of works like Llanos-Figueroa's *Daughters of the Stone*, the daughter never travels to Africa. Imagining matria means realizing a maternal Caribbean identity and subjectivity that does not negate but rather integrates African heritage. Historical novels written prior to the millennium show that Caribbean women like Dionne Brand were certainly engaging the period of slavery in nonconventional ways, but the millennium has ushered in what can only be described as a textual explosion. As the close readings that follow evidence, matrilineages like Brand's and Levy's mythologize the defiant African enslaved mother and centralize the Caribbean as the daughter's mother-land, her matria. The relationship between mother and daughter problematizes not only a psychological separation but also a physical one, both of which are inextricably linked to slavery. An Afra-centric notion of matria, therefore, emphasizes enslaved mothers' contributions to the forging of the Caribbean; rejecting paternal lines repositions and reevaluates the African mother as the hitherto unacknowledged founding figure of not only the daughter's but also the Caribbean's genealogy.

1

Maternal Genealogies and the Legacy of Nonhistory in Dionne Brand's *At the Full and Change of the Moon*

Written on the cusp of the new millennium in 1999, Dionne Brand's poetic novel *At the Full and Change of the Moon* fiercely counters historical and fictional accounts that ignore or denigrate the lives and voices of enslaved Afra-Caribbean women and their descendants. In centralizing Afra-Caribbean voices and their relation to the slave past, Brand builds on her first novel, *In Another Place, Not Here* (1996). *At the Full and Change of the Moon* directly engages with the fragmented historical record of a Trinidadian enslaved woman: the maternal genealogy also strategically repositions the Afra-Caribbean mother. Extending the work of earlier women's Caribbean historical fiction showcasing multigenerational, matrilineal families such as Simone Schwarz-Bart's *Pluie et vent sur Télumée Miracle*, *At the Full and Change of the Moon* joins an increasing number of contemporary "historical novels in which the protagonists come to terms with the haunting presence of an ancestor, often one who has been enslaved. Family and generation thus become tropes for rendering history in personalized and intersubjective terms" (K. C. Davis 728).[1] *At the Full and Change of the Moon* argues that Caribbean history must be rewritten to recognize the enslaved Afra-Caribbean mother and the critical bond between mothers and daughters.

The novel's paratextual matrilineal tree thus discloses Brand's postcolonial-psychoanalytic feminist framework for matria as mythologizing and reuniting enslaved mothers and daughters.

To demonstrate the complexity of Brand's matria as a matrilineal family tree, the analysis that follows brings together Caribbean writer Édouard Glissant's concepts of the rhizome and nonhistory with scholarship on slavery in the novel (e.g., Dhar, Evans, Garvey, Ryan). I argue that Brand reappropriates the traditional patrilineal family tree, defined as unified, filial, History, and single root, for her Black enslaved mother while simultaneously subverting that very same patriarchal tree from a feminist rhizomatic root perspective premised on stratification, kinship, nonhistory, and multiplicity. Refusing to privilege one theory over the other, Brand's novel concerns itself with the interplay between single root (continuity) and rhizomatic root theory (discontinuity), mimicked in the relation between the protagonists, the mother Marie Ursule (single root) and her daughter Bola (rhizome). This chapter thus begins with a theoretical discussion of root theory before closely analyzing Marie Ursule (her death, her name, and her religion), the daughter Bola (as daughter-mother, her absent father, and her children's absent fathers), and the late twentieth-century descendant, young Bola (her memories, her madness, and her song). Reading the novel's maternal genealogy in tandem with the mother-daughter relationships, switching back and forth between them, demonstrates the tensions between the rhizome and the single root as necessary to open up new spaces and attitudes in which to voice the political urgency of an Afra-Caribbean slave-centered matria and narrative.

While an arbolic root operates according to singularity, hierarchy, and linearity, a rhizomatic root expresses a circum-Caribbean space consisting of transnational migration and transgenerational time. Equally inspired by Gilles Deleuze and Félix Guattari's philosophy of the rhizome and Kamau Brathwaite's conceptualization of the tidalectic (*ConVERSations* 34), which captures the region's submarine unity (Brathwaite, *Contradictory Omens* 64), Édouard Glissant's "submarine roots" express the shared histories of slavery, colonialism, and migration (*Caribbean Discourse* 67). A rhizome is "an enmeshed root system, a network spreading either in the ground or in the air, with no predatory rootstock taking over permanently. The notion of the rhizome maintains, therefore, the idea of rootedness but challenges that of a totalitarian root" (Glissant, *Poetics of Relation* 11). In *Queer Roots for the Diaspora: Ghosts in the Family Tree*, Jarrod Hayes clarifies that "Glissant's notion of the rhizomatic ... not only is attached to a specific geocultural context—the Caribbean—but also allows for an identity rooted in that place ... he keeps rootedness" (11). Caribbean scholar Odile Ferly concurs that in Glissant's works, one can still perceive "traces of the root" (4).

Glissant's notion of the rhizome therefore proves appropriate for reading the novel's complex maternal family tree. For example, Lucy Evans writes that the rhizome "replaces hierarchical 'arborescent systems' with an 'anti-genealogy'" (6). Anti-genealogy rejects the notion of progress found in linear novels, "replac[ing] the fixed 'filiation' of the 'tree' with the shifting 'alliance[s]' of the rhizome" (Evans 8). This chapter, however, concurs with Ferly's poignant claim that, rather, "the whole Caribbean intellectual tradition oscillates between single root and rhizomatic thought" (4), and it argues that the novel does not subscribe wholly to either the tree or the rhizome. Concentrating on the mother-daughter plots further supports Evans's conclusion that "Brand's tidal poetics allow her to interrogate, if not to reformulate, existing conceptions of Caribbean communal identity" (15), such as Glissant's or Brathwaite's. Equally genealogy and anti-genealogy, *At the Full and Change of the Moon* thus exploits the space between family tree–linear paternal History and kinship rhizome–cyclical maternal history, demonstrated by the fact that Marie Ursule, the mother figure, anchors the genealogy and text in both linearity and cyclicality.[2]

One finds Brand's reworking of "rootedness" in the trace, which emphasizes the mother-daughter relation and the importance of the maternal to any theory of the Caribbean—rhizomatic, arbolic, or otherwise. Novels like *At the Full and Change of the Moon* attempt to "throw the fake fathers out of Caribbean history," as Clarisse Zimra puts it, so as to elect a matria in which the Afra-Caribbean enslaved mother is "the primal one" ("Righting the Calabash" 146, 156). The "symbolic ideological Mother" provides a strong countervoice to patriarchal-colonial authority and ancestry (Zimra, "Righting the Calabash" 156). Granted that rhizomatic Caribbean roots are "not fixed in one position in some primordial spot, but extend in all directions in our world through its network of branches" (Glissant, *Caribbean Discourse* 67), in *At the Full and Change of the Moon*, the Afra-Caribbean enslaved mother's position within her genealogy complicates this. Marie Ursule is connected by an umbilical cord–like line to her daughter Bola. Bola, however, is connected to the rhizomatic diasporic lives of her descendants, most of whom, for all intents and purposes, are motherless. References to three of Bola's children in the family tree exemplify the family's dispersal: an unnamed child finds Terre Bouillante (a quasi-historical maroon camp, which the enslaved father-figure, Kamena, dies trying to relocate), Eugenia goes to Bonaire in a basket, and an anonymous child is taken to Curaçao. Other brief mentions of place in the tree—a child running to the Rupununi in Guyana, one being taken to Venezuela, and two sisters going to England—equally "frustrate the tracing of a bloodline" (Evans 6), which is found in traditional patriarchal family trees. The fragmentation and the migration of the family stresses that the children are often motherless, nameless, anonymous.

Glissant's notion of the rhizome root also leads to an articulation of "non-history" as the underside or outside of History. He writes: "The implosion of Caribbean history (of the converging histories of our peoples) relieves us of the linear, hierarchical vision of a single History that would run its unique course" (*Caribbean Discourse* 66). The shared experience of an "imposed nonhistory" (65), which becomes that material that exists outside, while sustaining the (M)aster narratives of History, connects Caribbean communities. For Glissant, nonhistory begins with the slave trade: "[C]haracterized by ruptures ... that began with a brutal dislocation, the slave trade ... in the context of shock, contraction, painful negation, and explosive forces[,] [t]his dislocation of the continuum, and the inability of the collective consciousness to absorb it all, characterize what I call a nonhistory" (61–62). The matria in *At the Full and Change of the Moon*, however, invites the reader to interpret nonhistory as the maternal—silenced, unwritten, and effaced—exemplified in her family tree. Brand's text effectively replaces the lacuna in the planters'/colonizers' historiographic accounts, i.e., History, with "the voices and testimonies of slaves like Marie Ursule" (Dhar 33). Nandini Dhar adds: "The dominant models of historiography simply do not provide us with the tools to grasp the violence committed on the bodies of slaves by the machinery of the plantation.... [R]ather ... they are narratives which empathize with the victor" (33–34). Marie Ursule's genealogy and history therefore redefine matria as that which has been traditionally considered the nonhistory of the Black enslaved mother.

Repositioning the "black mother-of-history" (Rody 48) emphasizes her importance in both fictional and factual accounts of Caribbean history and to a conception of matria. Consider Eula's wish—young Bola's estranged mother who lives in the Canadian diaspora during the 1980s—"I would like one single line of ancestry, Mama. One line from you to me and farther back, but a line that I can trace" (Brand, *At the Full* 234). Caribbean critic Raphael Dalleo suggests that diasporic authors like Brand yearn through their "family tree novels . . . [for] a rooted link to ancestors and ancestral space" (2); that is, they yearn for matria. The daughter desires the single root that has historically been denied to her because enslaved women's lives have been deemed nonhistory. Brand's inclusion of the family tree then to some extent fulfills the daughter's wish to know her mothers and thereby know her history, her matria. The "fictionalized family tree . . . giv[es] readers a visual image of maternal and familial roots and an insight into the complex . . . diasporic genealogies that have emerged as a result of slavery and colonialism" in Trinidad (Beyer 131). Originating with and indebted to the enslaved Black mother, matria therefore importantly rejoins mothers and daughters and speaks to the imaginative power of the writer (Rody 55), as the novel clearly establishes Marie Ursule, the enslaved Afra-Caribbean mother, as the Caribbean root.

From the family tree, the reader sees that Marie Ursule is the origin of the matria. Critic Connor Ryan argues that "the novel offers . . . [an] Ur-mother in the person of Marie Ursule," "a strong female at the source of ancestry," and "a mythic chronotope . . . cast as the Maroon matriarch struggling in the dire environs of the slave plantation" (1236). The lineage, like the novel's chapters, however, springs not from Marie Ursule's birth or life but from her execution in Trinidad, 1824; from her death, the novel advances to narrate the lives of Marie Ursule's many descendants, including young Bola, the second-youngest child, born in 1982.[3] That this revised narrative begins with the death of the heroic enslaved woman cannot be overlooked, for it casts an ominous shadow over the entire genealogy. As much as the novel is a constructive recuperation of matria as an Afra-centric matrilineage, the implication is that Marie Ursule's enslavement and murder continue to define if not haunt her twentieth-century family.

Marie Ursule's murder adheres to the traditional contrast between "the single root and the rhizome. The rhizome [suggests] fertility and creativity, whereas . . . the tree or the single root only generates death and destruction" (Ferly 3). In Brand's matrilineage, Marie Ursule gives birth to one child, Bola, in 1821, while Bola gives birth to fourteen children. The single birth defies the planter's expectations, which placed a high value on the "slave woman's reproductive capacity" (Angela Davis 6–7). Given the historical time period and setting, and the plantation owner's vested interest in propagating his wealth, Marie Ursule's admission to previous abortions demonstrates a history of rebellion. Brand writes: "Like Marcelle Dauphine and Marie Bastien and Marie Rose, she had washed out many from between her legs. Like them, she had vowed never to bring a child into this world, and so to impoverish de Lambert with barrenness as well as disobedience" (8). Why Marie Ursule chooses to give birth to Bola is never explained in the text. One can, however, make two plausible inferences. One is that slave owner M. de Lambert (whose first name is never given) is not Bola's father; the other is that Marie Ursule believes that this daughter might escape to freedom via Kamena and the surrounding maroon camps. Marie Ursule's agency over her body, however limited, demonstrates her continued resistance to slavery and her essential role as the root of the matria.

Concretized in the novel's first lines, Brand writes: "Marie Ursule woke up this morning knowing what morning it was and that it might be her last. She had gathered the poisons the way anyone else might gather flowers, the way one gathers scents or small wishes and fondness" (1). We quickly learn that in 1824 Marie Ursule, in a deliberate act of individual and collective resistance to slavery, consensually poisons the plantation's slaves; this heroic act clarifies why Brand begins her genealogy with Marie Ursule's death: death means the end of physical enslavement for her kin.

> When they found her [Marie Ursule] she was sitting in the dirt near the bodies. Her burnt hands were outstretched soothing a face. She was cooing the song they used to hum at night in their meetings. She sat with the dead, cooing to them like babies . . . until someone came. The overseer, the driver, de Lambert. "This is but a drink of water," she told them when they killed her. "This is but a drink of water," they heard her say after they broke her arms dragging her. After they put the rope around her neck, after she confessed gladly to her own name alone, "This is but a drink of water to what I have already suffered." (21)

Marie Ursule embodies the trope of a mother caring for her children, a role that defies systemic slavery and revises historiographic accounts of slave mothers. She decides not to poison herself but instead to comfort the other dying slaves. Facing the wrath of de Lambert alone mythologizes Marie Ursule's maternal role and demonstrates her continued rejection of slavery.

Marie Ursule, however, Brand tells us, is a fictionalized historical figure who attempted to end her genealogy of suffering in the present and the projected future suffering of the island's Black inhabitants. After reading V. S. Naipaul's *The Loss of El Dorado: A History*, Brand claims to have "found the story of Thisbe who in 1802 was hanged, mutilated and burnt, her head spiked on a pole, for the mass deaths by poisoning on an estate. At her hanging she was reported to have said, 'This is but a drink of water to what I have already suffered.' She became my character Marie Ursule" (*At the Full*, acknowledgments). Exploiting the relation between fiction and history, the line referenced above, "but a drink of water," also constitutes the title of chapter 1, reinforcing the strategy of repetition, in terms of both time and space, histories and geographies, that Brand employs throughout her novel. In this context, drinking water, repeated thrice, is deemed routine; even, contradictorily, life sustaining. The cruel punishments, culminating in her death, that Marie Ursule will inevitably receive are ironically compared to nothing more than doing that which is necessary to survive: drinking water. Dying, like drinking water, is seemingly easy; yet, often, in asserting his power, the master would deny a field slave "a drink of water." Determining that death is preferable to a slave's existence, Marie Ursule refuses the master his labor force and his livelihood. Her voice undermines the master's power and prevents him from inflicting any more pain than that which he and the institution of slavery have already inflicted. What need do the dead have for a drink of water, Marie Ursule postulates. Her post-hanging speech also signals that she will survive posthumously, postslavery, foreshadowing her spectral appearances later in the novel.

Brand's inclusion and strategy of maternal genealogy in relation to Marie Ursule's death and the lives of her future generations affirms the enslaved mother's importance to matria. Matria thus entails writing nonhistory—reviving the maternal—as a postcolonial means toward imagining a collective memory, an Afra-Caribbean-centered consciousness. As Jennifer R. Thomas clarifies, "nonhistory can emerge as history for peoples of the Caribbean with the help of the writer who cultivates a historical consciousness unlimited by the traditional chronological and hierarchical understandings of experience" (88). Brand delves deeper into nonlinear maternal nonhistory when she writes on memory. Marie Ursule wonders, "and what was memory when she felt it loop and repeat, when what she was about to do she had imagined done already, like a memory" (9). To reiterate, Marie Ursule's position in the chronology reveals not only the maternal nonhistory of the untold Afra-Caribbean past but also that the lives of her descendants, her survivors, will be haunted, even if unconsciously, by slavery and the maternal. In Caribbean women's historical novels, maternal nonhistory as a certain kind of "dispossession, homelessness, and historylessness" (Rody 110) is countered through retracing one's matri(a)lineage and centralizing the mother. Glissant echoes such a sentiment when writing on nonhistory: "Because the Caribbean notion of time was fixed in the void of an imposed nonhistory, the writer must contribute to reconstituting its tormented chronology" (*Caribbean Discourse* 65). For Brand, chronology without the maternal is nonsensical. Historical novelists like Brand then have the difficult task of envisioning matria by repositioning the Afra-Caribbean mother as heroic, without replicating the same (M)aster-narrative framework the traditional patriarchal-colonial genealogy employs.

Acutely aware that her descendants will be linked to her and Bola's life, Marie Ursule perceptively realizes that she might be forgotten: "In another century without knowing her, because centuries are forgetful places, Marie Ursule's great-great-grandchildren would face the world too. But even that forgetfulness Marie Ursule had accounted for" (18): "she had taken account of forgetfulness and remembrances" (19). Even on the morning she poisons her fellow slaves and in turn is murdered by her master, Marie Ursule sees her future generations. In one poignant example, she predicts the abolishment of slavery and the diasporic condition: "The lives of her great-great-grandchildren, their lives would spill all over floors and glass cases and the verandas and streets in the new world coming. Their hearts would burst" (20). Like a violent birth, Marie Ursule foresees many of her relatives living scattered, separated from their matria—maternal ancestry and maternal homeland, Trinidad. The novel boldly asserts that both kinds of roots—arbolic and rhizomatic—inevitably lead back to the Black enslaved mother. The importance of recalling the maternal Afra-Caribbean slave then is paramount toward healing. Brand indicates that a willful forgetting of the maternal, denying her a root in History and relegating her to the realm of nonhistory, to haunting the margins, precludes moving forward—cyclically, linearly, or in some combination thereof.

Brand's novel suggests that not only were radical acts of rebellion necessary to the eventual abolishment of slavery but also that the legacy of slavery defines the present. The historical progress implied in a chronological genealogy, the single root, is highly dubious, but so is the allegedly liberating rhizome root. Resonating with the postmodern style of interlinked chapters, the genealogy feels at times as if it is spiraling out of control. The book's challenging structure/style nevertheless reinforces Brand's decision to anchor unpredictable, destabilized migratory lives and their sense of historylessness in a matria beginning with a slave-centered maternal genealogy. Well aware that "formal genealogies can interconnect with and reinforce colonial values, offering legitimacy to those who follow prescribed guidelines for establishing families" (Garvey 496), the text reappropriates patriarchal genealogy root theory if only to also undermine it. Yet, the novel resists resolution: it suggests that root theory—singular or rhizomatic—cannot accurately reflect the Afra-Caribbean slave maternal genealogy; only the interplay between the two can speak to the Caribbean past and present.

Neither cyclical time nor linear time, fictional nor factual discourses, can fully account for slavery and its aftermath. Glissant writes: "Because historical facts have been crossed out of collective memory too many times, the Caribbean writer has to '*root* around,' faintly guided by latent traces showing through the real" (qtd. in Zimra, "Righting the Calabash" 152, italics mine). Brand's fusion of historical places and persons with fictional ones adheres to Rody's contention that "[w]hile these fictions pay realist attention to the historical timeline, in moments they also reject linear time for time-stopped immersion in maternal reunion" (8). Indeed, in this matria, many of the female protagonists including Marie Ursule and Bola experience time nonlinearly. Marie Ursule's maternal response to caring for the dying slaves, quoted earlier, encapsulates one such moment. In many ways, Marie Ursule's matrilineage constitutes precisely an "unwritten chronology . . . of female time" (Rody 9). Yet, these maternal times-spaces are temporary respites, for the separation between mother and child, typically a daughter, persists. For instance, in exiling Bola prior to the mass suicide, Marie Ursule intimates that she still holds out hope for a better future.

Although Marie Ursule is the singular beginning of the matria, in *At the Full and Change of the Moon*, the traditional (M)aster narrative of continuity is subverted because any knowledge of Marie Ursule's date of birth or of her parents is either omitted or unknown. Whether Marie Ursule was born in Africa or the Caribbean is indeterminable: "the lineage cannot be traced farther back than Trinidad" (Laramee 2). Brief glimpses into Marie Ursule's past, however, allow for piecing together some of her genealogy. We learn that prior to being bought and brought to Trinidad by Ursuline nuns, she was owned and sold by M. Rochard in Guadeloupe. In Guadeloupe, "[h]er ears' tips had been cut for rebellion there ... and many charges laid against her for insolence" (Brand, *At the Full* 10). The Ursuline nuns "move[d] [Marie Ursule] from place to place, from Guadeloupe to Martinique and then here, Trinidad" (9).

Marie Ursule might be her baptized name, for, as Brand explains, the Ursuline nuns "Mére Marguerite de St. Joseph and Soeur de Clémy baptized all their slaves, hoping for obedience, but they could not depend on baptism strictly. The lash was handy" (11). Marie Ursule's name thus strongly suggests her status as the Ursulines' property and that her existence, her history, is defined primarily in relation to her slavers, in this case Christian women. Her "true-true name," to quote from Merle Hodge's *Crick Crack, Monkey*, or original identity remains unknown and unknowable (Hodge 21). Marie Ursule proves that names are a source of power and authority, however, when she takes responsibility for the deaths of her fellow plantation slaves, confessing "gladly to her own name alone" (21). Marie Ursule subverts the master's power to name, and thereby that control over her or any slave's life when she proudly reclaims that very same name, which was never hers to begin with. Additionally, that the name "Bola" is derived from the African (Yorùbá) name "Bolanle," which means "finds wealth at home, meets wealth at home" (NameDoctor), suggests that while Marie Ursule may not have been able to name herself, she did in fact name her daughter. A strong correlation between mother-home-Africa, matria, emerges in contradistinction to patriarchal-colonial society.

Another possible link to African roots can be found in the similarities between the Haitian Vodou goddess Erzulie and Marie Ursule. Evans notes the homophonic quality to their names, that Erzulie "fought in the Haitian slave rebellion in the late eighteenth century" (6), and that as "an independent childbearing woman ... [Erzulie] offers the possibility of having a child without a man" (6). Linking fluidity and the maternal, Marie Ursule, like Erzulie, "offers an alternative family structure" (Evans 6). When Rochard sells Marie Ursule to the Ursuline nuns, Brand's references to both Haitian Vodou and Christianity are strengthened. Marie Ursule whispers to her new masters, "*Pain c'est viande beque, vin c'est sang beque, nous va mange pain beque nous va boir sang beque*" (Brand, *At the Full* 11). As the only French phrase included in the text, Brand translates it for us: "Bread is the flesh of the white man, wine is the blood of the white man, we will eat the white man's flesh, we will drink the white man's blood" (11). This historical slave song references the

Haitian Revolution, but Brand omits the chorus line "St Domingo" (Brereton, "Resistance" 161), perhaps to reflect its applicability to the entire archipelago.

As Hortense J. Spillers's research on slavery shows, however, the partaking of bread and wine was also a Western Christian mark of civilization, of personhood, and of those with faith versus the faithless (70). Marie Ursule's utterance satirizes this Christian ideology and evokes the Haitian Revolution as inspiration for her role in orchestrating similar revolts in the various regions where she has been enslaved. The song is repeated in the novel two more times: by Marie Ursule's daughter, Bola, circa 1914, when she is ninety-four years old (Brand, *At the Full* 83), and when Marie Ursule's and her great-granddaughter's, Dear Mama's, ghosts sing to young Bola circa 1999 (271). The repetition of the song implies that a generation of Trinidadians, like young Bola, are still experiencing not only devastating inequalities caused by migration and globalization but more importantly the loss and separation of mothers from daughters. Considering Marie Ursule and her kin as a composite of Caribbean nonhistory (rhizome) and historical record (tree) is productive for understanding matria because it provides an alternative reading to Western patriarchal family structures, and it explains why other Caribbean women writers are actively resurrecting the Afra-Caribbean maternal past using similar textual strategies.

One can likewise interpret Marie Ursule's cannibalistic threats as directed toward the institution of slavery and by association, Christianity. Her threatening words refer to Catholicism's symbolic gesture during communion: eating the body and drinking the blood of Jesus Christ. Marie Ursule appropriates Catholicism's language and ritual for her own antislavery purposes and exposes the hypocrisy of slavery as conforming to Christian doctrine: here the white man is the slave owner, who supposedly, like the Ursuline nuns, serves his Christian god. Brand writes, "The industry of slavery was how they [Ursuline nuns] kept God and flesh together" (11). Marie Ursule, like the island, is hostile to the Ursuline nuns, particularly their religion and reliance on slavery. The plantation at Culebra Bay is a failure, which the nuns attribute to Marie Ursule and her rebellious plots against them. Merchants avoid Culebra Bay, the estate is sinking, and a rumor of leprosy circulates. The ruined plantation foretells the inevitable abolishment of slavery. Neither Trinidad nor the Afra-Caribbean enslaved mother, the novel intimates, can be defeated by a patriarchal foreign religion and foreign ownership. The leader of slave rebellions, Marie Ursule positions herself as a formidable counterforce, but as her words emphasize, she is not alone. The rebellion will come, literally and metaphorically, from "we," the other Black slaves who will band together in solidarity to defeat their cruel masters.

Although Brand's novel begins in matricide, literalizing its symbolic occurrence in psychoanalysis, it perseveres in monumentalizing the maternal through the mythologizing of Marie Ursule. Placing Marie Ursule at the beginning of the matria apotheosizes her. Rivaling the traditional paternal Christian monotheistic deity, Marie Ursule, a Black female, a mother, a slave, wields impressive power—her existence influences and shapes the present and future lives of Trinidadians and those in the Caribbean diaspora. Marie Ursule's pregnancy further contributes to matria because Bola's birth appears by parthenogenesis: this mother-daughter bond centralizes and mythologizes the African slave maternal figure within Caribbean history and memory. That the name "Marie" also multifariously means wished-for child, bitter, and rebellion and is a variation of Mary, Jesus's virgin mother (Behind the Name), strengthens reading Marie Ursule as a counter-Mary: in Brand's matria, a Black female slave mother gives birth to her daughter Bola, a Christ-like figure. The matria replaces the white, patrilineal lineage with a Black female-centered matrilineage. Marie Ursule thus aligns with Evans's descriptions of her as the goddess Erzulie and gestures toward a new maternal Caribbean identity.

Marie Ursule, the mother physically and psychically transformed by slavery, knows that she cannot join Bola and Kamena, but she can envision a better future, a matria, for them.

> Marie Ursule, could not go because of her limp. And even more because of her heart, so skilled now, so full of wrath. She could not think of escape for herself. She could not imagine the mountains or Arauc or Terre Bouillante where they said life was free. She could not imagine or believe any place like that. She was ruined already.... But sending Bola far into the hills and the impenetrable bush beyond, beyond the reach of de Lambert and his like, that was her one conceit now, her one little ambition. (6)

Born into slavery in 1821 and fleeing with Kamena to live as a maroon, Bola best embodies the pairing of the rhizome with single root theory to express a maternal genealogy.

Directly descended from Marie Ursule, the biological enslaved mother and the single root, Bola's father is not connected by filiation but by kinship. Bola is rescued by Kamena, a maroon, included in the genealogy but marooned/exiled on the page, so to speak. Kamena is not listed as the girl's biological father. Johanna Garvey argues that the "erasure of Kamena from the story, his placement at the edges of rather than within the family, . . . suggests that other ways of mapping connections are crucial to the disruption of colonial legacies and ideologies" (493). A rhizomatic reading of genealogy, which disfavors filiation, supports the notion of elected "kinship as a central part of its genealogy" (Garvey 491). The practice of kinship, historically employed by enslaved people, makes Kamena for all intents and purposes the father. This familial setup challenges the traditional family found in psychoanalysis, which depends on the laws of filiation as opposed to kinship. A postcolonial feminist reading of the family then includes not only biological members but elected ones, too.

Evans, quoting Glissant, makes a similar claim, that "the logic of the Oedipus complex cannot be 'replanted' in the context of the Caribbean since the Oedipal complex 'depends on laws of filiation, whereas an extended family is circular and meshed'" (5). The matria in this novel subverts the notion of "Family" as an arbolic root in which "the vertical transfer of a bloodline, of a patronymic, of titles and entitlements" takes place from father to son (Spillers 74) and instead focuses on mother-daughter relations. Not even an empty dash marks Bola's father's presence. The novel's exclusion of the father thus rejects the literal and symbolic weight of the Father in the traditional Freudian drama; omitting the overseer's and/or master's rape of the mother also sets it apart from other neo-slavery narratives. If the child's father is Marie Ursule's owner and master, M. de Lambert, then his erasure could also be attributed to the fact that the rape is too painful to recount or that the master denies the child is his. Barbara Fletchman Smith argues that slavery disrupted both maternity and paternity because infants did not belong to their parents and were routinely separated from their families (49).

Spillers insists that "captive persons were forced into patterns of dispersal, beginning with the Trade itself, into the horizontal relatedness of language groups, discourse formations, bloodlines, names, and properties by the legal arrangements of enslavement" (75). Slavery thus violently disrupted, among other relations, the mother-daughter one, making "working-through and resolution of the Oedipus complex difficult" (B. F. Smith 51). Although writing on slavery in the United States, Spillers's thoughts on genealogy are applicable to Brand's conception of matria. She writes: "[U]nder conditions of captivity, the offspring of the female does not 'belong' to the Mother, nor is s/he 'related' to the 'owner,' though the latter 'possesses' it, and . . . often fathered it, and, as often, without whatever benefit of patrimony" (74). Put slightly differently, the child's condition as slave is inherited from the slave mother, regardless of whether the father is Black or white, but the very same slave mother who ironically passes on her status as status-less cannot possess her child in any legal way—this is a right only the white master (irrespective of whether he is the biological father or not) possesses. That Brand's genealogy deliberately erases the white European man, and his violent rape (at least symbolically), from the Caribbean lineage is plausible. The erasure in all cases throws into sharp relief the violent exclusion of the Afra-Caribbean mother and the disruption of her family found in traditional accounts, fictional and factual.

Relegated to the margins of nonhistory, the maternal-slave genealogy is therefore unrecognized by the patriarchal-colonial Father—who simultaneously claims the child, like the mother, as his property but not as his Family. The genealogy in *At the Full and Change of the Moon* resonates with Spillers's radical claim, that

> when we speak of the enslaved person, we perceive that the dominant culture, in a fatal misunderstanding, assigns a matriarchist value where it does not belong; actually *misnames* the power of the female regarding the enslaved community. Such naming is false because the female could not, in fact, claim her child, and false, once again, because "motherhood" is not perceived in the prevailing social climate as a legitimate procedure of cultural inheritance. (80)

The institution of slavery therefore not only denies the mother *qua* mother but also denies a father *qua* father, Afro-Caribbean or European. That the mother passes on her status of slave, paradoxically, "in fact engender[s] the law of the Mother" (Ryan 1241), as Marie Ursule's genealogy demonstrates. Does this explain the ambiguity of the father in *At the Full and Change of the Moon*'s matria? Does the presence of the European master/Father de Lambert explain why Bola has no biological father named in her family tree?

If the child born to the enslaved mother is ipso facto the master's property, Smith deduces that according to this logic, "there was no such thing during slavery as the African father" (3). Although not necessarily biologically the father, legally the slave's master was the father, and his paternal line was the only one that mattered. By asserting the power of the white, European father as *the*

Father, slavery denied not only the Afro-Caribbean father his claim to his child and position within the family as father but also the Afra-Caribbean mother her claim to her child and position within the family as mother. Arguably, Brand's omission of the Black father accentuates his powerlessness, his nonexistence as a father as it were, suggesting perhaps that the white Father, not the Black Mother, as Frantz Fanon claims, symbolically, if not at times literally, castrates the Black Father. Losing the right to one's child, however, also led to the biological Black father relinquishing responsibility for that same child (B. F. Smith 34). Smith reminds us that during the time period of Brand's text (post-1824), the Slave Registration Act of 1815 would have required slave fathers to be acknowledged: "Under this law, which followed the Abolition of the Slave Trade Act (1807), all slaves were required to register the surname which he and his 'lawful issue' and she and her 'lawful issue' would be called" (34). Does this legal requirement mean that Kamena is indeed not the biological father?

By focusing primarily on mother-daughter relations, *At the Full and Change of the Moon*'s matria challenges the role of the white master, Father, and the subsequent blame the Black mother has received for causing not only the Caribbean family's problems but also, by extension, the region's. Michèle Praeger claims that it is not the Black mother or the law of the Mother, as alleged in psychoanalytic work like that of Jacques André, but rather the intersection of patriarchy and slavery that sustains the "maternal continuum" (26). The maternal continuum entails that the daughter, like her mother, reproduce fatherless children to appropriate the Father's power for herself.

Praeger writes that according to this fallacious logic, the Caribbean family is structured around incest:

> Mother-daughter incest has to do with the reunion of the mother and the daughter, the rebellious daughter who becomes pregnant and therefore shames her mother.... When the prodigal daughter comes home—that is, home to her mother—the two women become equal, so to speak: the daughter has become what her mother used to be, a mechanism (*rouage*) in the creation and maintenance of this vicious feminine circle: the production of fatherless babies. The daughter makes babies with (for) her mother in order to perpetuate the myth of the male-oppressed black woman. (27)

At the Full and Change of the Moon exposes the harm this kind of patriarchal thinking has on Caribbean mothers and daughters. The novel further refutes this cycle because Bola never sees Marie Ursule again. Marie Ursule does not assume power to criticize the Black father: "The slave mother assumes the role of the imaginary father in the absence of the African patronymic and the disavowal of the genetic (slaveholder) father" (Ryan 1241). The mother-daughter position and their voices then potentially offer an alternative maternal symbolic order to the traditional patriarchal one.

Drawing on Spillers's work, Gil Zehava Hochberg explains: "With the absence of the symbolic patriarchal figure . . . 'the monstrosity' of a strong maternal figure ('with the capacity to name') offers a radical identity position for . . . women and an alternative narrative of female empowerment, based on the specific (destruction of) the . . . family during slavery" (2). To reiterate, Brand's work demonstrates that the enslaved mother's power arises because fathers cannot be fathers according to the logic of slavery; slavery adheres to the matrilineal line. In the family tree, Bola is described as "Marie Ursule's vanity and whose eyes wept an ocean and who loved whales" (Brand, *At the Full* 8). By virtue of her many children, with different fathers, Bola carries on her mother's legacy within the Caribbean and the Caribbean diaspora. Distinctively missing, however, is a notion of ownership between Bola and her lovers or between Bola and her children. Bola's freedom, particularly her sexual freedom, combats the systems of slavery and religion in which she, like the island, is contained and defined. Bola's role as "abandoning mother and as abandoned daughter" (Moglen 211) nevertheless cannot be overlooked. Slavery perpetuates not only mother-daughter abandonment but also father-daughter abandonment. Bola gives birth to fourteen children, none for whom a father is named, with the exception of Augusta (b. 1881): her birth is a result of "the blind man whose head she [Bola] loved" (Brand, *At the Full* 8). Bola's relationships seem pre-, if not overly, determined by her separation from Marie Ursule, which asserts the centrality of matria in this novel.

Critiquing Freud's distinction between melancholia and mourning, Dhar claims that "like other post-colonial texts, Brand refuses to 'let go' of the colonial past" (30); instead, this work productively rethinks melancholia, "a pathological mourning," as a mode of resistance that allows one to retrieve and mourn the lost object—the enslaved Afra-Caribbean mother and her maternal genealogy (30). This further explains why in the novel's penultimate chapter, Marie Ursule reappears to young Bola. A deliberate though not identical link with the past emerges. The doubling or repetition of Bola characters expresses a mother-daughter connection, wherein both daughter and mother desire a reunion. This matria symbolically attempts to repair the damage slavery has caused to the mothers and daughters featured throughout the novel. The family tree affirms that the original Bola is young Bola's great-great-grandmother and Marie Ursule her great-great-great-grandmother. The political stakes for acknowledging the matria of mother, Marie Ursule, and daughter, Bola, are clear. Reimagining a historical maternal genealogy that begins in slavery is essential for young Bola to learn her personal history; that is, like Freudian psychoanalysis insists, she must discover her family's identity.

Young Bola's loving relationship with her grandmother, whom she mistakenly believes is her mother, sustains her; yet when the grandmother dies, young Bola's sense of "continuity, solidity, belonging and attachment to kin and place" is thrown into chaos and confusion (B. F. Smith 48–49). Young Bola becomes mad. While Sandra M. Gilbert argues that "a matria without men might become madly or maddeningly maenadic" (205), this proves untrue for young Bola. Is she mad because neither men nor fathers figure in her life? Or is it that a matria without Black maternal figures is more unimaginable? Didn't the *patria*rchy, in this case the white, colonial one, exile the maternal?[4] Young Bola, who simultaneously loses her mother and her mind, prefers living with maternal ghosts to an existent patriarchal postindependent island, which deliberately forgets them, justifying such forgetting of nonhistory as logical and sane. Feminist psychoanalytic scholar Julia Kristeva recognizes as much when she writes that "[t]he hysteric (either male or female) who suffers from reminiscences would, rather, recognize his or her self in the anterior temporal modalities: cyclical or monumental" (17), both of which are aligned with the maternal. According to Kristeva's view, young Bola dwells in a kind of women's time that seeks to recuperate a past, maternal nonhistory.

It is not only the family but also the nation, however, that must come to terms with its repressed maternal slave history. Both Trinidad and Bola must confront "the past that haunts" them (Vint 248). The late twentieth-century Bola, however, seemingly has less freedom than her namesake living in Culebra Bay in the nineteenth century, which implies that the postcolonial future has not delivered on its promises to the island's women. Unable to function in her postcolonial, patriarchal society, young Bola delves deeper and deeper into the past; she is imprisoned by a past and a present, inextricably linked to slavery, which forecloses her from knowing either her biological mother, Eula, who lives in Canada, or her matrilineage. Having sent young

Bola to Trinidad to live with her grandmother, Eula, the mother, also realizes that "it was as if I had left her completely and left this family" (Brand, *At the Full* 221). Similarly, the first Bola loses her connection to her mother Marie Ursule when Kamena takes her to Culebra Bay. Both girls, however, continue to keep searching for matria by imagining and mythologizing their mothers.

Although her diasporic mother is unreachable, young Bola's grandmother ostensibly becomes the mother figure, and her ghost appears at several key times. She will not simply go away and be forgotten. As a combination of nonhistory and maternal memory, the grandmother interjects and disrupts the flow of linear patriarchal History and realist ontology. More importantly, however, Marie Ursule also appears to young Bola: "A lady, came limping to our house as if one foot was sore.... She had a heavy ring around her ankle and a rope around her throat. I loosened the rope, I fanned her as I had fanned our mother when the sun was too hot" (285). In a daughterly fashion, young Bola eases Marie Ursule's pain by loosening the noose at her neck—essentially, she tries to undo the stranglehold of slavery and the burden of this past on not only Marie Ursule's life but her entire genealogy. Is this act enough to end the cycle of violence?

Brand reminds the reader that Marie Ursule received the ring around her ankle as punishment for organizing a rebellion in 1819: "Marie Ursule in Sans Peur Regiment to receive thirty-nine lashes, to have an ear cut off, and to have an iron ring of ten pounds weight affixed to one of her legs, to remain thereon for the space of two years" (14). The ring speaks to the physical and psychical impact of slavery: "But the memory of that ring of iron hung on, even after it was removed. A ghost of pain around her ankle" (4). Marie Ursule is a ghost of pain, suggesting that "slavery can be looked upon as a system which has permanently altered the black body to the point that not even Marie Ursule's phantom can be free of the fetters of her earthly bondage" (Dhar 40). Dhar speculates that because "the ring embodied slavery itself" (41), the appearance of Marie Ursule's scarred specter signals an urgent need to confront the brutality of the slave past and its enduring effects.

An engagement with the slave past must include the lives of mothers and daughters. The novel defies traditional space-time continuums when old Bola's and young Bola's mothers are present in the same time and place. Memory, and its association with the maternal, offer an alternative feminist history and space, which resonates with Kristeva's belief that a Western conception of time is typically reserved for men, symbolized in genealogies, history, progress, and teleological projects—arbolic root—while women are connected with space through reproduction and the body of the mother (17)—rhizome root. Recognizing two kinds of time linked with female subjectivity—cyclical time and monumental time—Kristeva nevertheless argues that they are at odds with a masculine conception of time as history.[5] Echoing these thoughts, Evans argues that *At the Full and Change of the Moon* manifests "an 'alter/native' historiography to linear models of colonial progress" (4). Marie Ursule's visit to young Bola thus speaks to both the cyclical and monumental nature of maternal time and maternal nonhistory. Portraying young Bola as controlled by a feminine, cyclical lunar time—and for this she is labeled a lunatic—further invokes the novel's title, *At the Full and Change of the Moon*, and the only chapter title repeated in the book. The moon, like the mother—in this case, the Afra-Caribbean slave, Marie Ursule—signifies both pregnancy and birth and a definitive matria defined by the relationship between mother and daughter: when the moon, a sign of the maternal, is full, the cycle repeats itself—the daughter inhabits the mother's space-time and the mother inhabits the daughter's space-time.

Kristeva explains: "As for time, female subjectivity would seem to provide a specific measure that essentially retains repetition and eternity from among the multiple modalities of time known through the history of civilizations. On the one hand, there are cycles, gestation, the eternal recurrence of a biological rhythm which conforms to that of nature and imposes a temporality whose stereotyping may shock" (16). Remember, too, that Marie Ursule's final appearance in the novel depicts her with "a heavy ring around her ankle and a rope around her throat" (285). The ring and rope, both circular, symbolize Marie Ursule's enslavement to and punishment by not only her master but also her master's linear History, that is, his-time, his-story. Maternal nonhistory and maternal time refuse to adhere to linear time, and thus they threaten the logic of grand (M)aster narratives and official History. This kind of maternal history for Kristeva entails that it exist "outside the linear time of identities which communicate through projection and revindication. Such a feminism rejoins, on the one hand, the archaic (mythical) memory and, on the other, the cyclical or monumental temporality of marginal movements" (19–20). Matria as an imagined tree root and rhizome, mother-time and mother-land, is realized through the mother's and daughter's memory demonstrated in Marie Ursule's and Bola's relationship prior to and after their separation.

Marie Ursule is sung and imagined into being by daughterly memory and revision. Of such historical fictions, Rody notes, "having begun with the death of the heroine's silenced mother, the novel concludes by restoring the sound of the maternal voice, as heard by her daughter" (55). Singing, particularly as it relates to the slave's song, connects the characters' lives and reflects a joining of nonhistory with maternal memory. For instance, on the morning of the mass suicide, Brand writes, "[w]hat woke her [Marie Ursule] also this morning was dreaming the thing she had to dream. Dreaming her generations. Dreaming a safe place for Bola. And she only remembered to dream when she heard the child singing in the damp ochre shade of the morning" (15). The daughter repeating the mother's name counters the white European Father's historiography and keeps the Black mother's genealogy alive. As such, it is an important aspect of Bola's identity and her connection with matria: "From the time she first spoke she sang Marie Ursule's name" (8). Marie Ursule is the center of Bola's life even after the latter arrives at Culebra Bay, the former plantation where her mother was enslaved. It is in this very same place of pain that Bola keeps time by way of the maternal: "[S]he only knows time in the memory of Marie Ursule now" (26). Singing Marie Ursule's name and keeping time through maternal memory mimics the genealogy included in the paratext and demonstrates the mother-daughter bond. Marie Ursule knows that creating an alternative maternal imaginary, a matria, is possible through her daughter, Bola.

From the beginning to the end of their lives, both Bolas cite the past, a personal history inextricably connected to the mother that is dependent on the slave's song. Near the end of the novel, young Bola hears Marie Ursule humming the French words she once spat at the Ursuline nuns, and she hears her deceased mother quickly joining in. For Zimra, this constitutes the "oral trace" evidenced by the "superimposition of the mother's 'song' over the father's 'place-time'" ("Righting the Calabash," 156). Together, these maternal ghosts invoke slavery and transplant this experiential knowledge to their young female kin. The oppression and repression of the maternal is reiterated in a confusion between mothers and daughters or mother-daughter doubling, when the first Bola, in old age, mistakes her daughter, Augusta, for her mother, Marie Ursule (83). Her grandson "heard her singing sometime. Marie Ursule. Just these two words were her whole song" (83). As Pamela McCallum and Christian Olbey note, "Brand uses the presence of the ancestor and the tradition of slave song to underscore the crucial connections between formations of collectivity and developments of Black resistance to domination" (19). Transmitted from one generation to the next, the slave song suggests continuity, but the fact that it is necessary suggests that patriarchal, colonial History continues to detrimentally affect the lives of Afra-Caribbean women.

Maternal genealogies need not indicate an eternal maternal return of the same if rooted in the singular and the rhizomatic root. The ancestral Bola, who always sang her mother's name, has her call answered when the phantasmal Marie Ursule visits the young Bola. With the future perfect before and behind them, the reunion between mother and daughter that takes place defies the time and space of slavery, which violently separated them in 1824, and which continues to haunt them in 1999, the novel's publication date. *At the Full and Change of the Moon* therefore imparts the political urgency for envisioning an Afra-Caribbean slave-centered matria, solidified by the strategic inclusion of the family tree, which simultaneously proceeds chronologically and cyclically. A matria of maternal memory, nonhistory, and genealogy symbolized/embodied by an enslaved Afra-Caribbean mother, Marie Ursule (arbolic root), and her daughter Bola (rhizome root), is therefore recuperated to break the "thick chain of . . . silence" (Stone 272) and to confront the traumas of (non)history.

2

Voice, Violence, and Masculine Suffocation in Andrea Levy's *The Long Song*

Andrea Levy, the author of five novels, including the critically acclaimed *Fruit of the Lemon* (1999), published her last novel, *The Long Song*, in 2010. This final novel's setting, however, marks Levy's first attempt to tackle the slave past directly: *The Long Song* takes place in nineteenth-century Jamaica both prior to and after emancipation in 1834. By returning to Jamaica's slave past, Levy's text joins a growing body of contemporary British women's literature—such as Laura Fish's *Strange Music* (2007)—creating a matria by rewriting the depiction of slavery from the perspective of Black women. Not only do these works revise the portrayal of slavery found in earlier Caribbean novels such as Jean Rhys's *Wide Sargasso Sea* (1966) but they also "attempt to bring more readers to a topic which until the 1990s remained almost invisible in . . . Britain [which] has traditionally chosen to remember its role in the abolition of the slave trade, rather than the way its wealth and industrial development was built on plantation benefits" (Muñoz-Valdivieso 39). Importantly, Levy's *The Long Song* constitutes one of the first neo-slavery novels to be set in Jamaica, to be told from the enslaved woman's perspective, and to be written by a British woman. The matria created by Levy hones in on the special bond between enslaved mothers and daughters. That the son (Thomas) edits his mother's (July's) first-person account of slavery, however, heightens why women's voices are crucial to matria.

The analysis of matria that follows first examines both historical and fictional slave narratives (audience, editor, and voice), then the daughter's origins and the mother-daughter relation (the mother Kitty's rape, July's birth, Kitty's heroism, and her death), and lastly, Thomas's role as editor of the novel. This chapter proposes a postcolonial-psychoanalytic feminist approach to reading the enslaved woman's/mother's voice as informed by Nicole N. Aljoe's, Gwen Bergner's, and Mae G. Henderson's scholarship on slave narratives. Contrary to much criticism on the novel (Beyer, Lima, Muñoz-Valdivieso, Tolan)—as well as comments by the author[1] and even by July, the protagonist/narrator who claims, "This story is of my own making"—this chapter argues that Levy's deliberate construction of the novel as primarily an oral tale remembered and written down by July but transmuted by a male editor draws attention to the fact that the maternal voice, the legacy of maternal history, and the matria remain problematically enclosed in, figured through, and contained by the violent, colonizing, white Father and his masculine parameters.

In defining its matria, *The Long Song* reexamines and combines two specific literary genres that employ the device of an editor as a means for asserting facts, legitimacy, and authenticity: historical novels and slave narratives. Both genres, particularly in the late eighteenth and nineteenth centuries, impressed upon the reader the factual nature of the text—distancing themselves from fantastical accounts. Historical novel critic David Buchanan notes that many authors such as Samuel Richardson "created a sense of objective distance by claiming to be editor rather than author. . . . In one way or another, fiction was repeatedly, consciously positioned as a form of history, which was framed as the only genuine representation of the past" (12). With historical slave narratives, for example Mary Prince's *The History of Mary Prince, A West Indian Slave* (1831), the moral stakes were much higher: the idea was that the more convincing and authentic a slave narrative would read—after having been compiled, edited, and then published in England—the more it would appeal to liberal-minded Europeans, and subsequently lead to abolishing slavery (Aljoe 3). Prince's editor, Thomas Pringle, pedantically claims that he edited and "pruned it into its present shape. . . . It is essentially [Mary's] own, without any material alteration farther than what was required to exclude redundancies and gross grammatical errors so as to render it clearly intelligible" (qtd. in Aljoe 4). Unequal power of course defines the editor's/European's relation to the tale-teller/slave, indicating in both cases that the woman's "natural" text must be civilized. Levy's novel suggests that when envisioning matria we must be attentive to and skeptical of the political underpinnings of texts—even slave narratives.

Importantly, Aljoe defines the region's factual slave accounts as follows:

> [T]hey are all set in the Caribbean and offer specific descriptions and details of Caribbean slavery (as distinct from the US context); they are all dictated texts; there is an emphasis on orality—slaves spoke in Creole therefore texts needed translation for British readers; formally they share a concern with legal structure and language, with religious discourse and imagery, as well as the question of black slave subjectivity, ethics, and citizenship. Further, most of the narratives relied on first-person narration and were purported to be "by" the slave or free black narrator. (3)

Levy's novel certainly draws on the genre of factual slave narratives described by Aljoe, but her historical novel diverges in important ways.

For one, realism was vital to the historical slave writer attempting to educate and then elicit an oppositional stance toward slavery from white readers (Vint 245); also, if the narrative was commercially successful, the revenue might allow authors to purchase their own freedom or someone else's. Levy's neo-slavery novel, by contrast, constitutes historiographic metafiction. Although comfortably shifting away from realism, *The Long Song* still desires to "show the continued traumatic effects of slavery, particularly in relation to the black female body," to demonstrate that "systemic racism persists [today] in ways akin to the continuation of slavery," and to recognize that "the audience for the neo-slave narratives includes contemporary black readers who must come to terms with their own personal, familial histories of slavery" (Vint 242, 243, 245). In an act Vivian Nun Halloran calls "self-reflexive historical revisionism" (7), Levy's neo-slavery novel thus undermines the very same genres she puts to use: rather than purporting to be fact (ironically drawing on historical slave narratives and records), the text draws attention to its ontological status as fiction.

The fictionalization of the maternal slave past, however, for critic Maria Helena Lima means that Levy's novel is a neo-slave narrative as opposed to a historical novel. She argues that unlike historical novels, neo-slave narratives privilege "re-imagining historical memory" over linearity ("A Written Song" 144). Lima draws attention to the paucity in historical documents as necessitating the writer's reliance on invention: "What July remembers cannot be found in history books . . . [T]he novel [is] a memoir of July's experience . . . based on memory. . . . We must remember that while the original slave narratives aimed to recover history, neo-slave narratives are based on re-imagining the subjectivity of the enslaved" ("A Written Song" 144). Lima correctly states that the novel's and the former slave's, July's, narration are at odds with traditional accounts of history, but she troublingly places limitations on the historical novel genre, such as linearity. This perpetuates narrow definitions of the genre and history, which historically have operated to exclude women's lives and texts, under the logic that they constitute nonhistory.

Such limits therefore exclude important Caribbean women's texts like Levy's—incidentally, *The Long Song* won the Walter Scott Prize for historical fiction in 2011—whose matria challenge the masculinist parameters of the historical novel genre, such as excluding the subjectivity of marginalized figures or denying a space for counternarratives. Lima, however, backtracks when she states: "Historical novels may function as counter-memory . . . enabling the process of reading history against its grain, of taking an active role in its interpretation rather than a passive one. Reading Levy's *The Long Song* as counter-memory allows us/her to intervene in history rather than merely chronicle it" ("A Written Song"145). That postcolonial feminist texts like *The Long Song* are set in the slave past further makes a distinction between the neo-slave and historical novel unnecessary—all neo-slave narratives by their very definition should be considered historical fictions. As such they expose the facile relation between fact and fiction, between history and (counter)memory, which is crucial not only to genre studies but also to the conception of matria.

The son as editor further alerts us to Levy's reworking of history and the slave narrative genre in relation to matria. Referencing Toni Morrison's essay "The Site of Memory," Sofía Muñoz-Valdivieso points out that "[t]he narrators of the original slave narratives, whose work was usually mediated by a white editor, 'were silent about many things, and they "forgot" many other things [that were] too terrible to relate'" (41). The ambiguity of the "they" in this quotation suggests that both former slaves and editors, by necessity of perceived social norms, were forced to keep some events and realities of slavery unwritten and/or unpublished. However, as a historical novelist in the twenty-first century, Levy can candidly relay and imagine the brutality of the slave past through her heroine's point of view. She notes: "[I]f history has kept them [enslaved women] silent then we must conjure their voices ourselves and listen to their stories" (qtd. in Beyer 132). *The Long Song*'s editor is not a distant European white man either but July's son, Thomas (born into slavery but raised in England before his return to postemancipation Jamaica). The novel's matria thus underscores that even Jamaican sons can colonize Jamaican mothers and the mother-tongue.

Consider that Thomas Kinsman's words begin the foreword to *The Long Song*. A publisher-editor in Jamaica, Kinsman reflects on the process of putting his mother's thoughts to the page: "The book you are now holding within your hand was born of a craving. My mama had a story—a story that lay so fat within her breast that she felt impelled, by some force which was mightier than her own will, to relay this tale to me, her son" (8). He continues to remark on his ability to present his mother's writing: "Let blades of grass blow together in the breeze and I will find words written in their flowing strands" (9). That there is the necessity of the author, of the mother, to pass on her family stories and her memories is established, but that the neo-slave narrative is framed by her son signals the metafictional quality of the entire work. Although July, the central narrator-protagonist, initially attempts to orally relay her experience of slavery to her son so that he will at "some other date, convey its narrative to . . . [his] daughters," (8) this proves to be a nuisance for Thomas. He therefore determines to "raise life out of her most crabbed script to make her tale flow like some of the finest writing in the English language" (9), which results in her account being preserved in "a printed book" (10). Because Thomas's foreword prefaces the story and his afterword concludes it, however, assertions that July is the central narrator and voice become untenable.

While understanding the slave Creole storyteller and English editor relation as collaborative, meaning that these texts are polyphonic and "hybrid products," is productive, the omission of gender in Aljoe's study remains problematic (7). Aljoe argues that "[r]eading for evidence of a dominant singular subjectivity—and for the voice of the historical figure—will necessarily constrict the heterogeneous nature of these narratives, effectively silencing the testimony of Caribbean slaves" (7), but one wonders how gender dynamics complicate "silencing." For instance, Mae Henderson argues that the editor as author demonstrates a racial identification with the Black mother and the subject of slave narratives on the one hand, and on the other hand nearly conceals "an oppositional relation between" male and female (290).

The representation of the slave's "voice as formal, poetic, religious-inflected prose links the slave rebel not with the vernacular of the other slaves but the highly literate author," which in this case would be the presumed male editor (290). Thus, we must "deconstruct a surface 'female' narrative . . . exposing it as a cover story displacing a deeper 'male' narrative of manipulation," writes Henderson (292).

Reputed to be published in 1898, "sixty years since" emancipation, July's narrative is thus set apart from most historical slave narratives. July wants to tell her narrative not to convince Europeans to abolish slavery (which has already happened) but because she wants her family, especially her granddaughters, to know her story, and subsequently their maternal history. Following the tradition of Afra-Caribbean oral storytelling and the importance placed on women as repositories of historical and cultural memory, July tries at various times to tell her son about his maternal genealogy. At the same time, July's desire to talk about slavery counters the typical portrayal of slaves and those colonized as reluctant to discuss their pasts, which in turn perpetuates a certain kind of silence and "historical invisibility" (Beyer 132). Thomas, however, explains that he is too busy to listen and that orality is ineffective for transmitting her story; she must commit it to writing.

Bergner's complex understanding of the intersection of race and gender, particularly "how race inflects the masculine subject's relation to the paternal metaphor" in *Narrative of the Life of Frederick Douglass, an American Slave, Written by Himself* (1845), is extremely useful for my analysis here. She writes:

> Under slavery, literacy assumes the role that performs in the symbolic order. . . . As an African-American slave, he is not authorized to speak or write, as such, much less to denounce slavery. By representing his exclusion from signification, however, Douglass begins properly to articulate his subjectivity; he appropriates symbolic dictates and thus partly subverts them. Indeed, by describing himself *as a slave*, Douglass resists the widespread assumption that slave identity is outside or beyond representation. (249)

Through writing the life of a former enslaved Black woman, however, Levy questions the gendered dimension of subjectivity. Her work begs the question, in order to achieve subjectivity, must one privilege masculine power because only the masculine is authorized to speak?

That Douglass's narrative also describes the whipping of his aunt, a fellow slave, by the master (reputed to be Douglass's father [M. Henderson 293]), importantly highlights a gender/race identification dilemma: "Douglass vacillates between identifying as a slave to authenticate his narrative (and African American identity) and shedding that identity to authorize his voice as a man" (Bergner 249). Bergner's argument is that the female slave's suffering authenticates Douglass's narrative. He must paradoxically hold onto both positions—slave and male—in order for his Oedipal narrative—master/Father, aunt-Mother, self/Son—to play out. For example, "[i]n the whipping scene, not only does the father figure represent the Law and the mother figure represent castration, but slavery and femininity seem to correspond as do freedom and masculinity. The aunt's powerlessness before the master mirrors the mother's castration relative to paternal Law" (Bergner 253). Not wanting to be castrated like the mother, Bergner contends that "to achieve 'manhood' . . . is to forsake not only the mother but her race, whereas to achieve 'blackness' is to forsake the father and his virility" (Jenny Franchot, qtd. in Bergner 254). This leads one to ask, does the female slave's suffering authenticate the male narrator's/editor's story?

The bodies of enslaved women incur the majority of violence depicted in Levy's novel, like in Douglass's *Narrative*. Reducing enslaved women to the body, which in historical slave narratives was sometimes necessary to show the inhumanity of slavery, however, forecloses them, according to a Western logic that privileges mind over body, from being authorized to speak as subjects (Vint 244). Arguably, "[a] woman's damaged body" permits "man's ability to make meaning"; thus she becomes the silent/silenced ground for signification (Bergner 257). Furthermore, if "masculinity bears a privileged relationship to the order of language," then white masculinity during the period of slavery doubly does (Bergner 257). Unsettlingly, July's narrative is framed by the son; but more problematic is that the son's narrative, and "his relation to the Name-of-the-Father which authorizes his voice" (Bergner 257–58), is dependent on the enslaved mother's condition.

Despite having a Black father (a free man named Nimrod, who is murdered by the white overseer, Tam Dewar, Thomas's grandfather), Thomas's alignment with the language of the adopted white father, including his surname, suggests that gender, not race, determines one's access to the symbolic order (Bergner 257). July's lack, her voicelessness, so to speak, because her voice must be filtered through a masculine one, can be starkly contrasted with her son's subjectivity and his access to the symbolic order of language. Although reluctant to have her words subject to public reading and criticism, July is eventually convinced by Thomas to publish her words. Thomas assures her that he will be "her most conscientious editor" (Levy, *The Long Song* 9), which "confirms the value and authority attached" to the editor (M. Henderson 294) and becomes "an articulation of male mastery through its manipulation and representation" of the hitherto unknown maternal slave past (M. Henderson 294–95). The mother's voice, the slave's voice, then is characterized as lack, as feminine. The neo-slavery historical novel, unlike its historical counterpart, therefore questions the role of the colonial editor, originally considered in paternalistic terms as providing legitimacy. Feminist postcolonial writing contends that these editors, unwittingly or not, participated in and perpetuated a tradition of failure when it came to discursively articulating the Afra-Caribbean voice.

Rewriting (M)aster texts is therefore essential to matria and further entails "discarding the Logos of the Father for the Silent Song of the Mother" (Zimra, "Righting the Calabash" 156), an act that resonates with the novel's title, *The Long Song*. Although writing on Levy's fiction prior to the publication of *The Long Song*, Michael Perfect's observation that "[s]ilences and the unspoken are ubiquitous in Andrea Levy's fiction" (32) still applies. Like her earlier work, this neo-slavery novel insists on the importance of narrating the past as opposed to continuing a legacy of silence, even if that maternal voice must be framed by a man's. Granted that July manages at times to interject and reject her son's interference with her core narrative, the novel still suggests that if July refuses her son's desire to have her story written down, her and her mother's voice, a synecdoche for the lives of slaves, will be lost or forgotten altogether. The "long song" in many ways then speaks to the history of the Mother's silence and her coming into history via her own voice, her own song. Levy shows how the Master's voice has edited the maternal past. This draws attention to the fact that every text is composed of several voices, even first-person slave ones (Aljoe 4). The fact that the English father's surname, Kinsman, introduces and concludes the novel demonstrates again that the Jamaican slave mother's voice is contained by not only the son's voice but a son who has been adopted by the English colonizer and has had to take on his name and language.

After Thomas's foreword, the link between language and voice continues as a dominant theme in *The Long Song*. Like many Caribbean women's historical fictions, the novel begins with an account of an overseer raping an enslaved woman. Unlike the previous times that Tam Dewar has raped Kitty, this time, in exchange for his "limp offering," she receives a bolt of yellow and black cloth (12). That Dewar shoves "a gift" (12) into the slave's hand highlights the unusualness of the situation and creates suspicion and uncertainty not only in Kitty but also in the reader, who wonders what to make of this exchange. Quite possibly Dewar wants to secure Kitty's silence and continued cooperation, although, as Fiona Tolan persuasively suggests, "as a synecdoche of slavery—a heinous abuse of power followed by a startling insufficient recompense—it condenses centuries of exploitation into a single, terrible moment" (99). After July's brief description of her mother's rape—to which she would not have had firsthand access (she has not been born yet)—she confronts the reader: "Reader, my son tells me that this is too indelicate a commencement of any tale" (12). July reveals that white men raping enslaved women, and the silence that follows, is commonplace.

July, however, also asserts matria by countering the typical characteristics of a historical slave narrative. As Lima reminds us, Lydia Maria Child's preface to Harriet Jacobs's *Incidents* "seemingly apologises for presenting a narrative that is so frank about sexuality—she may be accused of 'indecorum'—but in the narrative itself, Jacobs turns the issue of propriety against her white readers, emphasizing that the standards for chaste female behavior cannot be applied to a slave girl" (139). Once again, July's narrative demonstrates incongruity when it comes to race and gender expectations, especially as they relate to lives of enslaved women. According to patriarchal-colonial logic, she can neither fully partake in subjectivity because she is female nor fulfill idealizations of womanhood because she is Black. When the identity categories of Black, female, and slave intersect, as is the case with July, it forecloses her from entry into the colonial white (F)ather's symbolic order apart from being or constituting absence, an absence that upholds, yet at the same time undermines, the entire system.

July's Afra-Caribbean-centric matria therefore opposes traditional Anglo-European accounts of the West Indies (fictional and factual), especially the "meandering . . . puff and twaddle of some white lady's mind" (Levy, *The Long Song* 12). July contrasts the daily inconveniences of white plantation women, for instance the scarcity of beef, with the brutality and cruelty slaves, like she and her mother, endure. By writing back, Levy's postcolonial feminist novel questions the English canon and where both the Black female slave's narrative and the contemporary neo-slavery narrative fit. July tells the reader to "go to any shelf that groans under a weight of books and there, wrapped in leather and stamped in gold, will be volumes" of white English women's "hardships" while living in Jamaica (12). July taunts the reader to "not take my word upon it, peruse the volumes for yourself. For I have" (13). Exemplifying another hallmark of the postmodern neo-slavery novel, the slave-teller's anachronistic literacy (Halloran 17–18), July shows her mastery of scholarship (which Levy echoes by including examples of works such as *Lady Nugent's Journal of Her Residence in Jamaica from 1801 to 1805* in her acknowledgments).

July emphasizes that the prescriptive parameters of the canon do not come only from white women's journals and travelogues or from white men's official records and historical accounts because she knows that Thomas is reading her work and trying to censor it, redacting any writing about his grandmother's rape. Aljoe tells us that in historical slave narratives like Prince's, it was standard for "the editors [to] interrupt the narratives to assert the authenticity and authority of the speaking slave" (4), while at the same time ironically undermining the slave's authority. Certainly, the mother's oral-like Creole tale, framed by the son's formal English, draws attention to these complexities. When Thomas declares in his foreword, "*I will* find words written in their flowing strands" (Levy, *The Long Song* 9, italics mine), the need to contain the narrative, the mother, the matria, is evident: "The power of violence that forces and seizes" (Maurice Blanchot, qtd. in Bruns 70), amends, crafts, and packages the slave narrative into something more palpable for the reading public but in doing so perpetuates injustice and potentially the legacy of slavery by enslaving the narrative.

Despite Thomas's belief that rape is an unsuitable topic with which to begin a respectable narrative, he, as editor, permits it to stay, perhaps because July brings him directly into the story. To censor rape perpetuates a patriarchal, colonial attitude and, in this case, silences his maternal heritage. Muzzling women from openly talking about rape and naming their accusers commits violence on its survivors and permits the perpetrators to go unnamed and unpunished. For this reason, many Caribbean women's neo-slavery novels, such as Maryse Condé's *I, Tituba, Black Witch of Salem* (1986), do in fact begin with the mother being raped. As Sherryl Vint argues: "[S]lavery objectified black women through the debasement of two moments of significant human connection, sexual intercourse and mothering, demonstrating the degree to which they did not 'own' themselves" (247). The rape and the death, physical and symbolic, of Afra-Caribbean mothers at the hands of slavers most intensely shape these novels and play an invaluable role in imagining matria.

After the short paragraph describing Kitty's rape, which mimics and parodies the overseer's sexual act, the narrative switches to an account of July's birth. Several fantastical accounts compete for legitimacy, including that her mother birthed her daughter while working in the cane field. This claim, however, immediately follows: "Kitty, July's mama, gave birth to her in her dwelling hut" (15). The narrator explains that had she defended the previous invention, namely being born while her mama is caning, the rest of her story would be subject to accusations of falsehood. The competing narratives allow Levy to turn "away from the temporal restrictions of linear narrative" (Baxter 88) and effectively challenge the authority of (M)aster narratives. If the prevailing definition of History is the patriarchal (M)aster narrative, then to be heard, July's maternal voice must adapt accordingly. Thus, the narrator proceeds to provide realistic details about Kitty struggling to give birth.

Kitty experiences terrible pain, and her cries reach the overseer. Callous to the fact that she is in labor, Tam Dewar shoves rags into her mouth in order to "stop up her mouth" (18). The silk cloth, replaced by the dirty rag, participates in silencing the mother. Both physical and metaphorical, Kitty's painful screams remind Dewar of his violent role in impregnating Kitty and his violent role in enforcing slavery; thus, he attempts to silence her story. When he forces rags into her mouth, however, Kitty bites Dewar's fingers. Her defiance briefly alters the power balance between them, between man and woman, between overseer and slave. Kitty's physical assault shows Dewar that he cannot shut her up and that she will not go quietly. This is an early example in the text of the colonial patriarchy brutally attempting to confine and constrain the Black maternal, albeit not entirely successfully.

Kitty powerfully symbolizes the matria fighting back, biting, at the very structures that attempt to rule and to control her. Supporting this correlation between voice and maternal power, Dewar, upon leaving the hut, reminds her, "Hush, Kitty or I'll take a whip to you, so help me, God, *I will*, I cannot stand the noise.... And be careful with that wee baby—it will be worth a great deal of money" (19, italics mine). Again, Dewar's response to Kitty's voice expresses his, the colonial patriarchy's, and even Thomas's unconscious fear of the mother's voice. Dewar's threat of the *I will* echoes Thomas's assertion of the I will in his foreword. Comparing Tam Dewar with Thomas admittedly overlooks that traditionally the Black slave's subjectivity has been denied. To assert one's self as a speaking subject, as Thomas does, was historically rare not to mention punishable during slavery. Wanting to contain the maternal voice and conform it to their own ideological norms and conventions links the two men. The Afra-Caribbean mother's speech is met with physical violence, yet Kitty's power exposes a fearful white patriarchy; it is a cruel system acutely aware of being threatened and toppled by those it attempts to oppress and silence the most: the Afra-Caribbean enslaved mother.

Levy's writing further draws attention to July only having access to such details via another source, for instance the midwife, Rose, or perhaps Kitty relaying the story to her. July's inclusion of such events, however, further complicates the narrator's direct remarks to the reader. The narrator confronts readers on numerous occasions and assures them that her tale is accurate, yet the inclusion of Kitty's rape and childbearing presents significant challenges. How July learns this firsthand knowledge about her mother and her own birth is never revealed; and so Levy insists that the reader must question the narrator's reliability and her truth claims (ascertained from both first- and secondhand sources), knowing full well that one is reluctant to do so when reading slave narratives, fictional or factual. In addition to an anxiety about the narrator's reliability or that the sources are constructed, Levy's writing alerts one to the gap in the maternal memory and thus in the maternal genealogy; in the matria, memory and genealogy are strongly linked. One must have a memory for there to be a genealogy and conversely a genealogy for there to be a memory.

Genealogy and memory are necessary for the mother-daughter relation, matria, to survive, and they serve as a strong counterpoint to the masculine record and the transmission of its heritage (both Afro-Caribbean and Anglo-European). One must take into account not only that the genealogy begins with rape but also that it is unlikely Kitty has relayed her rape to July. July must therefore imagine her mother's rape and her own birth, which is no small feat, but in doing so, she restores the maternal genealogy and the voice, a countervoice and countermemory to the mother and her daughter. This act proves to be even more significant because July is "Kitty's only child" (21). As in other Caribbean women's writing such as Dionne Brand's, the plot hinges exclusively on a bond between a mother and her only daughter. The mother-daughter connection, therefore, establishes matria as a distinct matrilineage that vocalizes an unwritten maternal history that refuses to be silenced.

July lives with her mother until the age of nine. One day, however, while walking to market, the pair are spotted by the plantation's owners, John Howarth and his sister Caroline. The products of her labor, her market-worthy fruit (evoking reproduction and her daughter July), belong to her, which upsets the power balance between master and slave, man and woman. John introduces Kitty and makes a spectacle of her in front of his sister. Holding onto Kitty's strong legs, John claims, "It's the work on the cane pieces, they are absolutely made for it. This one will be in the first gang—cutting cane, holing, manuring, tasks that take a bit of strength" (37). The reader learns that this powerful woman, "a beast so ugly that she blocked out all sunlight before her," was as a baby called "Little Kitty" because she was frail and not expected to live (36). John boasts about purchasing her for nearly nothing from another slaver, providing a rare glimpse into Kitty's past.

July amuses Caroline so much, though, that she asks if she may pluck Kitty's ripe fruit and keep the child as a house servant. That Caroline must ask for her brother's permission to take in a slave highlights her lower position in the hierarchy. Although she exerts great power over the slaves and the overseer because she is a white woman, her social standing is lower than her brother's—emphasizing that her own genealogy and memory as a woman must submit to patriarchal authority. John consents, acknowledging that "[s]he would be taken soon enough anyway. It will encourage her [Kitty] to have another. They are dreadful mothers, these negroes" (38). John's words echo Dewar's earlier reply to Kitty that slave children have immense monetary value and that the mother has no stake or claim to ownership over herself or her children. The assertion that "negroes are dreadful mothers," however, highlights the complex and cruel treatment of enslaved women. The suggestion that Black women cannot mother as well as white Anglo-European mothers undermines its own logic because first, the slaver rarely permits a mother to have a meaningful relationship with her children, and second, among many other mothering roles such as wet-nurse or caretaker, slaves are for all intents and purposes mothers to the slaver's children. Kitty's reaction to Caroline kidnapping her child nevertheless emphasizes her lowly, near-invisible place in this system. Full of disbelief and anger, she is left on the side of the road, silent and helpless to intervene or bite back.

The narrator at this point disrupts the plot by inviting the reader to peer inside John's great house, a symbol for white colonial power and privilege. One sees "the fingers of Kitty's right hand as she leans against the window in anguish to glimpse her only child, July, there within" (40). Levy forces the reader to participate in this colonial mindset by adopting the slaver's perspective and having the privilege to see: inside the home, the reader is permitted to move around and to gaze outside. Meanwhile, the white patriarchy, ever fearful of the Black enslaved mother, keeps her confined to the margins—Kitty is literally on the periphery struggling for a glimpse inside. She is more than a mother eager to connect with her daughter; she wants to maintain and affirm the matria of genealogy and the memory of maternal life. And despite the midwife Rose's claims that the great house "be where Miss July belong" and that she "will at last feel to be a white man's child" (41), presumably the reader, like Kitty, feels differently. The great house, analogous to the master's language, is an undesirable space in which to dwell; it is an assimilating, suffocating, destructive place in which the slave-servant is found but always on unequal and harsh terms. In July's case, she comes to see herself as her master's gatekeeper and protector by keeping out those like her mother: "'No big black n----- gonna get past me, missus,' July said, holding up her fists" (83). Kitty, however, continues a nightly adventure of peering in on that which excludes her, which now includes her daughter. Her silent, rebellious behavior from the margins defines her character and her narrative, and in a broader sense serves as a metaphor for the novel's staunch postcolonial feminist position.

Excluded from the great home because of her status as a Black female field slave, Kitty's voice begins to diminish as the novel progresses. Her presence as a memory, however, is not so easily silenced or erased. Although commenting on Levy's corpus prior to the publication of *The Long Song*, Michael Perfect aptly recognizes the predominant relationship between history—that is, voicing/writing one's narrative—and silence as a kind of violence, to the extent that "the dangers of historical erasure . . . suggest that it is a kind of violence in itself" (38). He adds that "Levy stresses the importance of openly confronting the past rather than attempting to deny or disregard it, even when keeping what is difficult and hurtful unspoken seems to allow the world to 'stay intact'" (39). The world, however, is white and patriarchal, and for a matria of Black maternal history to come forth and break the confines of its containment, it must rail against the violence of forced silence. Matria must speak. It must speak the Father's unspeakable crimes against the mother: matria must name the mother and restore her genealogy.

For example, the beginning of part 2 of Levy's novel focuses on a misrecognition of the mother. Working as a domestic slave, July ruins a pocket.

Upon being stabbed with a sewing needle for her misdemeanor, July yells out "Mama, Mama, Mama!" (53). Having invoked her mother, Caroline shouts, "Your mama is sold away. She is sold away, you hear me? Sold away. You are mine now" (53). This exchange between master and slave echoes the earlier scene between overseer and slave and reinforces the connection between physical punishment and vocalization. The transfer of power from the biological mother, Kitty, to Caroline has not been entirely successful. Passing as authentic mother is crucial in this exchange. Caroline is the counterfeit or fraud mother, an analogy for the "false mother country, England" (Rody 135); she exposes that, like the British Empire, she does not have complete control over her disobedient daughter and her slave. The relationship between white English mother and Black slave daughter is a sham. July's utterance of the word "Mama" might also indicate that Caroline does not self-identify with this appellation. After all, she has no children of her own, or perhaps for reasons of reputation, she does not want to be deemed July's mother. Caroline threatens July when she declares that Kitty, the true mother, has been sold to another slaver: July should forget her Afra-Caribbean mother and forget her maternal heritage if she wants to remain in the great English house, which is of course situated in Jamaica. Caroline sees this daughterly forgetting as necessary for her to exert power, if not as a mother then at least as an owner and a colonizer. If Kitty, the mother, can be sold away then so, too, can July, the daughter.

Kitty reappears later in the novel, however, after several years have passed, when one plantation owner decrees: "[T]here is trouble.... A great deal of trouble. The negroes are burning plantations in the west" (78). John reports for militia duty to suppress the slave rebellion while Caroline remains in charge of the plantation. With the fighting intensifying and the whites' lives increasingly in danger, Caroline realizes that she has been "[f]orgot!... I am forgot" (93); "My brother has abandoned me! I am forgot" (93–94). When John does finally return to the house, he responds to the seriousness of the Baptist War and his inability to deal with it by committing suicide. Pragmatically, Caroline refuses to admit her brother's suicide, because as a woman she risks losing everything. Her neighbor Jane Glover "had lost her home, her prospects, and every penny that she ever had to squander upon those silk caps of hers, when her father was found dangling from a beam in their house. Jane Glover had everything seized!" (117). With Tam Dewar's help, Caroline attempts to pin the blame on Nimrod, but before she can manage to shoot him, July rescues him, and they escape together. The significance of this event, which Levy stresses, is that July rebels against her mistress and, by escaping, foreshadows her eventual freedom, which can commence only when July returns to her maternal roots and when Kitty, the maternal, returns to the narrative.

Levy writes, "For it is at this point within my story, reader, that we must once more seek out Kitty. It is at this time that we must walk again within the company of that field slave that is our July's mama" (122). The reader learns that Kitty, who has given up her dangerous nightly quests, has spent the past eight years hard-manuring, and because of her stench, she cannot sell her wares at market. The mother-daughter duo reunite when July and Nimrod arrive at the huts of the field slaves. July's return to her mother, to the maternal, coincides with the master's death (foreshadowing the death of slavery). July informs the slaves, "[M]assa be dead. Massa John be dead!" (126). The slave woman's voice acts as powerful alternative authority. Counter to Caroline's claims that her brother was murdered, July knows the truth. This dispute over the truth supports July's initial claims that her tale will not be in keeping with white women's journals; her story will be one of brutality and injustice. Like her mother before her, her facts are at odds with the establishment, and therefore she must be silenced and punished.

Upon hearing that July has fled with a wanted man and that the militia are making their way through the villages, Kitty begins to make her way to the mill yard to reunite with her daughter. The narrative offers several competing accounts of Kitty's journey toward July, such as tearing a white man off his horse or walking through fire. Finally, two slaves see "Kitty—for suddenly she stood up from within the legs of the horses, bold as Nanny Maroon" (129), and "she fly, oh she fly. Her feet no longer upon God's earth" (130). Fantastical accounts of Kitty reinforce her role as a powerful, supernatural-mythic maternal figure, which leads Charlotte Beyer to argue that *The Long Song* generally "presents a maternal counternarrative to the stereotypical image of the victimized slave mother" (136). The mother who will do whatever it takes to reach her daughter mimics July's search as author and narrator for her maternal heritage and that she will do/write whatever is necessary to get there. Kitty could not intervene on the day Caroline took her daughter to live in the great house, but this time as master of her own narrative, her own matria, July can refuse to let her mother go. Thus, in this matria, the enslaved mother's life is vindicated and written back into the official record and the literary canon via the daughter's affirmation of her Afra-Caribbean maternal genealogy.

When Tam Dewar, however, catches up to the pair, he attacks July because she pleads, "Him [Nimrod] no kill massa, him no kill massa" (130). Dewar knows that July is telling the truth, but as overseer of the plantation, he must ensure that this truth be silenced; thus, following her vocal protestations, he beats July and murders Nimrod. The white father's betrayal of the daughter copies his previous betrayal of the mother by sexual assault. As Levy notes, "the overseer could hardly hold her" (131), so Dewar shouts: "Shut up, you dead fucking n-----, shut up" (131). One sees that "man needs to represent [woman] as a *closed* volume, a container, his desire is to immobilize her, keep her under his control, in his possession, even in his house. He needs to believe that the container belongs to him. The fear is of the 'open container'" (Whitford, "Introduction to Section I" 28). Desire and fear become strongly linked to sexuality. The retaliation of patriarchal violence against maternal voice, a dominant theme throughout the novel and the genre, is evident again as Tam Dewar struggles to maintain control over the fierce female slave and her speech.

Enslaved mothers like Kitty are feared to the extent that the plantation system operates on an unspoken matriphobia, which can and often does lead to matricide. Kitty's imposing physical stature and her dignified attitude make her especially vulnerable to the overseer's violence. That Kitty and July represent a willful mother-daughter duo who, in countering the singular masculine subject, need to be tamed and to be contained is evident with Tam Dewar's solution to silencing July by attempting to brutally murder her: "It was as the overseer raised his hand to strike her with his pistol that Kitty flew" (131). The mother cannot, however, be fully controlled—there are always possibilities for fighting back. Kitty saving July's life is but one example of this disruption because it rewrites from a Black enslaved mother-daughter perspective, the mother as a hero rescuing her daughter. Unable to stop Caroline from initially stealing her daughter, this time Kitty refuses to let her daughter go.

Kitty's, the Black enslaved mother's, attack against Dewar, the white (M)aster-(F)ather, further symbolizes the slave revolt against the plantation owners and slavery in general. Dewar, a man who repeatedly raped and abused Kitty, is finally punished: "All that is known is that Tam Dewar was found, not yet dead, but spread upon the ground of the mill yard with a broken collarbone, a fracture in his skull, two broken ankles, two broken arms and his ribs mash up. Wounds he would die from two days later—fitting, spewing, and boiling hotter than bubbling cane liquor" (132). In this twenty-first-century text, the abolishment of slavery is indicated when Dewar chokes on his own bodily fluids, likened to the hot, sweet cane liquor produced by hard slave labor; the slavery in which he participated has destroyed him from the inside out. For her role as a heroic figure in the slave rebellion of 1831 and as a return of the maternal, Kitty is shackled and sentenced to hang. Hiding in the square, July sees her mother "kicking and convulsing at the end of her rope. . . . [H]er mama struggled, her mama choked. Until, at last stilled, her mama hung small and black as a ripened pod upon a tree" (136). The rebellious maternal is bound in chains and sentenced to die without so much as a burial: a matricide cannot be traced if it is left unmarked. This is why July's memory and/or reimagining of matria plays such a pivotal role in the novel. Her voice gives her mother a presence that History has attempted to erase and to degenealogize. Kitty's death foreshadows the death of slavery seven years later.

Levy fast-forwards time to make two events happen simultaneously: part 3 begins with a coffin, echoing Michelle Cliff's references to the burial of slavery in *Abeng* (1984), in which incidentally/coincidentally the mother is also named Kitty. As the coffin is lowered, a white Baptist minister, who in factuality is the historical figure Reverend William Knibb, declares, "The hour is at hand. The monster is dying" (138). He shouts: "The monster is dead. The negro is free!" (138). Kitty's death, the sacrifice of the monstrous Afra-Caribbean maternal, signals the commencement of freedom. Levy's matria retrieves "the maternal-feminine, said to be the sacrificial object, from being forgotten, repressed, confused, denied" (Whitford, "Introduction to Section II," 73). The casket bears the words of the pain and cruelty she and all slaves have endured: "Colonial slavery died July 31, 1838, aged 276 years" (138).[2] Including the month of July emphasizes the connection between the power to write and the power to name, which has traditionally belonged to the white male slaver.

We are reminded, too, that at the center of this domestic slave narrative is the mother-daughter bond, the matria. Kitty, despite her daughter being born in December, names her July because it is the only written word she can remember after having been taught to write the months of the year (19). As Muñoz-Valdivieso concludes, "[T]he narrator's name also has a symbolic meaning because of its association in her mother's mind with the forbidden skill of writing" (43). July's narrative, which holds accountable the omission and willful amnesia of British slavers and later Britain's retelling of its empire's histories, continues the forbidden act of writing begun by her mother. The lowering of the coffin ends her life as a slave. Joyously, the mechanisms of enforcing slavery and containing Black minds and bodies are thrown into the grave with all the slaves, including Kitty, their martyr, a witness and witnessed, a memory keeper and remembered. Although Kitty dies approximately halfway through the novel, her genealogy continues with July's life.

This traumatic event marks July's wish for her narrative to come to a close. Thomas, however, commands his mother to keep writing because he wants an account of his birth. Levy writes:

> We did step this fancy argument too long for my delicate stomach. And my son's finger did wave upon me for the whole time. It is not for a son to wave his finger upon his mama, but the other way about! And he huffed and puffed to me that I needs to tell why he was abandoned and that I must speak true. Sometimes his demands upon me are as constricting as the corset they bind me in to keep me as a lady. But I must do as my son bids. Else, I may wake to find my valise—with my piece of lace and my cracked plate placed outside the gates of this house, and my nagging bones cast out to join them. My son may shake his head upon this circumstance, but his old mama has now witnessed that possibility within his eye. (142)

July suggests that Thomas's family forces her to wear a corset to feign English respectability as a lady, and if she does not do as she is told, she will be evicted. The reference to July's corset, which acts like a serpent tightening around her waist, emphasizes that she, like her story, is tightly contained within dominant masculine ideology and rhetoric. If her work offends too many, she may likewise be ejected from or rejected by the great house of the English literary canon. This is to say that the confrontation, the contestation, that this novel offers to the historical-literary tradition is not a singular event, a short univocal song, but in fact participates in a wide range of polyphonic counternarratives—neo-slavery, historical fiction, and autobiography alike.

The neo-slavery novel, like "July's narrative, however, cannot be easily contained and it spills far beyond the limits of the 'chapbook—a small pamphlet' . . . that her long-suffering son had originally envisioned" (Tolan 96). When July gets to Thomas's part in the story, we already know that, like his mother and his grandmother, he was born into slavery. This might explain why July internalizes the rhetoric that Black children are undesirable. Not wanting to care for the "ugliest black-skinned child she had ever seen" (142) (recalling a similar description of Kitty), July leaves the unnamed baby on the doorstep of the Baptist minister's house. Revisiting critical race studies on the Freudian family is useful for thinking about July's reaction to Thomas. Recall that in *Black Skin, White Masks* (1952), Frantz Fanon articulates that in the family drama, the Black mother's presence and her desire for the white Father, dominate (25–29). Caribbean literary critic Michèle Praeger, however, problematizes Fanon's belief that "the black father has been castrated by the Mother" (20) and that "[t]he Caribbean woman . . . humiliates the black man with her desire for ever-whiter children" (21). According to this fallacious logic, Black mothers, not Black fathers, are to blame for the Caribbean family's troubles:

> [T]he "matrifocal" family in the Caribbean is not a result of the failure of the black father or of the roles slave men played in the reproduction economy of the plantation; it results instead from the forsaking of the black man by the black mother, who can only love and honor the white father-master. As long as the symbolic Father is fantasmatically present, the presence of the biological father is unnecessary. (Fritz Gracchus, qtd. in Praeger 23)

The Black mother, like July, becomes a scapegoat for the entire system of slavery that originates with and is perpetuated by "the white Father" (Praeger 28). If from a familial perspective the Black son must separate himself from the Black Mother to become independent, then politically the Black Mother Caribbean must be separated from the white Father Britain.

Levy leaves Thomas's story to refocus on July, who after the uprising watches her mistress Caroline marry the new overseer, Robert Goodwin (Emily's father). Robert rejects and betrays July (suggesting that the new, pro-abolitionist Britain is not ready to deliver on its promises of freedom or to accept the Caribbean on equal sociopolitical terms). Unable to make the plantation a success, Caroline and her husband flee to England. In the same way in which she stole July from Kitty, Caroline kidnaps July's daughter, Emily. Like Kitty before her, July the mother who must be forgotten is also the mother who must forget. July cannot save her daughter. As an Englishwoman, Caroline can return to her homeland. She does not have to suffer the consequences of a postslavery society. July, meanwhile, must forge life anew on the island in which the colonizer imprisoned and enslaved her. At the end of the novel, Levy portrays July as legally free but destitute, childless, and severely impoverished. As such, *The Long Song* offers a mimetic representation of historical slave narratives, like Prince's, "whose tales of survival depended for their success on the ex-slaves' presence as proof of the veracity of their account" (Halloran 19). The reality of slavery is not easily overcome, Levy reminds us.

Reestablishing Afra-Caribbean daughter-mother relations is the long song in this novel, though it remains incomplete. July loses her Afra-Caribbean mother, Kitty (murdered for killing the overseer/July's father), and she loses her children, Emily (stolen by the [M]aster/Father) and Thomas (given away to the master because he is a Black slave). Searching for the maternal, however, Thomas relocates and returns to his roots and his mother-island, Jamaica, which supports Caroline Rody's belief that "[t]he Caribbean mother-quest has been a visionary labor" (110–11) in the hands of women historical novelists. The novel's twist sees July reuniting with her estranged son Thomas, who, had he never lived in England with the minister's family, would never have learned the printing practice with which he edits and publishes his mother's narrative. Thomas to some extent takes back the power of the English master's words and narratives by publishing his mother's work alongside his own annotations, but his foreword and his afterword frame the text. One must not forget that the name *Thomas Kinsman* concludes the novel—reminding this reader that this is Thomas's narrative, not July's, and that July and Kitty do not have surnames, a legitimate genealogy—and that Kinsman is the name of Thomas's adopted white, English father.

In the afterword, Thomas reflects on his mother's cause by pleading for information pertaining to his half sister Emily Goodwin, whose whereabouts and well-being are never disclosed. The broken maternal genealogy cannot necessarily be repaired; the patriarchal record's empty spaces signify that the forbidden, rebellious, sacrificial, and powerful maternal can sometimes never be known or voiced. Foreshadowing Thomas's adoption of an English name, July's daughter, Emily, has had her Black maternal heritage erased from her lineage, so she remembers neither her mother nor her mother-island: without a memory, without a genealogy, there is no matria for the Black daughter to return to. Levy's long song therefore calls attention to and attempts to voice the slaver's deliberate violence/silence. Perhaps, then, it is precisely through writing *The Long Song* that Levy in fact creates a matria, because she diminishes the traditional male editor's voice by housing it between two women's voices: July's, the Afra-Caribbean enslaved mother, and Levy's, the diasporic Caribbean woman writer.

PART II
DECOLONIZING MATRIA

DISPOSSESSED DAUGHTERS

Searching for Caribbean Mother-Land/Tongue

In the 1970s, historical novels featuring young daughters questioning their Caribbean mother-land/tongue began to appear. Set during the period of colonialism, early bildungsromane such as Merle Hodge's *Crick Crack, Monkey* (1970) established "the colonized subject's awakening to her history" (Rody 168), a history linked inextricably to the maternal. Reflecting on this era's literature, Hodge asserts: "We never saw ourselves [young women] in a book, so we didn't exist in a kind of way" (qtd. in Gikandi 13). By writing young Caribbean women's lives from first-person perspectives, women novelists in the diaspora, however, have fully taken on and refashioned this previously male-dominated literary genre, which includes works by George Lamming, H. G. de Lisser, and V. S. Naipaul. While Afra-Caribbean historical bildungsromane flourished in the 1980s, Jan Lowe Shinebourne's works—*Timepiece* (1986) and *The Last English Plantation* (1988) (analyzed in chapter 3)—ushered in the beginning of Indo-Caribbean examples throughout the 1990s; new millennium bildungsromane such as Judith Ortiz Cofer's Puerto Rican historical novel *The Meaning of Consuelo* (2003) (studied in chapter 4) have radically shaped the genre by articulating an expanded vision of the region's voices and untold histories.

Caribbean women's historical bildungsromane follow Erna Brodber's directive to "correct images from the inside, destroy what should be destroyed, replace it with what it should be replaced with and put us back together, give us back our-selves with which to chart our course to go where we want to go" (110). Unlike in part I: Mythologizing Matria, matria is not characterized here by an explicit return to the enslaved Afra-Caribbean mother as maternal root, albeit the present remains haunted by the unresolved trauma of slavery, for example in Zee Edgell's *Beka Lamb* (1982) or Michelle Cliff's *Abeng* (1984). These Caribbean bildungsromane instead decisively return to colonial times and the daughter's separation from the mother. These works draw attention to and challenge the traditional understanding of the genre as formation building, one in which the protagonist's development follows a path of telos, subjectivity, and progress precipitated by the loss of or a break with the mother. Furthermore, as Rosamond S. King recognizes in *Island Bodies: Transgressive Sexualities in the Caribbean Imagination*, unlike men's novels, which typically prepare a young man for political leadership, Caribbean women's bildungsromane reflect "sexual maturation and sexual activity, with the former representing transition into adulthood and womanhood, and the latter often signifying rebellion against traditional conservative Caribbean upbringings and expectations" (131). As a result, the daughter ambivalently recognizes that her identity/sexual subjectivity is intimately attached to both her mother and her nation, both of which are subject to colonialism and patriarchy. Likewise, the colonized mother and the colonial nation attempt to "civilize" and oppress the daughter figure.

Frequently in this genre the daughter's rejection of her mother not only functions as an allegory for the colonized nation desiring independence but also signals the diasporic author's meditation on the lead-up to her leaving her Caribbean home. King's term "force-ripe"—"fruit picked before it's ripe and then forced to ripen early"—referring to the premature transition from girlhood into womanhood, also resonates here, especially when read in terms of mother-daughter ties (123). The matrias in these texts therefore attempt to reconceive the daughter's break with the mother so as to alert one not only to the problematic engendering-colonizing of the Caribbean mother-land/tongue but also to the possibilities for a return to mother-daughter intimacy. In rethinking the traditional Freudian Oedipal drama as a daughter-mother break precipitated and necessitated by patriarchy and colonialism, part II, Decolonizing Matria, provides close textual analyses of two pioneering works: Jan Lowe Shinebourne's premillennium novel *The Last English Plantation*

(1988), set in 1950s Guyana, and Judith Ortiz Cofer's postmillennium novel *The Meaning of Consuelo* (2003), set in 1950s Puerto Rico.

The publication of Caribbean novels concentrating on female protagonists searching for an authentic, independent self feeds into and coincides with the anticolonial concepts, antipatriarchal theory/praxis, and pro-independence movements circulating during the authors' lives. Born in the 1940s, Shinebourne and Ortiz Cofer were young women during the politically tumultuous times of their protagonists, June Lehall and Consuelo Signe, respectively. Written from the British diaspora, Shinebourne's novel constitutes the only work set on the Caribbean mainland that is closely studied in *Matria Redux* and that addresses the colonial history of her birthplace, Guyana. Ortiz Cofer, writing from the United States, returns textually to her island birthplace, Puerto Rico, a US territory, making it uniquely the only nonindependent nation that this book examines. Both writers are well known for exploring Caribbean women's identities and politics in their award-winning works, namely Shinebourne's *Timepiece* (1986) and Ortiz Cofer's *The Line of the Sun* (1989). Yet, the two historical novels examined here constitute the authors' most engaging treatment of the colonial past from postcolonial-psychoanalytic feminist perspectives. The young female protagonist's search for matria proceeds in divergent ways: uncovering and decolonizing her Caribbean mother's heritage and foreign-ruled land while remaining in the region (e.g., June stays in Guyana in Shinebourne's *The Last English Plantation*), or she parts with her mother/nation, favoring the colonial mother (e.g., Consuelo leaves the island for the mainland United States in Ortiz Cofer's *The Meaning of Consuelo*).

Set in 1950s Guyana, Shinebourne's premillennium text differs from traditional bildungsromane, which span several years, by honing in on a turbulent two-week period; significantly, the novel is one of the first Caribbean historical novels to centralize an Indo-Chinese girl's perspective. While the women and girls in June's life inform her postcolonial position, it is Nani, a grandmother figure knowledgeable in traditional Hindu healing practices, who plays the primary maternal role. *The Last English Plantation* venerates the granddaughter-grandmother relationship, as is characteristic of other premillennium novels (e.g., *Beka Lamb*, *Abeng*, Jamaica Kincaid's *Annie John*). A repository for the family's history as well as Hindu traditions and stories, Nani intervenes in and disrupts the colonial present's hold on June and fosters a decolonial matria in the novel. In "Caliban's Daughter: The Tempest and the Teapot," Michelle Cliff articulates that feminist postcolonial theory and practice "will open her [the protagonist's] mind and memory ... [and] will take her from the mother country back to the grandmother country, which is, in the end, her own" (48). The grandmother's counterknowledge, as opposed to the "compromised or alienated" mother's (Rody 121), contributes substantially to the granddaughter's postcolonial perspectives. The diasporic writer's return to the (grand)mother-(is)land as her subject throws into question the psychic consequences when female protagonists migrate from the mother-(is)land to the colonizing mother country, namely Great Britain or the United States.

Shinebourne's text stands out not only for writing the Indo-Chinese Caribbean girl and her grandmother into the literary tradition but also for acknowledging their shared past of indentured servitude. In part I: Mythologizing Matria, I demonstrated that novels that rewrite slavery emphasize the importance of the enslaved Afra-Caribbean mother and her maternal genealogy. Here, the concept of matria manifests in June's recuperation of her family's past, for she realizes that indentured servitude plays a crucial role in her own and Guyana's pursuit of decolonization. As chapter 3 argues, slavery and/or indentured servitude prove fundamental to the Anglophone premillennium text. Many postmillennium novels, however, particularly Hispanophone ones like Ortiz Cofer's text, omit the slave past. Ortiz Cofer's postmillennium work instead adapts the bildungsroman tradition to depict a young woman envisioning matria by leaving the island for the mainland. Spanning Consuelo's formative years, the novel captures her increasing frustration with Puerto Rico's conservative gender and sexuality norms. As a result, she resolves to live in New York City. *The Meaning of Consuelo* demonstrates an expansion in the genre, because the heroine's migration to the colonial country shifts from Britain—as found primarily in premillennium novels such as *Crick Crack, Monkey* and *Annie John*—to the United States, a pattern replicated in many postmillennium novels, like Sarah McCoy's *The Time It Snowed in Puerto Rico* (2009). As a whole, the genre reveals how colonization, like psychoanalysis, coerces, or as Rosamond King might say "force-ripes," daughters into leaving the colonized mother-(is)land for the colonizer's land.

In *The Last English Plantation*, enslavement and colonization form an inescapable tropical backdrop. In *Guiana and the Shadows of Empire: Colonial and Cultural Negotiations at the Edge of the World*, historian Joshua R. Hyles explains that seventeenth-century European colonization resulted in three Guianas: British Guiana, French Guiana, and Dutch Guiana (3); the three areas had concretized politically by 1814 (9).[1] British Guiana's dependence on slave labor for its plantations and settlements is indisputable, but as the 1833 abolition of slavery neared (Hyles 45), the British began seeking an alternative labor force. With Britain's imperial power extending to both China and India, it is no coincidence that people from both nations found themselves in Britain's Caribbean colonies. The presence of Chinese and Indian people in the Caribbean can therefore be traced to a British stop-gap solution to its labor shortage.

Caribbean scholar Judith Misrahi-Barak elaborates:

> The peak of Chinese emigration to the Caribbean occurred between 1853 and 1866, but it actually ended in 1884. About 3,000 Chinese went to Trinidad between 1853 and 1866; about 13,500 to British Guyana between 1853 and 1879; about 2,500 to Surinam between 1853 and 1873; and about 1,000 to Jamaica between 1854 and 1884. Comparatively, some 700,000 Indian people went to the Caribbean as indentured workers, or contract laborers, from 1838 to 1917. In the two cases of the Indian and Chinese migrations, push factors were stronger than pull factors, and the whole system of indenture contracts was state-sponsored and state-regulated by the British, often involving onsite government agencies. ("Looking In, Looking Out" 2)

Shinebourne's novel intimates that the historical women who made the crossing now serve as sources of inspiration for women like June fighting for gender/national autonomy in the twentieth century; both historical moments, nineteenth-century migration and twentieth-century postcolonialism, have since worked in tandem to provide a model for contemporary Indo-Caribbean women writers' literary transgressions and the means for "(self) knowledge" and "self-representation" (Mehta, *Diasporic [Dis]locations* 4, 5).

The major impetus for women's migration from China and India, as suggested in *The Last English Plantation*, was economic gain. However, "dissatisfied with their continued state of marginalization and oppression" in India and China, these women also sought "renegotiations of gender identity within the structural dissolutions of caste, class, and religion" (Mehta, *Diasporic [Dis]locations*, 5). Many women believed that social mobility was possible through reinventing one's self. Yet, in the Caribbean colony, the

British prioritized cultural assimilation, as they were eager to indoctrinate indentured servants and former slaves on supposed British superiority (Hyles 45). Britishness became a unifying thread between racially and ethnically disparate groups and the primary means for social mobility (Hyles 49). In Shinebourne's text, for instance, June's mother, Lucille, distances herself from her Indo-Caribbean familial past because she craves British acceptance and social status. "In the British colonies, there was no tolerance for being 'non-British,' so newcomers had to assimilate and adopt the mother culture," writes Hyles (49). Lucille's life also lends credence to Janet Momsen's claim that in the twentieth century, the church as well as the educational and legal systems increasingly called for women to marry and to stay at home (46), which is at odds with the fact that originally "most women migrants came to the Caribbean to be plantation workers not housewives, as field workers, not household servants" (45). Misrahi-Barak points out that Chinese assimilation differed from the Indo experience because over time they left their agricultural background to become merchants. New economic success abroad in the twentieth century meant that the Chinese were able to improve their social standing, which sparked anti-Chinese sentiments ("Looking In, Looking Out" 3). *The Last English Plantation* reflects this reality.

By the mid-twentieth century, the British-ruled Guyanese turned to local leaders for guidance, unification, and change. Shinebourne's novel is strategically set against the backdrop of Britain's waning power. In 1953, Britain suspended Guyana's constitution, sent in troops, and installed an interim administration after democratic parliamentary elections produced undesirable results—a victory for the left-wing Indo-Guyanese People's Progressive Party. As depicted in *Timepiece*, political troubles continued for the next decade. In 1961—in the era after the novel's end when June would be roughly twenty years old—Cheddi Jagan of the PPP became premier, and although Guyana was granted "full autonomy," Britain still retained control over defense matters. Violence continued to roil the country, particularly between rivaling Indian and African groups, even after British Guiana gained independence and became Guyana in 1966 (Hyles 7). In Shinebourne's *The Last English Plantation*, the struggle for autonomy plays out through the convergence and collision of female characters of differing races, ethnicities, and classes as well as linguistic, educational, and religious backgrounds. Each female character strongly influences June's budding postcolonial feminist concept of matria, which is imagined through her perspective on her Guyanese family's and nation's past, present, and future.[2]

Patriarchal familial discourses also reflect and reinforce national discourses in *The Meaning of Consuelo*. Consisting of two troubled daughters (Consuelo and Mili), the mother (Angélica), and the father (Carlos), the Signe family serves as a mirror of the island and its predicaments. As a US territory, Puerto Rico is neither a state nor an independent nation. Angélica, and by corollary her wayward daughters, lack autonomy, and yet ironically are held primarily responsible for the downfall of the patriarchal family/nation (resonating with the blame the Black mother has traditionally received in scholarship, e.g., Fanon). At the novel's end, Mili's death prompts Consuelo to envision matria by leaving her family behind and departing for the mainland.

Offering a succinct account of Puerto Rico's history, Susan C. Méndez writes: "Puerto Rico, of course, has been a possession of the United States since the end of the Spanish-American War in 1898 (more specifically Puerto Rico is an Estado Libre Asociado [Free Associated State or commonwealth] since 1952), and before this time, it was a colony of the Spanish Empire (late fifteenth to late nineteenth century). As an island nation, Puerto Rico has long-harbored frustrated dreams of independence" (38). Ortiz Cofer's work captures the Gran Migración that followed the granting of near universal US citizenship to Puerto Ricans in 1917, and Consuelo represents the large number of Puerto Ricans who emigrated to New York in the 1950s (where they are commonly called Nuyoricans).

Significantly "when the Commonwealth was institute[d] . . . Puerto Rico was dubbed 'the shining star of the Caribbean, a model to be emulated by Third World countries around the world'" (Lugo-Lugo 250). *The Meaning of Consuelo*, however, portrays young women's disenchantment with the island's territorial status by highlighting the transitionary time period of the 1950s when the cultural hold of Spain, the old colonial power, idealized by the mother as an "agrarian, precapitalist past" (Moreno, *Family Matters* 17), is rapidly waning, and the transition to the newer colonial power of the United States is firmly taking hold (symbolized by the daughter Consuelo).

Consequently, the break between daughter and mother, read allegorically as competing Puerto Rican national identities and ideologies of sexual agency, critically informs the novel. While the family and the nation may be patriarchal, the mother is responsible for her children. The mother's attempts to raise her daughters according to conservative patriarchal, colonial values, however, are predicated on "the cultural myth of *la gran familia puertorriqueña*, the great Puerto Rican family" (Moreno, "Family Matters" 76). Puerto Rican literary scholar Marisel Moreno explains the political importance of upholding this family ideal:

> The foundational myth of la gran familia puertorriqueña, deployed by the Generation of 1930 as a weapon against the threat of Americanization, emphasized the harmonious coexistence of different groups under a unified nation, the exaltation of the Island's past under Spanish rule, and the authority of a benevolent father figure who depended on the submissiveness of others to maintain his control.... "[T]he patriarchal icon of the gran familia puertorriqueña has emerged historically during times of crisis against the colonial presence of the United States." ("Family Matters" 77)

Ortiz Cofer's novel suggests that by the 1950s, the patriarchal mother and father were becoming less effectual; instead, those who had historically been excluded from the national myth—Americanized young women and sexually marginalized figures—were redefining Puerto Rican identity, both familial and political.

In the novel, the United States' increasing power becomes evident. For example, American cultural values influence the Signe family's decision to migrate from the rural to the urban; they settle in an American-type suburb of San Juan. Later, for economic and political reasons, family members join other, more established relatives in the United States, demonstrating the shift from island to colonizer's mainland/metropolis. At the time of the novel's publication and the writing of this book, there were more Puerto Ricans living off the island than on (Lugo-Lugo 238). The diasporic location of Puerto Rican writers like Ortiz Cofer strongly informs the novel's desire to identify the conditions under which that migration took place for women, principally repressive gender and sexuality norms.

The search for matria in the Caribbean bildungsroman emerges as a distinct link between gender, land, and language. For June, it means reconnecting with Guyana's "coolie" past and Hindi, while for Consuelo the United States and the English language promise to transform her identity. Diasporic writing such as that by Ortiz Cofer and Shinebourne "makes manifest the double-consciousness of the postcolonial, bilingual, and bicultural writer who lives and writes across the margins of different traditions and cultural universes" (Lionnet 26–27). Such attention to language further underscores each novel's innovative approach. For example, Shinebourne uses a third-person Creolized English in conjunction with Hindi words (the old mother-tongue), while Ortiz Cofer's first-person English text includes a glossary for the Spanish words of her mother-tongue that are woven throughout.[3] Both authors suggest that the search for a postcolonial feminist identity includes the Caribbean daughter's/writer's mother-tongue. As Kevin Meehan argues, "Caribbean writers have repeatedly turned to the *bildungsroman* to explore the promises and pitfalls of regional decolonization, the uneven participation of women in currents of social change, and the contemporary struggle to survive and thrive in the latest dispensations of globalization" (11). Importantly, then, these bildungsromane "depict reality as it is experienced by 'othered' subjects" (Ashworth 209), those who negotiate their identity across cultures, locations, and languages. Shinebourne and Ortiz Cofer demonstrate the ability of Caribbean women's historiographic fictions to not only uniquely question the maternal and colonial past but also reimagine matrias through daughterly eyes.

Matrias written from quasi-autobiographical, realistic postcolonial feminist perspectives further unite these foundational narratives and set them apart from, for instance, neo-slavery narratives, which use supernaturalism and/or postmodernism. Unlike traditional historical novels, which discourage or reject the inclusion of an author's personal history, autobiography in Caribbean women's bildungsromane effectively challenges the dominant discourses of fiction and the "tales of far darker iniquity" found "in history books" (Persaud 18). Because Caribbean women have been incompletely realized in both literature and historiography (Gikandi 13), Françoise Lionnet perceptively articulates that "autobiographical practice reflects absence" (25). Corroborating this thinking, J. Dillon Brown and Leah Reade Rosenberg persuasively argue in their introduction to *Beyond Windrush: Rethinking Postwar Anglophone Caribbean Literature* that rejecting the maternal and women's writing was often deemed necessary for both aspiring and newly independent nations to assert themselves as legitimate powers in the former colonizer's eyes:

> The need to assert or construct Caribbean manhood was very strong in the wake of slavery, indenture, and colonialism, all of which has denied Caribbean people the attributes commonly associated with masculinity—the ownership

of self and one's work, and the ability to be the patriarch of one's family. . . . [R]eestablishing these attributes was such an imperative that the recognition of women, women writers, and feminist concerns became unimportant, and was even seen as an outright threat to the era's nationalist projects. (8–9)

Autobiography is thus an essential tool in the hands of the Caribbean woman historical novelist recuperating her maternal past and contesting hegemonic patriarchal and colonial authority as well as cultural assimilation.

An adamant refusal to believe that "the past is buried and dead and done with" (Shah 12) underpins the postcolonial feminist turn to historical fiction. Collectively, these historical novels mark returns by women writers to the maternal past so as to symbolically recognize and, in some cases, repair the protagonist's loss of a mother-land/tongue. The young protagonist's journey toward maturity often mimics the nation's difficult transition from colonialism to independence, and the daughter's complex relationship with her mother is reflective of the daughter-island-mother-country paradigm. Historical novel scholar Caroline Rody observes that one cannot doubt "the centrality of maternal presences in Caribbean literature," but it is a "complex and ambiguous figuration, in which . . . [the] mother is . . . at once 'good' and 'bad,' beloved but terribly problematic. . . . It is her capacity to embody history that associates the Caribbean mother-island, in writings by both men and women, with sickness, death, abandonment, rejection, and failure" (113). Ambivalence, expressed in psychoanalytic and postcolonial terms, characterizes the Caribbean mothers and their (is)lands throughout these bildungsromane.

In this colonial context, a girl improves her socioeconomic status through her mother's dream of social mobility for the family, for instance an eldest daughter's colonial education won by hard work, intelligence, scholarship, and fluency in English. Consequently, the daughter's privileged position creates distance between her and her less-formally educated mother. Rebecca Ashworth notes that "the peculiar nature of this irony is that it is the result of her mother's own internalization of colonial values that caused the friction between them and has been experienced . . . as a betrayal" by the daughter (214). Often, the daughter is contemptuous of the mother who imperfectly ventriloquizes the colonizer's rhetoric, but, as Shinebourne's *The Last English Plantation* and Ortiz Cofer's *The Meaning of Consuelo* demonstrate, a dilemma emerges. If the mother mimics the colonizer, she is rejected by her anticolonial daughter (e.g., Guyana or Puerto Rico); if the mother does not mimic the colonizer, she is rejected by her colonial mother (e.g., Britain or the United States). The mother figure finds herself ironically in a no-man's-land and without recourse to speech. The mother-daughter, colonizer-colonized relationships found in the genre therefore speak to ambivalence in the psychoanalytic (Freud) and postcolonial (Bhabha, "Of Mimicry and Man") sense as "the conflict between the two primal instincts" (Freud, *Civilization and Its Discontents* 84). Simultaneous oppositional feelings—love/hate, attraction/repulsion, for an object or person, in this case the colonized mother—are readily found in these texts. That with few exceptions there are no sons, biological or symbolic, further emphasizes a reworking of the bildungsroman genre and Freud's mother-father-son triad in favor of mother-daughter dyads.

Daughterly distance occurs physically and emotionally. Caribbean literary scholar Carole Boyce Davies explains that the daughter's break is twofold—first from the mother and then from the mother-land/tongue: "The mother's seemingly brutal way of instituting this break produces emotions in the daughter which border on hatred, but actively produce an intense love/hate sequence with much pain and rejection for both women. Separation and loss throughout these texts follow a pattern of repetition which produce[s] her migration at the end" (*Black Women* 125). In Cofer Ortiz's novel, Consuelo leaves her colonized mother/land, Puerto Rico, for the mainland United States, not necessarily in search of a better socioeconomic position but for a more expressive and sexually liberating space for women. Given Consuelo's propensity for writing letters, presumably she becomes an author in New York City. Consuelo's relationships with several transgressive figures (her homosexual cousin, a transgender neighbor, and her exuberant sister) inspire her to find her voice and to defy traditional gender and sexuality norms for young Puerto Rican women (passive, silent, pious, virgin, maternal, and heterosexual).

Ashworth cogently states that such "novels establish the female body, women's sexuality, and the relationships between women as important themes in the region's decolonization" (216), while Rosamond King contends that the bildungsroman offers "an intimate counterarchive to official documents" (157). Granted that sexual desire and maturity remain by and large absent in Shinebourne's narrative (perhaps reflecting the nation-yet-to-come), reinforcing the author's novel approach to the genre, many Caribbean bildungsromane such as *The Meaning of Consuelo* articulate the protagonist's sexual experiences as integral to her conception of self. Consuelo subsequently perceives her sister Mili's madness as linked to the family's and the nation's policing of her sexuality/speech. Corroborating this reading, Ashworth writes that "female 'madness' signifies a crisis of identity for both the female subject and, symbolically, the nation. The fissure between the female body and psyche is not only indicative of cultural alienation and loss, but also the sociohistorical determinants of women's sexuality and self-possession" (209). To have the feminist life and independence she desires, Consuelo believes that she must free herself from Puerto Rico's rigid *patria*rchy, enforced primarily by the mother, acting on the (F)ather's behalf. Consuelo envisions matria as a sexually liberated space in which women have creative freedom, the mainland as opposed to the island. Bearing this in mind, my analysis engages gender theorist Judith Butler's insights into the compulsive heterosexuality of the Oedipal complex and the crisis this causes young women and men.

The mother-daughter's reimagined Oedipal complex must be considered in its colonial context. Critiquing the standard psychoanalytic interpretation of mother-daughters, Luce Irigaray argues that patriarchal societies exclude the law of the mother: "This means that love between mother and daughter, [is] rendered impossible by the patriarchal regime (and Freud, as it happens, tells us the same thing)" (*The Irigaray Reader* 199). Female characters experiencing psychic ruptures as a result of colonialism are pervasive throughout *Matria Redux*, and while in Shinebourne's novel June is healed by a wise, older Hindu woman, maternal mentors are missing in Ortiz Cofer's novel. Although writing explicitly on Ortiz Cofer's novels, Maya Socolovsky's assertion applies to Shinebourne's text too: "At the root of external migration lies internal migration: a legacy of displacement that becomes expressed . . . through examples of collective and personal exile both within and without the island itself" (96). Migration and exile are connected here with the mother. Both domestic novels intimate that a decolonial matria is possible when the colonial-patriarchal mother-land is rejected. The novels highlight that neither the legacy of patriarchal colonialism—which begins with slavery and indentured servitude—nor the transformation of the mother figure into a colonial informant has been adequately acknowledged.

Contrary to Consuelo in Ortiz Cofer's postmillennium novel, who seeks to distance herself from her patriarchal land's/mother's history, in Shinebourne's premillennial novel, June desires a connection with her maternal past. She regards learning about her Indo-Chinese heritage as a necessary part of her postcolonial feminist literacy. The novel thus raises another quandary for postcolonial feminism: if the land is under the colonial control of Britain as mother country, and it is engendered as a mother (Lucille), then, according to both postcolonial and psychoanalytic theory, she (Lucille and Britain) must be rejected, if the daughter/nation (June/Guyana) is to achieve independence. Rightly uncomfortable with excising the mother as a means toward self-determination, June reveals the patriarchal underpinnings of both theories. Instead, she turns to her foremothers—indentured servants from India and China—who inspire her to forge an anticolonial, antipatriarchal connection to the mother. June envisions an egalitarian Guyana, a matria, that is proud of its "coolie" (plantation laborer) Indo-Chinese heritage. In chapter 3, I analyze the novel in relation to Freudian mother-daughter conflicts and the postcolonial feminist theory of "coolitude." Chapter 4 posits that Consuelo's desire for gender and sexual equality cannot be realized by recuperating Puerto Rico's Spanish past. For Consuelo, the possibility for matria manifests when she emigrates to the US mainland. The protagonist in each novel carves out a path that is different from her mother's. The colonized maternal continuum in these texts is definitively broken by daughterly figures not so much to condemn their mothers directly but rather to challenge the patriarchal sociopolitical structures that colonized their mothers-lands/tongues and caused the rift to begin with.

3

Maternal Conflicts, Coolitude, and Colonialism in Jan Lowe Shinebourne's *The Last English Plantation*

Jan Lowe Shinebourne's novel *The Last English Plantation* (1988) imagines two critical weeks in the life of twelve-year-old June Lehall and her nation, Guyana. Set in the 1950s, a revolt at the sugar plantation in New Dam village prompts June, the Indo-Chinese protagonist, to begin seriously questioning British colonialism and its discriminatory social hierarchies based on race, class, gender, and culture. June's increasing gender-class-race consciousness coincides with the country's attempt to reject its British colonial-plantation system in favor of left-wing political independence. As such, this bildungsroman echoes the physic and political tensions Shinebourne depicted in her first novel, *Timepiece* (1986). Both texts importantly give the Indo-Chinese woman "a sense of history and rootedness" that directly undermines patriarchal, colonial power and entrenched ethnic divisions in Guyana (Arnold 97). Guyana's desire for national independence—signified by the titular last English plantation—and the Guyanese girl's awakening of a postcolonial feminist consciousness coincide with a break from the mother country. This chapter argues that in Shinebourne's *The Last English Plantation*, the daughter's psychic-physical break from the mother extends the traditional psychoanalytic Oedipal model to include the role of colonialism. *The Last*

English Plantation suggests that matria can only be achieved when the colonial mother/mother country is rejected and a decolonized maternal figure and space is envisioned.

Generally speaking, until the mid-1980s women subjects and authors were largely excluded from literary and historical discourses in Guyana. Writers like Grace Nichols, Beryl Gilroy, and Shinebourne, however, responded to this silencing with inventive works featuring young women. These authors caused a boom in not only Guyanese women's writing but also, in Shinebourne's case, Indo-Caribbean women's writing specifically. Literary scholar Brinda Mehta explains that "Indo-Caribbean women writers from Guyana and Trinidad have been subjected to a particular literary and cultural eclipsing by their black counterparts, by the diasporic hegemony of South Asian writers from North America and Britain, by Indian men and by women writers from India" (*Diasporic [Dis]locations* 1). She further notes that until recently "male prejudice and literary chauvinism" impeded Indo-Caribbean women writers' critical reception across the region (*Diasporic [Dis]locations* 23). This might explain why *The Last English Plantation* has not received the critical recognition it deserves. Early postcolonial fictions of Indo-Chinese women's history like Shinebourne's nevertheless have undeniably paved the way for many Indo-Chinese-Caribbean, and Guyanese women's historical novels, including those by Shani Mootoo, Ramabai Espinet, Denise Harris, Lakshmi Persaud, Oonya Kempadoo, and Ryhaan Shah.

Recognizing Shinebourne's literary contribution to the historical novel genre, this chapter combines psychoanalysis, feminism, and postcolonial theory to offer a new and nuanced reading of the novel's female protagonists; it draws specifically on Véronique Bragard's and Brinda Mehta's theories of coolitude/coolie-ness to argue that Shinebourne's novel revises the patriarchal Oedipal complex from a postcolonial feminist perspective and in doing so rewrites Guyana as a matria. I begin with an analysis of coolitude-coolieness theory before closely reading the multivalent lives and storylines of the five girls and women who, differing in their material (racial, class, ethnic, linguistic) positions, have the most impact on June: June's Indo-Guyanese mother, Lucille; the white English overseer's daughters Annie and Sarah Beardsley; June's Afro-Guyanese classmate, Lavender Jones; and, the elderly Indo-Guyanese villager, Nani Dharamdai Misir.

Revising women's history is fundamental to anticolonial literature like Shinebourne's as Caribbean feminist theorists (Baksh, Bragard, Mahabir,

Mehta, Misrahi-Barak, Pirbhai) have pointed out. Novels reimagining Indo and Chinese indentured servants' perspectives from the early/mid-nineteenth century to the mid-twentieth century have been particularly important to this anticolonial project, such as Shinebourne's recent novel *The Last Ship* (2015). Such writers have turned to "the fictionalization of history... slowly extracting out of oblivion the history of a forgotten slavery, all the more painful because it was not considered enslavement but indentured servitude" (Misrahi-Barak, "Looking In, Looking Out" 4). In a Caribbean context, like Guyana, *coolie* relates directly to those with ancestors who immigrated as indentured laborers; it is "a racialized epithet of inferiority and alterity to designate Indo-Caribbean populations, [and] remains, even today, a highly loaded and pejorative term that denigrates all things Indian" (Mehta, *Diasporic [Dis]locations* 2). Mehta elaborates that "[t]he term 'coolie,' as an original signifier of caste and class disparity in India and China, refers to the porter class of unskilled, cheaply-employed laborers, a readily exploitable mass labor force whose only value was located in its utilitarian capacities. Created by class-determined occupational necessities, coolies were situated at the very bottom of the four-tiered Hindu caste structure" (*Diasporic [Dis]locations* 125). In *The Last English Plantation*, however, June revaluates her laboring ancestors' lives and reclaims the word *coolie* for decolonizing purposes.

June understands that she "must gain knowledge about her Indian heritage before she negotiates biculturality, a process wherein the past's repressed traces can only be uncovered" through her female ancestors' memories (Mehta, *Notions of Identity* 146). Linking the Indian and Chinese experience together under the term *coolie* reinterprets the repressed trace as the Indo-Chinese Caribbean maternal; it "reveals the ontological urgency to recover a primary loss characterizing" June's position (Mehta, *Notions of Identity* 146). Quoting the Indo-Mauritian poet Khal Torabully, who coined the terms "coolitude" and "coolie historicity," Mehta notes that, for Indo-Chinese girls like June, problematically there "is no real founding text of their indentureship"; that is, there is no founding mother, or mother-text, to which they can return (146). Significantly, then, matria is envisioned in the novel as an imaginative reconstruction and decolonization of *coolie* maternal heritage so as to forge a new Guyana/Guyanese identity for women.

The only mother June knows is the one who has assimilated to British values and customs, resulting in a deliberate "cultural disinheritance" (Mehta,

Notions of Identity 147) of Indian values. It is, however, through other female figures like the Hindu elder Nani (discussed below) that June begins to seek a matria to "appease the pain of historical uprootedness" and to recuperate that "irrepressible trace," which is the psychic-historical Indo-Chinese maternal (Mehta 147). June's postcolonial feminism gives visibility to and integrates her indentured past, consequently establishing an "umbilical affinity with India" if not also with China (Mehta 148). Although focusing strictly on the Indo experience, Mehta's questions are applicable for the matria in Shinebourne's text; she asks, "[D]oes the Indian component constitute a separate or integrated track in the creolized imaginary of contemporary [Guyana] ... or will Indians be condemned to repeat the traumatic displacement of Otherness experienced by their ancestors?" (Mehta, *Notions of Identity* 149); "will an Indian-centered discourse of belonging offer a script of belonging for disenfranchised Indians, just as negritude offered a locus of cultural, political, and ethnic relocation for alienated blacks in the diaspora?" (149). These questions align with June's challenging of Guyana's "authorizing discourses," including patriarchal-colonial British and patriarchal Indian ones, which "marginaliz[e] women through their purist and confining notions of ideal womanhood located in reductive characterizations of Mother India" (Mehta 149). June's concept of matria instead retheorizes Guyana's coolie maternal past to foster anticolonial, antipatriarchal bonds between women in the present.

Racism and sexism, inherent in the leading discourses of this period, are discarded by June, who, preferring a theory of coolitude, envisions matria as Guyana's postcolonial feminist future. Resonating with but critiquing theories of Créolité for not integrating "coolies as fully fledged literary creations," Torabully explains that coolitude is "an aesthetic blend, a kind of mix of complex culture, bringing to the *imaginaire* a part of the other. It calls to attention 'Indianness' in relation with 'Otherness' as a premise which leads to a transcultural awareness" (Carter and Torabully 168). He further explains that in these texts, "a mirror is held to History, a moment of History, when the struggle between the descendants of slaves and the descendants of coolies was real, each fighting to carve out a place in the plantocracies" (168). In an earlier work, Mehta suggested that Torabully's notion of coolitude was an essentialist concept, lacked a political agenda, and offered "a displaced imaginary construction of nostalgia" ("The Colonial Curriculum" 126). Having since revised her thinking, Mehta concedes that coolitude might offer the potential to "transcend the limitations of local identity politics by embracing a larger diasporic consciousness, while retaining Indian distinctiveness at the same time" (*Notions of Identity* 151). While Mehta remains skeptical whether coolitude can accurately express women's lives, Bragard adopts the term precisely for advocating for cultural pluralism; coolitude's insistence on revising History further lends itself to conceiving postcolonial historical fiction like *The Last English Plantation*.

According to Bragard, "Coolitude gathers but also illustrates how most literary works from the coolie diaspora are concerned with the poetic retrieving and imaginative re-exploration of the past. The emergence of coolie literature enables readers to discover what has been hidden or shrouded in silence, the truth of what has ensued since thousands of Indian indentured laborers crossed the Kala Pani (dark waters)" ("Coolie Woman" 14). Helen Scott, quoting Bragard, therefore shows how "a reclaiming of the racist term [i]s a 'means of palliating what history, in its western conceptualization, has not been able to do'... to describe Shinebourne's 'remembering of the past, of Indian values and rituals... as a healing process' that uncovers 'an identity that is plural and migratory'" (H. Scott 95). Bragard's understanding of coolitude in the novel further supports reading the novel's matria as one of women's multiplicity, cyclicality, and subjectivity in contradistinction to a singular, linear, objective rendering of history that is conceived as Western and male.

The novel demonstrates how coolitude informs maternal history and vice versa through June embracing a pluralistic Guyana—in which "racial self-centeredness gives way to transformative relational intersections with the Other" (Mehta, *Notions of Identity* 151)—experienced primarily through her encounters and engagements with girls and women. Thus, while Mehta recognizes the male biases and masculinist aspects of coolitude, suggesting that as a theory it "colludes with the male-centredness of negritude, indianite, and créolité to displace Caribbean women in general, and Indo-Caribbean women in particular from the politics of representation" (*Notions of Identity* 152), Shinebourne's alteration of the definition for postcolonial feminist purposes remains unexamined. I suggest instead that we consider how coolitude can not only establish the means for gender equality but also function as a bridge between competing theories like Négritude and Indianité, and in doing so put forth an "egalitarian cosmovision" (Mehta, *Notions of Identity* 151) for the region; by focusing on women's lives and voices, Shinebourne's historical novel thus envisions a feminist coolitude, one that proposes a postcolonial feminist future for the nation, a matria.

The novel's main focus, however, is on June's disagreements with Lucille, her hard-working stay-at-home mother. Lucille pins her "ambitions and hopes" on her daughter (Shinebourne, *The Last* 15). She tells June that she can be a "doctor, or a lawyer, or a teacher—anything at all. Although Lucille was careful not to say it, June knew she meant she could leave New Dam where it was not possible to be anything but poor, which meant being scorned and treated . . . like an animal" (32) by the British. Mehta explains that in the 1930s and for a few decades later, in Indo-Caribbean contexts, "a sustained culture of male domination had reduced female participation to the private, domestic sphere of the family and family-related duties" (*Diasporic [Dis]locations* 5). Confined to and silenced in the domestic sphere, Lucille projects her own personal dreams and foiled aspirations onto her daughter. For the duration of the novel's two-week period, Lucille is heavily pregnant, and she rarely travels beyond the fringes of the village. She works tirelessly, cleaning, cooking, and child-rearing, but her economic and other contributions to the home and family largely go unnoticed; further, "she is expected to accept the unchallenged authority of the patriarch" (Mehta, *Diasporic [Dis]locations* 6). However, because Lucille is Christian and embraces colonial assimilation, she wields some, albeit limited, social power over her husband.

Voyeuristically, the reader sees Lucille closely watching June from a small window when her husband's friend enters her yard. When Boysie Ramkarran calls June "Muluk," she sees "her mother straighten and drag her soapy arms from the wooden tub. She saw too her look of coldness and dislike . . . Lucille spoke her English English . . . 'And please don't call June "Muluk." That is not her name. Her name is June'" (Shinebourne, *The Last* 7). Shinebourne explains, "'Muluk' . . . meant 'India'" (7). Having the connotation of an "'ancestral home' or 'motherland' [also] suggests a sense of rootedness" (Mehta, *Diasporic [Dis]locations* 52). This brief interlude expresses the central conflicts of the novel as the reader sees Lucille struggling to distance herself and her daughter linguistically, culturally, racially, and economically from the mother country, India, as well as other New Dam villagers, whom she perceives as uneducated Hindi/Creole-speaking Hindu plantation-mill laborers. June's mother is preoccupied with an "enslavement to a materialist ethic" and "sacrificial labor" (Rahim 741). In a desperate attempt "to escape poverty and anonymity," non-English families and individuals, like Lucille, compete for coveted opportunities by hyper-assimilating to Britishness (Rahim 741). June, too, is inculcated in this highly competitive system as we learn that she earns a scholarship to a prestigious school in New Amsterdam. As Josephine Arnold's research on Guyanese literature and Shinebourne's *Timepiece* intimate, to be successful one has to first attend a respectable school in Guyana and then one in Britain (Arnold 100); will June be compelled, post-novel, to go to England?

When Boysie returns, however, he argues with June's father, Cyrus, over his meeting with the British overseer Beardsley. Boysie humbly states, "[T]he fact [is] that they were still slaves on the estate" (Shinebourne, *The Last* 156). Attempting to organize the villagers to rebel against the British plantation overseers and owners, Boysie sees Cyrus as undermining his authority and goals. He suggests that Cyrus is out of touch with the other men because he doesn't work on the sugar plantation or labor at the rice mill. Defensively, Cyrus, a self-employed mechanic, reminds Boysie that his father, Lou, "was one of the few Chinese immigrants who had stayed on the sugar plantations as [a] labourer" (11) and managed to work his way up to foreman. This is one of the rare mentions of the Lehalls' Chinese background, as their Indian heritage dominates the novel. It also establishes that among the laborers a link to one's coolie past is a sign of socioeconomic authenticity and solidarity, which runs counter to the British, who consider coolie-ness a sign of inferiority. The third-person narrator explains that Cyrus's mother was a Hindu orphan named Narain, and that prior to his marriage to Lucille, Cyrus had been called by his Indian name, Dushyand, and maintained Hindu customs. Lucille, ethnically Indian, by contrast is Anglican, and she renames her husband Cyrus (ironically a Persian name) in an attempt to further separate herself and her family from their non-English familial background. Her awkward imitation of an English accent, ventriloquizing an imagined mother-tongue, participates in this distance, and she continually reminds June to speak properly so that the family may socially and economically advance.

Cyrus reveals that in fact the overseer did not come to discuss his fear of strikes or the British calling in the militia. He says, "He got a sick daughter June age. He ask if June could go an' visit she, see if she could raise the child spirit" (Shinebourne, *The Last* 14). Given the rigid racial, cultural, and class dynamics, that the overseer chooses June to befriend his daughter Annie confounds both Boysie and Lucille, not to mention Cyrus. Reputedly, Annie is bullied at school, has no friends, and "don' eat at all" (16). June, who will soon attend Annie's high school, is expected to remedy the girl's problems. That an Indo-Chinese girl is perceived as having the ability to save a white girl adds complexity to the narrative (however, the novel's ending complicates this idea, as I discuss later, when it returns to the notion of Europeans civilizing racialized others or Britain's attempt to bring the Indo populations on side against other ethnic groups, primarily the Afro-Guyanese).

Although traditional doctors and Annie's parents have failed to alleviate the situation, June, despite her class and ethnicity, is seen as a last resort: "She could raise the child spirit" (Shinebourne, *The Last* 14) symbolically suggests that June will perform as a kind of healer, a revivalist or a spiritualist even, which solidifies her contiguity with Nani (grandmother), not Lucille (mother). The white English girl blurs the line between the living and the dead, the present and the past. As such, Annie embodies the eventual demise of British colonialism in Guyana. If she revives Annie, is June responsible for giving life back to the colonial system? Does this mean the young girl is complicit with the very same British system that oppresses her family and the other villagers? June is of course put in an impossible position, forced to choose between her family's desire for socioeconomic mobility on the one hand (subscribing to colonial education, language, and religion) and supporting the struggles of the villagers (with whom she shares a common culture, if not also ethnicity and class) for socioeconomic equality and political autonomy.

Ultimately, June's parents feel compelled to do the overseer's bidding. The plantation owners' and overseers' power over the villagers' lives is clear and reminds one of the slave past and indentured servitude periods, in which Cyrus's and Lucille's ancestors toiled. Forcing certain members to associate with the overseers also causes internal conflict among the villagers, and June, like her parents, is viewed suspiciously by both sides. June is forced to occupy the tenuous position of female translator/traitor, a common trope in postcolonial women's historical fiction: presciently, June realizes her insider/outsider position: "Why was she feeling sorry for the white girls? There was a traitor somewhere inside her to make her feel sorry for them" (31). Though befriending Annie and Sarah could potentially heal the cultural wounds caused by colonialism and create a more meaningful relationship between colonizers and colonized, it could also be another instantiation of cultural servitude, maintaining the colonial order, and be viewed as undermining the villagers' political goals for independence.

Shinebourne writes Annie and Sarah Beardsley into and against a notable mid-twentieth-century Caribbean women's literary tradition portraying

English/Creole white women on failing plantations, for instance Ada Quayle, Jean Rhys, Phyllis Shand Allfrey, or Lucille Iremonger (O'Callaghan 137); here, however, Annie and Sarah are described from the unique perspective of an Indo-Chinese girl. Wearing her best dress, June arrives at the Beardsleys' security gate to receive permission to enter the premises (20). The isolation of the "European quarters" (14) from the village again reminds one of the region's gothic literary texts as well as the enduring slave-indentureship past and the hierarchies of race and class. A victim of racial segregation, June is prohibited from using the front door and must enter and exit via the kitchen, where several anonymous servants, under Mistress Beardsley's orders, are working, silently.

Unlike Annie, rumored to have leukemia and who remains silent for the entirety of June's visit, Sarah incessantly laughs at and criticizes June for her way of speaking and her ignorance of English manners (24–25). Mimicking the tensions between overseers and villagers, Sarah calls her a coolie and makes fun of her poverty (27). June, reappropriating the term, lambasts Sarah:

> You! You are a bad, wicked, evil little child! God will punish you! You will roast in hell for your nasty mind! You should count your blessings and feel humble for what you have instead of slandering poor people who can't help themselves. You should feel shame! You wicked, nasty, wicked, shameless child! And who tell you to call people *coolie*? Who give you the right to call people *coolie*? They are *not coolies* They are workers and if they did not work you would not have what you have! (28)

Addressing "the thinly disguised disdain for the Indian presence in the Caribbean" (Mehta, *Diasporic [Dis]locations* 2), Sarah's use of the word "coolie" is ironic given that, as June rightly points out, without the Indians and Chinese, there would be neither plantations nor sugar. After Sarah bursts into tears, June feels sorry for her, again suggesting white girls'/women's manipulative tactics used to make racialized girls/women feel guilty when they experience white women's racism.

Accompanying June back to the gate, Sarah reveals a secret hiding place, which contains several items that speak to a stereotypical version of white femininity as vain, infantile, and domestic: a blanket, dolls, a mirror, a hairbrush, and a pair of binoculars (29). Sarah explains, "[T]his is my spying quarters . . . Everyone has binoculars here. They are always spying on each other when it is the workers they should be spying on, Mummy says. So I spy, I spy on the coolies and n-----s..." (29). Sarah's spying makes her a self-appointed colonial authority on the workers, who should be mimicking her definition, the colonial definition, of labor. To use Homi Bhabha's phrase, the workers become "the object of colonial surveillance" ("Of Mimicry and Man" 130). Sarah's comments show that the British distrust each other; hence they monitor not only their workers but also themselves, which signals the latter's paranoia and their accelerating loss of control and power.

When June leaves the overseer's compound, the security guard offhandedly comments—again employing a common trope of young white women in the Caribbean—"That child mad, both'a dem mad" (29). For June, this signals the British girls' "unbelonging and vulnerability in the period of anticolonial nationalism" (Brown and Rosenberg 10). Looking back over her shoulder, June sees Sarah pressing against the high-wire fence, mired in anger and frustration: "Now the look on Sarah's face was like her sister's—a dead look, a look that made June feel as if she herself had put them there, behind the fence" (30). Shinebourne leaves the reader with an image of two lonely, sick, and spoiled British girls. Their literal failure to keep June from leaving applies metaphorically to Britain failing to keep Guyana from breaking away. The girls' silence, coldness, and abuse mirrors Britain's treatment of the Guyanese and their blaming the Guyanese for their behavior rather than taking responsibility for their violent actions.

This upsetting experience has repercussions later in the novel. For instance, while sitting on the Dolphin Swingbridge, June reflects:

> It was such a miserable country, poor people living like prisoners in crowded villages where they could not plant or settle as they pleased, could not speak as equals, as men, women, human beings, to the overseers.... [T]he ruling army and the sugar plantation workers were the prisoners. If you did not live on a plantation village you did not have to put up with that, your freedom was limited too, you did not get far before you came up against one kind of restriction or another.... Was Guyana really just a big prison camp run by the British? If it was, all the freedom of the land that your eyes saw was just an illusion, a dream. (88)

The novel emphasizes that both girls, while differences and hierarchies exist between them, come to understand, because of race, gender, and class, what it means to be locked in and to be locked out. Mehta notes that "[c]olonial pathology finds its power in enclosure or confinement" linking "the prison, army barracks, . . . plantation," and school as all prohibitive and restrictive colonial spaces under surveillance, by guards, overseers, wardens, or teachers ("The Colonial Curriculum" 116). The analogy extends to the mother-daughter relation; June is imprisoned by Lucille's rules just as Guyana, under British rule, is seemingly a prison for everyone.

June, however, begins to learn that social categories and divisions like race and class are constructed and as such they can be contested; thus, Shinebourne's novel, as Anita Baksh writes, "promotes a model of Indo-Guyanese identity that acknowledges racial and cultural exchange without the erasure of Indianness, thereby challenging essentialist notions of cultural identity and authenticity. . . . Shinebourne's fiction uncovers the impossibility of dividing the different groups existing in Guyana along distinct racial and cultural lines" (218). Despite the privileges that the Beardsley sisters enjoy, the novel shows that this way of life is slowly driving them toward illness and madness. As such, they are symbols of the decaying, dying English plantation system in Guyana, while for June, her inability to feel at home within a single identity results in being "lonely . . . like the two white girls" (Shinebourne, *The Last* 32). This realization prompts June's conception of a matria founded on coolitude, meaning that she can embrace cultural multiplicity without rejecting her Indo-Chinese heritage. Literally and figuratively June shuttles between several cultures, classes, and religions evidencing her specific liminal position but also the Indo-Chinese woman's more generally. Like the many bridges she crosses daily, she "balances within and between traditional racial and ethnic discourses" (K. Kempadoo, "Negotiating Cultures" 109), preferring "transcultural and intercultural" modes of being (Mehta, *Diasporic [Dis]locations* 17)—that is, a feminist coolitude—to inflexible demarcations. For instance, June's school journey sees her meeting workers, overseers, foremen, and various other commuters, including her classmate Lavender Jones, who comes from an Afro-Guyanese village.

Despite coming from different villages, the two girls are "united by their poverty" (Shinebourne, *The Last* 59–60). The classroom, however, amplifies the division between country (poor) and town (wealth): "There was so much scorn in the class, June felt more anxious than ever. The country villages were targets of scorn here too, as they were to the overseers and their children, children like Sarah Beardsley" (71). June remembers Sarah's harsh stereotypes about the materiality of the plantation workers and their families' lives: "cowdung, coconut oil, latrines and lice" (79). Social acceptance "often means that the Indo-Caribbean must lose that which marks her as Indian, in order to 'belong' to the urbanised Creole culture which still despises her un-creolised ways" (Ramabai Espinet, qtd. in Mehta, *Diasporic [Dis]locations* 17). June learns that it is the village children with Indian names who receive the most abuse, often from the town Indians with Christian names (Shinebourne, *The Last* 71): "[T]he presence of rural girls in school becomes a source of embarrassment for other Indian students who are anxious to forget a 'shameful' history of cooliehood," Mehta explains (*Diasporic [Dis]locations* 46). Racial, gender, class, and ethnic differences determine social-spatial hierarchies and thus weaken attempts at collective anticolonial action and an anticolonial matria.

Within the classroom, racial slurs and insults travel back and forth. For instance, Lavender yells "Coolie! Coolie water rice!" at some boys. June is called "Chinky chinee" (Shinebourne, *The Last* 72) and "Country Bacoo" (73). When June proudly retorts: "I am Indian too!" (72), further abuse is heaped on her as she is deemed not a "'pure' Indian" (72). As Mehta underscores, "June's identity is located in a double dislocation that highlights two colonized histories in the Caribbean: Indian and Chinese indentureship. Her origins are thus located within a dual source of shame or embarrassment," not for herself necessarily but for others like her mother (*Diasporic [Dis]locations* 51). June is further singled out because she brings her lunch in a saucepan, an instant giveaway that she is a country girl—meanwhile, Lavender is ridiculed for her inability to buy new books, her cheap dress, and her overdeveloped breasts (Shinebourne, *The Last* 82).

Annie's situation at school also continues to worsen. Lavender complains, "She [Annie] is too damn stuck up. I talk to her and she 'in say one word to me" (82); "She sick! She nearly vomit" (83). Annie's doll-like silence angers Lavender to such an extent that in addition to the ridicule she receives from the other children, she declares, "I don' like this stuck-up school. I not coming back, you see all these chil'ren here? All is doctor or lawyer or overseer chil'ren. They don' want we here" (82). Annie's refusal to speak may also indicate the inability of the British plantation owners to converse with and understand the needs and well-being of the plantation workers, particularly the Afro-Guyanese communities. Annie's stone-like refusal to answer cements the fact that communication is impossible; the distance between the British and the

Guyanese girls, let alone adults, cannot be bridged. When the son of a white English overseer speaks up for Annie, the power of the colonial-patriarchal voice and June's failure as cultural mediator are doubly highlighted.

Any solidarity felt between June (Indo-Chinese) and Lavender (Afro) is short-lived as they argue over books. Reinforcing her mother's point of view, June knows that education is one of the only ways a young racialized girl from the country can socially advance. Instead of the two reaching an understanding, however, a fistfight ensues, mimicking the outcome of arguments between her father and Boysie, poor villagers against plantation overseers and owners (English and local Indo- and Afro-Guyanese), the communists versus the capitalists. Lavender, "hysterical, screaming, shouting, tears streaming down her face," beats her fists against June (85). When Lavender retreats, she warns June that just because she dresses like the white girls and talks to them and "rich coolie[s], . . . [t]hey is not you friend . . . you will find out you 'in no big shot . . ." (85). Distraught, June leaves Lavender with their differences unresolved, suggesting that an alternative matria is necessary for Guyanese women.

The absence of matria is seen again when June snaps at Lucille: "Lavender has no books. We have to get her some books, and her uniform look terrible. Tell her mother to buy a good uniform for her. She had on yatching [*sic*] shoes, old ones. Nobody comb her hair properly. All her bubby showing through her blouse. . . . Everybody look at her like she dirt" (89). Lucille might sympathize with Lavender's position, but she reminds her daughter that she has to scrounge money together just to pay for June's necessities. She cannot afford to be clothing other children. June comes to see her privileged position in comparison to others, and even Lavender's privilege, as most children in the village do not attend school after primary. Only those with enough money can attend school, yet a colonial education remains one of the few vehicles, particularly for a girl, to socially advance.

Rather than taking seriously June's decolonizing questioning of an unfair system that disadvantages the villagers and keeps them oppressed, Lucille tells her daughter that Lavender "has an inferiority complex and I can see you are anxious to have one too" (92). Lavender's calling out of the classist, racist, violent English system resonates with June, and unlike her mother, she begins interrogating cultural assimilation and colonization. As Bragard writes, "[Lucille's] blind material concerns and allegiance to western materialism are lampooned" by June ("Gendered Voyages" 111). But June also contradicts herself by wishing aloud for Lavender to have what her own mother, Lucille, has given to her: social acceptance based on education and wealth, as demonstrated by a new uniform and new books. Unlike Lucille, however, June values her Hindu heritage and begins to question its cultural erosion and suppression in Guyana; this questioning occurs simultaneously with the arrival of the British army in the village (Shinebourne, *The Last* 107).

A matria for Guyana is also repressed by June's teachers, who demand obedience and exert their power by beating the most vulnerable students (Mehta, "The Colonial Curriculum" 116). When Lavender is beaten, June remarks that there is "no justice in this school, only madness" (Shinebourne, *The Last* 112). Lavender "had been whipped too"; now she "was lying across her desk. She [June] touched her on the shoulder and asked what happened. Lavender raised herself and showed June the welts which were beginning to rise along the inside of her arms. Annie Beardsley stared at Lavender's welts" (112). While Annie ineffectually stares, Lavender, evoking the rhetoric of slavery, says that she was "beaten like a mule" (112). Foreshadowing the tensions between the military and the villagers, between colonialism and postcolonialism, rich and poor, Lavender reaches her breaking point. Caught by a group of schoolboys, Lavender is outnumbered and overpowered; the boys (foreshadowing British military strength) begin "pushing her towards the door then shoving her down the stairs. Lavender rolled halfway down, picked herself up then ran away" (114). The excessive force inflicted on Lavender, a young, poor Afra-Guyanese girl, sends a message to others who try to claim their dignity and their presence in this colonial space and time; this again foretells that British military might will be directed at villagers deemed unruly and disobedient.

After witnessing the brutality against Lavender, June does not return to school. Instead, she and Lucille bitterly fight about June's life chances if she does not receive an education. Baksh notes that "June becomes caught between the Indian, British, Chinese and African influences that exist in her community," essentially "turning her against herself," the result of which is an extreme feeling of "alienation" (217). Mehta concurs that June's alleged coolie-ness (inferior) is juxtaposed with civilization (superior) ("The Colonial Curriculum" 126). Lucille exclaims: "You used to be a coolie and I manage to turn you into a civilised person, now you want to turn coolie again!" (Shinebourne, *The Last* 123). Here, the "ambivalence of mimicry—almost but not quite—" plays out (Bhabha, "Of Mimicry and Man" 130). Lucille has "fetishized colonial culture" to the extent that she expects June not only to mimic her so-called Britishness but to surpass her—to perfect the mother's mimicry of the colonizer (Bhabha, "Of Mimicry and Man" 130). Despite being racialized, gendered as Other by British colonialism, Lucille attempts to renounce her Indo maternal heritage, her coolie history, and she wants June to do the same by emulating her assimilation to Britishness. Ironically, Lucille's mimicry has the unintended effect of disavowing British authority; her imperfect mimicry has the effect of mockery, of coolitude, that is, subversion.

Distraught and nearly suffering a psychological breakdown, June takes refuge at Nani Dharamdai's house (Shinebourne, *The Last* 125). Nani calls June "Muluk" and rocks her "like a baby" (126). June, in turn, uses "Nani," the Urdu term for maternal grandmother (Pirbhai 39). Throughout the novel, however, Lucille denigrates Nani for her allegedly backward Hindu practices and lower-class status as a threat or warning to June. Nani is talked about frequently, but she is not seen until late in the novel when June chooses her over Lucille. Nani's life troubles Lucille because she reminds her of her own past, her Indian heritage, and her deceased mother: after all, Nani "had known Lucille's parents" (Shinebourne, *The Last* 41). Nani's marginal voice in the narrative speaks also to a past in which the writer/reader has little recourse because "there are no indenture narratives to revisit: neither the Indians nor the Chinese found it possible to voice any of their concerns and suffering at the time of indenture" (Misrahi-Barak, "Looking In, Looking Out" 4). Shinebourne exploits this fact because June's grandparents are dead before the narrative opens, thus pushing Nani's indispensable memories to the margins.

Ambivalence toward the mother is demonstrated because Nani provokes Lucille's inner conflicts. Although Freud's initial analysis of ambivalence described a son's feeling toward his father (*Civilization and Its Discontents* 79), his later work "Female Sexuality" recognizes that the daughter's "intense attachment to her mother is strongly ambivalent" (28). Bhabha suggests that ambivalence likewise refers to the relationship between colonized and colonizer. Just as Freud did not consider ambivalence in relation to colonialism, Bhabha does not consider ambivalence in relation to the maternal; combining both usages, however, sheds light on the colonized/colonizing mother figure, Lucille. Importantly, Bhabha connects ambivalence to mimicry, which can also characterize the mother-daughter relation. The daughter is expected to mimic her mother just as the colonized is expected to mimic the colonizer. But, as Bhabha's work demonstrates, mimicry has the potential to be subversive, parodic even: "[C]olonial mimicry is the desire for a reformed, recognizable Other, as a subject of a difference that is almost the same, but not quite. Which is to say, that the discourse of mimicry is constructed around an ambivalence; in order to be effective, mimicry must continually produce its slippage, its excess, its difference" (126). Coerced by colonialism to repress her Indian maternal heritage, Lucille evidences a "desire to emerge as 'authentic' through mimicry" (Bhabha, "Of Mimicry and Man" 129). She lashes out at Nani and makes her a scapegoat for the village's and June's difficulties assimilating to an imagined Britishness.

Revealing her own anxieties, Lucille rants about June wanting to become "a coolie woman" and describes the inevitable suffering June will endure in the patriarchal Hindu family. An exasperated Lucille cries, "This is the West Indies, not India, not Africa, not China, the West Indies! We are British!" (Shinebourne, *The Last* 124). To Lucille, figures like Nani who continue to affirm their connections to the past, for instance by speaking Hindi, are "a threat" (41). Knowing the struggles her family endured as indentured servants, Lucille is terrified of poverty and of becoming her mother: she will renounce her past, her former friends, mother-figures like Nani, and possibly her daughter if it means escaping the real and imagined risk of material poverty. Bragard rightfully identifies that contradictorily, Lucille "rejects the domination of men, [yet] she consciously accepts colonial domination" ("Gendered Voyages" 111). Shinebourne's feminist reinterpretation of coolitude, however, rejects both patriarchy and colonialism, which, to reiterate, facilitate the daughter's distance from her mother, and her subsequent entrance into patriarchal-colonial subjectivity. A feminist reappropriation of coolitude reveals the novel's contention that June is entrapped by patriarchy, colonialism, and postcolonialism. Feminist coolitude asks whether the path toward independence and subjectivity must entail a rejection of the mother; can an alternative mother, an anticolonial, antipatriarchal matria exist?

The Last English Plantation offers a potential clue as to what feminist coolitude and a Guyanese matria might look like through its recuperation of the Indo-Caribbean grandmother figure. When Nani lays a feverish June down on a soft bed, she recites mantras and performs rituals such as lighting incense (127). Part of June's healing, then, is learning her ancestral history via maternal storytelling. Nani explains that "[h]er Chinese name was Li-Hau but the immigration officer could not spell it and wrote it 'Lehall'" (128). Nani, a reminder and rememberer of the past, warns of the risks when one forgets from where and from whom one comes. This information is even more salient given that it is an elderly Hindu Indian woman who interprets and transmits the Chinese Caribbean past. Further, Lucille's father cannot speak Chinese (Baksh 217), and Lucille's mother remains June's only living grandparent, but she is neither named nor mentioned. Was her maternal grandmother a cane cutter? A "*mati coolie*" (Shinebourne, *The Last* 123) like Nani? The invisibility of the lives and voices of Chinese minorities in the Caribbean, and June learning indirectly that she has had her Chinese heritage concealed, constitute a double erasure. By keeping this past alive, Nani shows solidarity between those with Chinese and Indian heritage and gestures toward the postcolonial feminist future matria.

Nani therefore constitutes an *aji*, a sage who has mastered ancestral knowledge and who initiates "transformative re-evaluations of women's history and cultural resistance" (Mehta, *Diasporic [Dis]locations* 138). Proud of her heritage, Nani is a strong countervoice to British colonial racism and sexism; as an "ancestral mother" (Mehta 138), Nani lists various egregious acts of assimilation forced upon the villagers in order to find work, such as changing their names and changing their religions. Insightfully, Nani knows that Lucille scorns her, maybe that she even fears her, and that Lucille increasingly seeks to distance herself and her family from its Hindu roots; but she asks June not to repeat the mother's actions. The matria that Shinebourne constructs thus refuses to perpetuate violence against the mother. Nani asks June to accept Lucille, to accept the mother, seemingly in an attempt to disentangle the mother figure from patriarchal (post)colonial discourses, even if it means her own relationship with June will suffer.

While Shinebourne's novel highlights a link between Nani and India as a mother country, Judith Misrahi-Barak argues that "[s]uch a dialectic construction did not exist between mainland China and the Chinese diasporic community in the Caribbean" ("Looking In, Looking Out" 9); seemingly, because the dead cannot speak—Cyrus's Chinese father is deceased—the potential link to China is broken and/or forgotten. *The Last English Plantation* also corroborates that

> [t]he Chinese intermarried or had interethnic relationships much more frequently than Indians, who married within their own community. . . . [I]t was necessary for the Chinese to assimilate because of the early absence of women among the migrants. They also allowed their languages to disappear,

more than the Indo-Caribbean people who tended to speak Hindi among themselves. This is probably due to the difference in their socio professional activities. (Misrahi-Barak, "Looking In, Looking Out" 10)

Shinebourne's novel captures a crucial moment in Guyana's history when cultures were colliding and powers were shifting. The loss of language is also closely linked to the loss of memory; therefore, the loss of Cyrus's Chinese language and heritage serves as a distinct warning that Hindi and Hinduism, too, are under threat by colonial English. While Nani resists this loss, Lucille embraces it.

These tensions between anticolonialism and colonialism are evident when Lucille and Cyrus come to collect June from Nani. Nani says, "[W]e must pray for June, we must look after her spiritual welfare" (Shinebourne, *The Last* 129), while Lucille claims that Nani is poisoning June's mind by not speaking English (129). When Lucille grumbles to June, "I send you to school to be educated, not to defy me" (130), an unintended irony arises, as certainly education will turn June against Lucille. Education from both Nani (maternal, informal, oral, Hindu) and school (paternal, formal, written, colonial) will allow June to articulate the postcolonial feminist position she is already developing. Unlike Lucille, however, June will not tolerate that "Nani's voice . . . a voice from the past . . . [be] shoved aside" (146). In psychoanalytic terms, the reader understands June's new independence as a young daughter as an allegory for her nation. Developing a strong sense of postcolonial feminist coolitude, June challenges the colonial British mother (symbolized by the Beardsley sisters) and her colonized mother; instead, she envisions a matria in which women and Guyana are independent. Informed by feminist coolitude, June's notion of matria thus integrates several intersecting, nonhierarchal aspects of identity such as culture, gender, ethnicity, religion, and class. June's return to the indentureship period and the legacy of her ancestral mother countries, specifically India and China, also importantly gives voice and consideration to a suppressed and repressed part of not only the young woman's familial history but also the nation's history. The novel intimates that the previous mother countries (India, China, or Britain) are unsuitable authorities for Guyana; the young June must integrate her maternal heritage but still define her own identity, her own matria.

June's criticisms of colonialism are solidified after violence erupts among striking workers, British soldiers, and local police. The conflict results in some of the cane fields and the overseers' homes being burned, an unmarried, economically independent Hindu village woman named Mariam Mootoo being killed, and June's friend Ralph being wrongly imprisoned. June's precarious position as cultural mediator is evident, because she accompanies overseer Beardsley and Sarah to visit Ralph at Good Land Police Station (153). Annie, meanwhile, is back in England (155). Annie's departure foreshadows the physical and psychical beginning of the end of British control in Guyana but that political challenges for the Guyanese still lie ahead. Consider Ralph's declaration: "I will stay right he'. Let we people strike and strike and strike and burn down everything. Let it be the last plantation" (157). Ralph's comment reflects the novel's title and the literal and figurative end to British rule in Guyana. The novel's major protagonists thus gather at the prison in the novel's final scenes. For instance, Lavender coolly tells June that the sergeant has to keep Ralph in jail so that Mariam's death can be pinned on him and not on the police force or British army (168). The conservative backlash against not only independent women but also young Guyanese men further reflects British colonialists' fear of revolt and their inability to acknowledge their patriarchal-colonial actions in Guyana; Mariam's British murderer, for instance, goes unpunished.

The novel's penultimate chapter is anticlimactic, yet cautiously optimistic. When the true causes and culprits of the uprising are revealed, overseer Beardsley returns to the prison with Ralph's mother, Bibi Mahadeo, to free her son (171). Curiously, critics have largely ignored the implications of this part of the novel, but surely one must ask: does a white man save the day? As an allegory for British interference in Guyana's independence, the novel suggests yes. For without Beardsley's overseeing, Ralph would remain in prison, and no one would believe his mother's words. The Indo-Caribbean woman's words are only heard when legitimated by the white colonial male, simultaneously expressing the predicament of the Indo-Chinese Caribbean woman historical novelist who writes her history from within but against the colonial, patriarchal system. One wonders whether Beardsley's participation is an attempt to quell his conscience for the many wrongs the British have inflicted on the Guyanese. The looming departure of several overseers including Beardsley certainly feeds into the novel's title symbolically but not necessarily historically: although the English plantations may disappear with time, the British, and the ever increasing presence of the Americans, will, as twenty-first-century readers know, continue to hold cultural and economic power over Guyana.

The novel concludes with June, having returned to school, celebrating Diwali. Sitting on Nani's porch, she takes in the village, recognizing that "[o]n this one night of the year, the darkness was completely banished from New Dam and the power of the lights gave a feeling of hope and happiness which she felt the more for the feelings of loss and the dramas of the year" (177). The strategic placement of Nani's yard, a woman-centered space, further reflects a sense of coolitude, dependent not on a narrow or singular vision but rather on a "broad perspective of her community" (Mehta, *Diasporic [Dis]locations* 148). Mehta thus calls Nani "the communal mother," for she "passes on her education to future generations to ensure the preservation of female cultural knowledge" (148). Nani's teachings thus illuminate a new psychic and physical path for June and for Guyana. Having literally and metaphorically had a "light [shone] on the silent histories" of her ancestors (Misrahi-Barak, "Looking In, Looking Out" 7), June's burgeoning sense of a matria thus integrates the coolie past with the postcolonial present, the Guyanese girl within the larger social collective.

Yet, is a feminist coolitude, a matria, truly possible? Will June have to leave her family and home behind, reminiscent of her exilic ancestors' crossings? Will June, who could not save Annie Beardsley, be able to save herself? Given Guyana's precarious political and economic position, will she be able to withstand the many forces (sexism, racism, classism, colonialism, cultural imperialism) that threaten her identity and autonomy? Or, does June celebrating Diwali with Nani gesture toward a reconciliation between Nani (old Indian traditions) and Lucille (new British ones), and a resolving of the novel's material and maternal conflicts? The novel suggests that the dream of a future Guyana, the matria, will value a coolie matrilineage as a source of strength, recognizing women's contributions (maternal and material) to the nation. Although *The Last English Plantation* remains open-ended, with June's and her country's futures uncertain, an important takeaway for the reader is that Shinebourne's postcolonial feminist novel vividly voices Guyana's plantation past and is one of the first to do so from an Indo-Chinese woman's perspective.

4

Matriz, Transgressive Sexuality, and National Ambiguity in Judith Ortiz Cofer's *The Meaning of Consuelo*

Judith Ortiz Cofer's *The Meaning of Consuelo* (2003) is a classic coming-of-age historical novel. Set predominantly in San Juan, Puerto Rico, during the 1950s, this bildungsroman privileges Consuelo Signe's, the eldest daughter's, voice. Despite the critical and commercial success of Puerto Rican women historical novelists like Rosario Ferré, Ana Lydia Vega, and Esmeralda Santiago, as well as receiving acclaim for her earlier semiautobiographical work, *The Line in the Sun* (1989), Ortiz Cofer's *The Meaning of Consuelo* has received little scholarly attention (Méndez 33). Resonating with other contemporary Puerto Rican women writing bildungsromane, such as Sarah McCoy (*The Time It Snowed in Puerto Rico*, 2009), Ortiz Cofer challenges the exclusionary patriarchal, nationalistic Puerto Rican literary canon and the "rhetoric of paternalism that envelops the cult of la gran familia" by spearheading open discussions of women's sexuality (Moreno, "Family Matters" 83). This chapter's return to Ortiz Cofer's novel therefore emphasizes its contribution to Caribbean women's historical fiction and to the concept of matria by discussing literature, nationhood, and sexuality. I argue that the titular character and her social circle's interrogation of normative gender and sexuality create a counter feminist-postcolonial discourse on the patriarchal, colonial Puerto Rican family/nation and in turn envision matria on the mainland.

My specific concentration on the eponymous protagonist and the sexually transgressive figures in her life (her transgender neighbor, her mad, sexualized sister, and her gay cousin) assigns importance to both gender and sexuality as shaping and being shaped by *la gran familia* and the nation. Dialoguing with Maya Socolovsky's examination of transgression in relation to the nation, Susan C. Méndez's reading of woman as nation trope, and Carmen R. Lugo-Lugo's inquiry into queer subjects and the colonial state, I, too, think through how expressions of gender and sexuality reflect the politics of both familial and national situations. This chapter nevertheless takes a different approach to *The Meaning of Consuelo* by reading Puerto Rico in relation to the maternal and the concept of matria. Informed theoretically by Judith Butler's *Gender Trouble*, my analysis reveals that *The Meaning of Consuelo*'s notion of matria expresses a complex feminist body politic consisting of transgression, gender, sexuality, and nationhood that disrupts and opposes the traditional, heteropatriarchal Puerto Rican nation and family. I begin by examining transgression as it relates to nationhood, sex, and gender. The next section closely reads Consuelo's relationships with the aforementioned socially othered—that is, sexually transgressive—protagonists to emphasize the novel's matria as a feminist refusal to comply with or reinforce the heterosexual-androcentric family/nation.

Ortiz Cofer's novel suggests that the daughter's break from the mother correlates to different Puerto Rican national identities. For this reason, Méndez productively reads the mother and her daughters as allegories signifying different national statuses: an independence-seeking Puerto Rico corresponds to the mother, Angélica (who remains in Puerto Rico), while the "stagnant commonwealth status" is embodied by Mili (the younger daughter, who drowns), and Consuelo (the elder daughter, who leaves for the mainland) symbolizes "the possibilities and challenges of an ethno-nation"—"a community with a common history, culture, and language, . . . [that] has a dual conception of itself as a minority and majority population" (Méndez 34, 40). Influenced by postcolonialism and feminism, it is educated young women and minority figures—people traditionally excluded from the national myth—whom Ortiz Cofer depicts as redefining Puerto Rico's identity (both familial and political). The novel recognizes that truly excluding transgressive figures from a national imaginary is an impossibility. As Butler notes,

"[T]he construction of an 'outside' that is nevertheless fully 'inside' . . . [is] nonsensical" (105). Ortiz Cofer's figures therefore are not so much excluded as they are marginalized (Butler 105); fully within culture but excluded from the dominant culture (105) or Master narrative more accurately describes these figures' positions and, by extrapolation, also characterizes the tenuous status of Puerto Ricans on the mainland.

In the text, physical transgressions manifest in taboo sexual behavior accompanied by migration to the mainland. Several characters in *The Meaning of Consuelo* defy the heteropatriarchal nation and family, proving their fragility. Socolovsky's study on this work insightfully contends that "[t]ransgression, the violation of a law or command that involves crossing over a limit, is of course inextricably connected to understandings of place and national identity, as normative cultural and physical borders determine and demarcate social and moral behavior" (98). The limits and definitions of acceptable or unacceptable behavior in *The Meaning of Consuelo* begin within the patriarchal *gran familia*. Socolovsky remarks: "[W]hen the characters transgress, they highlight the boundaries that they cross and make them more, rather than less, visible, destabilizing the cultural and national identity on which such limits depend" (98). The political potential of such transgressions for matria is clear. Challenging normative ideology, for instance about sex and gender, in one's patriarchal family thus prospectively alters and disrupts the very same ideology espoused and reinforced by the patriarchal nation.

Although sexual transgressions precede national transgressions, which culminate in moves to the United States, migration scholars have "'ignored the question of non-hegemonic sexualities' when discussing migration patterns" in Puerto Rico (Lugo-Lugo 237). Critic Lawrence La Fountain-Stokes writes: "Sexuality is a key factor in shaping and defining Puerto Rican migration to the United States, . . . as relevant as economic, political, and social factors" (9). The novel supports this argument by depicting several characters like Consuelo and her homosexual cousin, Patricio, as defying the island's gender and sexuality norms, being punished—Patricio is excommunicated from the family—and then leaving the island.

A gender and/or sexual consciousness leads many figures in this text to reject *la gran familia* and then their island home. Rejection and migration create a sense of national, not to mention familial, unbelonging: "The characters' experiences of home are thus based not on settlement but on an expectation of migration to a fictional space that is preceded by a commodified process of unbelonging on the island," writes Socolovsky (113). Consuelo sees exile as a necessary part of her future because she refuses to subscribe to the sexual norms of *la gran familia*. For her, the mainland offers an escape. Nevertheless, *The Meaning of Consuelo*'s conception of matria covertly indicts the patriarchal, colonial nation that causes the break between mother and daughter—the daughter's exile from the family—and correlates to her migration from the island mother-land/Spanish mother-tongue to the United States, the neocolonial mainland mother-land/English mother-tongue.

As Lugo-Lugo notes, there is a distinct sense that "[a]s literary and cultural documentarians, Puerto Rican women writers create works that directly contest coloniality, but also works in which the queer Puerto Rican subject is able to transcend the limitations of the colonial state" (241). Ortiz Cofer creates a narrative of crossings related to gender and sexual agency, thus "troubl[ing] and disrupt[ing] the U.S.–Puerto Rican colonial dynamic" (Socolovsky 97). A certain form of rootlessness that we might interpret as motherlessness thus comes to define this generation of young Puerto Ricans, as is evident in several characters, but certainly in Consuelo's belief that a better future exists in New York City. An underlying sense that the novel is not necessarily unfolding in real time but may be an older Consuelo's return through memory and writing to her youth and her mother-island, however, complicates such a reading.

In keeping with the bildungsroman tradition identified by Rosamond S. King, we might postulate whether Consuelo, like other young Caribbean women, discovers "that sex alone cannot liberate them from a restrictive society and that they have greater affinity for their Caribbean culture than they had realized" (132). Also supporting the belief that once on the mainland (post-novel), Consuelo may indeed not experience the liberatory or welcoming space she imagined, Marisel Moreno writes:

> [T]he myth of la gran familia was characterized by "Hispanophilia, anti-Americanism, racism, androcentrism, homophobia, and more recently xenophobia," and remained a cornerstone of Puerto Rican nationalist discourse throughout the twentieth century ... [leading] to the exclusion of minorities from the national fold.... In the last few decades, the myth has been revitalized to exclude diasporic communities from the Island's national imaginary. ("Family Matters" 78)[1]

The *gran familia* excludes young Puerto Rican feminists, like Consuelo, on both the island and the mainland. The novel prompts one to ask: could the family/nation be organized in ways that are more inclusive? Can women have a role that is not predetermined by patriarchy and colonialism? Is matria possible? Consuelo implicitly asks, if the patriarchal *gran familia* is no longer viable for Puerto Rican women, on or off the island, then how should the country envision its future political status?[2]

Méndez and Lugo-Lugo pose similar questions. Méndez believes that "'[b]eyond the purview of patriarchies' lies the character of Consuelo and her portrayal as the ethno-nation of Puerto Rico" (37). Accordingly, the ethno-nation can potentially "break the colonial/nationalist binary of thinking for Puerto Ricans, so as to nurture and include the agendas of subject groups that find themselves outside of the colonial/nationalist framework" (38). This is to say that the ambiguity of the ethno-nation, as opposed to hyper-masculine nationalism (mother-Angélica) or hyper-feminine commonwealth (daughter-Mili), potentially offers a matria for the young feminist, Consuelo. Alternatively, Lugo-Lugo reads Puerto Rico's ambiguous political status as queer and regards queerness as a tool to challenge colonialism:

> Queerness is about asserting and embracing ways of being and behaving that are deemed deviant by mainstream ideologies. When it comes to the island's political status, Puerto Ricans seem to have embraced (or at the very least come to terms with) its deviance as a political entity: the deviance of not being a recognized nation state or not being fully embedded within a powerful nation state (i.e., the U.S.).... This imperfectly produced colonial subject and metropolitan citizen is, then, bound to feel at home with ambiguity, with subordinated forms of existence, and with political queerness, to use Negrón Muntaner's concept. (236)

Certainly, the diverse expressions of sexuality by Ortiz Cofer's characters reflect Puerto Rico's "queer" nation status, but an oppressive heterosexual-patriarchal policing and regulating of bodies and behaviors dominate their lives. Ortiz Cofer's *The Meaning of Consuelo* suggests that the nation is not ready to confront its queerness, let alone embrace it. For one, Mili's tragic death tempers such a reading, for it is she who symbolizes the commonwealth and embodies such transgressions and ambiguity.

Both Signe sisters, Consuelo and Mili, have identity crises as young Puerto Rican women living in a patriarchal-colonial nation/family that attempts to impose strict gender norms and expectations. Mili's and Consuelo's defiance against familial/national rules shows that they are forming their own ideas about Puerto Rican identity when it comes to gender and sexuality. That is to say, they are conceiving a matria that seeks to transform patriarchal Puerto Rican society through rethinking *matriz*—"meaning both matrix and womb in Spanish" (Cámara Betancourt 8)—and redefining the mother. Consuelo's, and to a certain extent Mili's, sexual awakening is attained through an increasing awareness of gender, experienced in the transition from girlhood to womanhood. Sexism leads Consuelo to develop an early sense of gender consciousness and to understand that her experiences are also shared by other women, like her mother and her grandmother. She questions and revises her notions of gender and sexuality in relation to her mother and her mother-island, but instead of mimicking her foremothers, she searches for an autonomous, gendered self within a collective, a matria, that possesses an open and nondiscriminatory attitude toward sexuality and gender.

Butler's notion of the matrix, as a complex system of gender, sexuality, and power, is useful for understanding this matria. According to Butler, "the heterosexualization of desire" reinforces and is reinforced by a gender-sex-hierarchal binary pair that "requires that certain kinds of 'identities' cannot 'exist'—that is, those in which gender does not follow from sex and those in which practices of desire do not 'follow' from either sex or gender" (24). Gender and sex, deemed social constructs by Butler, are upheld by the matrix of heterosexuality. She writes, "[U]nivocity of sex, the internal coherence of gender, and the binary framework for both sex and gender are considered throughout as regulatory fictions that consolidate and naturalize the convergent power regimes of masculine and heterosexist oppression" (46). *La gran familia* is a "regulatory regime" (46)—while a sociopolitical fiction—that dictates appropriate gender, sex, and sexuality practices and boundaries for men and women. As Rafael Ramírez notes, in patriarchy "asymmetrical relations are established when the masculine domain is privileged with the consequent subordination and devaluation of the feminine domain" (237); in Puerto Rico, women, homosexuals, and gender nonconformists all fall into the realm of the feminine. While noncomplying genders and sexualities are penalized, they still "open up within the very terms of that matrix of intelligibility rival and subversive matrices of gender disorder" (Butler 24), which is evident in so-called sexually deviant characters like Consuelo. Ortiz Cofer's novel therefore challenges the "matrix of intelligibility" that insists on a heterosexual, cisgender identity for *la gran familia*.

Like Méndez's reading of the ethno-nation as a possible undoing of the binary between island independence and commonwealth status, a possibility for subverting reified notions of gender and sex emerges. The "recourse to an original or genuine femininity is a nostalgic and parochial ideal that refuses the contemporary demand to formulate an account of gender as a complex cultural construction" (Butler 49), and is analogous to the nostalgic desire for a Puerto Rico founded on the myth of *la gran familia*. Additionally, this myth is strongly informed by the Catholic Church (Kevane 46), which, according to Consuelo, provides only two gender models: Mary Magdalene ("whore who betrays self, family, and culture") or Virgin Mary ("feminine purity ... the virtues of nurturing and self-sacrifice)" (Cobb 134). Studying the influence of Catholicism on Ortiz Cofer's female characters, Bridget Kevane concurs that in Puerto Rico "[t]he role of women is like that of a priest in the church as they instill moral values and disseminate the gender and spiritual expectations of the community" (54). That women are compared to priests who make a promise of celibacy further emphasizes that sexual desires and/ or committing sexual acts, except when between married adults attempting to procreate, are immoral and sinful. Since "women's sexual agency 'signals danger to respectability' and thus threatens conventional notions of the Caribbean family and nation" (R. King 128), a great deal of shame and anxiety over female sexuality, not to mention nonconforming gender and transgressive desire, manifests throughout the text.

Kamala Kempadoo argues that women are generally "marginalized, scorned, and disrespected as loose women within local cultural logic if they appear explicitly sexual and engaged in multiple sexual relationships, without this being attached to procreation and economic needs of the family" (79). Furthermore, a correlation between women's sexuality and nationalism emerges, since both prescribe "'female sexual containment through compulsory heterosexuality, marriage and motherhood.' And as 'disciplining the body is at the heart of bourgeois nationalist projects,' women's sexuality in the Caribbean is often connected to class and respect" (R. King 126).[3] While Angélica, called "Mami," occupies the preferred Virgin Mary, *la mujer sufrida* position, Consuelo, who loses her virginity, occupies more or less the position of Mary Magdalene. If the ethno-nation, as Méndez argues, might offer a way out of the binary of colony/territory, then matria gestures toward women's empowerment and agency as an alternative to the virgin/whore dichotomy.

The Meaning of Consuelo suggests that the break between mother and daughter in this patriarchal-colonial Catholic society reproduces the traditional Oedipal complex. The feminine Oedipal complex mandates that mothers and daughters are first separated from each other, but then the daughter's life replicates her mother's when she becomes a mother herself. As Consuelo notes early on, "It was a woman's burden and her privilege to sacrifice her own needs and desires in order to one day reach that pinnacle of praise: *Se sacrificó por su familia*. It helped to have company in your misery, to have a group of female relatives with whom to compare your progress toward martyrdom, [and] to share generational wisdom about babies and husbands" (Ortiz Cofer 59). Further, it seems that Consuelo's independence hinges on rejecting her mother: she literally leaves her mother behind when she leaves for New York. Tensions between mothers and daughters in this novel demonstrate anger and anxiety over patriarchal (national and familial) expectations for women. Transgressive acts of sexuality and gender therefore destabilize the traditional *matriz* (matrix and womb) of heteronormativity and indicate that certain maternal aspects can be stifling. Ambivalence marks this daughter's relation to her mother-land/tongue.

While the island, as a space, is gendered and sexualized, so, too, are places within the heteropatriarchal nation: Consuelo having permission to join her female relatives in the kitchen, Mili being punished for infiltrating prohibited spaces, Patricio proudly making his sexuality public, and María Sereno having the nerve to walk the streets of suburbia wearing women's clothing are all key examples. These protagonists trouble the demarcations of acceptable spaces determined by gender and sexuality, but they also provide insight into gender and sexuality determined by spatial metaphors. The novel takes the body as a space in and of itself to show how labels such as gender are social constructs that are yet nevertheless tightly regulated, hierarchized, and systematized by the heterosexual-patriarchal nation.

The first page of the novel, for instance, begins with a definition of *fulano*: "so-and-so, what's his/her-name; tart, whore; Mr./Miss/Mrs. Nobody" (3), followed by this line: "the *fulano* of our neighborhood . . . born [as] Mario Manuel Santiago Sereno . . . [and] he or she never called by name" (3). María Sereno is a nonconformist, gender-bending figure shunned publicly but tolerated privately by the *"gente decente"* (31). Unbeknown to her husband, Angélica, like her neighbors, receives manicures from María Sereno. As Consuelo explains: "[I]t was up to me as the oldest to keep Mili, who was only four, from telling. Mili liked María Sereno. She had confessed to me that she wanted to be a nail-painter like him when she grew up" (5). The reader, like Consuelo, understands that Mili's future sexuality and gender expression are foreshadowed by the transgressive acts of María Sereno.

Coinciding with Consuelo encountering hypocritical attitudes toward María Sereno, she learns that her mother needs help minding Mili. Described as "high-strung, [but] artistic" (19), Mili impulsively runs away, usually toward water. For instance, on a car ride to the festival of the patron saint San Lázaro, Mami gets out along the way to taste the sugarcane (23). While tasting the sweetness, Mili, seduced by "the sugarcane field that extended toward the horizon like a green sea," runs off (22). The reference to sugarcane alludes to Puerto Rico's slave plantations, a brutal history that undergirds the novel but goes unexamined. At the same time, the pleasure from sugar allegedly leads the mother-daughter duo physically and morally astray. This sentiment is expressed again when, while at her grandmother's, Consuelo overhears her mother admit that while working at the hotel, "Mili had slipped away from her. . . . They had found her at the edge of the swimming pool . . . mesmerized by the play of the sunlight on the water, chanting '*Azul, azul, azul*'" (19). The sea, like the field an open, seemingly infinite, natural space, entices Mili rather than the confining, artificial space of suburbia.

Natural landscapes tempt Mili, as do persons labeled harmful by the *gente decente*. It is during the same holiday trip that Consuelo decides to leave Mili with her cousins. While riding the Ferris wheel, Consuelo suddenly spies Mili: "She was behind a kiosk sitting on Néstor's lap, eating an ice-cream cone. He was holding a cigarette in one hand and holding her like a large doll with his other hand behind her back. When I saw—or did I just think I saw?—what he was doing to my sister, I yelled" (33). Mili's sitting on the lap of a fifteen-year-old boy horrifies Consuelo. Mili's taboo behavior, such as eating ice-cream, however, exhibits "wild instinctual impulse[s] untamed by the ego" (Freud, *Civilization and Its Discontents* 26). Freud refers to the "pleasure principle" (*Civilization* 23) as being at odds with the expectations of the external world. The young girl's desire for pleasure prevails over her concern for patriarchal social norms and punishments. Thus, while Mili experiences pleasure from the outside world, she likewise turns increasingly inward, away from restrictive external rules, so as to defend herself (*Civilization* 25). She "withdraw[s] from the pressure of reality and find[s] refuge in a world" of her own (*Civilization* 25). The "connection with reality is . . . loosened" (*Civilization* 27), meaning her "satisfaction is obtained from illusions" that "arise in the imagination" (*Civilization* 27), not with the external world around her. Mili's withdrawal, however, also takes her back to a prelinguistic, pre-Oedipal stage. Her nonsensical language is muddled, like baby talk. Reading Mili as an allegory for Puerto Rico's commonwealth status suggests that the young girl is stuck. Likened to a beautiful doll who does not speak or resist, Mili has not and cannot differentiate or defend herself from her mother—neither Spain nor the United States.

As mentioned previously, Lugo-Lugo perceives Puerto Rico's ambiguous nation status as allowing for a certain vantage point and a certain kind of "political queerness" (235), yet, like Méndez, I read Mili's encounters with predatory men as a cautionary tale against Puerto Rico as a commonwealth: "Subjugated individuals in Puerto Rico such as Mili are forced to contend with a double coloniality of power that consists of the sexist, racist, and classist structures of the United States and the local elites in Puerto Rico. . . . In other words, Mili's representation of the commonwealth reflects an endangered and rarely empowered body. Mili's mental illness further portrays the commonwealth's vulnerability" (Méndez 39). Mili thus literally and metaphorically embodies Puerto Rican identity; her fragmented psyche puts into question whether Puerto Rican culture and its political future is something that can be easily, if at all, remedied.

Mili's urge to break free—physically and mentally—is partly a response to the patriarchal family's/nation's restrictions on young girls' actions and bodies. A young *niña* is not permitted to run wildly or to exert herself. Instead, she is to be poised and demonstrate restraint. Mili, however, overtly flies in the face of any attempts to control/colonize her. A failure to restrain/contain Mili, and to a certain extent Consuelo, reflects badly on Mami. Not once is Carlos inculcated in Mili's disappearances or Consuelo's rule breaking. Instead, in the hotel example, "Papi had been anguished, then embarrassed and angry with her [Mami] for her *descuido*. A terrible accusation to make of any woman, that she had been careless with a child" (Ortiz Cofer 19). Papi scolds Mami as if she, too, were a girl. Mili reflects the mother and the Puerto Rican *matriz*. A bad *niña* is the mother's fault. While fathers typically give their daughters their genealogies for patriarchal reasons, Papi seems to attribute Mili's problems to her maternal heritage. The intersection of racism and sexism reveals itself, for it is the "mother's darker skin tone" (Ortiz Cofer 62) rather than the "father's European roots" (62) that is causing Mili's issues. Highlighting the maternal line instead of the paternal one absolves Papi and any father of responsibility if the lineage produces unruly women. Tellingly, Papi does not intervene in Mili's upbringing: instead, Consuelo is enlisted to help guide and watch her sister.

The traditional woman's sphere, like the kitchen, is initially a liberating space for Consuelo as she is permitted to serve coffee and overhear her mother's gossip, but this same space soon becomes stifling. For instance, Consuelo's task to mind Mili stems from her being a sister and not a brother. She is forced to become a shadow mother, or perhaps more accurately a shadow father, so that Mili avoids danger. Mili's adventurous, fearless personality contrasts with Consuelo's, as the extended family compares the sisters according to well-known binary pairs: "pretty/mature; cute/smart; spontaneous and creative/thoughtful and dependable" (Ortiz Cofer 51). Neither sister is complete, however. Does this correlate to a new Puerto Rico as a synthesis between commonwealth and ethno-nation? After all, it is only when paired together that a full, complex *señorita* comes into view. This is mirrored by the literal physical closeness of the sisters, necessitated in part, however, by Consuelo acting as guardian. Because the younger sister yearns for freedom and takes space, Consuelo's physicality is limited and constrained. As the example of the Ferris wheel shows, Consuelo's movements are severely hindered by her sisterly responsibilities.

Consuelo's responsibilities also increase when she begins menstruating and becomes a *señorita* at the age of twelve. Ventriloquizing the women in her extended family, she claims, "*I could have children and carry out God's will; so I could fulfill myself as a woman!* Then I was warned as to the many things I could not and should not do—an endless list of warnings" (50); she also learns that "[w]hen a man breaks something in anger, the next thing he grabs may be one of your limbs; we had heard that said by women in our own house" (58). Noteworthy is that menstruation catches Consuelo unawares, and Mili is held accountable. Mami explains: "She [Consuelo] thought she was hurt from a fall she took running after Mili" (50). Consuelo's rationalizing that Mili's physicality indirectly causes her to bleed, and Mami's inability to question why Consuelo is running after Mili in the first place, emphasize the tenuous relationship between mothers and daughters and between sisters, and Puerto Rico's fragile political position. Neither the old Spanish ways, symbolized by the mother, nor the ethno-nation, arguably symbolized by Consuelo, however, are able to care for the commonwealth, signified by the mentally unwell Mili.

Other figures deemed deviant by their gender expression and sexual behavior like María Sereno and Patricio serve as a distinct backdrop for Mili's increasing remove from reality and Consuelo's search, as a cisgendered, heterosexual teen, for freedom of expression. A pattern emerges: the Signe sisters with childlike innocence engage with the social outcasts they have been cautioned against, defined primarily by transgressive gender and sexuality, and in doing so begin to challenge these seemingly fixed labels. Lauren Cobb articulates that it is not necessarily other women in the novel but "marginalized and nonconformist men [who] instruct her [Consuelo] in how to subvert the power of cultural and familial narratives" (135). María Sereno and Patricio draw attention to the taboo status of homosexuality and certain gender identities. As Lugo-Lugo notes, Puerto Ricans "see the figure of the homosexual as a symbol for that which is—or should be—outside the configuration of nation" (133). Furthermore, Puerto Ricans consider homosexuality deviant (Lugo-Lugo 239) and illegal (Crespo-Kebler 192–93). Including marginalized figures like Patricio and María as part of the national fabric "insist[s] upon the extension of . . . legitimacy to bodies that have been regarded as false, unreal, and unintelligible" and "expose[s] the tenuousness of gender 'reality' in order to counter the violence performed by gender norms" (Butler xxv). Ortiz Cofer's matria thus contests rigid gender and sexuality norms and expands the definition of the Puerto Rican family/nation.

Consuelo conceives matria through her friendship with her closeted homosexual cousin, while Mili learns it through her openness toward outsiders such as Néstor and María Sereno. Butler writes that "the resolution of the Oedipal complex affects gender identification through not only the incest taboo, but, prior to that, the taboo against homosexuality" (86). She explains that in traditional Freudian theory, the child must renounce the object of desire, which would be the parent of the opposite sex (avoiding the incest taboo—"forbid[ding] sexual union between members of the same kinship group" [Butler 99]), but that this presumes heterosexuality: "It would appear that the taboo against homosexuality must *precede* the heterosexual incest taboo; the taboo against homosexuality in effect creates the heterosexual 'dispositions' by which the Oedipal conflict becomes possible. . . . [They] are effects of a law which, internalized, produces and regulates discrete gender identity and heterosexuality" (87). Butler's work argues that this matrix makes heterosexuality "legitimate" and homosexuality "illegitimate" (99) and as such informs the gender/sexuality permissions and prohibitions of Puerto Rican culture and identity.

Butler also traces the enforcement of heterosexuality and acceptable gender performances back to the family, creating an opportunity to make an analogy between sexuality and nationhood. Butler explains, "For heterosexuality to remain intact as a distinct social form, it *requires* an intelligible conception of homosexuality and also requires the prohibition of that conception in rendering it culturally unintelligible" (104). This logic applies to Puerto Rico's political status, and to who is and who is not considered Puerto Rican. Méndez concurs that "[s]pecifically, the characters of María Sereno and Patricio Signe further the argument for a reconceptualization of a more inclusive body politic although they also problematize the use of the woman as nation configuration and possibly offer an alternative to nationalist and colonial discourses other [than] the ethno-nation" (38). Revisiting this theory at the end of her article, however, Méndez poses an intriguing question: "Might María and Patricio be examples other than 'woman' who offer their own conception of and relationship with nation?" (42). Yes, is the simple answer. María Sereno symbolizes "something else entirely, some configuration based on deception, exclusion, and division but still potentially effective" (Méndez 43), while Patricio highlights "exclusion and change" (Méndez 43). Unfortunately, Méndez does not fully explore how these marginalized figures complicate the allegorical reading of woman as nation or how both gender and nationhood are sociopolitically constructed.

Both María Sereno and Patricio are rejected as the Puerto Rican masculine ideal: male, cisgendered, heterosexual. Butler articulates that it is "the institution of a compulsory and naturalized heterosexuality [that] requires and regulates gender as a binary relation in which the masculine term is differentiated from a feminine term, and this differentiation is accomplished through the practices of heterosexual desire" (31). Furthermore, "the viability of *man* and *woman* as nouns, is called into question by the dissonant play of attributes that fail to conform to sequential or causal models of intelligibility" (Butler 33). Their challenge to masculine ideals implicitly marks them as feminine or nonmasculine—that is, inferior. In the case of cisgendered, heterosexual women, femininity (described ideally as nonsexual, weak, nurturing, maternal, martyrlike, white, and virginal [Crespo-Kebler 200]) is rigidly imposed, and it is up to the masculine ideal as superior to protect her. Importantly, however, "María Sereno and Patricio help Consuelo understand and resist the narratives molding her into a submissive *mujer decente*" (Cobb 141). Consuelo realizes that if she remains in Puerto Rico, then she can become either *la fulana* or *la sufrida*. If she leaves, then a matria of alternative gender and sexuality may be possible.

Figures like Patricio and María Sereno adhere to Socolovsky's reading of the US–Puerto Rico relation in gendered terms: "Ortiz Cofer's texts disrupt U.S. national identity by showing the ambiguity of Puerto Rican presence on and off the island" (99). Patricio's and María Sereno's ambiguous gender and sexuality constitute their "unbelonging" (Socolovsky 111) and complicate Puerto Rican gender identity, suggesting that reading the nation without taking into consideration non-cisgendered and non-heterosexual people has serious political implications. Deemed feminine and/or nonmasculine, they are at the same time considered neither appropriate sexual objects of masculine desire nor appropriate desiring subjects. Patricio and María Sereno fall outside both the masculine and the feminine ideal, exposing the binary and the trope of woman as nation as fictional and false.

After having been seen leaving *los baños* with "*el fulano*" (Ortiz Cofer 53), for instance, Patricio's sexuality is considered by the family to be "a real *tragedia*," even an "*escándalo*" (52). At the same time, as Consuelo notes, no one in her family recognizes the real tragedy: Mili. Ortiz Cofer writes: "Perhaps it's impossible to say to a mother, Your child is sick beyond our help. She needs help we [the family] cannot give her. The *familia* cannot save her" (55). This reader wonders whether the capitalization of "Your" is a typo. Assuming it is intentional, however, reinforces the idea that the child belongs to the mother and not the father. The family only turns its attention to Mili once Patricio is labeled damned and lost. Seen frolicking in the hotel pool with a young man, Patricio "had stepped over the imaginary line" (Ortiz Cofer 70). The imaginary line refers to this society's rigid gender and sexuality demarcations, with acceptable norms and morals categorized on one side of the binary and unacceptable ones on the other. A homosexual and a "transvestite" displaying their desire publicly, places them on the wrong side, the illegal side, of the binary (Crespo-Kebler 207). As Socolovsky explains, "Transgression, the violation of a law or command . . . involves crossing over a limit" (98). Patricio's transgressive sexuality, interestingly enough, is also blamed on his dead mother. Without a maternal figure, Patricio apparently loses his way, as if his sexuality were a choice and a response to maternal absence. The father bears little if any responsibility, with the exception that he is criticized for not surrounding his son with maternal figures, essentially the eroticized mother-lover figure in the Oedipal complex. If the mother is the only meaningful parent, then the mother is also implicitly blamed or held responsible for the child's problems.

Prepared to lose Patricio, the family refocuses on Mili. Described as "learning the language of birds" (Ortiz Cofer 70), Mili tells Consuelo that the birds communicate with each other: "'Fly for your life.' Sometimes they repeat the word *volar* all day . . . *volar, volar, volar, volar*" (71). The birds fly "because the sky is too blue, they can't see anything but *el azul, azul, azul*, and they get lost in it" (71). Echoing her response to the hotel swimming pool (19), the very same pool where Patricio publicly showed affection for a young man, Mili utters the word "*azul*." Mili conflates the sky and the sea by calling them both *azul*. Beyond being blue, however, sky and sea are open spaces, with the sea's color reflecting the sky, much like Mili reflects, or rather attempts to deflect ideals of Puerto Rican womanhood and femininity.

Mili imagines the birds not only escaping into the blue but also becoming disoriented by it because there is no distinction or reference point. This mirrors her Puerto Rican society, which denies sexual and gender difference so that the sky and sea in their endlessness, homogeneity, and symmetry (cisgendered, heterosexual society) become oppressive. As Elizabeth Crespo-Kebler argues, girls and women during this time would be "punish[ed] for desiring forbidden activities and forbidden places. It was intended as a way to control and produce shame" (200). Mili, who is learning to speak and to identify with the birds, understands this violence, and she, like Patricio, longs for escape from her mother-island, the "nest" (Ortiz Cofer 70), which is controlled by misogynistic, transphobic/homophobic beliefs.

La Señora Platasi also claims that at school Mili has "been playing bad games with boys" (75). Defending herself to Consuelo, Mili claims, "It's the *muchachos* who lie about me" (75). When pressed about which *muchachos*, Mili becomes silent. The teacher and adults in Mili's life blame the girl for encouraging the older boys, forgetting that Mili is a child; the victim blaming Mili experiences is symptomatic of the larger problems in a sexist society in which women's bodies are policed and controlled, mirroring Papi blaming Mami for Mili's issues. When Mili, Mami, Consuelo, and La Señora Platasi later meet in the Signe kitchen, the domestic once more becomes a site for sexual politics. Mili reports that she hears voices and is often distracted by "the birds singing the same song over and over" (80). The birdcalls emphasize the need but also the futility for Mili to have a voice and to escape her constraints, especially those at school. *La gran familia*, however, strongly suggests confining/silencing Mili.

The mother once more attempts to remedy Mili's alleged immorality and educational failures. Papi notes: "[I]t was a mother's duty to shape a daughter's character—a woman's job" (82). As the child-bearer, Mami is expected to be the child-carer. But Mami also holds down a job at the hotel and is thus tasked with balancing work inside and outside the home. Is Mami a bad mother because she works outside the home? Mami finds herself in the paradoxical position of being responsible for Mili because she gave birth to her while also being expected to let go of any authority over and any meaningful connection with her daughter that does not serve her heteropatriarchal Puerto Rican society. Rather than obediently bending to such roles, Mili retreats further and further from reality, listening to the language of birds, while Consuelo, too, feels a sense of "dislocation" in relation to following gender expectations (Ortiz Cofer 84).

Suspicious of outsider perspectives, Mami turns to her mother for advice about Mili. Consuelo's *abuela*, like her husband, holds Angélica accountable for her daughter's behavior and dismisses the notion that Mili needs medical help. She tells her daughter "to show her the way.... Spend time with her; teach her how to live a creative life" (89). The insinuation is that Mami has failed to instruct her daughter in womanly arts; if the sea reflects the sky, the daughter's failures reflect the mother's failures, suggesting that no distinction between the two exists. Abuela's advice is rendered pointless, however, when Mili slaughters a chicken in her grandparents' yard, and no change in her behavior occurs. Desperate, Mami secretly enlists the help of Doña Sereno, María Sereno's mother, reputed to be a spirit medium. A missed opportunity in the novel to be sure, Ortiz Cofer leaves the encounter between Mili and the *espiritista* (105) for the reader to imagine, although we are privy to her advice: Mami must "confront the *malas influencias* trying to destroy this family," while the "father's *aventuras* are at the core of all our troubles" (121). Doña Sereno is the only one to implicate the father in his daughter's actions, though she, too, sees the patriarchal family as the answer to or savior of the family's problems generally, and the women's problems specifically.

Certain characters in the novel suggest that patriarchy is at fault for Mili's mental illness. Doña Sereno's belief is that an illicit affair the father has indulged in, possibly an analogy for his increasing support for American culture as opposed to Spanish culture, is causing Mili's erratic behavior. If the father were to remain faithful to his wife, Mili would heal and become psychologically stable. The father's deeds, his past, his betrayal, and by extension Puerto Rican history haunt Mili, causing her difficulties, according to Doña Sereno. The suggestion is that sexual transgressions are at the heart of the family's and nation's troubles and that suppressing this past bears psychic consequences. After a visit by a nurse and a psychologist, however, Consuelo learns that Mili cannot return to school and that she needs professional help (120). Resistant to such outside authority, most likely out of fear, or selfishness to save her marriage, Mami instead heeds Doña Sereno's advice and tells Consuelo that the family will be moving to New York so as to put the past behind them. The decision to emigrate to the mainland coincides with Mili's first menstrual cycle, Papi leaving his lover, and Consuelo losing her virginity—all taboo bodily-sexual experiences.

It is at this time of sexual maturity that Consuelo increasingly questions her mother's decisions and starts to distance herself from her. Like Mili, who desires physical, psychical, and sexual freedom, Consuelo, too, comes to see herself differently. Consuelo concludes: "I belong to myself. I was not like my mother who had to get the permission of all her relatives and ancestors before making any decisions about her life. She was ruled by ghosts and their dead words: *la decencia, el sacrificio, el deber de la mujer Buena, para la familia.* . . . It was time to learn a new language" (132). The language is an embodied one. Consuelo seeks a new way of defining her sexuality and gender via language but also her Puerto Rican identity through the language of gender and sexuality. As Kevane suggests, Ortiz Cofer's novel offers us a young woman who, no longer a virgin, rejects *la familia* and all that entails, so that the new Puerto Rican "woman emerges" (55). But does this new language and woman, this new matria, reflect an American-style feminism?

The family concurs that possibly Americanization and a move to New York is the only option. With the Signes preparing for their departure, María Sereno reenters the narrative. Having recovered from a collapse a few months earlier, after injecting oil into her chest (Ortiz Cofer 133–35), María Sereno now works as a manicurist at one of the American hotels. Mami reveals that "[he and] his mother have been a comfort to me during these past months.

... He has a special touch with Mili, you know. Some days I just could not stay alone with your sister" (148). Mami reveals that the responsibility to take care of Mili normally assigned to the mother and the elder sister has been taken up by a transgender person. On the one hand, the narrative opens up a conversation about who can parent or be a legal guardian to a child in this traditional heterosexual, conservative society, but on the other hand, it reinforces uncertainty and possibly willful ignorance when it comes to correctly identifying her identity. For example, Mami refers to María Sereno with the feminized form of her birth name but then uses the pronouns "he" and "she" interchangeably within a matter of a page (148–49). Is the switching between pronouns evidence of the novel's refusal to subscribe to gender or gender-sex binaries?

How do we make sense of María Sereno's transformation into a manicurist dressed in a "white cabin mate's parade uniform with shoulder decorations of braids and fringe[?] His chest was flat but was covered in medals and ribbons. He looked stunning" (147). Ortiz Cofer suggests that resistance in terms of gender and sexuality is limited because María Sereno finds a way to fit into her society, albeit this alternative space is occupied by American tourists and dependent on capitalism. Thus, it may be that Puerto Rican capitalism, modeled on American capitalism, tolerates María Sereno in this space, but not once she travels beyond it. As Socolovsky argues, "acts of resistance" prove nearly impossible because "the commercialized subaltern identity represents a repetition of (rather than a departure from) U.S. economic dominance"; thus, these actions "end up becoming part of the system of colonial capitalism on the island" (112). Ortiz Cofer's text thus questions whether transforming stereotypes, sexism, and transphobia/homophobia is possible in this Puerto Rican culture, and if so, whether it is only made possible by American capitalism-colonialism.

Poignantly, Socolovsky asks: "As the boundaries between tourist and native, home and hotel, and self and other grow more muffled, who determines the limit that will establish and keep in place social, moral, and ethical practices? ... And what is the efficacy of transgressive acts that operate within the boundaries of U.S. economic and cultural consumerism?" (116). Attempts by Puerto Ricans to disrupt either the island's or the United States' hold over the characters' lives remain limited because of the latter's colonial power over the former. That during the novel's time frame homosexuality and feminism were seen as a result of an American-style capitalism, and thus anti–Puerto Rican by nationalists (Crespo-Kebler 205), must also be considered. One should also seriously doubt that exile from the island correlates to being free from patriarchy in the United States in the 1950s. Believing the mainland to be a more liberating space for women, the novel proposes, might be another myth.

The novel's climax occurs, however, when Consuelo and Mami are packing their belongings, and Tía Divina takes Mili to the beach (171), where, true to her habit, she runs away. Tía Divina's "gaze had shifted a mere seconds from her niece—who had been singing to herself at the edge of the water—toward an American cruise ship that had appeared. . . . Our María Milagros vanished" (178). The aunt's diverted attention suggests that she has been seduced by American culture and the promise of luxury. For this brief lapse, she is saddled with extreme guilt for losing Mili. Consuelo joins the now multiple search parties out looking for Mili. Ortiz Cofer writes, "I put my head under the nearly black water of the Atlantic. I swam in ever-widening circles until I was completely disoriented. . . . Under the gently rocking waves, I called my sister in words from her private language: *Mar azul, aguabuena, aguamala, azul, azul,* please return my sister" (179). True to the bird parable Mili told Consuelo earlier in the novel, Mili's body is never found.

Mili's disappearance proposes a form of socio-sexual resistance. She will not be the beautiful, dutiful, happy, doll-like, and silent beauty queen that her parents desire: she refuses to be theirs, and by corollary, Puerto Rico's *milagros,* miracle. She disappears as if she were never real to begin with. Just as Patricio, María Sereno, and Consuelo trouble the static definition of heterosexual womanhood/femininity and the notion of the nation as a woman, Mili, too, rejects this label. Instead, she fights back, speaks out loud, takes up public space, and refuses to have her body and sexuality exploited or policed. Perhaps, as Méndez suggests, Mili signifies an outdated, impossible Puerto Rican dream of fame and fortune and/or the failure of Puerto Rico to successfully fit in with and gain the United States' respect: "Just as the body and life of Mili, as a female figure of the commonwealth, are lost, so can Puerto Rico lose its sense of being a national community" if its status as commonwealth continues indefinitely (Méndez 40). The risk, Méndez concludes, is that in attempting to please and imitate the United States, much like it did with Spain previously, Puerto Rico risks losing its sense of identity, its orientation, instead occupying a liminal, confused space.

Socolovsky goes one step further to argue that when Mili "disappears at the end of the story and is mourned as if dead, [she] becom[es] not only the text's central tragic figure but also a significant metaphor for Puerto Rican displacement. Rather than commodifying her exile, the narrative illustrates, through Mili, the alienating and frightening depths of the colonized psyche" (125). This indeterminacy is likewise echoed in the novel's ending when we perceive Consuelo embarking "on her migration to the mainland, but with no actual narrative of arrival" (Socolovsky 112). Resonating with maternal imagery, Consuelo reappears as a child in her mother's womb. Alone, on the plane to New York, she watches her island fade "[u]ntil there was nothing below or ahead but *mar azul y cielo azul*" (Ortiz Cofer 185). The new Puerto Rican woman has neither been fully separated from her mother-island, nor has she been born into her new self-mainland. This also suggests that attempts like Consuelo's to fully leave the mother-land/tongue will always in some sense fail because Puerto Rico is a commonwealth of the United States. Nevertheless, to realize her dream of matria Consuelo feels compelled to move to the mainland, where her status as a racialized minority is another challenge in and of itself that the novel leaves for the reader to imagine.

Perhaps, Mili's death (symbolized as the commonwealth status) makes Consuelo's freedom possible. The younger sister is "responsible for saving Consuelo from perpetuating the myth of the perfect Puerto Rican woman," writes Kevane (48). As Kevane notes, however, "for Ortiz Cofer, the tragedy is *not* the death of Mili, but rather a community of women who are so paralyzed by their beliefs in sacrifice and suffering that they are silent accomplices in Mili's death" (51). Does this impart too much blame on the mother? For example, Consuelo recalls her female family members circling around Mami: "They told and retold old stories as if they were giving my mother back her old vocabulary. She had to learn how to be a strong woman again. I was not a part of this, I chose not to be a part of this. I did not need to hear the old stories again" (Ortiz Cofer 181). This quotation also summarizes the matria perfectly—Consuelo seeks distance not only from being "defined by a man or a church" (Kevane 56) but also from her mother and her patriarchal (maternal) genealogy: she desires her own language and her own life without rejecting her mother(s) entirely.

The gendered roles that Mami subscribes to, the old stories, are therefore not the same ones the diasporic daughter desires. Consuelo cannot find her consolation on the island. She cannot commit to "a submissive act of consoling others, the family, the husband, and children"; instead, she performs "an assertive act of consoling the self" (Kevane 56), thus reinforcing the suitability of the bildungsroman for Ortiz Cofer's historical fiction. The title of the novel also reflects the eponymous character's journey toward self-definition. While Consuelo physically distances herself from her mothers and her mother-island/tongue, an embodied psychic connection to the maternal remains. That is to say, she does not embody a radical form of individualization. Consuelo realizes, "I was no more like my mother than Mami was like Abuela, than Abuela was like Mamá Isadora. Yet we each carried all the others in our bodies and minds" (181). Consuelo thus challenges and redefines from a postcolonial-psychoanalytic feminist perspective the Puerto Rican family's and nation's *matriz* of sexuality and gender. Embracing the label "*la fulana*" (185), she alters its meaning from signifying female shame to signifying female empowerment. Between island and mainland, she gains the promise of an imagined matria where she and her mothers might express their true gendered, sexual, and creative selves.

PART III
REVOLUTIONIZING MATRIA

POLITICIZED MOTHERS

Dreaming the Matria

Caribbean women's historical novels set in the mid-twentieth century during the time of dictatorships, anticolonialism, and communist revolution acknowledge women's contributions to both history and the nation. Evocative of the Haitian woman's revolutionary spirit depicted in Marie Vieux-Chauvet's early historical novel *Dance on the Volcano* (1957), contemporary texts take a direct postcolonial approach to writing about the militarization of the nation from women's points of view. Although many of these events are well documented by historians, the "task of recovering and representing the female perspective" has undeniably fallen to Caribbean women historical novelists (Bellamy 77). Revisiting Caribbean nations in crisis, these revolutionary novels depict not only the politicization of women across the region and their fights for social justice but also their desire for a new Caribbean as a matria.

Caribbean women's novels of revolution began materializing in the 1980s, principally with two works published in 1987: Merle Collins's *Angel*, set in Grenada, and Michelle Cliff's sequel to *Abeng*, *No Telephone to Heaven*, set in Jamaica. Following Cliff's and Collins's publications, other pioneering texts appeared throughout the 1990s including Cristina García's *Dreaming in Cuban* (1992), Julia Alvarez's *In the Time of the Butterflies* (1994), Oonya Kempadoo's *Buxton Spice* (1998), and Margaret Cezair-Thompson's *The True History of Paradise* (1999). The two revolutionary novels I examine in the following chapters tell the stories of women who, after having survived dictatorships and trauma, search for a depoliticized and demilitarized matria. In Edwidge Danticat's premillennium novel *The Farming of Bones* (1998), the motherless daughter seeks her matria in the maternal waters that flow between Haiti and the Dominican Republic. In Andrea O'Reilly Herrera's postmillennium text *The Pearl of the Antilles* (2001), the Cuban American mother-daughter pair imagine matria through recovering and reclaiming their Cuban herstory.

Danticat and O'Reilly Herrera have consistently addressed race and gender politics within Caribbean history, for example Danticat's *Breath, Eyes, Memory* (1994) and O'Reilly Herrera's scholarly and creative compendium *ReMembering Cuba: Legacy of a Diaspora* (2001). The two novels I examine, however, constitute the authors' most explicit and direct treatment of the revolutionary past in literary form. Writing from the Haitian diaspora in the United States, Danticat returns to the catastrophic effects of Dominican leader Rafael Leónidas Trujillo's dictatorship on her island birthplace. *The Farming of Bones*, partly inspired by Haitian novelist Jacques Stephen Alexis's *Compère Général Soleil* (1955) (*General Sun, My Brother*), is the first historical novel to retell the Parsley Massacre of 1937 from a Haitian woman's perspective.[1] Thus, scholars often read the fictional heroine's account of Trujillo's regime in Danticat's novel in relation to Alvarez's polyphonic novel *In the Time of the Butterflies*, which is narrated by four historical Dominican women—the Mirabal sisters—three of whom were murdered by Trujillo's men. Meanwhile, American-born O'Reilly Herrera, whose mother was Cuban, primarily reimagines the dictatorship of Fulgencio Batista (1952–1959) in *The Pearl of the Antilles*.

O'Reilly Herrera's only novel to date uses a feminist postcolonial lens to retell Cuba's storied revolutionary past. This critical account of Cuban women's lives complements García's earlier novel, *Dreaming in Cuban*, about the lead-up to and aftermath of the Cuban Revolution. O'Reilly Herrera's novel, however, focuses more on the power of matrilineal herstory, specifically how mother-daughter relations can challenge the oppressive patriarchal family and patriarchal nation—Cuban and American, communist and capitalist. The authors' returns to the revolutionary past emphasize the detrimental effects patriarchy and dictatorships have on mother-daughter bonds, literally and discursively. Novels like O'Reilly Herrera's or Ana Menéndez's *Loving Che* (2003) thus support Elena Machado Sáez's claim that "[a]nticolonialism's public project of intimacy domesticates the masculine collective and excludes women from the project of revolution. When women do appear, they can be articulated only as objects that reassure the heteronormative subjectivity of the male revolutionary" (128). Conversely, by creating postcolonial tragic romances, which often take the form of matrilineal herstories, contemporary Caribbean women's writing rejects patria, specifically Fatherland, violence, misogyny, and white supremacy. This leads to "a feminist revision of anticolonial movements while also tackling the rhetorical shortcomings of revolutionary discourse" (Machado Sáez 129). The genre replaces the heteropatriarchy with the romance of a mother-daughter reunion, which effectively rewrites the shared maternal past to imagine antipatriarchal democratic-socialist maternal futures.

Generally, postcolonial novels envision matria as a means to begin healing psychically and physically from the personal and collective wounds of a past replete with human rights violations, murder, imprisonment, rape, and exile. This section thus builds on part II's consideration of girls in bildungsromane whose budding autonomy is analogous to the independence-seeking Caribbean nation. Part III demonstrates that the revolutionary novel portrays the effects of extreme right- and left-wing politics, capitalism and communism, and patriarchal nationalism on women's lives. Told from Amabelle's first-person perspective, Danticat's novel centers on the heroine's experiences as a young Haitian woman living in the Dominican Republic during Trujillo's regime. After surviving the Parsley Massacre of 1937, Amabelle spends the rest of her life in Haiti experiencing guilt and reflecting on losing loved ones. Meanwhile, unlike Danticat's text, O'Reilly Herrera's novel is at a "geographic and generational remove" from its dictatorship history, facilitating what Jennifer Harford Vargas calls "a double vision of state violence both abroad and domestically" (*Forms of Dictatorship* 6). O'Reilly Herrera's work, written in the third person, provides a multigenerational account of women's lives in one Cuban family. Margarita's herstory includes the life of her mother, Rosa, and then transitions into an account of her own exile from her family and her island—at the onset of the 1959 revolution, Margarita's father banishes her for being pregnant and unwed. Cuba is no longer a viable homeland, so she emigrates to the United States. For Harford Vargas, this move "enlarge[s] the geographic scope transnationally" and "extend[s] the temporality of the dictatorship by exploring its afterlife" (*Forms of Dictatorship* 10). *The Pearl of the Antilles* concludes with Margarita's American daughter Lilly learning and writing her matrilineal Cuban past in novel form.

Caribbean women's narratives of historical trauma demonstrate how patriarchal families and nations perpetuate the loss of matrilineage. Machado Sáez insightfully notes that "[w]ith nation and diaspora defined by homosocial kinship, the filiation of a female community appears to have no alternative lineage to root it, so that the women remain unmoored from the postcolonial nation and marginalized within the ... diaspora" (192). The texts under consideration in this section strategically employ memory to repair the broken link between mothers and daughters. Amabelle, for instance, finds herself without parents, children, or partner (her fiancé Sebastien and his sister are murdered by Trujillo's men), while Margarita's son dies during an exchange of fire between rival political factions. *The Pearl of the Antilles*, however, also highlights Margarita's illustrious line of Cuban mothers, and then daughter Lilly, demonstrating that the maternal genealogy continues postmigration. As a result of political instability, violence, and social unrest, the female protagonists oscillate between a feeling of rootedness and rootlessness in both their birth islands and their respective diasporas. The strategy of alternating between realistic depictions and antirealism modes such as dream and memory to relay the traumas of the mother-island's past is crucial to both writers and to the genre more broadly.

In this third section of *Matria Redux*, I locate in the novels a common historical experience in Haiti, Cuba, and the Dominican Republic of sugar plantations, slavery, US occupation, and dictatorship. In *From Sugar to Revolution: Women's Visions of Haiti, Cuba, and the Dominican Republic*, Myriam J. A. Chancy notes the influence of both the Haitian Revolution (1804) and the Cuban Revolution (1959) on each nation—Haiti's revolution coincided with independence and the abolishment of slavery, while Cuba's constituted a distinct economic and political break from the United States. All three nations, too, were ruled by dictators in the late 1950s: François Duvalier in Haiti; Trujillo in the Dominican Republic; and Batista, supplanted by Fidel Castro, in Cuba. Further, there were violent clashes between the Dominican Republic and both Haiti and Cuba. The historical entanglement of the three nations is found in both *The Farming of Bones* and *The Pearl of the Antilles*, which draw attention to and cross hostile national borders, such as the island of Hispaniola's.

Hispaniola is composed of two nations: Haiti and the Dominican Republic. French-imposed slavery ended in 1804 after a successful slave uprising, which led to independence. This momentous event made Haiti the first in the region to abolish slavery and the first independent nation in the Caribbean. Moreover, Haiti was the first to be governed by former slaves, who included Jean-Jacques Dessalines and Henri Christophe. The Dominican Republic gained independence from Spain in 1821 (Fernández Olmos and Paravisini-Gebert 27), but in 1822, Haitian president Jean-Pierre Boyer unified the island (Eller x). Haiti dominated and occupied the Dominican Republic— then called Santo Domingo—until 1844. That year, the Dominican Republic regained its independence (Wucker 36–37), but struggled to maintain its autonomy and fell under Spanish control again in 1861. Michele Wucker in *Why the Cocks Fight: Dominicans, Haitians, and the Struggle for Hispaniola* contends that Spain's control was relatively short-lived because Dominicans sought independence; this time, they enlisted the support of their former enemy, Haiti. A shared concern about European threats to sovereignty led to their joining forces and defeating Spain in 1865 (Wucker 64). Several presidents in both nations throughout the nineteenth and early twentieth centuries were deposed, murdered, or resigned, contributing to a volatile political climate. Danticat's novel places its heroine's birth around 1912, just prior to the US occupation of Haiti, which began in 1915 and lasted nineteen years (Wucker 67). Meanwhile, Amabelle's life in the Dominican Republic begins circa 1922 (Danticat, *The Farming* 38).

After facing a series of political setbacks, the Dominican Republic was occupied by the United States from 1916 to 1924 and then later was ruled by American-backed dictatorships (Fernández Olmos and Paravisini-Gebert 27), as Alvarez's historical novel *In the Name of Salomé* (2000) recounts. Danticat explains: "[D]uring the 1929 U.S.-guided border negotiations, Haiti lost some land, and many Haitians suddenly found themselves on Dominican soil" ("The Long Legacy of Occupation"). Danticat thus directly links occupation by the United States in both nations as contributing to the socioeconomic and racial tensions between Haiti and the Dominican Republic. In 1930, Trujillo, head of the armed forces, launched a successful coup and became president of the Dominican Republic. Meanwhile, Sténio Joseph Vincent became president of Haiti, although that country was still under US occupation (Wucker 68). Supported by Trujillo, Vincent remained Haiti's president until 1941—despite being widely criticized by Haitians for his weak, ineffective handling of the 1937 Parsley Massacre (Wucker 77), in which Dominican army troops, on Trujillo's orders, killed a large number of Haitians living in the Dominican Republic's northwestern frontier region. As far as Dominicans were concerned, the massacre was not racially motivated but a result of "a migratory-control problem" (Wucker 78). Nevertheless, it resulted in "fifteen to twenty thousand Haitians [and Haitian Dominicans being] slaughtered in an operation known in Spanish as *el corte* (the cutting), in Kreyòl as *koutkout-a* (the stabbing), and in English as the Parsley Massacre because the Trujillo regime identified ethnic Haitians by their inability to trill the 'r' in *perejil*, the Spanish word for parsley" (Harford Vargas, "Novel Testimony" 1164). In 1938, the Dominican Republic "agreed to pay $750,000 to the Haitian government, which in theory would distribute the money among the survivors of the massacre" (Wucker 77), but in 1941, Vincent was replaced as president by Élie Lescot, "a light-skinned mulatto" who "shared Trujillo's racial biases" (Wucker 78). Wucker notes that during Trujillo's regime, Dominicans came to call themselves *"blancos de la tierra"* (whites of the earth) (56).

The current border between the two nations was drawn in 1929 (Wucker 67), and tensions between Haitians and Dominicans continue. For instance, Dominicans celebrate independence not from Spain but from Haiti (Wucker 63), and more recently, a 2013 Tribunal Court sentence in the Dominican Republic (known as TC-1068/13) retroactively deprived Dominicans of Haitian descent of Dominican "nationality" (Inter-American Commission on Human Rights 11–12). Referencing Silvio Torres-Saillant's work, literary scholar Kelli Lyon Johnson writes that "Dominican national identity is dependent upon Haitians, against whom they define themselves and thereby construct 'a nation-building ideology based primarily on self-differentiation from Haiti'" ("Both Sides" 141). As such, "anti-Haitianism becomes a form of Dominican patriotism" that "manifests itself also as a declared contempt for blackness" (Torres-Saillant 55). O'Reilly Herrera's novel recounts historical anti-Blackness in Cuba as well. Cuba was the last Spanish colony to abolish slavery, not long before it ceased being a Spanish colony in 1898 (Fernández Olmos and Paravisini-Gebert 26).

Cuba, as O'Reilly Herrera's opening scene with an elderly woman's vision of the island as a pearl lost to colonization indicates, had a rich Indigenous history prior to late fifteenth-century European colonization. Despite several rebellions throughout the following centuries, Cuba remained a Spanish colony for almost all of its colonial period and surpassed Santo Domingo as the center of Spanish power in the Caribbean. Sugar was the island's leading export, and its cultivation depended heavily on slave labor from Africa

Politicized Mothers: Dreaming the Matria   153

and then on indentured labor from the Yucatán and China (Gott 69). With other European colonies abolishing slavery in the nineteenth century, Cuba became "the greatest slave-importing colony" and the epicenter of slavery in the Caribbean (Gott 59) until abolition in 1886 (Sadowski-Smith 130). Spanish rule came to an end when Cuban rebels declared independence in 1897, "an event that helped incite the Spanish-American War [1898–1902]" (Sadowski-Smith 130) and led to US military rule of the island. Cuba gained independence in 1902, but Guantánamo Bay was leased to the United States as part of the Platt Amendment, which allowed the Americans the right to military intervention in Cuba (Gott 110).

American military interventions in 1906, 1912, and 1917 attempted to "prop up unstable and insecure governments" (Gott 129), making Cuba, according to Richard Gott in *Cuba: A New History*, "a colony" of the United States "in all but name" (129). The next few decades saw Cuba changing leadership between only a few individuals, but several social reforms were implemented, such as a minimum wage for cane cutters, an eight-hour workday, a restoring of land to Cuban citizens, autonomy of the university, and a rejection of the Platt Amendment in 1934 (Gott 110). Sadowski-Smith argues that it was "[t]he 1933 uprising, known as the 'Revolt of the Sergeants,' [that] ultimately led to the installation of a Cuban government under Fulgencio Batista y Zaldívar," a leader "officially recognized by the United States" (130). By the 1950s, Cuba was a considerably wealthy, educated nation with a healthy middle class influenced by American culture. From 1952 to 1959, Cuba found itself under Batista's leadership once more, this time as a US-backed dictator, who remained in power until he was overthrown by Fidel Castro (Sadowski-Smith 130). Castro ushered in the Cuban Revolution, brought the new socialist state under his power, and cut ties with the United States. While the revolution renounced wealthy and foreign landowners, forcing many to flee the island, mostly for the United States—a storyline O'Reilly Herrera deploys in her novel—Castro also unified Cuba and brought together an island formerly "divided by race and class and ethnic origin," where "endemic violence[,] . . . ingrained racism," and pernicious sexism had once been the norm (Gott 5).

Close readings of Caribbean women's revolutionary novels suggest that the region's violent political past has been falsely captured, in part because women's lives and voices have been disregarded. These postcolonial feminist counternarratives thus serve "to inscribe an alternative history" emphasizing "female power" (Lima, "Revolutionary Developments" 41). The dearth of women-centered and -authored novels can be attributed to male-dominated conceptions of the historical novel genre, which suggest that war and military campaigns pertain to men, not women. As Cuban American writer Cristina García reminds us, "[H]istory does not just happen to men on a battlefield but ... politics really lie ... at home" (qtd. in O'Reilly Herrera, "Cristina García, *Dreaming in Cuban*" 93). Violent patriarchal-national politics mimic violent patriarchal-familial politics in these works, reinforcing an interpretation of their interconnectedness. This interconnectedness can be found between the individual and her collective of female friends and family as well. As Maria Helena Lima argues: "[T]he collectivity of the *testimonio*, [is] a literature of personal witness and involvement designed ... to make the cause of these movements known to the outside world.... Because *testimonio* is not so much concerned with the life of a 'problematic hero' as with a problematic collective social situation, the narrator in *testimonio* speaks for, or in the name of, a community or group" ("Revolutionary Developments" 43). The *testimonios* found in Caribbean women's fictions of revolutionary history not only strategically link the "marginalization, oppression, and struggle" of the "individual subject" with the experiences of her community but also signal the writer's "process of destabilizing and transforming fixed ideas of history" (Lima 44, 36), such as patriarchal-imperial ones.

Women's pre- and postmillennium returns to the region's military past reveal that a "new breed of bilingual, bicultural, mestiza writers, who are political, *tercermundista*, *feminista*, and familial," has emerged (Gatto 84). Unlike the traditional bildungsroman, discussed in part II: Decolonizing Matria, these novels adopt a polyphonic and multigenerational approach, writing "in the voices of mothers as well as daughters" (Lima, "Revolutionary Developments" 45).[2] The result is that "the novel [is] not only less teleological but more politically effective" in challenging masculine (M)aster narratives (Lima 47). Furthermore, the novels in my close readings tactically employ the analogy of mothers giving birth to fraternal twins with the subsequent death of the son and survival of the daughter as not only coinciding with the birth of a new national/masculine revolution but also its inevitable failure, a failure for which women are directly responsible, such as Trujillo's 1961 assassination. For instance, chapter 6 posits that O'Reilly Herrera's family saga chronicles the lives of a Cuban grandmother, mother, and daughter to displace and replace the lives of fathers and men. As Adriana Méndez Rodenas explains, these postcolonial feminist works expose "the 'underside' of the nation, the antiheroic (and mostly silent and *silenced* story of mothers and daughters)" (57). Rejecting the singular male hero and focusing on the collective political potential of women-mothers-daughters is a defining characteristic of this genre, both pre- and postmillennium.

Although military coups d'état, "successful or otherwise ... [continue to] form an inescapable part of the contemporary political history of the region" (United Nations Economic Commission 17), Danticat's *The Farming of Bones*, published in 1998, signals the genre's diminished emphasis on women combating political injustices with violence, as in *Angel* and *In the Time of the Butterflies*.[3] Typical of postmillennium novels, O'Reilly Herrera's *The Pearl of the Antilles* denounces violence and is fairly cynical of "the possibility of revolutionary social transformation" (Lima, "Revolutionary Developments" 35) through military action. One reason might be that, following major economic and social reforms in the 1980s, the region experienced economic growth in the 1990s and attained relative political stability in the new millennium. Disillusionment with Marxist ideology has further meant that the revolutionary novel of the late 1980s and 1990s has noticeably dropped off—the exception being postmillennial women's novels set mainly in Cuba, such as O'Reilly Herrera's.

Caribbean women's historical fiction alerts readers to how genocides, uprisings, and violence radically transform and reinforce traditional gender expectations. Stereotypical images of women as "maternal, emotional, and peace-loving," for instance, become complicated by the "monstrous" violent woman (Sjoberg and Gentry 1). Feminist scholars Laura Sjoberg and Caron E. Gentry suggest that the woman who commits violence is "incompatible with traditional explanations of all women as the 'peaceful people' whom 'war protects' and who 'should be protected from war'": a "woman is expected to be against war and violence, but to cooperate with wars fought to protect her innocence and virginity" (3–4). *The Farming of Bones* and *The Pearl of the Antilles*, as is typical of Caribbean women's fictions of revolutionary history, productively question the socioeconomic, gendered, racial, and political motives for women to either take up or not take up arms. They also question how gendered tropes, particularly those of the maternal, are used contradictorily and conveniently in heteropatriarchal societies to legitimize and/or denounce violence by and against women.

With heroines as witnesses and/or participants in the struggle against injustices, these postcolonial feminist texts depict the psychological and physical effects of war and trauma, including survivor's guilt. Drawing on Freudian ideas of the "returning traumatic dream" (48), Cathy Caruth's scholarship suggests that figures like Amabelle and Margarita may suffer from a neurosis that involves "the repetitive intrusion of nightmares and relivings of... events... whose symptoms seem to reflect, in startling directness and simplicity, nothing but the unmediated occurrence of violent events" (48). This is to say that rather than dreams being symbolic or covering over a repressed past, the events literally manifest. With Amabelle, this is evident in her nightmares of her parents drowning. Caruth suggests that in the moment of the traumatic experience, the person cannot fully comprehend what is happening; there is a delayed response, so to speak, between the actual event and one's consciousness of it. For instance, in *The Farming of Bones*, Amabelle does not initially grasp the weight of her struggle to survive the Parsley Massacre of 1937. It is only years later while in Haiti that she finds herself at a loss to come to grips with the violence she has witnessed and experienced.

That Amabelle and Margarita are survivors significantly influences their conceptions of trauma. Caruth clarifies: "What Freud encounters in the traumatic neurosis is not the reaction to any horrible event but, rather, the peculiar and perplexing experience of survival. If the dreams and flashbacks of the traumatized thus engage Freud's interest, it is because they bear witness to a survival that exceeds the very claims and consciousness of the one who endures it" (49). Both Danticat and O'Reilly Herrera reflect the difficulty of processing traumatic events, including recurring violent dreams and other psychic experiences that severely disrupt mother-daughter bonds. In *Beyond the Pleasure Principle* (1920), Freud suggests that the survivor's inability to deal with the magnitude of the threat of death at the time of the trauma has lasting effects on the consciousness. One result is the survivor being forced "continually, to confront it over and over again. For consciousness then, the act of survival, as the experience of trauma, is the repeated confrontation with the necessity and impossibility of grasping the threat to one's own life" (Caruth 51). Amabelle and Margarita, in their failure to fully comprehend or speak their trauma individually, function synecdochally for displaced Haitian and Cuban woman, respectively.

The heroines occupy liminal spaces between Haiti and the Dominican Republic, Cuba and the United States, and their lives contest national and cultural borders. Postcolonial critic Homi Bhabha writes that "we find ourselves in the moment of transit where space and time cross to produce complex figures of difference and identity, past and present, inside and outside, inclusion and exclusion" (*The Location* 2). New possibilities for selfhood are located in these postcolonial "in-between spaces" (Bhabha, *The Location* 2). Rejecting the notion of monolithic, homogeneous nations, Bhabha refers to their identities as "narratives." "It is in the emergence of the interstices—the overlap and displacement of domains of difference—that the intersubjective and collective experiences of nationness, community interest, or cultural value are negotiated," he writes (*The Location* 2). Danticat's and O'Reilly Herrera's novels adhere to Bhabha's notions of cultural hybridity, interstitial spaces, and "domains of difference" from which new identities, personal and communal, can emerge, but the impact of violence on their female protagonists' lives cannot be overlooked. As I explain in chapter 5, hybridity can come at great personal and collective cost, not least of which is a loss of the maternal and/or mother figure. For this reason, Amabelle comes to symbolize neither Haiti nor the Dominican Republic but rather the Massacre River, which flows between the two countries. In both chapters I read matria in relation to postcolonial theories of home/unhomeliness, island/exile, feminism, and psychoanalytic theory—Freud's theory of the uncanny and trauma in Danticat's novel and the incest taboo in O'Reilly Herrera's.

Historical novels concerned with women's lives during political upheaval, dictatorships, and periods of nationalistic agitation almost exclusively centralize the heroine's political awakening and her commitment to social reform. Frequently, the female protagonists, like many of the authors, live in exile or emigrate to the United States. For instance, Danticat left Haiti as a teenager for the United States during Jean-Claude Duvalier's (Baby Doc's) dictatorship, while Amabelle flees to Haiti under Trujillo's threat of deportation and genocide. In the postmillennium novel, Margarita struggles to build a life for herself in the diaspora. She has meaningful relationships with neither her maternal relatives in Cuba nor her daughter in the United States. *The Farming of Bones* and *The Pearl of the Antilles* then certainly constitute what Caruth calls "a kind of double telling," "the oscillation between a crisis of death and the correlative crisis of life: between the story of the unbearable nature of an event and the story of the unbearable nature of its survival" (12). Caruth elaborates that "what returns to haunt the victim . . . is not only the reality of the violent event but also the reality of the way that its violence has not yet been fully known" (12). For example, Amabelle spends several decades reliving painful memories after surviving the massacre. In *The Pearl of the*

Antilles, the reader learns at the end of the novel that Margarita's daughter, Lilly, has penned the story. Bringing together disparate narrative threads, Lilly writes the heartbreaking lives of her Cuban foremothers. Lima suggests that "by reworking the narratives that connect and separate mothers from daughters," these novels go so "far as to suggest that a return to a pre-oedipal, preverbal moment of origin can provide an instrument for binding the fragments of self" ("Revolutionary Developments" 38). Because mothers' and daughters' lives are cut short or stunted by the militarization of their nations, and neither capitalism nor communism delivers on their promises to women, these novels revisit the maternal as a source for healing. For Amabelle, wading in the womblike river functions as her matria, and for Margarita, matria is realized through sharing her maternal herstory with her daughter, Lilly.

The polyphonic aspect to these works underscores that vocalizing and sharing one's trauma with others is a necessary path toward realizing the yet-to-be matria. Contemporary Caribbean authors undoubtedly take on the difficult task of fictionalizing women's lives during tumultuous periods. Telling these stories of violence can be potentially cathartic for writers, readers, and protagonists. Such novels productively suggest that narrating women's lives can fundamentally challenge oppressive political authorities and regimes. Importantly, within this subgenre the attempt to disrupt nationalist-masculinist discourses means that political/military dictators remain shadowy figures, never full-fledged characters; the result is a deglorifying and silencing of the offender/(F)ather and a restoring of subjectivity to the victim/survivor mother-daughter. Caribbean women's novels thus alert one to the devasting violence committed against women and serve to "break pervasive silence surrounding abuse and exploitation" (Donahue 3). For instance, Danticat's novel never gives Trujillo a voice; instead, he is referred to indirectly, such as when Amabelle claims that he is giving a speech in a nearby church when she and her fellow Haitian refugees are accosted in the town's square. Meanwhile Castro, like Batista, is only referred to metonymically with ironic names like "el cura" in O'Reilly Herrera's work. Thus, these counternovels invert "hierarchies of power by making the dictator a minor character and the marginalized subject a major character" (Harford Vargas, *Forms of Dictatorship* 17). Given the impact of military operations and political violence against women as foregrounded in these domestic novels, matria manifests doubly in a demilitarization of the region and of the historical novel genre.

Caribbean women's countervoices contribute to an antipatriarchal, demilitarized, revolutionary matria. Unlike texts in this genre that depict women actively taking up arms, Danticat's and O'Reilly Herrera's works show the effects of violence on women's lives over several generations. While they do not necessarily critique the woman's novel by challenging patriarchal beliefs that women are passive and incapable of violence, they do prioritize resistance through memory, storytelling, and narrative. For Margarita, sharing her Cuban past with her daughter begins the healing process. For Amabelle, it is revisiting the river at the borderland and remembering the loved ones she lost decades earlier. The feminist postcolonial potential of transnational, transcultural dialogue is thus found in *The Farming of Bones* and *The Pearl of the Antilles*—two historical novels that actively seek a feminist space, a matria that exists outside of or beyond the violence of the patriarchal nation.

5

"Mother of the Rivers": Maternal Tropes in Edwidge Danticat's *The Farming of Bones*

Edwidge Danticat's novel *The Farming of Bones* (1998) describes the murder of Haitians and Haitian Dominicans from Amabelle Désir's perspective. Amabelle is a fictional, young Haitian domestic servant living in the Dominican Republic up until the Parsley Massacre of 1937. Forced by the ensuing genocide carried out by the Dominican Republic's dictator, Rafael Leónidas Trujillo (ruled 1930–1961), Amabelle escapes to Haiti, her birth country. To search for her fiancé, Sebastien, a Haitian cane worker, who disappears during a military roundup, however, is the main reason Amabelle returns to the border. In Haiti, Amabelle lives out her days haunted by the massacre, which claimed the lives of tens of thousands of Haitians including her loved ones. As Danticat writes in her acknowledgments: "[T]he very last words on the page but always first in my memory, must be offered to those who died in the massacre of 1937, to those who survived to testify, and to the constant struggle of those who still toil in the cane fields" (266). Comparable to precursory Haitian novels such as those by Marie Vieux-Chauvet, Danticat's narrative voices Haiti's fragmented history and mourns an event for which "there were no graves, no markers" (231).[1] A postcolonial feminist historical novel, *The Farming of Bones* (re)writes, from a

Haitian woman's perspective, a significant traumatic event in Haiti's and the Dominican Republic's past, radically counters conventional discourses pertaining to Trujillo's dictatorship, and criticizes nationalist and patriarchal gender tropes that violate the maternal.

Scholarship on this groundbreaking novel is significant and rightfully pertains mostly to trauma, memory, *testimonio* (e.g., Harford Vargas; Johnson; Martin; Shemak), and/or reading the woman's body as a metaphor for the nation (e.g., Simone A. James Alexander; Shemak). These modes of reading the novel argue that the island's violent past must be spoken and written as a means toward sociopolitical justice. They also suggest that the Haitian woman's voice is essential to countering official patriarchal records and to holding accountable those responsible for the genocide. Guided by April Shemak's and Kelli Lyon Johnson's literary scholarship on the nation, the maternal, and memory as a means toward personal and collective healing—particularly Amabelle's precarious position as a Haitian-born domestic servant living near the border in the Dominican Republic—this chapter offers a new analysis by honing in on the role of mothers and birth. I argue that Amabelle can be read allegorically as the Massacre River, which, described in maternal tropes, flows between the two nations; like/as the river, Amabelle gestures toward a matria that consists of an alternative postcolonial feminist position for the Dominican Republic and Haiti.

Consider the novel's epigraph: "In confidence to you, Metrès Dlo, Mother of the Rivers Amabelle Désir." Not only is Danticat's book dedicated to her fictional character, but Amabelle is also referred to as the "Mother of the Rivers"; in her interview with Danticat, Haitian literary scholar/writer Myriam J. A. Chancy comments that Metrès Dlo, "goddess of the waters," protects Amabelle throughout the novel (120). By the end of the novel, when Amabelle lays herself down in the Massacre River, Danticat clearly claims Amabelle as an incarnation of the Haitian Vodou deity. As goddess and mother of the rivers, Amabelle embodies the maternal and its revitalizing powers. The novel thus revolutionarily envisions matria in the plural as an ethical maternal space—archive-river-womb—that connects and brings together the two nations and the peoples who share the same island. Her search for mother figures, as she loses one mother after another, culminates at the end of the work when she finds her own maternal self and becomes a spiritual, healing mother to others—particularly Haitian women. Offering an alternative vision of Haitian and Dominican identity, Danticat's concept of matria centralizes births and mothers.

Reflecting on Danticat's first novel, *Breath, Eyes, Memory* (1994), set during Haiti's Duvalier dictatorships from the late 1950s to the mid-1980s, is productive when thinking about the intersection of nationhood with the maternal in *The Farming of Bones*. This first novel suggests that in many dictatorial regimes in Latin America and the Caribbean, the political ideologies implicitly, if not explicitly, conflate nationalism with rigid gender roles for men and women: while men must defend and protect women and the state, "women are burdened with the task of maintaining the nation's (read men's) honor and integrity. As a result, they are accorded the title 'mothers of the nation,' an assigned designation that surreptitiously further justifies controlling women's sexuality" (S. A. J. Alexander, "M/othering the Nation" 373). Simone A. James Alexander further suggests that patriarchal nationalistic rhetoric and laws consign women and mothers to a certain kind of silence in "the private, domestic sphere," while patriarchal leaders "design the public, political arena to accommodate men and their nationalist pursuits" ("M/othering the Nation" 373). In this earlier historical novel and in *The Farming of Bones*, maternal motifs disrupt the "male narrative of history" (Johnson, "Both Sides" 77).

The Farming of Bones' reconceptualization of maternal history "has strong historical and cultural resonance for black women who have been socialized or pathologized as deviant, corrupt, and unfit" (S. A. J. Alexander, "M/othering the Nation" 374). Danticat's complex depiction of the maternal does not include any young Haitian women getting pregnant or giving birth, most of the biological mothers in the novel are deceased, or the women have reached postmenopausal age, such as Man Rapadou and Man Denise. For instance, when asked by Juana, a fellow servant (who incidentally, despite her wishes, never has children), if she wants children, Amabelle recalls her response: "I shook my head no. Perhaps because my parents had died young, I never imagined myself getting older than I was, much less living long enough to bear my own children" (38). Danticat's novels suggest that an enforced patriarchal motherhood—and all the violence and death that come with it—problematically silences/oppresses Haitian women.

The Farming of Bones is thus often considered a riposte to Julia Alvarez's Dominican-set novel *In the Time of the Butterflies* (1994)—which recuperates four historical sisters who were, with the exception of one, brutally murdered on November 25, 1960, by order of Trujillo. Alvarez's work is told from each woman's perspective, including Dedé Mirabal's, the sister who survived. While exceptional for emphasizing women's political and personal sacrifices specifically and Dominican women more generally, Alvarez's novel only superficially and indirectly mentions racism, the massacre, or violence against Haitians; furthermore, characters of Haitian heritage remain marginalized and incompletely realized, for instance Fela, the family servant.[2] While Danticat's novel tells another side to the Dominican Republic's history, both novelists' concentration on the lives of women during Trujillo's dictatorship provides a much-needed critical feminist discourse, rarely captured in either Haiti's or the Dominican Republic's fiction and history (Johnson, "Both Sides" 77).

Johnson productively claims that the two novels articulate in-betweenness as an alternative feminist political strategy to patriarchal nationalism. Quoting from Homi K. Bhabha's work *The Location of Culture*, she writes:

> [P]ostcolonial cultures must create and inhabit "in-between spaces" that "provide the terrain for elaborating strategies of selfhood—singular or communal—that initiate new signs of identity, and innovative sites of collaboration, and contestation." . . . [T]hat in-between space is entextualized in the novel: between history and memory, the vernacular and the official, fiction and fact. The novel thus becomes a new narrative space. These novelists create and claim a new, literary space in which collective memory expresses a national identity that includes members of the memory community previously excluded from historical discourse because of racial, class, sexual, or national identity. ("Both Sides" 76)

In reference to matria, Amabelle as/like the river, a maternal space, importantly qualifies as an in-between place, a postcolonial position wherein the familiar (home) and unfamiliar (unhomely) overlap and commingle (Bhabha, "The World and the Home" 141).

Historically, the Dominican Republic and Haiti, as already noted, were subject to European colonialism, which entailed that Indigenous people were enslaved and murdered, Africans were transported as slaves to work plantations, and both nations had to fight for independence—from France (Haiti) and Spain (the Dominican Republic)—and later were subject to occupations by the United States. The legacy of tensions between slaving colonial regimes indelibly left its mark not only on the Haitian landscape but also the Dominican Republic's. Furthermore, *The Farming of Bones* demonstrates that to survive, Haitians in the Dominican Republic were forced to assimilate by mimicking the Dominicans. For example, Haitians who cannot pronounce the word *perejil* the Dominican way face dire consequences, like when Amabelle and other fellow Haitians are fleeing toward the border and are publicly beaten and humiliated by having parsley shoved down their throats.

Judith Misrahi-Barak points to the double meaning of "translate," arguing that it refers both to bodies being moved and to the rendering of words in one language to a different one ("Biopolitics and Translation" 350). The massacre, because it is racially and linguistically motivated, strongly resonates with slavery. Misrahi-Barak argues that Haitians living and working in the Dominican Republic, like Amabelle, were not so much relocating to Haiti, which implies choice, as they were being "re*translated*, back to Haiti," because the migration was "forced" ("Biopolitics and Translation" 350). The novel depicts the Dominican Republic as paranoid about its culture being contaminated by the Haitians, and, therefore, it attempts to ethnically cleanse itself through genocide: the Dominican Republic defines and determines Haiti as an othered space, an exiled space—a feminized/emasculated space—which should not necessarily be taken over by force, but force should translate into guaranteeing that Haiti remain culturally, linguistically, and racially separate.

Chancy, quoting from Katherine McKittrick, addresses a similar point by arguing that Black Haitians like Amabelle "are located, assessed as deviant, punished, erased and cast beyond the nation," in this case the Dominican Republic, but also "beyond the regional borders of Latin America and the Caribbean" (xvii). Worth noting is that for Amabelle, Haiti, despite being an independent nation, has quasi-national status. Amabelle's memories of Haiti, for example, make much use of ghosts, and she describes a postslavery past that is in decay, making its location appear peripheral, a hinterland, as if it, too, is "beyond the nation" of the Dominican Republic. In a sense, Haiti ironically and deliberately becomes unhomely, that is, uncanny. Sigmund Freud's term "unheimlich" literally means unhomey, so that Haiti becomes uncanny, "that species of the frightening that goes back to what was once well known, and had long been familiar" (*The Uncanny* 124)—a diaspora to the Dominican Republic homeland, despite and in spite of Amabelle being born in Haiti. Amabelle is at home neither in the Dominican Republic nor in Haiti. The novel's matria thus troubles the notion of one's birth country as inherently home as opposed to the adopted homeland. Amabelle instead gestures toward the fluidity of borders, homelands, and identities, and she shows the harmful effects of national delineations: young Haitians' futures are dramatically altered. The desire for children, the future, is thwarted by violence, the death of loved ones, and the inconsolable loss and guilt experienced by the women and mothers who survive.

The Farming of Bones, like the other contemporary Caribbean women's historical novels studied in this book, weaves maternal tropes with memories and loss, producing what Freud calls "an uncanny effect [which] often arises when the boundary between fantasy and reality is blurred" (*The Uncanny* 150). Consider the novel's opening sentences:

> His name is Sebastien Onius. He comes most nights to put an end to my nightmare, the one I have all the time, of my parents drowning. While my body is struggling against sleep, fighting itself to awaken, he whispers for me to "lie still while I take you back." "Back where?" I ask without feeling my lips moving. He says, "I will take you back into the cave across the river." (1)

Thrust into this disorienting scene, we sense Amabelle's confusion: Is this a dream? Is Sebastien a ghost? Is this an account from the past, the present, or the future? The blurring of boundaries in *The Farming of Bones* repeatedly contests binaries such as Haiti and the Dominican Republic, romance and history, private and public, Spanish and French, rich and poor, Black and non-Black, and so on. The in-between space of the river that Sebastien names, and his promise to safeguard her across it, further sets the tone for the novel's maternal tropes.

Sebastien serves as both a ferryman and a midwife, two positions that "ensure the safe passage" from one place to another—the dead to the afterlife, the unborn to life, respectively (Jonte-Pace 70). Sebastien delivers the quasi-dead Amabelle in a way that mimics birth: she will, by going back to the womb, back to the cave, be reborn. By taking her back, Sebastien guides Amabelle into the past, which allows her to tell the narrative, to tell the truth of her life and of the losses she and her fellow Haitians have endured; but at the same time, the river/cave is also a future space, a matria—reachable only once the past has been let go. The cave across the river, a metaphor for the womb and birth canal, is a sacred space of rebirth and peace, in which Amabelle and other Haitian Dominicans might come to terms with the traumatic patriarchal past.

From Sebastien's visit, the reader also learns that Amabelle's first major loss is her parents drowning in the river. After traveling to Dajabón—a border town in the Dominican Republic—to buy cooking pots from a Haitian master craftsman, Amabelle's parents die when her father tries to carry her mother across the river back to Haiti. One can read this as a warning to Haitians who travel across the newly mapped border: it is dangerous and deadly, naturally as a strong river and politically as a dividing line between nations. The parents' drowning foreshadows the death of thousands of Haitians, attempting to flee Trujillo's regime, in the very same water. That the cooking pots are coveted as the best in the area—"there is a gleam to Moy's pots that makes you think you are getting a gem" (Danticat, *The Farming* 50)—alludes to the notion that the parents are possibly lured by money and false advertising, a similar ploy used by the plantation and mill owners to entice Haitian cane workers. The best pot maker, a Haitian, possibly having been displaced by recent border changes, no longer lives in Haiti but on the other side. This signals a promise of wealth and social mobility in the Dominican Republic, which again draws thousands of Haitians each year to the neighboring country's cane fields and mills. The novel not only critiques economic disparity between Haitians and Dominicans but also questions the existence of a dangerous border that so many Haitians risk their lives to cross.

Arguably, Amabelle's parents are searching for a prosperity that eludes and excludes them: "Once he is in the river, he flinches, realizing that he has made a grave mistake" (51). Bringing Moy's pots back into Haiti, for practical and symbolic reasons, is impossible. If Amabelle's parents can attain these high-quality goods, then the Dominican Republic will potentially lose its economic upper hand. Haitians are therefore subsequently blamed for threatening the Dominican Republic's prosperity and future. Amabelle's father senses his mistake too late, but her mother is the one who causes the final collapse: "My mother turns back to look for me, throwing my father off balance.... My mother tightens her grip around his neck; her body covers him and weighs him down at the same time" (51). The father fails to carry the mother through this perilous river. She weighs him down—the suggestion is that a Haitian man cannot support his family, and when he tries to, he sinks. By implication, the mother cannot cross alone; her survival is tied to the father.

The mother's look at her daughter guarantees her demise. After this transgressive act, the mother will never see her beloved daughter again, and her daughter will be stranded in the Dominican Republic. One might read this as the "mother is literally the instructor in mortality" (Jonte-Pace 76), as this loss catalyzes Amabelle's search for a mother figure and a return to the womb, the cave across the river, so to speak, throughout the rest of the novel. From this initial trauma, Amabelle becomes motherless and stateless. When a Dominican father-daughter duo, Papí and Valencia, however, happen to be near Dajabón visiting friends, they take her in. The intention is that Amabelle will act as a servant and a sister-mother substitute because Señora Valencia's mother and her unborn son have recently died (91).

From this dream-like opening, the narrative switches to an assertive, realistic tone and refocuses on the maternal. Amabelle claims: "[B]irths and deaths were my parents' work. I never thought I would help at a birth myself until the screams rang through the valley that morning" (5). The reader learns that Amabelle's "mother and father were herb healers in Haiti. When it was called for, they birthed a child" (19). Set in a Dominican town called Alegría (an ironic synonym for happiness given the massacre that occurs and/or that happiness is reserved for the privileged few), the novel at this point starts in medias res with Amabelle attempting to deliver her employer's, Señora Valencia's, premature baby.

The only birth in the novel constitutes a strong narrative element for thinking about in-betweenness. The Dominican Señora Valencia, married to Señor Pico Duarte, one of Trujillo's military men, gives birth to fraternal twins. Amabelle acting as midwife makes the births possible. Although Amabelle facilitates birth, she physically never has children herself. Distressed and helpless, Señora Valencia, however, depends entirely on Amabelle's knowledge to help her through the difficult birth. The imbalance in the relationship is clear as Amabelle remembers a happier time, before she was a domestic servant and when she and the Señora were girls who slept in the same bed (6). The relationship between would-be sisters is analogous to the relation between Haiti and the Dominican Republic: where peace and friendship might rule, the latter exploits and depends upon the former instead for its success and growth. When questioned by her employer if she is going to die, Amabelle remarks, "I had to calm her, to help her, as she had always counted on me to do, as her father had always counted on me to do" (7). Amabelle later realizes, "I had called her Señorita as she grew from a child into a young woman. When she married the year before, I called her Señora. She on the other hand had always called me Amabelle" (63). That Señora Valencia will die in childbirth if Amabelle doesn't aid her delivery emphasizes the Dominican Republic's dependence on Haitian knowledge, personal sacrifice, and labor.

The analogy is more complex, however, when one considers that neither Señora Valencia nor Amabelle have mothers. When Amabelle attempts to soothe her employer with these comforting words, "Señora, this child will be yours.... You will be its mother for the rest of your days. It will be yours like watercress belongs to water and river lilies belong to the river" (9), Señora Valencia snaps: "Like I belonged to my mother" (9). The implication is that mothers die in childbirth and abandon their children; thus, she is at risk of being torn away from her child like her mother was torn away from her when she was pregnant a second time, in an attempt to have a son, an heir. There is resentment on Señora Valencia's part for having grown up without a mother—and in many ways, Amabelle functions as both a surrogate sister and a mother figure, although she, too, is sisterless and motherless. If Haiti, like Amabelle, is an orphan (Danticat, *The Farming* 56), then the novel implies that the Dominican Republic, like Señora Valencia, remains problematically firmly rooted in the rule of the Father—her Spanish-born father, Papí, and her Dominican-born army general husband, Pico.

Reading the maternal, familial relationships in the novel as symbolic of their nations proves fruitful again when Señora Valencia gives birth to a son. Amabelle begins severing "the boy from his mother" (10), a psychoanalytic necessity in patriarchal society, when another cry interrupts her work. Inexperienced, Amabelle remembers one of her mother's favorite expressions, "*The baby's old nest took its time coming out. It was like another child altogether*" (10), but it is not the afterbirth that emerges but indeed "another child altogether." A girl is born with the caul over her face and the umbilical cord wrapped around her neck, interpreted by Señora Valencia as a curse; furthermore, she is smaller and darker skinned to the extent that the Señora asks: "Amabelle do you think my daughter will always be the color she is now[?] . . . My poor love, what if she's mistaken for one of your people?" (12). The Señora echoes the general sentiment of racial discrimination in the Dominican Republic in this time and place and foreshadows the massacre that will claim not only the lives of thousands of Haitians but also those of darker Dominicans mistaken for Haitians (Shemak 90). In this social context, the lighter one's skin color, the better, and thus the daughter serves as a symbol of Haiti, or African roots, in the Dominican Republic, while the son represents the other half of the island, the Dominican Republic, or Spanish roots in the nation. Despite her dark skin, however, the baby is named after the deceased maternal grandmother, Rosalinda Teresa, perhaps attempting to negate her skin color by suffusing it with the bloodline of an alleged prestigious Spanish ancestry.

Xenophobia is latent throughout the novel, as recognized by several protagonists. For instance, after having been arrested and tortured during the genocide, Father Romain, a Haitian priest, is forced to ventriloquize the Generalissimo, stating:

> Our motherland is Spain; theirs is darkest Africa, you understand? They once came here only to cut sugarcane, but now there are more of them than there will ever be cane to cut, you understand? Our problem is one of dominion. Tell me, does anyone like to have their house flooded with visitors, to the point that the visitors replace their own children? How can a country be ours if we are in smaller number than the outsiders? Those of us who love our country are taking measures to keep it our own.... We, as Dominicans, must have our separate traditions and our own ways of living. If not, in less than three generations, we will all be Haitians. In three generations, our children and grandchildren will have their blood completely tainted unless we defend ourselves now, you understand? (260–61)

The concern over the lineage being tainted is clear, from Señora Valencia's worry over her child's skin color to her husband's, Pico's, masculinist preference for his son over his daughter, his national pride in the Dominican Republic, and his disdain for Haitians, especially those living on his side of the island.

April Shemak astutely reads the birth scene along race and class lines, with Amabelle upholding Señora Valencia's privileged position as a "bourgeois Dominican mother figure, cleansed of the blood, sweat and labor of childbirth" (89). Referencing Señora Valencia's inability to imagine giving birth alone and then having the doctor and her father see her undressed results in "a kind of bourgeois 'mother-of-the-nation'... desire to protect herself from voyeuristic invasions [and] also symbolizes the Dominican nation's patrol of its racial borders from Haitian 'invaders'" (Shemak 90). Señora Valencia's role as mother is to uphold patriarchal nationalist discourse by reinforcing sociopolitical differences between Haitians and Dominicans such as race, class, and mother tongues. When the doctor arrives, though, Señora Valencia haughtily informs him that "Amabelle and I have done it.... We have given birth to the children, twins" (Danticat, *The Farming* 15). Señora Valencia's claim implies that she and Amabelle are both mothers, equally responsible for the birth of new life, signaling a potentially new relationship between the two countries. Had Amabelle not been present and exercised her midwifery knowledge, the Señora and her twins would likely have died.

Yet, the Señora is not the only one concerned by her daughter's skin color. Javier, the doctor, tells the family, "She has a little charcoal behind the ears, that one" (17), to which Papí retorts that it must be from her father's line. Papí defends his lineage by saying that his daughter "was born in the capital of this country. Her mother was of pure Spanish blood. She can trace her family to the Conquistadors, the line of El Amirante, Cristobal Colón. And I, myself, was born near a seaport in Valencia, Spain" (18). Naming his daughter after his Spanish birthplace reinforces the family's/nation's connection to Europe as opposed to Haiti and the Caribbean. Javier's implication that the little girl, Rosalinda, has African blood creates anxiety in the family. Rosalinda reminds Pico of his African heritage, which he and other Dominicans try so hard to erase and deny. Sensing the increasing disdain by the Dominican government for people with darker skin and/or an inability to speak Spanish correctly, Javier proposes that Amabelle return to Haiti's border and become a midwife (20). A midwife, Shemak reminds us, "is one who facilitates the crossing of borders of the mother's body in childbirth" (92–93): "This positioning constructs the border [river] as a kind of womb, which needs help in 'giving birth' to the people there. Amabelle would be the appropriate person for this job because she herself is a child of the border—of both nations—and could potentially help the people of the border-region 'give birth' to a new transnational identity" (93). Javier's recommendation has dire consequences, however, as later in the novel when the violence escalates, Amabelle's lover, Sebastien, and his sister, Mimi, die trying to join her on her way to Haiti.

Consider, too, that when Pico arrives to see the babies, he does not comment on his daughter but examines his son's testicles and declares: "I will name him Rafael, for the Generalissimo" (36): in this way the father takes on the role of birth to which he is physically denied. The naming of the son with not only his own surname but also the personal name of the general expresses doubling and suggests that dictators beget dictators. This act is amplified by the fact that Trujillo has erected numerous monuments to honor his name and regime. The maternal line, the mother, is unnecessary, even though it sustains the credibility of Pico and his children. Writing on *The Farming of Bones*, W. Todd Martin notes that "Pico's rejection of his daughter reflects not only his misogynistic attitudes, but also demonstrates his racial and nationalistic prejudices—the same prejudices that underlie the rationale for the massacre, itself" (71). The irony, according to Papí, is that the African heritage comes from Pico's lineage, much like Trujillo denied that his paternal grandmother was Haitian; the "attempted erasure of paternal racial origins is similar to that of Trujillo, the self-proclaimed 'father' of the nation, who attempted to camouflage his African heritage through the application of cosmetics," observes Shemak (91). The Dominican men therefore demonstrate a colonized psyche, and as a means of shielding themselves from criticism, overcompensate via military actions against Haitians, expressing a certain kind of hatred for an undeniable/inerasable part of their identity.

The meeting between the Dominican father and son also coincides with violence against Haitians: the death of a Haitian mill worker named Joël. Luis, who works for Papí, witnesses Pico, driving too fast in "the type of vehicle the Generalissimo himself loved to be driven in at that time" (Danticat, *The Farming* 59), kill Joël. Essentially a hit-and-run, Luis tells Amabelle about this crime, while Pico, unfazed, tends to his son (39). As a representative of the military arm of Trujillo, Pico's lack of concern or respect for Haitian lives is evident, and his act of murder foreshadows the massacre Trujillo will order him to carry out in his name: "[V]iolence and the law fuse together: it becomes lawful to kill" (Misrahi-Barak, "Biopolitics and Translation" 354). Joël's death is merely the beginning. Haitian lives in this slavery-like social system are dehumanized and deemed expendable or disposable.

By presenting characters who reject and conceal their African roots and heritage, Danticat depicts the Dominican Republic as an emerging powerful force, symbolized by the birth of Pico's son. Joël's death, however, prompts a heated debate in the Haitian community as to whether they should retaliate against the Dominicans. As Sebastien's sister, Mimi, notes: "[W]e should do something to keep them from taking others" (66). This sentiment is echoed by Unèl, a stonemason who lives in a nearby area inhabited by "non-vwayajè Haitians, the ones who were better off than the cane cutters but not as wealthy" (68) as the rich Haitians like Doña Sabine, a famous dancer, and her husband, Don Gilbert, a rum-maker. Amabelle explains that many of these people, like the landowners, farmers, dressmakers, and so on, had been born in and lived in Alegría for generations. When Amabelle approaches Unèl, she learns that even people like him are not safe from deportation by Trujillo. Trujillo is sending anyone without papers or anyone who is not working for an American cane mill back to Haiti (69). Amabelle soon realizes that few people possess papers, and often "the mill owners keep their papers so they have a rope around their necks. Papers are everything. You have no papers in your hands, they do with you want they want. I thought of my own situation. I had no papers to show that I belonged either here or in Haiti where I was born" (70). The likening of papers to a noose suggests the powerful legacy of slavery. The official record refuses to recognize Dominicans of Haitian descent and excludes them from the nation.

Amabelle thus reflects on Joël's death, Sebastien's claims that this will be his final year cutting cane, and her own fragile migrant status, all of which make her take seriously Doctor Javier's proposition that she be a midwife in Haiti. When the doctor arrives the next day to check in on the twins, she thinks, "[M]aybe I too had been waiting for an escape, looking out the corner of my eyes for a sign telling me it was time to go on to another life, a life that would fully be mine. Maybe I had been hoping for a voice to call to me from across the river, someone to arrive saying 'I have come for you to bring you back'" (79–80). Amabelle's imagining that she is being called back to her roots echoes Sebastien's opening lines when he whispers, "[L]ie still while I take you back" (1), and her mother's look before she drowns. It is bittersweet that Sebastien, who to reiterate dies in the massacre, and Amabelle's mother, who drowned more than a decade previously, are the ones to call Amabelle back after she has already fled the Dominican Republic for Haiti and has been living there for many years. In this way, Sebastien comes to embody her mother, to take her place, and to echo her maternal voice.

Birth and death, joy and sadness coincide again in the text as, the morning after the twins' birth and Joël's death, a birthday party is planned for the doctor's mother, the cane harvest has begun for another season, and Señora Valencia's son dies (86–87). According to the doctor, Rafi dies because he lost his breath (90), but this also links back to Amabelle's account of the birth and the "'badly placed' umbilical cord" around Rosalinda's neck (19). Javier proceeds to press his point: "It's as if the other one tried to strangle her" (19). Javier implies that the Dominican Republic is attempting to murder its Afro-Caribbean brothers and sisters, but he later adds that sometimes one twin will sacrifice itself for the other (19). The male heir's death by asphyxiation thus symbolizes the loss of the Dominican Republic's future: it is suffocating itself; or perhaps the stronger, darker twin, Rosalinda, as a symbol of African roots, has outlived her weaker brother, a symbol of Spanish ancestry in the Dominican Republic.

Shemak also considers national implications in relation to the symbolic significance of *marasa*, the Haitian Kreyòl word for twins. She argues that "seen through the lens of 'marasa consciousness,' Danticat's text reworks the genealogy of the island by symbolically erasing the border between the nations and revealing their singular origin. The Dominican Republic is no longer a separate entity with separate mythical Amerindian origins; its history and people must be read in conjunction with its Haitian 'twin'" (92). Conceiving the island as a single womb is productive for thinking about the importance of matria in the novel not only in terms of national allegory but also in terms of Amabelle's in-between position, symbolized by the river. It also complicates a straightforward interpretation of Haiti's position (a Black feminine nation) dominated by the Dominican Republic (a white masculine nation). Referencing Marilyn Houlberg and VèVè Clark's work, Shemak elaborates:

> [T]wins are considered "powerful and dangerous" in Haitian Vodou and "are associated with transitional spaces such as thresholds." ... In the novel, the river border between Haiti and the Dominican Republic serves as a kind of threshold for these "twin" nations, and Valencia's own body represents this border and the reproduction of these twin affiliations.... "*Marasa* consciousness invites us to imagine beyond the binary.... On the surface, *marasa* seem to be binary. My research of Haitian peasant lore and ritual observance has revealed that the tension between oppositions leads to another norm of creativity—to interaction or deconstruction as it were." (92)[3]

The novel's concentration on maternal tropes and on mothers and daughters as another iteration of twins emphasizes that binary positions are unstable and ethically untenable. The son, named after Trujillo, likewise foreshadows the dictator's eventual demise, which comes near the end of the novel.

The link between the son and the general is strengthened by the fact that Señora Valencia has a large, flattering painting of the Generalissimo in her home. A sign of a patriotic Dominican, she has painted the work herself—and upon the death of Rafi, she remarks that next she'd like to paint a portrait of her son (Danticat, *The Farming* 149). Señora Valencia does in fact keep her promise; when, decades later, Amabelle sees her for the first and only time since the massacre, she notices that the portrait of Trujillo has been replaced by one of Rafi (294). The doubling of images highlights that

"Mother of the Rivers": Maternal Tropes in *The Farming of Bones*   175

the love of the son, of the male heir, extends to the Father of the nation, the patriarch. Yet, as matria shows, the worship of such militaristic masculinity and patriarchal patriotism has deadly and dangerous consequences. Further, Señora Valencia's son dying mirrors her own mother's son (Señora Valencia's brother) not surviving either and signifies an effeminate genealogy, accentuated by Señora Valencia dressing Rafi in her old baptism gown and bonnet.

Following Rafi's death, Pico informs his wife that he must leave for the border to complete a military operation (99). According to the Haitian cane workers, this mission entails that the "Generalissimo, along with a border commission, had given orders to have all Haitians killed. Poor Dominican peasants had been asked to catch Haitians and bring them to the soldiers" (114). Doctor Javier confirms that Amabelle must leave immediately (140). As Joël's father, Kongo, notes, Rafi's death supplants his son's death to the extent that Pico neither discusses killing Joël with anyone nor informs his wife about the act. The priority of lives is clear; the death of a Dominican son brings the household into mourning, while the death of a Haitian cane worker goes unmentioned.

Amabelle, Sebastien, and Mimi, taking heed of the doctor's offer to transport them across the border that very night, prepare to leave. Amabelle, however, is too late and fails to meet everyone at the chapel because Señora Valencia had begun to hemorrhage. Señora Valencia's postnatal complications and Amabelle's loyalty save her life, but at the same time, Valencia's "spilled blood becomes tied to the Haitian blood spilled" (Shemak 105). Beside her employer, Amabelle witnesses army trucks rushing to the border and violently rounding up Haitian workers on their way. She also learns that the doctor, two priests, and those with them, including Mimi and Sebastien, have been arrested and forcibly taken to the border (Danticat, *The Farming* 155, 163). It is at this point in the narrative that Amabelle, along with Sebastien's fellow cane-cutting friend Yves, decides to leave the Dominican Republic in search of her fiancé and his sister.

After a harrowing account of trekking through the mountains and crossing the river—in which Amabelle, in a scene reminiscent of her parents' demise, must cover the mouth of another Haitian woman because she tries to scream when witnessing her lover being murdered; Odette, "half-dead" (174), drowns, while Amabelle lives (174)—the pair, physically and psychically beaten and humiliated by Trujillo's men, barely survive. Arriving in Cap-Haïtien, Amabelle lives the rest of her days like a ghost with Yves and his mother, Man Rapadou. Man Rapadou is the wise and gentle mother figure Amabelle never had but throughout her life has been continually searching for. She also seeks maternal guidance from Man Denise, Sebastien's mother, but Man Denise, overburdened with her own loss and trauma—having been told by many strangers that Sebastien and Mimi died at the hands of the soldiers (241–43)—is unable to offer much comfort. After meeting Amabelle and knowing that her future with her children has been taken from her, Man Denise silently returns to her people in Port-au-Prince (251).

Although Amabelle begins to accept that Sebastien and Mimi are dead, haunted by her memories of them, she continues to search for answers. In her introduction to Haitian writer Lilas Desquiron's historical novel *Les chemins de Loco-Miroir* (*Reflections of Loko Miwa*) (1990), which incidentally focuses on spiritual twin sisters during François Duvalier's rule in Haiti, Marie-Agnès Sourieau writes, "The living dead haunt the imaginary space of Haitians. No fate is more feared than to be made into a soulless body" (xxi), yet this is precisely what Amabelle and the Haitian national body have become. "Disembodied ghosts," Misrahi-Barak calls the Haitian survivors ("Biopolitics and Translation" 356), while Sourieau refers to Haiti's "living dead" as zombies. According to Margarite Fernández Olmos and Lizabeth Paravisini-Gebert, zombies are "symbolic of the Haitian experience of slavery, of the separation of man from his will, his reduction to a beast of burden at the will of a master" (153), yet for Sourieau, "zombification is the symbol of the collective amnesia and silence imposed by Haiti's long history of violently repressive dictatorships" (xxvi). Undoubtedly, a strong link between enslavement and dictatorships is found in *The Farming of Bones*, but the text uniquely references the Dominican Republic's dictatorship and its treatment of Haitians as slaves/zombies, particularly during and after the massacre.

The most "uncanny" thing of all is to be alive while appearing to be dead, to paraphrase Freud (*The Uncanny* 150), and he further links the uncanny with the castration complex (150), so that when gender is taken into account, another layer to zombification emerges. In Freudian terms, the zombie-woman/mother is doubly castrated—"[S]he's female, she's dead"—and as such she evokes Oedipal "anxieties centering on separation, abandonment, and loss" (Jonte-Pace 67). When Freud writes of "severed limbs . . . a hand detached from the arm" (*The Uncanny* 150), the cruelties of slavery and genocide are likewise evoked as uncanny. The intersection of gender and race, which Freud does not concern himself with, is nevertheless an important aspect of the uncanny in *The Farming of Bones*. Freud's zombie fantasy, however, which arguably Amabelle plays out, becomes a transformation of another fantasy, which was not originally frightening but rather was filled with a certain "lasciviousness; this was the fantasy of living in the womb (*The Uncanny* 150). Does this explain Amabelle's desire, as a living-dead survivor of the massacre, to return to the river, a passageway to her mother's womb?

One must also bear in mind that Amabelle frequently relives her "fears of maternal death," particularly in her "dream-world encounter with the dead mother" (Jonte-Pace 69, 68). Dead maternal bodies throughout the novel remind one that the patriarchal nation—much like psychoanalytic theory—is founded paradoxically on both literal and metaphorical matriphilia and matricide. Amabelle, for instance, never fully recovers from losing the love and romance she experienced first with her mother and then with her fiancé. Her far-reaching and relentless pursuit of Sebastien shows that the victims' names will not be forgotten, and her memory of them attempts to reveal that the two nations share a history, emphasized by their mutual forgetting of the massacre—"commemorated by [neither] monuments [n]or ceremonies" (Johnson, "Both Sides" 78)—which is another kind of violence in and of itself.

Amabelle's narrative thus voices the undocumented history of the massacre, but Danticat cautions that the marginalized who historically experienced the massacre, particularly women, were never, nor perhaps ever can be, fully accounted for or fully represented by traditional historiography. For instance, consider that the Haitian government fails to hear Amabelle's testimony because her narrative does not conform to their official one. Desiring closure, after the Generalissimo's assassination in 1961, Amabelle illegally travels to Alegría and to Señora Valencia's house to see the waterfall and cave where she and Sebastien first made love. The meeting between former mistress and servant is tense and brief, primarily because Señora Valencia does not accept accountability for her part in the genocide. Amabelle realizes that reliving her happier past, as was the case with her mother's failure to return, with Sebastien is impossible: there is no going back and that past, that life, is gone. As Amabelle remarks, "Sebastien, I couldn't find. He didn't come out and show himself. He stayed inside the waterfall" (Danticat, *The Farming* 306). With rebirth in the Dominican Republic denied, upon reentering Haiti, she stops at the border. In the darkness of the night, she wades into the river, which like an archive houses "thousands whose graves are here" (308), including her parents' and her lover's.

The river, shared by both nations of the same island, is a site of in-betweenness and attests through its "materiality ... a historical record" (Johnson, "Both Sides" 79) of the dead. Submerging herself "like a newborn in a washbasin" (Danticat, *The Farming* 310) in this river of decay and death, Amabelle looks "for the dawn" (310). Floating in the birth canal, Amabelle, one of the living dead, too, joins her kin, Sebastien, Mimi, and countless others. "To embrace death as one embraces a mother," as writes Diane Jonte-Pace (77), means both to come to terms with the death of the mother (as well as Sebastien, Mimi, Odette, and countless others), which Amabelle has tried so hard to repress—hence the reason for her dreams—and also to recognize that the idea of death is closely linked with the "fantasy of return to the womb" (Jonte-Pace 82). *The Farming of Bones* thus suggests that "the idea of death and the idea of the afterlife involve a notion of return to the mother, to the uncanny home or the home in the uncanny. Death, afterlife, and the mother are intertwined in the uncanny" (Jonte-Pace 82), which in this novel is both Amabelle and/as the Massacre River, which flows between Haiti and the Dominican Republic.

Amabelle's matria refuses solid ground and to split marginalized individuals, like herself, in half. The novel's ending intimates that the river, like Amabelle, belongs to no nation, no man. Amabelle's body thus functions metonymically as "a counter-discourse by operating within the existing (patriarchal) structures of state violence, using [her] mutilated, abused bod[y] as [a] weapon to resist and rebel against the nationalist agenda[s]" of both Haiti and the Dominican Republic (S. A. J. Alexander, "M/othering the Nation" 373–74). Embracing the fluidity and fecundity of the water, Amabelle, experiencing a womb-like encounter, as daughter, mother, and midwife, gives birth to herself. As a river, as a woman, she gives new life and meaning to the words she once ushered to Señora Valencia: "You will be its mother for the rest of your days. It will be yours like watercress belongs to water and river lilies belong to the river" (Danticat, *The Farming* 9). Amabelle's spiritual baptism, a potential symbol for the rebirth of both nations, fittingly concludes the novel; by placing a fictional woman at the center of Haitian history, Danticat's *The Farming of Bones* suggests an opportunity for Haitians and Dominicans to rebirth themselves, too, to confront the traumas and ghosts of the past, and to dream of matria, a revolutionary alternative feminist future.[4]

6

Revolutionary Herstory and Martial/Marital Law in Andrea O'Reilly Herrera's *The Pearl of the Antilles*

A sprawling herstory of the lead-up to and the aftermath of the Cuban Revolution, *The Pearl of the Antilles* (2001) by Andrea O'Reilly Herrera centers on two mother-daughter duos, Rosa and Margarita and Margarita and Lilly. *The Pearl of the Antilles* shuttles between Cuba and the United States and offers a unique insight into the experiences of Cuban women in a family and a nation in political flux. While Cristina García's pioneering novel *Dreaming in Cuban* (1992)—chronicling several generations of a matriarchal family against the backdrop of the Cuban Revolution—is credited with inaugurating the "Cubana Boom" (Rivero 117), O'Reilly Herrera's only novel to date has not, with the exception of Latina literary scholar Claudia Sadowski-Smith's work, garnered substantial criticism.[1] Remedying this scholarly neglect, this chapter focuses on the mother-daughter relationships as influenced by the patriarchal husband/father figure, Pedro. Drawing on Luce Irigaray's psychoanalytic feminist criticisms of incest and patriarchy as preventing meaningful mother-daughter connections, I show how Pedro's marital/martial law, likened to Cuba's dictatorial national leaders (Batista and Castro), shapes Rosa's prerevolution relationship with her daughter, Margarita, and then Margarita's post-revolution relationship with her American-born daughter, Lilly. In this family romance, the mother-daughter bond, not the wife-husband or daughter-father bond, is the most meaningful relationship in all three women's lives. The retelling of "herstory"—that is, women's history—between mothers and daughters (O'Reilly Herrera, "Women and the Revolution" 71), not only disrupts the cyclical violence of the patriarchal family but also criticizes Cuba, as an insular nation, for being patriarchal and incestuous. *The Pearl of the Antilles* thus seeks alternative "ways to imaginatively reconstruct both the psychic structure at the core of female identity and an as yet unrealized '*isla possible*' infused by female creativity and energy" (Méndez Rodenas 48), therein highlighting matria's revolutionary potential.

In in her article "Women and the Revolution in Cristina García's *Dreaming in Cuban*," O'Reilly Herrera suggests that herstory tells of a Caribbean woman's "past denied . . . by the official records" (69), not only in Cuba but also in foreign narratives of Cuba, like those of the United States. Herstory directly confronts traditional History's methods and subjects, which privilege men's lives and consequently ignore women's contributions to Cuba's past. Like García's novel, O'Reilly Herrera's *The Pearl of the Antilles* "offers a feminized . . . re-emplotment not only of the Cuban Revolution, but of the powers that have dominated her" since Spanish colonialism (O'Reilly Herrera, "Women and the Revolution" 71). This approach adheres to Irigaray's recognition that "[i]f we keep on speaking the same language together, we're going to reproduce the same history" (*This Sex* 205). While challenging (M)aster masculinist narratives, O'Reilly Herrera's "post-modern herstory" recognizes that historical discourses, even when told from women's perspectives about women, are constructions that closely follow the narrative patterns of literature (O'Reilly Herrera, "Women and the Revolution" 71). O'Reilly Herrera writes that herstory "is rooted in paradox and thereby undermines . . . the very History which she [the author] feminizes and claims for her female characters ("Women" 71). *The Pearl of the Antilles* alerts us to its constructed nature as historical fiction; the reader learns that the matria, a compendium of letters, family heirlooms, maternal storytelling, and imagination, is penned by Lilly, Margarita's American daughter.

Herstory plays an essential role in this matria not only for Lilly but also for O'Reilly Herrera; Eliana Rivero reminds the reader that the author has never been to Cuba: "[T]he island nation and its culture are known to her through her mother in Philadelphia and her maternal great-aunts in Miami" (118). Mirroring her Cuban American protagonist, O'Reilly Herrera thus "delve[s] into family history to create a world that is imaginary and yet very real, both for the writer and for her readers" (Rivero 118). An American teenager growing up in the 1980s, Lilly knows neither her mother nor Cuba. As such, the narrative's style, again closely following García's *Dreaming in Cuban*, "examine[s] three important dimensions of the Cuban exile: the story of the Cubans who remained in Cuba [Pedro, aunts, and sisters] . . . the story of the Cuban exiles who came to the U.S. in the sixties [Margarita] . . . and, finally, the story of the children of exile," which is Lilly's story (Alvarez-Borland 43). It is learning about her mother's Cuban past, however, that frames Lilly's sense of matria and dictates the order of the narrative's structure; while loosely chronological, the narrative downplays major events in Cuba's national history in favor of familial events such as Margarita fleeing Cuba in the early 1960s, shortly after the revolution. Tasked with keeping alive both her matrilineage and her family's history in Cuba as a means of protesting "women's exclusion from patriarchal Historical discourse" (O'Reilly Herrera, "Women and the Revolution" 71), Lilly writes a herstory. A matria composed of finding the daughter's voice/place in and through her Cuban maternal genealogy thus becomes her means to challenge patriarchy/History.

The Pearl of the Antilles refuses to "appropriate a revolutionary, male hero as a means for developing a creative exploration of love, culture, history and the female imaginary" (Alvina E. Quintana, qtd. in Rivero 119). O'Reilly Herrera's work rarely mentions any political leaders by name, although the maternal great-aunt ironically calls Castro "el cura"—the priest or the curer (echoing the male savior trope). Male historical revolutionary figures are background material in this mater-familial saga. It is, however, arguably not the revolution that tears the family apart, physically and emotionally, but the patriarchal father. For example, before her exile from the nation, Margarita is "exiled from . . . her family" (McAuliffe 5); she is banished by her father and rejected by her lover. O'Reilly Herrera's polyphonic, transnational, and transhistorical novel thus subverts any unitary, singular, dictatorial voice.

The matria of this herstory narrative "replace[s] the phallic hero at the center of the frame of representation" with mother-daughter lives and voices (Anderlini-D'Onofrio 160). Lilly's narrative contextualizes that the exile of women from history is already in the making when the novel begins. An argument between Margarita's parents, Pedro and Rosa, in 1949, indicates that the family dynamics are shifting toward the absolute power of the Father. The couple have, however, had this argument before: Rosa does not want to leave her Edenic ancestral home, Tres Flores, and move to her deceased mother-in-law's home in Havana (O'Reilly Herrera, *The Pearl* 7). Patriarchy necessitates that Rosa symbolically leave her mother. Commenting on Sigmund Freud's lecture "Femininity," Marianne Hirsch in *The Mother/Daughter Plot: Narrative, Psychoanalysis, Feminism* claims that "the mother-daughter bond must be abandoned in favor of a strong attachment to the father, which, in turn, must be superseded by the adult love of another man and the conception of a child, preferably male" (99). Although Rosa manages to refuse Pedro a first time, perhaps signifying a more nuanced role for a woman/mother in the home and the nation, it becomes clear that there will be no second time.

Pedro states, "Excuse my impertinence, Señora, but didn't your mother teach you that it's a wife's duty to respect and obey her husband's will?" (O'Reilly Herrera, *The Pearl* 8). Pedro's comments, expressing his latent desire to mother, suggest that patriarchal ideals tightly regulate and police motherhood and mothers. Rosa's mother's failure to instruct her daughter properly means that now the husband must supplement his wife's insufficient education. That Pedro can readily tell his wife how she should act implies his moral, educational, and intellectual superiority—he is the better mother. One wonders how Pedro knows how a wife and mother should act, but then one remembers that his own mother serves in exemplum. The suggestion is that mothering is not necessarily biological but social. Women may be the biological mothers, but fathers are the social mothers. Of course, the idea of Pedro as mother to his wife infantilizes Rosa, but it also transgresses patriarchy's strict sexual norms. The incest taboo's implications thus present themselves when the father plays mother to his wife. One mustn't also forget that Pedro, the son, literally wants to rehouse his wife in the house of his dead mother. His desire for his dead mother is transferred onto his wife, who now becomes his poor substitute mother.

In *Speculum of the Other Woman*, Irigaray criticizes and revises Freud's psychoanalytic work, particularly on women. She writes that the girl's pre-Oedipus attachment to her mother is problematically forgotten when realizing her mother's and her own symbolic castration, therein affirming "the superiority of the male and her own inferiority" (67). All "desires for identification with her mother" and her self as woman "are eliminated" (79). By contrast, a boy in "the Oedipus complex . . . desires *his* mother and would like to get rid of *his* father as being a rival, [he] develops *naturally* from the phase of his phallic sexuality" (Irigaray, *Speculum* 81). Irigaray explains that, unlike a girl who must transfer her desire away from the mother, "[a] boy's mother is the first object of his love, and she remains so too during the formation of his Oedipus complex and, in essence, ALL THROUGH HIS LIFE" (31). Consider the following remark by Rosa: "Honestly, Pedro, the older you get, the more you sound like your mother" (O'Reilly Herrera, *The Pearl* 114). In Pedro's eyes, Rosa will always be an inadequate mother or daughter. She can neither replace Pedro's biological mother, Josefina Amargo, as his primary love object, which is really why he wants to live in Havana, nor can she function as a good mother to her daughters, because her own mother, Rafaela, has failed her.

In Freud's controversial work *Totem and Taboo*, which undeniably denigrates and stereotypes Indigenous peoples, he nevertheless proceeds to explore how the son/brother is prohibited from "incest with the mother or the sisters" and other totem blood kin (7). For Freud, incest is one of the foremost "taboo prohibitions" (20), yet with "the basis of taboo is a forbidden action for which there exists a strong inclination in the unconscious" (20). He writes:

> Psychoanalysis has taught us that the first object selection of the boy is of an incestuous nature and that it is directed to the forbidden objects, the mother and the sister; psychoanalysis has taught us also the methods through which the maturing individual frees himself from these incestuous attractions. The neurotic, however, regularly presents to us a piece of psychic infantilism; he has either not been able to free himself from the childlike conditions of psychosexuality, or else he has returned to them (inhibited development and regression). Hence the incestuous fixations of the libido still play or again are playing the main role in his unconscious psychic life. (13)

Drawing on Freud's ideas, Irigaray explains that "[d]espite the incest taboo, it seems that man has not sublimated the natural immediacy of his relationship with his mother, but has transferred it on to his wife as mother substitute" (*The Irigaray Reader* 199–200). Yet, the complexity does not end here. One must also take into account that although Pedro desires Rosa to be a stand-in for his dead mother (a role she can never fulfill), his desire to mother her also makes Rosa by default his daughter, and he is "in some sense the *brother* of his children" because they all share the same love object: "the maternal" (Irigaray, *Speculum* 31).

According to patriarchal law, Pedro does not want woman to be "anything but *his daughter* . . . or *his mother*" and arguably simultaneously both, as Rosa's case suggests (Irigaray, *Speculum* 129). Pedro is supposed to be a strong father whose voice and decisions go unquestioned, and one realizes that mothers have little say in how they raise their daughters. In fact, it is fathers like Pedro who regulate and control mothering. The father-husband's desire to be mother, to be that which biologically he can never be, pervades symbolically instead. So, it turns out that these men do not want to be fathers: they want to be mothers of the family and nation, even if this can only be achieved metaphorically. The actual wife and mother in this logic, however, should ventriloquize the Father's interdictions.

Believing himself to be superior in every way, Pedro knows what is best for his family—mimicking the role of the nation's leader to the Cuban people. Pedro, like Batista for instance, expects undisputed loyalty and obedience. One of Pedro's sisters informs Rosa, "No need to explain, dear, . . . we *all* know how Pedro can be. He's just like our father. He *always* had his way" (O'Reilly Herrera, *The Pearl* 16). If Rosa rebels against the supposed natural order of men ruling women, then paradoxically it is not the father acting as mother who has failed but in fact the mother who is fallible. Resonating with my discussion of Judith Ortiz Cofer's novel *The Meaning of Consuelo* in chapter 4, Rosa's mother is at fault for failing to control and instruct her daughter in the arts of subservience and silence. The flipside of this is that Pedro implies that Rosa's mother has indeed given her daughter a voice. That the mother can in fact teach her daughter to be subversive threatens Pedro and shows the fragility of patriarchy. Pedro's rule, like Batista's, can be undermined when the mother-daughter dyad refuses to mimic the roles laid out for them. The cyclical pattern of static women's lives, daughter-wife-mother, as inferior to the father-husband is put into question in O'Reilly Herrera's novel. Patriarchy, though reinforced by the father-husband, is to be taught not by him but by the daughter's mother. The mother is to be complicit in her own subordination, and to prove it she is tasked with silencing herself. Pedro's determination that Rosa will obey him foreshadows the increasing power of Batista, a man who by the time the novel picks up Rosa's story again is the nation's dictator (ruled 1952–1959).

In spite of and despite patriarchy's violent hold, in this matria's feminist postcolonial revision of the Freudian model, a daughter's mother matters more to her than her father or husband. Referencing Irigaray's work, Hirsch concludes the following: "[T]he father functions as obstacle, as the antagonist who makes the continued connection between child and mother impossible" (134). As a mother herself, Rosa, prior to 1949, refuses Pedro's demand that they move to the city because she must care for her ailing mother (will this happen to Lilly, too?). When Rosa's mother dies, however, in this logic the daughter is no longer a daughter. Irigaray argues that the wife's/mother's mother poses the greatest threat to the husband's desire for his mother (*Speculum* 32). A woman must let her love for her mother go in order to become a stand-in for her husband's erotic desire for his mother. Rosa feels that she has no choice but to submit to her husband's will: "When patriarchy is established, the daughter is separated from her mother and, more generally, from her family. She is transplanted into the genealogy of her husband, must live in his house, must bear his name, and so must her children etc." (Irigaray, *The Irigaray Reader* 199). Rosa's story picks up again in Havana, 1954, with the transformation from the maternal realm to the patriarchal one complete.

Perturbed that Pedro is managing the sugarcane fields of Cienfuegos without consulting her, Rosa decides, despite being heavily pregnant, that she will go to him. Rosa is not really returning to her husband, although this is how she justifies her unnecessary travel to her sister and sisters-in-law. Appearing the ever-loving wife on a quest for her beloved husband, Rosa is in fact returning to her mothers' home, so that "their first son would be born in her mother's bed, just like his sisters before him" (O'Reilly Herrera, *The Pearl* 59). Rosa travels to the lush countryside of her grandmother's home, Tres Flores, supporting Hirsch's claim that in such novels "it is the connection to the mother that carries emotional weight, not the shift to the father or husband" (133). That this is a matria, a femino-centric, womb-like space, solidified by the mother's bed in which no son has ever been born, eludes Rosa: she forgets that her maternal genealogy is composed solely of daughters, which foreshadows that a son will not be born.

Pedro, a landowning member of Cuba's gentry and born in 1908 during the second occupation of Cuba by the US military, is described by the women in his life as a tyrant, mirroring the emergence of Batista's political dictatorship. Despite Pedro's sister's, Nélida's, contestations—"He's the man of the house now. You don't want to go against him, do you?" (O'Reilly Herrera, *The Pearl* 19)—Rosa undermines her husband's authority. The "man of the house" is a strange comment because technically speaking, Pedro is not physically at home in Havana, and Tres Flores, though legally his by marriage, is for all intents and purposes his wife's home. In this sense, when Pedro is at Tres Flores, he is not the man of any house. It is also worth noting that Nélida uses the word "now" to describe Pedro's position. Who was the man of the house before him? His recently deceased mother? Nélida presumably means that because their mother is dead, Pedro is the owner of the Havana home, and whether he is physically at home is irrelevant: he is omnipotent and omnipresent.

Irigaray argues that "mothers, reproductive instruments marked with the name of the father and enclosed in his house, must be private property, excluded from exchange.... Mothers cannot circulate in the form of commodities without threatening the existence of the social order" (*This Sex* 185). Rosa's pregnancy is also high-risk; although the doctor has warned her that "after three consecutive miscarriages her body, let alone her heart, couldn't bear the strain of carrying and giving birth to another child" (O'Reilly Herrera, *The Pearl* 19), Pedro insists that his wife's body house his baby. Pedro forces Rosa to continue trying to have another child with him: "[T]he Amargos need a boy to carry on our name, otherwise the family line will die out with Pedro" (57). One assumes that Rosa is not willingly pregnant, unless she, too, buys into Pedro's logic. Does she believe in his rule so much that she is willing to die? Irigaray argues that the singular focus on the son "collapse[s] into a single genealogy: that of the *husband*" (*The Irigaray Reader* 200). The result of this genealogy is a loss of relation between mother and daughter that is not defined by the single genealogy, and that "the cult of the mother of the son ties our tradition to the horizon of mother-son incest" (*The Irigaray Reader* 200). That Pedro will risk his wife's life highlights that the life of the child, a potential son, is more important than that of the wife and mother: "The mother is sacrificed to the begetting of the phallic order" (Pollock 6). Both Pedro's and Rosa's sisters question her about the unborn baby: Nélida asks, "And if this one's a boy will you name him after his father?" (O'Reilly Herrera, *The Pearl* 55). Again, the idea is that the son is a mirror image of the father, but it is interesting that the sister-in-law thinks Rosa will have any input into her child's name, as the reader, like Rosa herself, highly doubts this will be the case.

Rosa's sister, María, quips: "*If* it's a boy? It had better be a boy this time, or Pedro will divorce her. 'Bring me an heir, your husband needs an heir,' he always tells her" (55). Rosa, as symbolic mother of the nation, the titular pearl of the Antilles, is reduced to being merely the child's vehicle. Pedro reminds her, "[W]omen are made to carry children" (55), a line that connotates both childbearing and child-rearing. Rosa's own life, or her potential daughter's, is seemingly of little importance. Irigaray explains: "Woman is nothing but the receptacle that passively receives his *product* . . . Matrix—womb, earth, factory, bank—to which the seed capital is entrusted" (*Speculum* 18). One is reminded that prior to the last miscarriage, Pedro, too, was convinced it would be "a boy the size of three green melons" (O'Reilly Herrera, *The Pearl* 55). Melons under no circumstances make one think of priapic symbols; they are symbols of the mother's breasts, and like the confused image, Pedro is wrong. Symbolically, Pedro's inability to produce a son up to this point in the novel, in conjunction with his wife's defiance, signals that his power, like Batista's, is waning.

Although Pedro manages to restrict and to rule Rosa in many ways, he fails to confine her to his house. With her two teenage daughters, Caridad and Margarita, Rosa makes the arduous journey back to the countryside of Tres Flores. Of the two daughters, Margarita is the one who resembles Rosa the most (47), and the two share a special bond. In one poignant scene, while gazing at the sea, Margarita senses her mother's desire to run free toward the shore; Rosa recognizes that her daughter has apprehended her thoughts correctly; although neither woman moves physically, Margarita "returned her mother's gaze" (35), "feeling as though they were bound together in a secret tryst" (35). The urge to break free from his-story, Father-nation, male-gaze, from marital/martial law, is intensely felt by both mother and daughter. Matria is envisioned as a mother's gaze that does not reduce the daughter to her mother.

Irigaray's notion of "labial mimesis" best describes O'Reilly Herrera's herstory and matria because it rejects the masculine subject as universal. It exposes through a deliberate ventriloquizing of the feminine style how patriarchal definitions of the feminine are restrictive, repressive, prohibitive, reductive, and problematically always defined already and in advance as inferior and subordinate to the masculine subject (Whitford, "Introduction to Section II" 76–78). Irigaray insists upon "contiguity, the two lips touching . . . the contiguity of mother and daughter" (Whitford, "Introduction to Section I" 28), which constitutes a differentiated relationship between daughter and mother outside of patriarchal representation and phallic penetration, which forces separation (Irigaray, *This Sex* 24). The labial lips "in continuous contact" (Irigaray, *This Sex* 24), mirrored by the text's mother-daughter narratives placed side by side and in contradistinction, gesture toward a "feminine imaginary," a matria, which will potentially disrupt patriarchal designations and categorizations (*This Sex* 212, 216).

Rosa's arrival with her daughters at Tres Flores is met with bitter silence: the reader learns that Pedro is having a nonconsensual sexual relationship with a teenage domestic servant whose name "he had never bothered to ask" (O'Reilly Herrera, *The Pearl* 95). Sitting at the breakfast table, with the nameless girl serving him, Pedro reflects on the time he "had first taken her" in the cane fields (91). Finding her too "wild and unbridled," Pedro decides to bring her into the house to "be domesticated" (93). Using the rhetoric of slavery, Pedro sees himself and his acts of rape as civilizing the racialized young woman. Much like he makes Rosa live in his dead mother's house, he forces the girl, who is his eldest daughter's age, to come into his dead mother-in-law's house. As master of both houses, he assumes to be master of both women. But as with Rosa, Pedro's experiment to tame the girl fails: she is insolent, violent, and secretive.

The reader also learns that the girl's name is Casandra and that she has newly given birth to a child with "eyes . . . as blue as the sea" (94). Knowing full well that no one in his family has blue eyes, Pedro refuses to entertain the idea that the child is not his: "[S]he wouldn't dare give herself to another man in my absence" (95). The notion of Casandra's power to "give" her body sexually is ironic, because Pedro has essentially been raping Casandra; what makes him think that another man is not capable of doing the same? It becomes clear that Pedro interprets their sexual acts as consensual, and that she should willingly want to submit to her master, when the reader knows that Casandra, if she has any choice in the matter, is merely avoiding working in the cane fields. As Rosa astutely perceives, "the mulata with blue-black hair" had been "brought in from the fields like some war trophy" (181). Pedro's arrogance and ignorance make him genuinely believe that because Casandra is a woman, *his* woman, she owes him loyalty, sexual or otherwise; he, of course, despite the possibility of being the father of her child, owes her nothing. He instead mistakenly believes that it is his job, as if he were the girl's mother, to train Casandra to be his respectable servant.

The blue-eyed child's gender, however, potentially remains unknown to Pedro, for Casandra never allows anyone to see the boy (only the reader discovers the child's gender on page 189—immediately following Rosa's death). The birth of a son, albeit an illegitimate one, coincides with Rosa's pregnancy, which helps explain why Pedro does not want Rosa present at Tres Flores. Pedro's betrayal of Rosa corresponds to Batista's betrayal of his people, arguably because during his dictatorship between 1952 and 1959, he was supported by the United States. The implication is that both men are abusing their power and betraying Cuba's trust by being more interested in forging ahead with their own agenda, despite the pain and suffering it will cause and being unwittingly betrayed in turn. This reader is convinced that Pedro is not the father, and that Batista is not fully in charge of the Cuban people.

Adopting a similar strategy to the one she noted in García's work, O'Reilly Herrera readily explores "[t]he theme of maternal loss [a]s metaphorically linked to the larger losses that Cuba, as mother country, sustained both prior to, and in the wake of the Revolution. For example, children are lost to their mothers both physically, through death and miscarriage and emotionally through . . . desertion" and isolation ("Women and the Revolution" 73). The morning of Pedro's departure for the fields coincides with Rosa awakening to the "sensation of drowning" (97). The image of water relates to both childbirth and death—foreshadowing that this child will be the death of Rosa. The feeling of drowning also prompts Rosa to remember her painful wedding night with Pedro and the oceanic void between them: coincidentally on this same night, she conceives her first child, Caridad. A girl child in Pedro's "imperialising 'phallic logic'" (Pollock 6) signals Rosa's failure as wife and mother.

The theme of incest and history repeating itself, however, also emerges during the wedding night memory: bitterly disappointed, Rosa internalizes patriarchal definitions of sex for respectable women, which cause her to feel "wounded" and "unclean" (O'Reilly Herrera, *The Pearl* 100). While Rosa silently cries, Pedro falls asleep, at which point "it struck Rosa that from behind Pedro resembled her father" (100). It is not surprising that Pedro resembles her father: her father is the one who selected Pedro as Rosa's husband (104). Daughters marry their fathers and husbands their mothers in this novel. Sadowski-Smith argues that "[O'Reilly] Herrera depicts a Cuba that, to borrow Antonio Benítez-Rojo's concept, is caught in a cycle of endless 'repetition,' which is tied to Cuba's colonial history" (134), but that this History is patriarchal and incestuous needs emphasizing. The implication is that it does not matter who is in charge of the family or the nation: it is always the same man and the same marital/martial control that dominates women. Aware of this fact, Rosa realizes that she is trapped in this genealogy, trapped on this island, and the weight of history drapes over her shoulders as heavily as "the veil [—] the same veil her mother and her grandmother had worn"—that she wears on her wedding day (O'Reilly Herrera, *The Pearl* 104).

Although committed to projecting a patriarchal image of holiness and purity, Rosa can control neither the messiness of sex nor pregnancy. Passing out suddenly from a sharp, shooting pain (183), "[w]ith one great heave she emptied her womb, sprinkling her white nightgown with water and blood" (188). Rosa dies drenched in her own and her child's bodily fluids. Whether the baby has also died, however, the reader does not learn until the narrative picks up ten years later in 1964. True to a revolutionary herstory, the novel skips over Batista's fall from power (though foreshadowed literally and metaphorically when Pedro, out riding in the cane fields, collapses and is dragged by his horse at the exact moment when Rosa dies) and the communist revolution's beginning in 1959 under its leader, Fidel Castro. Rosa's death and Pedro's fall definitively signal the end of the Edenic Tres Flores and the wealthy landowning Cuban class.

The novel switches styles, too, moving from third-person narration to letters from María, Rosa's sister, to her niece, Margarita. María remains at Cienfuegos while Margarita, the reader learns, has left the island and had a son, and her father's mysterious anger toward her is unvanquished. María holds Pedro responsible for the dissolution of both his family and his country: "It's people like him—who have money—who put el cura in power, Margarita, not the guajiros or the negritos, as most people believe. And it's pigheaded people like your father who will keep him in power. Take my word for it, your father has been deceived and he will die alone and disillusioned, having lost everything that he treasures in life, including his daughters" (199). María, of course, is right. Pedro's refusal to see Castro as another dictator mirrors his own inability to see himself as a dictator.

Pedro, more than anyone, should know that if the family's father cannot be challenged, then the government's leader cannot be, either: "Beard and all, el cura insists that he has no home, no wife, no family. Cuba is his home and the revolution is his bride (and, of course, the Cuban people are his children . . . ha! . . . one big happy family, no?)" (211). If Pedro's broken family is any indication of Castro's status as Cuba's husband, the answer is obvious. The letters written over nearly two decades detail the revolution's effect on the family's life. María recounts experiencing violence, food shortages, imprisonment, labor camps, censorship, and the confiscation of property, which now belongs not to individual families but to "the Cuban people" (196). That the letters are unilateral demonstrates the great communication gulf slowly emerging between the United States and Cuba and Margarita's increasing break from her family and her past. In fact, Margarita never reads her *tía*'s letters, although she does occasionally provide brief updates about her new family (her American husband, Joey, and two children, Peter and Lilly).

Part II of the novel begins on March 26, 1986, four years after the letters from Cuba have ceased. At this point, the full circumstances surrounding Margarita's departure remain unknown, but we learn that not much earlier her aunt María had died. María's death ends Rosa's Cuban family ties. With her estranged father having died in 1970, all of her relatives are now dead, and it is this realization that prompts Margarita to think: "[F]or years she had successfully held her memories at bay . . . but the telegram . . . brought her face-to-face with a past she had tried to bury" (248). The unearthing of her past comes out in this part of the novel as we follow Margarita's memories back to the time when her mother died. Margarita recounts Rosa's funeral as a solemn day: "María had given her and Caridad roses to place in their mother's casket just before their infant brother was laid at Rosa's side and the coffin lid was sealed shut" (253). Rosa's death constitutes "[t]he rupture of the mother/daughter bond" and prefigures "the irreparable break between island and diaspora" that occurs in the novel afterward (Méndez Rodenas 54). Exploring a symbolic terrain similar to Edwidge Danticat's *The Farming of Bones* when the Dominican Señora Valencia gives birth to fraternal twins—as discussed in chapter 5—in O'Reilly Herrera's novel, we learn that Rosa gave birth to twins: the longed-for son died, but the daughter survived (255). That he is "strangled in her womb by the umbilical cord" (255) suggests that Rosa may have somehow played a part in murdering her son, her Pedrocito, perhaps living out a fantasy to kill her husband and the stranglehold of patriarchy on her life.

Meanwhile, Pedro takes command of his property, his pearls, his daughters. Pedro refuses to look at his youngest daughter, Violeta, however, seemingly because he believes that she has betrayed him. Not only is Violeta blamed for Rosa's death but more importantly she is blamed for Pedrocito's death. Pedro gives Violeta away to the same Carmelite nuns to whom he abandoned his eldest daughter, Caridad (254). He leaves Margarita at Tres Flores. The desertion and enclosure of his daughters, with all its military connotations, is another paradoxical attempt to deny and exert patriarchal control over women's lives. Sentenced to virginity, Violeta and Caridad are exiled from the wife-becoming-mother trope; but they are fetishized in ways that "permit incest (she isn't my mother because she isn't a mother yet)" (Irigaray, *Speculum* 33): the daughters will presumably never have sexual relationships, and as virgins they will be unable to carry on Pedro's family lineage. A counter-genealogy to the patronym, Rosa's, the mother's, line, however, manages to survive through the birth of daughters. Staring at her young daughter Lilly, for instance, Margarita begins to see "her mother sitting before her once again" (O'Reilly Herrera, *The Pearl* 258). Reminded of when she left Cuba, Margarita muses that "Rosa's living spirit had not been able to cross the watery passage that now separated them" (258). Margarita speaks literally of the exilic waters between Cuba and Miami but also the water of birth, the break and separation that can only be mended through the relationship with a daughter. Seeing her mother's face reflected in her daughter's floods Margarita with memories.

The reader learns that Margarita became "pregnant with Cuba's future" (Bellamy 102), out of wedlock, in 1958, making her son's birth in 1959 coincide with the revolution's birth. Refusing to give up her lover's name, Pedro kicks her out of his house (O'Reilly Herrera, *The Pearl* 287). Pedro tells her, "You worthless whore . . . As long as I live you will never set foot in your grandmother's house again!" (287–88). Pedro's invocation of his mother once more allows him to appropriate the alleged but false power of mothers over daughters. Margarita has shamed her grandmother, Pedro says aloud, but he really means that she has shamed her father, who stands before her as mother. Because her womb has broken patriarchy's rules, Margarita is exiled from the father and his house. The lover, whose identity is never revealed, is a revolutionary supporter and student at the university, but he, too, breaks his promise: "All that you and your family represent go against the ideals of the revolution, Margarita. Your father's money—your name—all of it is stained by centuries of exploitation and abuse. I simply cannot afford to be associated with you any longer" (278). While these class criticisms are justified, and the reader admittedly feels little if any sympathy for the former slave-owning privileged family's downfall, the implication that Margarita is definitively marked and defined by her father and his sins is problematic. The suggestion is that there is no escape from the father's control if she remains in Cuba.

The irony, too, is that Pedro does not value giving Margarita his name—that name is temporary and transferrable as she will take on her future husband's name (arguably the only acceptable way to keep the father's name is to be a virgin nun like Caridad). In this society, only the son's, a mirror of the father's, name matters, "in the procreation of the *son*, this same of the procreating father. As testimony, for self and others, of his imperishable character, and warranty of a new generation of self-identity for the male seed," writes Irigaray (*Speculum* 27). Denying any responsibility for his child, in words that mimic Pedro's, her lover shouts, "Go back to your rich father. Eras una puta" (O'Reilly Herrera, *The Pearl* 278). Once again, regardless of political allegiance, and that the communist revolution in theory makes men and women comrades, Cuban men continue to subscribe to heteropatriarchal ideology.

Margarita "discovers that infidelity, abandonment, and, as a result, psychic and emotional estrangement characterize each succeeding generation of women" caught in this patriarchal, incestuous nation (O'Reilly Herrera, "Women and the Revolution" 74). Cast out by the father, Margarita has no choice but to prepare to leave Cuba after the birth of her son. When a cousin writes to Pedro to inform him of his grandson's birth, Pedro casually communicates through his lawyer that "his only daughter was now living in a convent in Cienfuegos" (O'Reilly Herrera, *The Pearl* 288). As Margarita realizes, according to the patriarchal family and nation, "she has ceased to exist. He had banished her just as he had banished Caridad and Violeta" (288). The three flowers of Tres Flores have been exiled—Rosa, Violeta, and Margarita (who in the United States renames herself Daisy). Subversive women, however, are banished by the militant patriarchal family and expatriated by Castro's new nation. Not only does Margarita bring shame upon her family by having a child out of wedlock but she also refused to marry the man her father chose because she was already pregnant. In this patriarchy, she is "[s]tained. Spoiled, like overripe fruit...beyond redemption" (287). Cuba's national rebirth thus coincides with Margarita giving birth to a new kind of Cuban woman and family. Aware of her inferior status in Cuba's patriarchy, she determines to be reborn in exile.

Margarita, renamed Daisy, keeps her Cuban son a secret from her American family. She remembers in 1960 making the difficult decision in the American consulate in Havana to leave her son behind—once she had established herself, she would send for him. Both the American officer and Margarita miscalculate Castro's power: "[T]his madman will never succeed. Once we cut off the sugar market he will fall like all the others. We're his lifeline. In no time at all, you will be able to freely return to your country with your child" (275). As Margarita struggles to make a life for herself in the United States, she learns that her son has died: a grenade was thrown into a park during a skirmish between pro-Castro rebels and anti-Castro civilians (283). Both sides are responsible for murdering Cuba's children, its future.

Determined to "forget her son—forget her island—forget even her own name," ten years pass before Margarita gets pregnant again (289). On March 29, 1973, she gives birth to Lilly. Disappointed at the time that she has not managed to replace her Cuban son, as if she could replicate the past, Margarita realizes thirteen years later in 1986 that she has regrettably "shut Lilly out all of these years and denied her knowledge that she needed to guard herself while searching for her place in a world of men" (293). Margarita recognizes that, much like her mother before her, her unquestioned adherence to patriarchal ideals has exiled her from her own daughter, suggesting that "mothers, themselves motherless, can only perpetuate a cycle of abandonment" (Hirsch 48). If patriarchy is allowed to go unchecked and women are complicit, the cycle of violence will continue. As Sadowski-Smith notes, patriarchal history/family "continue[s] to shape the outlines of the Cuban diaspora in the United States" (134). A renewed relationship with Lilly, however, promises Margarita a future, a matria, different from her patriarchal past: "This fantasy of the woman-daughter conceived between mother and daughter would mean that the little girl, and her mother also, perhaps, want to be able to represent themselves as women's bodies that are both desired and desiring—though not necessarily 'phallic'" (Irigaray, *Speculum* 36). Questioning "the maternal function as it has been cathected by man" finally gives Margarita the courage to read her aunt's letters (Irigaray, *Speculum* 36).

While Margarita reads, Lilly writes. Literally adding her own voice to the maternal narrative, Lilly addresses her mother, Margarita, as the presumed audience: "I've always felt somewhat neglected by you, Mother—made to take second place to Peter—and now I feel—even more than ever—that there is an ocean between us" (O'Reilly Herrera, *The Pearl* 341). Like her mother before her, Margarita obsesses over giving birth to a son: "[G]iving life to one who has the right to power, she wins the right to be perfectly happy. Proud of having willingly assisted in revealing her own anatomical inferiority. An accomplice . . . of the destiny that her 'own' womb re-enacts by perpetuating the domination of the penis and sperm" (Irigaray, *Speculum* 107). Lilly's first-person, confessional-style accounts recognize that "love between mother and daughter, [is] rendered impossible by the patriarchal regime" because it "transform[s] the woman into the obligatory cult of her husband's children, and her husband as male child" (Irigaray, *The Irigaray*

Reader 199). The emotional gulf between the husband's daughter and the husband's wife begins to heal, however, when Margarita tells her daughter about her Cuban past. The mother-daughter speaking-listening begins to fill in the gaps; previously there had been "only imagination where our history should be" (García 150). Matria emerges as Margarita transfers her love to her daughter; she rejects desire for and identification with the father/husband/son in favor of searching again for her lost maternal origins, which is more or less a searching for her story as a woman, as a mother-daughter.

That the lost tie with the mother, the trace of the pre-Oedipal, the familial/political history haunt the narrative means that it cannot be completely severed or erased. By naming her daughter Lilly, which is an altered, not quite identical, standard spelling of the flower, Daisy further suggests a potential new maternal home for Cuban Americans in the diaspora. But like that difficult return to the trace of the mother-daughter pre-Oedipal, how do Cuban Americans like Lilly "recapture a past that is marginal to [their] present?" (Alvarez-Borland 43). This raises the question, does the Cuban woman's tradition require a medium to make its message public? Consider for instance that, like Pilar in García's work, who may dream in Cuban, Lilly can neither speak nor write in Spanish, and she identifies as Cuban American. According to Rocío G. Davis, the shift in language (English) and geopolitical position (United States) for the Cuban American daughter is less important than the daughter's memory and imagination: "Separation and death may be overcome by reconstructing the cultural past and the image of the mother, achieving a reconciliation with the maternal through and within language and by recreating the idea of home. The final section suggests the protagonist's appropriation of the foremothers' voices and stories to bring the cycle of generation and regeneration to completion" (61). The question of whether the daughter's voice comes to speak for/over her mother's remains, and leaves ambiguous whether O'Reilly Herrera's novel suggests that the story of Cuban mothers-women can only be transmitted by American Cuban/Cuban American daughters-women.

Nevertheless, the patriarchal cycle in O'Reilly Herrera's text is disrupted when the mother-daughter's history and fiction intermingle, suggesting "symbiosis and fusion" (Pollock 5). Margarita experiences this realization when embracing her daughter: she "felt as though time had stood still, for Lilly was an infant once again" (O'Reilly Herrera, *The Pearl* 353). It is only when the daughter begins to tell her story, that is herstory, through her mother's that a return to a pre-phallic mother-daughter experience is imaginable and a renewed bond between Cuba and its diaspora might be realizable. Margarita "reached for her daughter's hand and together they stepped into a world she had left behind for what seemed to her a thousand and one lifetimes" (349). The dream of matria in *The Pearl of the Antilles* thus results in a desire to live in a world in which mothers and daughters are no longer weighed down by and caught in a violent marital/martial history that veils their very existence.

PART IV
RETURNING MATRIA

ANCESTRAL MOTHERS
The Caribbean Daughter's Homecoming

The subject matter of the Caribbean women's historical fiction discussed in this final section, Returning Matria, coincides with the authors' lifetimes. Testing the limits of the genre, they force readers and critics alike to question when a work ceases to be historical fiction and becomes contemporary. Exploiting this indeterminacy, each novel carefully engages with the distant maternal past and the female protagonists' present. Indebted to early Caribbean women's novels of return like Phyllis Shand Allfrey's *The Orchid House* (1953), set in 1930s Dominica, recent historical fiction also expresses the "'popular' or 'unofficial memory'" (Danyté 36) of family/community-based narratives. A rich oral tradition including spirituality, myth, songs, and stories relaying the power of female ancestors, African-derived or other non-Western religions, and African-centered Christianity further defines this genre. Most often penned by writers in the diaspora, these works feature heroines who, feeling homesick, nostalgic, or disconnected while living outside the region, seek their matrias by recuperating their maternal heritage in the Caribbean.

The two works considered in this section were both published by authors living in the United States. I closely read Paule Marshall's groundbreaking premillennium text *Praisesong for the Widow* (1983), set in 1970s Grenada and Carriacou. My second analysis is of Marie-Elena John's award-winning postmillennial novel *Unburnable* (2006), set in Dominica's recent past. Born and raised in Brooklyn, Marshall was the daughter of Barbadian immigrants, while John, born and raised in Antigua, currently splits her time between the island and Washington, DC. Prior to writing *Praisesong for the Widow*, Marshall published the well-received debut novel *Brown Girl, Brownstones* (1959), followed by the formidable *The Chosen Place, the Timeless People* (1969). Like these earlier texts, *Praisesong for the Widow* powerfully insists that daughters in the diaspora must recover their Afra-Caribbean ancestry, particularly the slave past; for the protagonist Avey, this means traveling from North White Plains, New York, to Grenada and Carriacou. Meanwhile, John's only novel to date portrays Lillian's determination to uncover the truth about her matrilineage. Arriving in Dominica from Washington, DC, Lillian's search for her mothers directly challenges the island's colonial legacy, specifically the intersection of race, sex, and history. Both novels emphasize that "the non-written social memory embedded in African Diasporan rituals is crucial to the excavation of the region's submerged histories" (Ashie-Nikoi 6), particularly maternal ones. That the "recurrent . . . figure of the revisionary 'daughter,' who, transcending time in a quest to contact lost . . . foremothers, embodies the newly born power of feminist reimagination" (Rody 4) is also evident. These two fictions of history thus exemplify the return of a daughter figure to her maternal Caribbean roots/routes as constituting matria.

Unlike the protagonists in part II: Decolonizing Matria, who reject their mothers and head for the colonial mother country—for instance, Consuelo moving to the United States—these diasporic daughters physically make their way to the Caribbean, the home of their mothers and/or maternal ancestors. A sense pervades that the daughter, having been born outside the region or lived away for most of her life, is disconnected from her matrilineage/communal history and that until she reconnects with her roots, she will not feel at home anywhere. Carole Boyce Davies insightfully observes that the daughter's "migration creates the desire for home, which in turn produces the rewriting of home" (*Black Women* 113). This is true of Marshall's African American protagonist, Avey, a widow who mysteriously falls ill on a Caribbean cruise after dreaming of her deceased great-great-aunt Cuney. Out of sorts, and much to her friends' vexation, Avey suddenly disembarks in Grenada. A charismatic man named Lebert Joseph, "whom Marshall connects with Legba—trickster and Vodou deity of the crossroads" (Andrea Davis 531)—convinces her not to return home to New York but to join him for a short homecoming celebration in the neighboring island of Carriacou. Evocative of the Middle Passage, Avey falls violently ill en route. Once on land, however, her healing and awakening to an anticolonial consciousness begins.

Avey's dancing to the drums in reverence of her African Caribbean ancestors supports Margarite Fernández Olmos and Lizabeth Paravisini-Gebert's assertion that "Caribbean writers and intellectuals . . . have turned to the discourse of healing through African-derived religious and cultural practices—to articulate a contestatory discourse of cultural and political liberation" (xx). In *Unburnable*, Lillian returns to Dominica to solve the mysteries surrounding her grandmother's and mother's deaths. Once on the island, Lillian begins to piece together the misogynistic and racist oral tales (unofficial history) and written records (official History) about her maternal kin. At the end of the novel, Lillian performs the myth of the *soucouyant* and jumps from the cliffs of her foremothers' maroon-camp-turned-secret-settlement. Postcolonial feminist fictions of history like Marshall's and John's thus imagine matria through reviving Afra-Caribbean myths, rituals, and storytelling.

Unlike the daughters in part III: Revolutionizing Matria, whose returns to the region are mostly symbolic, the daughterly homecomings to history in this section (Grenada and Carriacou, and Dominica, respectively) are physical and psychical. Like all Caribbean nations, Grenada (an archipelago composed of the islands of Grenada, Carriacou, Petite Martinique, and some smaller islands) was first settled by Indigenous people (Ashie-Nikoi 22)—in this specific context, the Arawak and Carib peoples. French settlers first arrived from Martinique and colonized Grenada (Ashie-Nikoi 22), establishing plantocracies dependent on slaves from Africa. While Grenada was known for sugar, Carriacou produced cotton (Ashie-Nikoi 14). With the conclusion of the Seven Years' War and the Treaty of Paris in 1763, Grenada came under British rule (Davidson 2). Edwina Ashie-Nikoi's research suggests that under the British, Grenada became an important hub for "re-exporting . . . [enslaved] African laborers . . . to other colonies" (27), including the American ones, which resonates with Avey's familial roots on (fictional) Tatem Island, South Carolina.

During the American War of Independence, Grenada and Carriacou suffered great economic hardship and were militarily vulnerable. For instance, the islands passed back into French hands before being restored to the British in 1783 (Ashie-Nikoi 31). Tensions between "free colored," French, and British planters remained high. Conflicts included the infamous Fédon's Rebellion in 1795—inspired by both the French Revolution and the Haitian

Revolution—which was led by Julien Fédon, "a free colored coffee and cocoa planter" who had been "disenfranchised by [British] stipulations that all candidates for office be white males over twenty-one, 'a natural-born subject,' and a Protestant" (Ashie-Nikoi 32). Because "[t]he growing number of Africans was felt to be dangerous," the colonial government sought to dismantle and suppress African heritage, religion, and pride, including African dances (McDaniel 30). Although "the legal code of 1808, inscribed in the Laws of Grenada from 1763 to 1805, made the ban on drumming and therefore dancing very clear" (McDaniel 30), these rebellious acts as well as expressions of convening with the sacred continued. Fédon's revolution was quashed, and slavery in Grenada, as in other British colonies, was not abolished until 1833. Conceptually resonating with the neo-slavery novels studied in part I: Mythologizing Matria, novels of return like *Praisesong for the Widow* emphasize that an unacknowledged Afra-Caribbean history and ancestry extends to many in the diaspora, for instance in Britain or the United States.

Grenada was a British colony until independence in 1974, the auspicious year Avey begins her unexpected journey to Grenada and Carriacou. Avey's voyage also happens shortly before Grenada's Marxist revolution, which put Maurice Bishop and the People's Revolutionary Government in power in 1979—as Merle Collins recounts in her novel *Angel* (1987). In an act of anticolonial defiance, the Grenada government forged strong socialist links with Castro's Cuba. The revolution came to an end when Bishop was killed in a military coup in 1983—the same year Marshall published her novel— and the United States invaded the islands (McDaniel 6). In 1984, however, democratic elections were held.

Meanwhile, Lennox Honychurch, historian and grandson of Dominican writer Elma Napier, contends that because of its rugged landscape of volcanoes and forested mountains, Dominica was the last Caribbean island to be colonized (*In the Forests* 3). Throughout the seventeenth and eighteenth centuries, however, the island did experience colonization by rival European forces: French, Spanish, and English. Dominica officially became a British colony in 1763, but the French had a lasting impact and even briefly recaptured the island in 1778 (Honychurch, *In the Forests* 3, 8). As with Grenada, in Dominica "most people still speak a patois of French as well as English, and are Roman Catholics rather than Protestants" (R. Alexander 179). Europeans developed plantations and forced Africans into slavery. Yet, as Honychurch's research suggests, the island's landscape, while proving difficult for plantocracies, was conducive to the growth of maroon societies (communities of runaway slaves and those born into that society, who thereafter lived outside of the slave system) (*In the Forests* 3). These maroon societies were distinct: "Most of the senior chiefs had been born in Africa, for unlike the Creole, Dominican-born slaves these Africans had once lived in and experienced a society other than the plantation society. They knew that an alternative system existed and they had no difficulty imagining that it could be recreated here on the other side of the Atlantic" (Honychurch, *In the Forests* 4). While not engaging with the slave past directly, John's protagonist Matilda, a fierce, matriarchal maroon-like figure who lives "Up There" in the forested mountains, functions as a synecdoche for the historical maroons who successfully waged several wars (1785–1786 and 1812–1814) and fought for freedom, until slavery was abolished in the 1830s (Honychurch, *In the Forests* 73, 6).

Honychurch insightfully notes that, postemancipation, maroons, former slaves, Indigenous people, and other marginalized groups were subject to harsh land laws favoring British planters and slavers: "A raft of laws, such as the wide-ranging vagrancy acts, were passed to keep control of the masses. The aim was to deprive them of land so as to tie them to reliance on estates, to limit the right to vote and to determine everything in their lives from the rates of their labor to the nature of their sexual activity" (*In the Forests* 6). These details are recounted in the novel's discussion of overlapping Indigenous, slave, and maroon pasts. Noteworthy is that, as *Unburnable* alludes, Dominica is the only Caribbean island "in which the Carib Indians still are a recognized part of the national community," underlined by the fact that in 1903, "the British set aside a small portion of the island as a Carib 'reserve'" (R. Alexander 179). Such land politics, however, in no great way benefited the Indigenous Kalinago and majorly displaced them. For instance, in *Unburnable*, Lillian's grandfather is a Carib Indian who joins Matilda's Afra-Caribbean matriarchal, mountaintop village of Up There, in part because he refuses to live on the reserve.

The maroon camps and societies of Dominica's interior, like Matilda's Up There, remained largely mysterious to outsiders until the 1950s, when colonial land became more accessible to and attainable for the independent smallholder: "Plantations that had featured during the Maroon era were taken over and occupied by the descendants of those who had participated in the struggle" (Honychurch, *In the Forests* 183). This new generation of Afro-Dominican landholders and small farmers spurred universal suffrage, education opportunities, increased construction and development, an emerging middle class, and a more active political role for islanders (184). Postcolonial and pro-African attitudes—such as the Rastafarian movement, which entailed "a back-to-the-land ... lifestyle marked by self-sufficiency and a composite of selective African traditions that rejected the colonial-based society" (184)—fed into an increasing demand for national independence (which occurred in 1978). The 1970s were a time of "great local upheaval" (184). Dominica from the early twentieth to the early twenty-first century thus fittingly serves as the backdrop for a novel set in and on "an island of fire" (Honychurch, *The Dominica Story* 1). Lillian articulates the novel's postcolonial feminist engagements by simultaneously retracing the legacies of slavery, marronage, and colonialism while uncovering the truth about her Afra-Caribbean maternal ancestry.

Praisesong for the Widow and *Unburnable* demonstrate how the Caribbean woman's historical novel of return provides the necessary vision or map to ensure that maternal memories and voices are included in the region's imaginary. As in many contemporary novels such as Michelle Cliff's *No Telephone to Heaven* (1987), Andrea Levy's *Fruit of the Lemon* (1999), Julia Alvarez's *In the Name of Salomé* (2000), or Ramabai Espinet's *The Swinging Bridge* (2003), the spiritual dimension of matria is expressed by the daughter returning to her mother's land. While critics have studied the various discourses of migrant/home/diaspora/exile in Caribbean writing, the importance of the maternal often gets overlooked. Yet, in many a Caribbean woman's historical novel "it is in the moorings of spirituality and spiritual consciousness" (Reyes 9), intimately connected to the mother and her mother-land, that the daughter's sense of self and home is fully realized. In John's novel, Lillian travels to the now defunct Up There, the Dominican home of her deceased mother, Iris, and maroon grandmother Matilda. Meanwhile, for Avey in *Praisesong*, her participation in Carriacou's Big Drum ceremony and her dancing a Juba reconnects her with her long-deceased Aunt Cuney, whom she used to visit on Tatem Island. Very much reterritorialized, the homeland becomes jointly linked with the spiritual and the maternal (matria), instead of the colonial and the paternal (patria).

A deliberate postcolonial feminist remapping replaces patriarchal-colonial-named locations with female Caribbean ones: Ibo Landing in *Praisesong* and Noir in *Unburnable*. Both locations are associated with women's resistance to slavery. In the case of Marshall's novel, Aunt Cuney's enslaved grandmother imagines that she, like the Ibos, will walk across the water back to Africa; and Noir, in John's work, is a notorious maroon camp in which Lillian's grandmother, Matilda, presides as magistrate (294). Carissa Turner Smith adds that "in the diasporic spiritual geography of these African American women writers, 'home' is still a possibility when the subject grounds herself in both the roots and the routes of the African diaspora" (715). A critical aspect to a daughter's return, then, is a connection to land that belonged to the maternal family. Chapter 7 therefore argues that Avey comes to prioritize ritual, spirituality, and myth as the means to reconnect her mind and her body with her Afra-Caribbean past.

Blending realism with spirituality and myth, Caribbean women's historical novels make visible women's contributions to preserving and validating the region's oppressed histories, cosmologies, and epistemologies. For example, Marshall provides a postcolonial feminist revision of Freud's understanding of ritual and the unconscious by expressing a version of the Crossing that links the spiritual with one's maternal ancestors. The book's four parts, "Runagate," "Sleeper's Wake," "Lavé Tete," and "The Big Pardon," further reflect a sacred dimension, for not only do they "indicate ritualistic process but also a change in Avey Johnson's character and context" (Christian 75). Both Marshall's and John's novels constitute a specific form of antiracist, antisexist intervention that contemporary novels enact when relocating their maternal roots/routes. Rejecting the false hierarchies and categorizations placed on women's lives by patriarchy and colonialism, such postcolonial fictions of history allow Caribbean women to define themselves both within and outside of their communities. The historical novel thus becomes a medium for the Caribbean woman writer to transform both island and diaspora into matrias.

By returning to Caribbean settings that are visibly connected to maternal land and matrilineage, each novel visibly resists "the pathologization of matrifocality" (Esnard 260)—the "cultural and affective centrality of women within their kinship group" (Rowley 24)—prescribed by "Eurocentric notions of the family" (Esnard 260) such as Freud's. Scholar Michelle Rowley writes that "the Caribbean has never been a matriarchal region, by virtue of its matrifocality" (24), a claim substantiated in John's novel.[1] Caribbean women's novels of return routinely depict women encountering institutional, ideological, and state "patriarchal exercises of power" (Rowley 22) as well as the effects of "multiple European colonial legacies" (Momsen 45). Marshall and John provide heterogeneous accounts of unconventional women to demonstrate the impact of "the intersections of empire, migration, and globalization" on their protagonists' lives (Machado Sáez 27–28); Lillian has no children, is unmarried, and is on the cusp of turning forty (John 48)—the same age her mother was when she died (9) and most likely the same age her grandmother, Matilda, was when she was hanged (39–40). At one point in the novel, Lillian even compares marriage to slavery: "[T]he reason they [women] did not marry was a simple matter. Descendants of slaves, of course, had a natural aversion to slavery" (79). Meanwhile Avey, a widowed grandmother in her mid-sixties, reflects on her marriage as a means to gain social acceptance and respect in white America. The patriarchal-colonial past bears an undeniable weight; hence the daughter protagonist realizes that "in order to find herself, she must first find her mother[s]" (Haigh 65). This search entails a return to her enslaved foremothers' lives, like the ones found in the neo-slavery novels discussed in part I: Mythologizing Matria.

Writing on the importance of returning to one's Caribbean maternal heritage, Samantha Haigh argues: "The quest for Motherland embarked upon by the narrator . . . becomes a continuation of that attempt to articulate an undefinable 'homesickness.' . . . This homesickness, emblematic of women's social and symbolic dereliction, can be articulated only through a (re)invention of the maternal genealogy, that broken line of mothers and daughters which the narrator is here attempting to restore" (69). In *Praisesong for the Widow*, Avey learns that matria is vital when she becomes her family's "ancestress as storyteller and healer" (Andrea Davis 532). She passes on her Afra-Caribbean culture and history to her grandchildren because, after all, she knows firsthand the painful consequences when the bond is broken or lost.

As much as a premillennium novel like *Praisesong for the Widow* offers hope by restoring the broken maternal genealogy, postmillennium novels such as John's *Unburnable* frequently explore the psychological consequences when the Caribbean daughter is "unable to fulfill her desires for the Caribbean mother" (Rody 144).[2] *Unburnable* offers a radical departure from most novels of return because there is no obvious cathartic moment for Lillian. Although matria in these novels consists of returning to the Caribbean in an attempt to "ma[k]e peace with the mother and the mother's land" (S. A. J. Alexander, *Mother Imagery* 25), for Lillian, her return to her birthplace, Dominica, proves tragic. Unlike for Avey, the oral culture is a source of shame for Lillian. She hears the distorted "history . . . recorded in chanté-mas songs" (John 202) about her mother (hypersexualized, mad, and alcoholic) and her grandmother (an Obeahwoman and murderess). She can overcome neither the disparaging Dominican folksongs about her maternal kin nor the corrupt archives founded on and privileging modernity, colonialism, and whiteness. Unable to exonerate her mother figures who have been vilified, hystericized, misrepresented, and marginalized in both official (written History) and popular discourses (oral culture), Lillian's death implies that a spiritual or a maternal homecoming can have heartbreaking consequences.

Consider Caribbean critic Josephine V. Arnold's skepticism: "The dream of homecoming is just that—a dream; for not only have the emigrants been changed by the land they went to, but the land they left has changed as well. The home to which they dream of returning exists only in their memory. Home is for the people who go on living there; all else is shadow of what might have been or can never be" (101). The disappointing homecoming or lack thereof informs my argument in chapter 8 that *Unburnable*'s complex advancement of *hystérie* (a triangulation of womb, madness, and history) functions as a counterdiscourse to traditional, hegemonic History and psychoanalysis, evident when Lillian searches for answers regarding her matrilineage.

Caribbean critics Hena Maes-Jelinek and Bénédicte Ledent's thoughts on female madness further lend context to Lillian's position:

> The madwoman is a recurring image in texts by Caribbean female novelists, often conveying an inability to cope with the stereotypes imposed from the outside. But while in many of them fragmentation of the self marks the beginning of a new wholeness . . . [sometimes] it only leads to self-destruction . . . represent[ing] the "schizophrenic nature of Caribbean society." . . . [H]er bleak end may therefore symbolize the impossibility of getting over the rifts caused by colonialism and patriarchy. (183)

Lillian's ambiguous fate has led some scholars like Carol Bailey to conclude that "Lillian has lost faith in the stories and by extension the oral tradition as sources of 'truth' and healing" (38). To an extent this is true, but Lillian's decision to leap from the historical maternal space (Noir) also demonstrates her agency over her own body as/and her own narrative.

Through her death, Lillian imagines turning herself into a folkloric figure, and that as such she will "join her ancestors, and create another song" (Bailey 46). This act suggests solidarity with her foremothers and draws attention to Lillian's inability to live in a patriarchal, colonial world, in which both the oral and written traditions disparage Black females who dare to defy Dominican societal norms and expectations. At the same time, the novel indirectly reveals the oral and mythical, not to mention fictional, underpinnings of European modernity and/as historical progress. By rewriting the Afra-Caribbean maternal past, *Unburnable* demonstrates the potential of the Caribbean woman's historical novel to subvert a traditionally Western male literary genre. John's text, like all Caribbean women's historical novels of return, evidences that the past can be reopened and remade for present postcolonial feminist circumstances.

Such texts highlight the importance of physically connecting with the maternal past, for the protagonist to "[l]iteralize through her body . . . [the] psychic condition" (Hunter 471). Neo-slavery literary scholar Sherryl Vint argues that "like any repressed content, the root cause must be acknowledged and dealt with before the individual—or collective—subject can be free. The body becomes the site through which the work of recovering and healing is done" (245). In Marshall's novel, for instance, Avey refinds herself spiritually by dancing the rituals of the Big Drum ceremony and retelling Aunt Cuney's narrative about the Ibos to her grandchildren. Meanwhile, Lillian in John's *Unburnable* engages with the *chanté mas* or masquerade songs about her maternal kin, which paradoxically relay not only the scandals involving the women but also the injustices committed against them. The novel's inclusion of a masquerade with songs, drummers, and dancers, all of which were deemed illegal during European colonialism, connects it to the other texts in this genre. Avey's and Lillian's embodied acts therefore take on substantial symbolic weight when considering how these subversive traditions survived, reinforcing that the slave past and the oral tradition are vital to the contemporary setting in both texts.

In pre- and postmillennium narratives, matria is disclosed through the revival of myth in novel form. Having attempted to confront or atone for the mother's pain and past, these novels of returning daughters end in two ways.[3] Typically, in the premillennium text, the daughter and her maternal kin embrace embodied ritual, which signals moving past the legacy of matrilineal trauma through a return to the diasporic home. Examples include Avey's return in *Praisesong for the Widow*, Faith's in Andrea Levy's *Fruit of the Lemon*, and Sophie's in Edwidge Danticat's *Breath, Eyes, Memory* (1994). In the postmillennium novel, the daughter recognizes that her own and her mother's stories belong together, and she dies in her Caribbean mother-land, for instance Lillian in *Unburnable*, Camila in Julia Alvarez's *In the Name of Salomé*, and Miriam and Micaela in Ana-Maurine Lara's *Erzulie's Skirt* (2006). Postcolonial feminist novels of return convey the significance of women's roles as practitioners and transmitters of non-Western or African-derived religions, rituals, and folk cultures in the Caribbean and its diaspora, past and present. Such countertexts novelize matria by distinctively remapping the inseparable link between the history of place and of people, between mothers and daughters, and between fact and fiction.

7

The Return of Daughterly Reincar(nation) and Rituals in Paule Marshall's *Praisesong for the Widow*

Although Paule Marshall is best known for her masterpieces *Brown Girl, Brownstones* (1959) and *The Chosen Place, the Timeless People*, published in 1969, her novel *Praisesong for the Widow* (1983) has steadily garnered critical praise (Alao; Christian; Ferguson; Pollard; Rogers; and Sandiford, among others). Reworking the returning daughter trope found in earlier works like Phyllis Shand Allfrey's *The Orchid House* (1953), Marshall's *Praisesong for the Widow* relays Avey's, an African American widow's, spiritual and physical journey to the Caribbean. This chapter rereads *Praisesong for the Widow*'s celebration of Afra-Caribbean heritage and "African diasporic cultural rituals and myths" (Alao 51) as historical fiction. I argue that by privileging ritual and myth as preservers and conveyors of the Afra-Caribbean past, the novel participates in decolonizing the genre and colonial historicization. Guided by M. Jacqui Alexander's conceptions of the Crossing and the spiritual, I argue that Avey's reverse migration from the United States to Grenada and Carriacou, before going back to the United States, entails a deliberate reconnecting with and reincarnation of her ancestors, her maternal roots, her matria, and the "burgeoning color" and "warm waters of the Caribbean" (Marshall 16–17).

The following passage from M. Jacqui Alexander articulates the importance of African belief systems to the region and provides a critical framework for making sense of the relationship between the divine and the individual that is found in Marshall's novel:

> [There is] an intimacy of lived experience in which the Sacred is embodied. ... Sacred energies intervene in the daily lives of human beings; they surround, protect, push, strengthen, and bring a sense of purpose so that the individual is attuned to the Soul's purpose; they are present both everywhere, as in the Wind, and at specific moments, as in dreams; they mediate a process of interdependence, of mutual beingness, in which one becomes oneself in the process of becoming one with the Sacred; and they manifest their sacredness in nature as well as in their relationship with human beings both of which take shape in a process of mutual embodiment. (301)

Avey's journey in the novel, however, begins not with her accepting the "idea and practice of Sacred accompaniment, Sacred guidance, and Sacred identity" (M. J. Alexander 301) but with her assimilation to and/or complicity with patriarchy, imperialism, and white tourism.

Praisesong for the Widow thus opens with Avey Johnson about to board a cruise ship. Marshall writes: "It had been 1974 then, and Jerome Johnson had been dead only a little over a year.... [W]hatever doubts ... [were] in Avey Johnson's mind had vanished the moment she saw the *Bianca Pride*" (15). Marshall continues to emphasize Avey's feelings of reassurance from this symbol of white supremacy: "Amid the burgeoning color stood the liner—huge, sleek, imperial, a glacial presence in the warm waters of the Caribbean" (16–17). Yet, once aboard, and a few days into having a good time with two friends, Avey is quickly overcome by nausea, anxiety, and a nightmare about her great-great-aunt Cuney. For instance, Avey becomes ill when dining in the Versailles Room: "Of the three dining rooms on board, the Versailles with its Louis XIV décor and wealth of silver and crystal on the damask-covered tables was the most formal" (46). At the back of Avey's mind, her daughter Marion's postcolonial claims ring: "*[D]o you know how many treaties were signed there, in that infamous Hall of Mirrors, divvying up India, the West Indies, the world?*" (47). When the dessert, a "*Peach Parfait à la Versailles*," arrives, Avey's nausea returns (49–50). Patriarchal colonialism and imperialism literally begin to sicken, if not poison, her.

Unable to control her physical and psychical unease, Avey feels compelled to immediately return to New York.

Critically, we also learn that Avey's dream about her maternal relative proceeded from having spent the day in Martinique and hearing a distant language that vaguely reminded her of her childhood. The language and the dream both suggest the Freudian idea "that in the unconscious there exists an archaic heritage" (J. Henderson 4), and as Lorna McDaniel notes, "unconscious messages and dreams . . . [are] much valued in Caribbean cultural practices" (2). In the dream, an impeccably dressed Avey sees her great-great-aunt Cuney summoning her. Refusing to obey her aunt, Avey finds herself accosted by "a hand with the feel of a manacle . . . close around her wrist"; she finds herself "being dragged forward in the direction of the Landing" (Marshall 43). As I discuss in more detail below, the dream leads to Marshall depicting Avey's memories of Tatem Island and her Aunt Cuney. Aunt Cuney's wide-brimmed hat and field-worker clothing also mark her as a figure of the Crossing, one who will guide Avey's unconscious desire for initiation toward embracing her repressed Afra-Caribbean roots/routes.

The reader knows that Avey is sixty-four years old at the time of the cruise in 1974; therefore, she was born in 1910. This means that her great-great-aunt was born probably in the antebellum South in the 1840s. The Civil War (1861–1865) and Aunt Cuney's life as a slave are briefly mentioned in the text, but curiously scholars have not paid much attention to this context, despite the fact that the legacy of slavery is a distinct theme that runs throughout all of Marshall's fiction. Avey's memories of her summers spent on Tatem Island (1917–1921), for instance, place Aunt Cuney at about eighty years old. Avey distinctly remembers how they would make their way toward the Landing, while Aunt Cuney would talk about the past (36–37). First, they pass the only church in Tatem: significantly, the church also functions as the only school. Its dilapidated appearance speaks to the community's poverty and the cultural wane of African practices and deities.

For example, Aunt Cuney recounts getting in serious trouble as a young girl when accused of "'crossing her feet' in a Ring Shout being held there and [she] had been ordered out of the circle" (33). A "Ring Shout" or plantation dance (Juba/*giouba*) "is a ritual connected to African forms of song and dance, and in the Americas, it served as a way for slaves to preserve some of these traditions" (C. T. Smith 721). That Aunt Cuney is participating in the Ring Shout further indicates her status as a plantation slave. The Ring

Shout, as with all rituals, includes "repeated, sacred, formalized, traditional and intentional (meaningful actions)" (Merkur 15). Guilty of transgressing the Ring Shout's rules, Aunt Cuney decides to leave the church indefinitely.

Aunt Cuney becomes disconnected from her African heritage and her spiritual community: an outsider, with her great-great-niece beside her, she sometimes looks in "through the open door [on] the handful of elderly men and women still left, and who still held to the old ways . . . slowly circling the room in a loose ring" (Marshall 34). Surreptitiously watching the performance, Aunt Cuney recalls that "it felt like dancing in her blood, so that under cover of the darkness she performed in place the little rhythmic trudge. She joined in the singing under her breath" (35). The result is that Aunt Cuney is cut off from her ancestors and from participating both collectively and individually in the memory of her heritage; the church and the elders who perform the cultural ritual are aging, and there is a sense that soon enough the connection will be irrevocably lost. Aunt Cuney, however, partially replaces this loss with a daily walk to the Landing—"People in Tatem said she had made the Landing her religion after that" (34)—but one wonders how Avey and the younger generation will locate their heritage if there is no one left to teach or guide them.

The past is also symbolized by the walk, which chronicles the legacy of slavery's history. For example, Aunt Cuney shows Avey a former cotton plantation; after referencing William Sherman, a Union Army general, Aunt Cuney notes that after the Civil War, which fundamentally ended slavery in the United States, the field was never replanted. After passing this abandoned field and trekking through a pine forest, however, the pair arrive at the marshes and the river, and they stand at Ibo Landing: "the point where the waters in and around Tatem met up with the open sea" (37). Ibo Landing is "where they brought 'em. They taken 'em out of the boats right here where we's standing . . . 'cording to my gran' who was a little girl no bigger than you when it happened. The small boats was drawed up here and the ship they had just come from was out in the deep water. Great big 'ol ship with sails" (37). Aunt Cuney speaks of a time at the turn of the eighteenth century when slaves from Africa were forcibly brought to work on both Caribbean and American plantations, and undoubtedly Avey's great-great-aunt's "gran" was a slave. Writing on Marshall's text, Folashade Alao argues that the peripatetic becomes a means for gaining cultural knowledge and experiencing a spiritual awakening: "[E]nding their walks at Ibo Landing suggests that walking and conscious awareness of physical and cultural places, like traditional forms of storytelling, are also essential for preserving and conveying cultural memory and a diasporic world-sense that may guide political and social responses" (55). Thus, Aunt Cuney serves as a didactic spiritual guide.

The twist in Aunt Cuney's story, however, is that the Ibos, despite their shackles and chains, see the future and the slavery that awaits them:

> They just turned ... all of 'em ... and walked on back down to the edge of the river here. Every las' man, woman and chile.... They just kept walking right on out over the river.... When they realized there wasn't nothing between them and home but some water and that wasn't giving 'em no trouble they got so tickled they started in to singing.... [M]y gran' declared she just picked herself up and took after 'em. In her mind. Her body she always usta say might be in Tatem but her mind, her mind was long since gone with the Ibos. (Marshall 39)

Marshall's repetition of the word "mind" emphasizes the "magnitude of their defiance ... communicated in mythical terms of corporeal transcendence" (Rogers 80). The value of myth to matria in countering colonial History becomes increasingly clear.

Critical race studies scholar Barbara T. Christian likewise notes that the novel shifts between the material and the immaterial: "external reality" and "memor[ies], dream[s], [and] hallucination[s] ... in which the past and the present fuse" (75). The novel suggests that mind-body dualism, in which mind is privileged, is a Western concept that holds little value or meaning in African-based cosmologies and epistemologies. Tracing the division between mind/body to the slave colonial past, for instance, Aunt Cuney's gran's body is enslaved, but in her mind, she is free and imagines being in Africa. Separating her mind from her enslaved body becomes a means for survival and keeping alive her heritage. Yet, the novel does not downplay that the Black woman's mind, over the course of slavery and its legacy, by being compelled to forget the past, to reject its ancestors, and to cut ties with African traditions and rituals is a type of slavery, too—Avey Johnson's body and mind at the time when she boards the *Bianca Pride* demonstrate this, and the novel shows how she must rejoin them if she is to be whole and "healed" (Christian 78). This is to say that Avey's body and her mind must relearn their maternal history, however fragmented, by returning to African-derived rituals and the sacred, and to a notion of "embodied knowledge" (Rogers 79). Aunt Cuney's description of the defiant Ibos, and her gran's imagining that she has sailed with them back to her African roots, is likewise pertinent to the dream Avey has fifty years later while aboard the cruise ship. For much of the novel, "Avey's mind may be in one place while her body is in another," writes Christian (76), suggesting a conflict between the intellect and the unconscious, as is the case with Avey's dream (J. Henderson 7).

The dream, however, may indicate not only Avey's guilt for separating herself from her heritage but also Aunt Cuney's. After all, Aunt Cuney isolates herself and never attends the Ring Shout dances again—logically, if people stop participating in the rituals, then the past (history) will be forgotten and not passed on. Daniel Merkur's research on Freudian theories of ritual proves useful here because he argues that "the popular misunderstanding of Freud's position" is that "ritual is a culturally congenial form of compulsion neurosis" (26). Instead, he argues that Freud believed that "people have an innate and unconscious sense of guilt" (20) that can be traced to the "primal crime" of sons murdering their father. Rituals were thus undertaken to atone for this violence (Merkur 20). Guilt here is linked with loss, yet Merkur goes further to contend that "ritual is invariably an evasion of unconscious guilt" (29). Reading the novel in relation to matria, however, connects Avey's guilt and her participation in ritual not to the primal father's murder but to abandoning and losing the primal mother, in this case, the enslaved Afra-Caribbean mother/African mother-land. Consider, too, Freud's contention in *Civilization and Its Discontents* that one of the origins of a sense of guilt arises "from fear of an authority" who, in this case, would be the mother figure, Aunt Cuney (74). Thus, for Avey ritual invariably confronts and replaces unconscious guilt. Merkur concludes that although "ritual entails an obligatory element" (24), which is exactly what Aunt Cuney in the dream tries to explain to Avey, it can be a healthy or liberating means to cope with traumas such as those caused by slavery.

Taking on a maternal role, Aunt Cuney attempts to force Avey once more to confront her slave past and to follow the initiative of the Ibos. As literary critic Moira Ferguson notes, "Cuney is an appropriate chronicler of the Ibos landing since linguistically as well as historically, she is linked to the original crossing from Tatem Island to Africa" (60). Beyond the specificity of the Ibos, there is still "[a] cultural unity which joins the black people of the Sea Islands or the Southern US to the black people of the

Caribbean and, by implication, to all diaspora people—a unity resulting from the cultural retentions from a common ancestor, one or other of the kingdoms of the African continent from which the black populations were taken" (Pollard 58). Velma Pollard further argues that anthropologists and linguists "have studied Gullah, the Creole language of the Sea Islands, which lie off the coast of Georgia and South Carolina. Comparisons between Gullah and the Creoles of the Caribbean have established relationships that are undoubtedly the result of similar linguistic histories" (58). In Marshall's text, interestingly, this language is mostly a "creole of French" (Pollard 59), evident in the Big Drum song titles, for instance. Yet, French Creole is "rapidly disappearing" (11), as McDaniel observes, because of the increasing socioeconomic impact of US imperialism and the use of English in the region.

An important cultural marker, the Landing is nevertheless where myth and history offer conflicting tales and "struggle for hegemony" (Sandiford 374). Aunt Cuney's ritual of repeating the Ibos' story is at odds with written colonial History. Edwina Ashie-Nikoi convincingly intimates that in lieu of written records there is oral storytelling and ritual practices like the Big Drum, which function as subversive texts capable of conveying a counter-hegemonic past (6). Avey, however, at first sees herself as outside of and apart from this heritage. Neither her mind nor her body identifies with her maternal heritage or her African roots. Refusing to obey her aunt's wishes, in the dream, Avey and her aunt trade blows, literally wrestling each other, with Avey beating Aunt Cuney for reminding her of a past she'd rather forget. In a sense, Aunt Cuney initially functions as the mother figure toward which the daughter in the Oedipus complex feels aggression and antagonism. Avey is wrestling not only with the mother, however, but also with her daughterly self, as she has not come to terms with that, either.

In the dream's fight sequence we see older values confronting newer ones, "a confrontation between the historical remnants (the archaic heritage) and the immediate needs of the personal psyche" (J. Henderson 10). "Archetypal images," like Aunt Cuney, as psychoanalytic scholar Joseph L. Henderson indicates, are important vehicles for initiation, in this case Avey's simultaneous return to and rebirth of her archaic maternal heritage: archetypal images "can then be accepted or rejected by the individual's own choice; this is of the greatest importance . . . for no one can experience the archetypal images without being temporarily fascinated, terrified, or possessed by them" (10). The unpleasant images, likewise, when rendered accessible "to consciousness" can be integrated and function "as organs of healing" (J. Henderson 10). Avey, however, is not ready to confront her maternal slave past: instead, she feels chained to it, that it unbearably physically and mentally restricts her (Rogers 81), and at this point in the dream she leaves her aunt bereft on the road, or the unconscious. *Praisesong for the Widow* nevertheless proposes that there is no escaping the past. The image of the manacle suggests that her unconscious refuses to confront her past/present links to slavery.

Venetria K. Patton, in *The Grasp That Reaches beyond the Grave: The Ancestral Call in Black Women's Texts*, contends that Aunt Cuney manifests as a healing ghost "to remind Avey of her history": she "facilitates a spiritual rebirth that allows her [Avey] to reconnect with her ancestors" (60). Thinking of the spirit(ual) in terms of the maternal further makes sense because "the ghost is primarily a symptom of what is missing . . . a loss," but it likewise signals hope (Gordon 64). The loss is Avey's contact with the maternal, the spirit world—she has dwelled too much, too long, in the patriarchal world of earthly possessions and materialism (evident by the fur stole she is wearing in the dream). Marshall's novel confronts the problem that "[i]n the realm of the secular, the material is conceived as tangible while the spiritual is either nonexistent or invisible" (M. J. Alexander 307), for example ghosts, dreams, the pre-Oedipal mother. Furthermore, the logical conclusion is that Avey has neglected her duty as a medium to the spirit world; in forgetting and/or refusing to transmit the story of the Ibos (Patton 62), she has refused to be an avatar. Her aunt's ghost reminds Avey that in African-based cosmologies, a barrier between the past and the present, like the living with the dead, is nonsensical (Sandiford 375).

Consequently, Avey takes her dream seriously enough that she believes she has indeed spoken with her Aunt Cuney as if she were present. Writing on *Praisesong for the Widow*, Keith Sandiford elaborates that

> African cosmology supports this assumption. In that system spirits of the departed are denominated the *living dead* for up to five generations and considered to exist in the *sasa* time frame, guarding, observing, and communicating with the living. Because of the relative recency of Great-aunt Cuney's death, we may infer that she is in the *sasa* of her life cycle, capable of contact with and exercising power over now time. (391)

Thus, while Avey dismisses and suppresses her heritage, she does not rule out that the past can still communicate with her, and that there is a force beyond the secular that can influence and impact the present. The daughter's ability to speak back to the past and through it is intimately bound to and connected with the maternal, and, like other novels studied in *Matria Redux*, constitutes an important aspect of matria. Women are cultural bearers, and it is only through reconnecting with one's maternal ancestry that the past can be confronted and reclaimed.

Marshall's novel supports M. Jacqui Alexander's complex notion of the Crossing, particularly how it relates to African-based cosmologies and the sacred. She contends that "African-based cosmological systems are complex manifestations of the geographies of crossing and dislocation. They are at the same time manifestations of locatedness, rootedness, and belonging that map individual and collective relationships to the Divine" (290–91). The break in Avey's heritage follows Alexander's claims that slaves carried their spiritual world with them during the Middle Passage but that these deities and rituals inevitably transformed over the course of their journeys. This is to say that the cosmology did not remain static but rather adapted and found ways to survive in different permutations and migrations. One sees this in Marshall's work when Aunt Cuney attempts to impart the lessons of the sacred past onto her niece.

As Aunt Cuney mentions in the dream, Avey's full name, Avatara, is the same name as Cuney's grandmother. Marshall explains how Aunt Cuney told her parents "months before her birth that it would be a girl and she was to be called after her grandmother who had come to her in a dream with the news" (42). The repetition of self-fulfilling prophecies via women's dreams once more emphasizes the spiritual's syncretism with the earthly world and vice versa. A sense of history already written pervades, and it is merely a matter of one accepting it and submitting to its forces: in this case, Avey must come to recognize her ancestors' traumas and enslavement, including those of her Aunt Cuney and Cuney's gran, so that she can fulfill her duty and fully engage in the world. Marshall thus very much turns the tables: it is not so much the case that Aunt Cuney is a ghost but that Avey, living under the spell of white Anglophone capitalist imperialism (very much in the habit of forgetting and erasing its role in the slave past), is a ghost. Sucked dry of her cultural soul, so to speak, so as to present respectability to the outside world, Avey comes to recognize her grave mistake. Her African-based heritage, including its mythologies, cosmologies, and traditions, is a priceless part of who she is and who her descendants are. If she represses who she is, she cuts off her maternal past from her future, the result of which is both matricide and "spiritual suicide" (Christian 77). Marshall's resurrection of alternative ways of knowing thus counters hegemonic historiography, subverts traditional historical fiction, and critically informs matria.

The meaning of "avatar" also bears spiritual importance in Marshall's historical novel. The *Oxford English Dictionary* defines the word as "an incarnation, embodiment, or manifestation of a person or idea"; it stems from the Sanskrit words *ava*, which means "down," and *tar*, "to cross." Avey in the twentieth century, like her aunt's eighteenth-century grandmother, must go down to the water—down to the Landing—and defiantly cross, like the Ibos, both literally and figuratively. The invocation of an avatar relates to the Crossing because, as the gods traveled from Africa to the Caribbean and the United States, they were often transformed, fused, and exchanged to the extent that "[o]ften there are multiple avatars of the same Sacred force" (M. J. Alexander 292). Similarly, this argument supports "the idea of a multiply manifested or multidimensional god, avatars, that make the Sacred tangible.... [M]anifestations ... inhabit physical elements as well as human beings" (M. J. Alexander 299). It is her going vertically down, that is, back in history and time, against linear time, and crossing horizontally in space by way of water that marks Avey's journey in the narrative. But in the early stages of the text, Avey embodies neither her maternal ancestor nor the sacred.

Unlike her ancestor, Avey has little recourse to her African past and its mythologies. The thread between her and the past has been disrupted. For instance, she painfully recalls when she was ten years old and hearing Aunt Cuney's now stale story, finally asking: "But how come they didn't drown?" (Marshall 39). Aunt Cuney meets Avey's question initially with silence and bitter disappointment. Then, she asks if anyone ever questions why Jesus didn't drown when he allegedly walked on water (40). Avey's skepticism indicates that Christian doctrine has replaced/displaced African cosmologies. Believing Jesus to be the true son of God also suggests a rejection of other religions and belief systems. That Aunt Cuney is critical of African Americans internalizing this belief system is further supported when Avey's mother (who remains nameless) sends her daughter to Tatem each summer with a Sunday School Bible (40).

In this time and place, Avey is unable to see that "Great-aunt Cuney's unwritten story parallels the biblical story documented in the Sunday-school book. Marshall's incorporation of the biblical scripture is her questioning of this script as the ultimate truth, and in so doing, she simultaneously renders authenticity to the untold and unwritten story of slavery" (S. A. J. Alexander, *Mother Imagery* 166). As a transmitter of African history and culture, Aunt Cuney passes down her knowledge orally, which is in direct contrast with the European written word—a word that has been used to enslave, silence, and misrepresent the realities of her ancestors and descendants. Simone A. James Alexander argues that "African-based cosmological systems become subordinated to the European cosmos, [as they are] not usually expected to accord any significance to modernity's itinerary" (296). Put slightly differently, Alexander clarifies that Avey, like her Aunt Cuney and Cuney's gran, is expected to counteract "the effacement of history and the historical past, the discrediting of the ancestral world, and the deeming of this 'other ways of knowing things' inconsequential and insignificant" (*Mother Imagery* 168). The novel thus concerns itself with Avey reestablishing a knowledge and belief in her African heritage (oral) and the sacred that has been suspended and displaced by European empiricism, logos, religion, and secularism.

Likewise, Avey's anonymous mother disparages the great aunt, claiming exasperatingly that "my child comes back here looking like Tar Baby from tearing around in the sun all day behind that old woman!" (Marshall 42). Avey's following her aunt extends beyond the physical. Class anxieties—Aunt Cuney dresses like a field worker, a reminder of her days as a slave and as a laborer, postemancipation—cause Avey's mother distress, a distress that Avey mimics in her dream when she refuses to follow her aunt. Beyond class concerns, Avey is being indoctrinated into Aunt Cuney's ways of being: her world views, her knowledge, her pedagogies, her mythologies, and her rituals, all of which are at odds with the dominant Christian, patriarchal, Western imperialist view. Racialized gender anxieties further exhibit themselves, for in following in the footsteps of her aunt, an authority on the old ways, versed in African-based cosmologies and Creole traditions, under a hot sun, Avey's skin darkens, which her mother reads as indicative of one becoming more African and therefore less socially desirable and possibly less attractive.

The reference to Tar Baby elaborates on the subversive politics of Marshall's novel. "Tar Baby" suggests that Avey is, like in the original 1881 story by Joel Chandler Harris, someone, or more accurately a thing (again resonating with notions of the slaves as property), that one wants to avoid. A tar baby is a dark-skinned doll composed of tar and turpentine that is used as a hunting trap. In Harris's story, a fox uses a tar baby to ensnare a rabbit: the rabbit, however, after becoming entangled with the baby, outwits the fox and manages to escape. The *Oxford English Dictionary* thus defines "tar baby" as "a difficult problem which is only aggravated by attempts to solve it," but the pejorative use of it refers to African Americans. The term, however, also has currency in African-based cosmologies with the figure of Anansi (a trickster spider) playing the role of the hunter and using a wooden doll as bait, which implies in the case of Harris's story and the cultural allusions it spawned, a Western appropriation of the African sacred and Avey's mother's internalization of and complicity in disavowing African cultural roots. Because her daughter toils in the old plantation fields and follows in the footsteps of her aunt, Avey, according to her mother, transforms into a Tar Baby; the implication is that Aunt Cuney is the fox and the archetypal trickster figure. Avey's nameless mother attempts to dissociate herself and her daughter from any connection not only with African deities, traditions, and belief systems but also with the racist stories promulgated by white writers like Harris. In both cases, she buys into racist, classist, and sexist attitudes toward African Americans.

African American and Caribbean historical fiction expert Caroline Rody argues that in Marshall's novel, like Toni Morrison's novel *Tar Baby*, "the plot of physical or mental return to the Caribbean—rather than Africa itself—[i]s the site of cultural and spiritual renewal" (89). Echoing this sentiment, Susan Rogers states that the novel "does not propose a literal return to Africa, but rather a return to America with a renewed awareness of African origins" (91). With timeless deities like Papa Legba, the Caribbean becomes reconceived as "a mythic space" capable of transforming Avey (Rody 89). This recognition plays a large part in the novel, particularly when, after Avey's violent dream, she leaves the pristine, white cruise ship. Like her African ancestors, who, foreseeing the traumas of slavery, return to Africa, Avey, unconsciously feeling the traumatic effects of a lost heritage, never once looks back at the ship as she makes her way to the shores of Grenada, a nation that shares her Ibo African ancestors (McDaniel 37).

Avey unwittingly retraces the journey of early colonizers and slaves as she travels by water from Martinique to Grenada. Marshall thus sets her protagonist up at an exact moment of crisis. Crises are important because not only are they provoked by guilt but "rituals surround crises" as well (Merkur 29). Pollard rightfully identifies Avey's dilemma of choosing "between the cultural values of the black great aunt and the target values of white America" (61), which read allegorically suggests that both Avey and Grenada must embrace their revolutionary spirit and gain independence from colonizing Western powers. *Praisesong for the Widow* suggests that the moment Avey leaves the *Bianca Pride* for Grenada and Carriacou, she chooses to embrace a supralinguistic, embodied means of communicating with others who share her African heritage.

Before her excursion to Carriacou, however, Avey meets an elderly man named Lebert Joseph, a reincarnation of the "West African god Esu-Elegbara" who "crossed the Atlantic to the New World during the most horrific instant of globalization: the Trans-Atlantic Slave Trade" (Russell 9, 11). Some of his New World manifestations include "*Papa Legba* in Haitian Vodoun" (Russell 12). Legba is another trickster-tempter figure, a gatekeeper between human and spirit worlds, "the mediator between the divine and the earthly" (McDaniel 117): he is the god of crossings, and as "the guardian of the crossroads [he] grants travel and communication" (McDaniel 117). Being deemed "the divine linguist" makes Legba the ideal candidate to serve as intermediary between the multiple languages spoken by those during slavery and those in the contemporary African diaspora such as Avey, her Gullah-speaking aunt, and the Grenadian and Carriacouan peoples she meets (Russell 9).

It is the reincarnation of Legba who insists, like Aunt Cuney before him— who incidentally wears a Legba-like broad-rimmed hat—that Avey accompany him to Carriacou for the annual homecoming and the Big Drum ritual.

> Big Drum (also called Nation Dance) is a ritual complex honoring the ancestors performed as the nucleus of communal events—baptisms, marriages, *saraca* (a sacrificial ancestral feast), maroon (a community project or feast), stone feasts (the last funerary rite), the opening of a shop, new house, launch of a new boat, and as part of Carriacou's Carnival activities. The ritual is sometimes held as a result of a dream in which an ancestor appears or specifically asks for a performance. (Ashie-Nikoi 7)

Ashie-Nikoi's sociohistorical remarks on the Big Drum imply that in Marshall's novel, Lebert Joseph may in fact appear as a result of Avey's dream about her Aunt Cuney, as if he, too, has been summoned by the ancestors.

Similarly, the Big Drum in Carriacou that Avey participates in might intimate that she is in fact her own reincarnated ancestor; her current self is honoring her past self, and as her own ancestor she requests this ritual performance.

If, as Ashie-Nikoi argues, "[w]hatever the reason for the ritual being held, the underlying purpose is to seek and receive the ancestors' blessings" (7), then Avey is seeking blessings from her previous self; she is asking for her past self to forgive her present self. Put slightly differently, "the Sacred becomes a way of embodying the remembering of self" (M. J. Alexander 298). Emphasizing the spiritual, the "Vodun Introit" from Haiti that opens this section, "*Papa Legba, ouvri barrière pou' mwê*" (Marshall 148), serves as a gate or door to the spirits for Avey. Pollard remarks that the invocation of Legba has been used in "the literature of the diaspora" as a kind of physical and psychological "cry for help" to be released of "certain aspects of colonialism" (62). Papa Legba will clear a path and (re)introduce the African pantheon to Avey: he will put her in touch with the gods and the gods within herself.

The journey to Carriacou, however, causes Avey to suffer from severe seasickness. Ferguson observes that "this boat annually carries people who work in Grenada back to Carriacou where they hail from. The extravagant pageantry of the expedition includes a display of huge unfurled sails, suggesting spectacle on a ritualistic scale. But this anti–Santa Maria flotilla is afloat, not with 'bianca' but with black pride" (68). Evocative of the horrific conditions slaves of the Middle Passage would have endured, Avey becomes one with her ancestors. She relives, even if briefly, the cruelty of transatlantic slavery, "crowded in with her in the hot, airless dark, packed around her in the filth and stench" (Marshall 209). The climax of the journey occurs when Avey, mentally and physically broken and attuned to the traumas of her ancestors, humiliatingly experiences encopresis. The shame she initially feels is negated by its cathartic effect: she has literally purged herself of the white American culture that has increasingly, predatorily, been taking over her life, to the extent that white pride is likened to a disease or illness.

For this reason, "the journey on the water must be made if the total cultural connection is to be achieved. It was water that broke the connections over the middle passage. It was water that separated the Mainland and Avey's parents from Aunt Cuney's Tatem. The homecoming had to be across water" (Pollard 66). The connection is to birth imagery, as water breaking further signals the importance of renewing the maternal dimension. Once on the island under the tutelage of Legba and the cleansing/healing hands of his daughter, Rosalie Parvie, Avey begins to recover. Barbara Christian reminds the reader that "[c]entral to African ritual is the concept that body and spirit are one. Thus sensuality is essential to the process of healing and rebirth of the spirit.... Rosalie washes her [Avey's] body as if she were a new-born" (81). She continues to note that "[t]he bathing ritual also takes Avey through childhood to womanhood" and thus functions as an important moment of initiation (81). On the night before her cyclical return to Grenada and then to the United States, Avey musters enough courage and energy to not only witness but also participate in the Big Drum ceremonial rituals of song, prayer, and dance.

Previously, when asked by Lebert Joseph, "And what you is?" (Marshall 166), Avey has no answer. Lebert Joseph rephrases his question: "What is your nation?" (167). The substitution for what one is with what one's nation is suggests that they are one and the same. Who a person is directly correlates to where one is from, demonstrating the convergence of time (history-lineage) and space (island/mother-country). Lebert Joseph begins to call out several nations to Avey as if he thinks he might be able to call her home in this private Big Drum ceremony. To his dismay, Avey remains ignorant of the names, but he comforts her by adding, "[Y]ou's not the one only one, oui.... People who can't call their nation. For one reason or another they just don' know. Is a hard thing. I don' even like to think about it. But you come across them all the time here in Grenada. You ask people in this place what nation they is and they look at you like you's a madman. No, you's not the only one ..." (175). Lebert Joseph argues that the loss of African heritage is a problem not only for African Americans but also for those living in the Caribbean.

The legacy of slavery, colonialism, and now postcolonial imperial economic policies and tourism continue to erode the old traditions. As the old man gets to the Creole dances, in particular the Juba (177), he locates it as both an ancestral name and a place, the White Nile in Africa (178). Significantly, the Juba is a woman's dance: an aggressive performance by women in long skirts, which the old man playfully dances for her. McDaniel claims, "He sings and dances a Juba to display the ancient codes of Carriacou and introduce a new world, or rather, the old world, to the novel's central character, Avey" (119). The novel suggests that the Juba is an important link between Avey and her maternal lineage. In performing the dance, she embodies her ancestors and manifests reincar(nation); like Avey, Caribbean women's historical fictions importantly make the old genre anew. The name Juba also connects Avey to her Aunt Cuney. When Aunt Cuney appears in her dream, Avey remembers her as "beckoning to her with a hand that should have been fleshless bone by now: clappers to be played at a Juba" (Marshall 40). When on the island of Carriacou and seeing the Juba firsthand, Avey experiences an indescribable magic.

Watching the elders perform their slow shuffle as Lebert Joseph calls the different nations to the circle, Avey, as if drawn by the same push and pull of the past she has experienced her entire journey, her entire life, slowly joins in. She begins to speak the languages of the past through her corporeality. Although Susan Rogers has some difficulty with Marshall's inconsistent references to Avey's bodily knowledge (79), she does remark that "events in the novel present a body's inherent knowledge as a resource for overcoming social and cultural disenfranchisement" (78) and that "Avey's physicality [i]s integral throughout her process of rediscovery ... and understanding her culture" (79). She points out, however, that although Avey renews a mind-body connection with her African heritage, she "does not recover a complete or unadulterated knowledge of African ceremony and ritual, far from it. It is clear that the celebrations in which she takes part, and the memories she recovers, offer only fragments of an African heritage" (92). Participating in the Big Drum, however limited, nevertheless recuperates for Avey both African roots and an identity that is not defined by white, patriarchal Western imperialism. This time when Lebert Joseph calls "And who you is?," she proudly responds that her nation is her mothers: "Avey, short for Avatara" (Marshall 90). The reclaiming of her name and her maternal heritage is her matria, and it breathes life into the Sacred and further awakens her spiritual ancestors. Avey thus reconnects with her repressed Afra-Caribbean maternal past through daughterly reimagining and reincarnation.

This self-identification, simultaneously a connectedness to others and to the gods, "is also essential to ritual, for in African cosmology it is through *nommo*, through the correct naming of a thing, that it comes into existence" (Christian 83). The Ring-Shout dance, which was denied to Avey's Aunt Cuney, is finally and powerfully enacted by her great-great-niece. The result is that Avey, in dancing her spiritual ancestors, comes to know herself. As M. Jacqui Alexander argues, "[T]o know the body is to know it as a medium for the Divine, living a purpose that exceeds the imperatives of these plantations. Put differently, it is to understand spiritual work as a type of bodily praxis, as a form of embodiment" (297). Embodiment therefore "functions as a pathway to knowledge, a talking book, whose intelligibility relies on the social—the spiritual expertise of a community to decode Sacred knowledge" (M. J. Alexander 298). Important points stand out: one cannot know one's self without a connection to the sacred, and "such memory [is] necessary to distill the psychic traumas produced under the grotesque conditions of slavery" (M. J. Alexander 293). To make sense of one's self, there must be a community—spiritual work is both private and collective. Finally, the feminist postcolonial implications of Avey's embodiment of the sacred should not be overlooked. Understanding "the body as a source of knowledge" irreducible to commodification and capitalism (M. J. Alexander 329) offers an alternative epistemology and corporeality, the sacred body as a matria.

In this way, the novel comes full circle, or full Ring Shout: it does not cross its legs or lift its feet from the ground but rather rhythmically shuffles toward a palpable destination. Marshall writes: "[S]he moved cautiously at first, each foot edging forward as if the ground under her was really water—muddy river water—" (248). Thus, Avey, who has psychically and physically traveled back into and relived her ancestral past from the time of slavery to a scattered diaspora, has learned to do that which her Aunt Cuney and Cuney's gran always knew was not only possible but inevitable: she has learned to reinhabit, to reincarnate her maternal ancestors, and she has understood that one can only make sense of the present and the future foretold by returning to the past. Avey has wrestled with her self (and all of her previous incarnations), she has laid her ghosts to rest, she has learned to walk on water. *Praisesong for the Widow* suggests that the patriarchal, white slaver society can be challenged. Marshall fittingly concludes the novel with Avey in Tatem reciting to her grandchildren the lessons of her past and the Middle Passage: "'It was here that they brought them,' she would begin. . . . 'They took them out of the boats right here where we're standing'" (256). Africa as a pure, ancestral place is unreachable, but they have put down roots in the diasporic place. Avey's encounter with people who are rooted/routed in their diasporic identity connects her to her nearer roots in Tatem. Marshall's novel therefore navigates its own space. Much like the unsteady, rustic sailboat, which Avey underestimates, the novel poignantly brings one to an alternative Afra-Caribbean space and time, a mythic, sacred matria that defiantly through ritual and collective memory revitalizes, revolutionizes, and reincarnates the genre.

8

Cartography, *Hystérie*, and Matrilineage in Marie-Elena John's *Unburnable*

At first glance, *Unburnable* (2006) is a curious title for a novel set in Dominica in which no fires, flames, or smoke occur. Yet, the reader soon realizes that the title applies to Marie-Elena John's protagonists—women who cannot be beaten or destroyed, despite the adversities they face. Compellingly, the three female protagonists—Matilda (grandmother, an Obeahwoman, hanged in 1950), Iris (mother, a beautiful mistress, dies in prison in 1971), and Lillian (daughter, the main protagonist, who works in Washington, DC, for a United Nations–type agency for girls and women at risk, commits suicide in the 2000s)—meet a violent end. The majority of the novel portrays the psychological effects of the past on the granddaughter Lillian, who returns to Dominica to recover her Afra-Caribbean maternal roots. Bringing together scholarship on female madness—Luce Irigaray, Kelly Baker Josephs, and Valérie Orlando—with Graham Huggan's postcolonial analysis of cartography, this chapter advances criticism on the novel (Bailey, Josephs, Down, Amy King) and the genre. I argue that John's postcolonial feminist novel *Unburnable* strategically employs what I refer to as *hystérie*, a triad of history, madness, and womb, to write matria.

Certainly, John's debut historical novel is indebted to Jean Rhys's masterpiece, *Wide Sargasso Sea* (1966)—a postcolonial rewrite of Charlotte Brontë's *Jane Eyre* (1847). Historical novel scholar Caroline Rody argues that through writing her white Creole protagonist, Antoinette Cosway Mason Rochester (Bertha), Rhys lit a way for new Caribbean voices, countertexts to the English classics and canon, to emerge. While this is true, other Dominican women writing early historical novels of the fallen plantation, such as Phyllis Shand Allfrey and her novel *The Orchid House* (1953) set in Dominica roughly during the interwar years and narrated by the Black nurse, Lally, also should be considered influential. John's novel, however, proposes that while earlier Caribbean writers like Rhys needed to burn down the old canon—symbolized by the former slaves burning the great plantation house (Coulibri) and the imprisoned Creole woman (Bertha) burning the English estate (Thornfield Hall)—in order to make way for new writing, contemporary authors must bring the fire back to the Caribbean.

The new Caribbean historical novel, therefore, is indebted to mother-texts like *The Orchid House* and *Wide Sargasso Sea* but at the same time sits uncomfortably in this white Creole women's literary tradition. For example, John's heroine does not die a discarded wife, isolated in a foreign country, but she does, similarly to Bertha, transform herself in/into fire. John describes Lillian's suicide as manifesting the *soucouyant*, a Caribbean folkloric figure—a visual fireball, she is "a woman who takes off her skin at night and flies around in search of victims whose blood she sucks" (John 299). In solidarity with her Afra-Carib foremothers, who were disparaged and maligned in traditional literary and historical discourses, Lillian dies in her Caribbean birthplace. As a broad symbol for Caribbean women, however, John's work intimates that women like Bertha and Lillian do not in fact burn in fire: they, like all Caribbean women who dare to revolt, are unburnable. As a postcolonial feminist novel, John's *Unburnable* develops matria as an Afra-Carib matrilineage, which rewrites traditional, colonial History as/through *hystérie*, that is, female hysteria.

Lillian's multigenerational history of marronage, slavery, and colonialism can be read in relation to female madness. Consider that in *Unburnable* Lillian perceives that her image reflects her grandmother: "Lillian had never seen a photograph of her [Matilda], although once, as a child, she had looked into a mirror and seen her swinging from a rope" (17). The rope not only literalizes Matilda's hanging in 1950 but also references the slave past, in which those enslaved and marooned were hanged by planters. Likewise, Lillian believes that she has "inherited some part of . . . her mother's [Iris's] madness" (206). In *Disturbers of the Peace: Representations of Madness in*

Anglophone Caribbean Literature, Josephs contends that hysteria and madness are prominent themes in postcolonial Caribbean fiction, particularly women's: "[T]wenty-first-century fictions by writers of the Caribbean diaspora situate madness as central to representing both the still-ongoing process of decolonization and the (more) contemporary concern with the residues of migration" (5). For the purposes of my argument here, I revisit and draw both on the etymological origins of "hysteria" as stemming from the *hystera* or womb (Sykes), and on hysteria as a condition most often associated with the psychoanalytic work of Sigmund Freud.

In *Studies on Hysteria*, for example, Freud and coauthor Josef Breuer name hysteria as the effect of psychological trauma and sexuality (manifest through hallucinations, anorexia, daydreaming, convulsions, and/or other signs). They write that hysteria can result from "the memory either of a single major trauma (which we find par excellence in what is called traumatic hysteria) or of a series of interconnected part-traumas (such as underlie common hysteria). Or, lastly, the attack may revive the events which have become emphasized owing to their coinciding with a moment of special disposition to trauma" (10). Hysteria further encompasses "behavior exhibiting overwhelming or unmanageable fear or emotional excess" (Sykes), the remedy for which Freud and Breuer recommend hypnosis and "talking" (17).

That hysteria can be linked with the Oedipal moment when a young girl must transfer her love from her mother to her father is further noted: "[T]his phase of attachment to the mother is especially intimately related to the aetiology of hysteria.... [I]n this dependence on the mother we have the germ of later paranoia in women" (Freud, qtd. in Hirsch 99). In *The Mother/Daughter Plot: Narrative, Psychoanalysis, Feminism*, Marianne Hirsch clarifies that the girl's "difficulty" in surmounting the "pre-Oedipus or the Oedipus complex adequately" might very well "derive from the fact that, for her, maturity is a passive subordination to male superiority" (99). John's novel traces the cause of Lillian's hysteria not just to patriarchy but to slavery and colonialism, particularly its violent treatment of her Afra-Carib maternal kin; hence, my term *hystérie* signals not only John's vision of matria but also the novel's distinct postcolonial feminist approach to female madness and history.

Importantly, I see John's postcolonial feminist notion of *hystérie* as engaging with the "the untold story and the retold story" (Newman 24). The folk oral tradition, the literary tradition, and official historiography are all equally challenged. The "untold" emerges as much from these retellings as it does from imagining and recuperating unknown/silenced voices. John's novel diagrammatically provides a vivid description of lineage, emphasizing the preeminence of matrilineage and *hystérie*. John writes:

> Lillian's mother, Iris, was known throughout the island for a number of distinct characteristics: the women would say that chief among them were her uncommon beauty, the fact that her skin was reputed to actually glow in the dark, and the nasty cussing she directed at anyone who crossed her path when she was drunk beyond a certain point. Others insisted that Iris was known best as the daughter of Matilda, who had been tried, convicted, and, one typically rainy day in Dominica in 1950, publicly hanged. (8)

Lillian finds herself in a line of marginalized women characterized by madness, drunkenness, and violence.

Through hysteria—female madness—history repeats itself: the daughter will become her mother. In *Unburnable*, this comes to fruition not necessarily because of an inherited trait but because of pernicious patriarchy, racism, and colonialism. The project of reclaiming the maternal in the novel involves this recognition and by extension disruption. Feminist psychoanalysis critic Luce Irigaray writes that "there is a revolutionary potential in hysteria" (*The Irigaray Reader* 47), and this is why it is vilified. Patriarchal colonial society is a form of madness because it symbolically murders the mother, and women are compelled to live in such madness (Irigaray, *The Irigaray Reader* 48). Women who transgress in their gestures and speech such as Matilda, Iris, and Lillian are labeled mad by hegemonic society, which in consolidating power attempts to silence revolutionary potential. This is why *hystérie*, that is, history, erupts through female madness: hysteria and history are one and the same—both are founded on "women-mothers, the silent substratum of the social order," as Irigaray's title of her essay phrases it (*The Irigaray Reader* 47). The Afra-Caribbean woman is thus a major threat to the patriarchal-colonial system.

Commenting on Irigaray's notion of hysteria, Margaret Whitford writes, "If a woman cannot express her relation to her mother and to other women, she may become 'hysterical'; but Irigaray sees hysteria as a culturally-induced symptom" ("Introduction to Section II" 77). The erasure of one's matrilineage participates in denying women an ability to relate to one another. This prohibition leads "to women's exile in the male imaginary" (Whitford,

"Introduction to Section II" 77). John's novel draws on these ideas but refuses to privilege gender over race. The racialized female body is particularly at risk of hysteria, as Angelita Reyes argues:

> Madness, a nonclinical term for emotional dysfunction and a catch-all label for mental illness, is a marker overused to designate women who act strangely and who do not submit to the social correctness of the day; they are women circulating on the perpetual margins of their societies. Ranging from associations with temporary depression to complete bipolar dysfunction, "madness" has become a layman's all-encompassing, gender-driven metaphor for anger, depression, levels of insanity, and emotional disenfranchisement. In feminist literature, madness has been labeled as a valuable defense mechanism that subverts enforced silence and patriarchal authority. (87)

Lillian, for example, lives in exile in the United States. Granted, she is not exiled because of feared political persecution, but the folk songs about her female relatives like "Matilda Swinging" and "Bottle of Coke," which depict their subjects as murderous, crazy, and/or raped-alcoholic prostitutes, traumatize Lillian.

The traumatizing effects of these lyrics, which chronicle the violence inflicted by Mrs. Richard (who is discussed in detail later) on her mother and her grandmother, make it "almost impossible, even in post-colonial Dominica," for Lillian to reclaim her maternal heritage (A. King 211). Worth noting is that both the official, written record and the folk-oral culture condemn Lillian's family: "Matilda is hanged because she confesses to a crime that is based on a narrative constructed by the local community and from within the oral tradition: the story of John Baptiste's murder 'was chronicled into song'... derived from local gossip and this is the story that the official legal system uses to convict Matilda" (Bailey 39). John's novel shows the interplay between speech and writing, and how sometimes the "spoken word is the more powerful mode of representation" (Bailey 40). After all, Dominican characters like Mrs. Richard choose to believe the events chronicled in the folk culture, for instance Matilda murdering John Baptiste, when it suits; when it does not offer an advantage, Mrs. Richard and others privilege writing to denigrate or question that very same oral culture and tradition.

John's inventive pairing of the oral, unofficial record with the written, official record makes clear that for Lillian, who seeks the truth about her mothers, neither mode is entirely reliable or preferable—the Afra-Caribbean story seemingly cannot be told in her own voice, as if it were not hers to tell. Although Bailey's analysis of narratology in the novel astutely identifies the complexity of voice and questions its veracity, she takes neither gender nor patriarchy enough into consideration. That the gossip, songs, and official accounts pertain to but cannot accurately reflect the Afra-Carib woman is significant. In some sense, she eludes representation in patriarchal texts, which, of course, for a postcolonial feminist position, proves problematic.

Bailey writes that "John problematises the notion that one might turn to the oral tales for a recovery of perspectives missing from official written representations" (46). The oral tradition in this time and place, *Unburnable* suggests, is also suspect/corrupt when it comes to expressing the Afra-Caribbean past: "As would be true of written colonial representations, the oral tradition's representation of events does not acknowledge the African religious dimension as a legitimate or wholesome culture. Therefore, a shared belief system underpins both dominant and unofficial modes of representation" (Bailey 43). I liken the inability of speech here to Freud and Breuer's infamous case study of the hysteric Anna O., which recounts how the patient experienced aphasia as well as an unaccounted-for fluency in foreign languages. Offering a psychoanalytic feminist interpretation of the hysteric's speechlessness and disruptive speech demonstrates her refusal to "integrat[e] into a cultural identity" she "want[s] to reject" (Hunter 468); we might read her "as enter[ing] a world repressed by patriarchal consciousness" (Hunter 474), which is more or less the world of the maternal and matria. For Lillian, again, it is not only integration into a patriarchal world that confounds her and her kin, but slavery and colonialism as well.

Caribbean scholar Valérie Orlando links the inability to speak with insanity and hysteria: "Insanity is often caused by the heroine's exile, isolation, and/or marginalization—either forced by masculine power or self-imposed—as she seeks to challenge age-old traditions in her culture. In some instances, hysteria is a positive catalyst toward a truer self-knowledge . . . and acts as a force that empowers and allows her to overcome debilitating obstacles" (13). In the United States, Lillian is siloed (that is, exiled) from her Afra-Caribbean maternal culture and maternal space, her history, which results in a kind of hysteria. Lillian's hysteria then can be accredited in part to a lack of postcolonial feminist support in her life. This means that "hysteria is feminism lacking a social network in the outer world. . . . [N]either hysterics nor feminists cooperate dutifully with patriarchal conventions" (Hunter 485). Disorganized speech and nonverbal expression, however, connect back to the mother and the body.

Dianne Hunter explains that "prior to our accession to the grammatical order of language, we exist in a dyadic, semiotic world of pure sound and body rhythms, oceanically at one with our nurturer," our mother (473). That the body functions as a text, that it tells a story, is key for John's novel. "Hysteria is a self-repudiating form of feminine discourse in which the body signifies what social conditions make it impossible to state linguistically," writes Hunter (485). Both verbal and nonverbal communication then supply a kind of catharsis for the hysteric, too, as evident when Lillian "dramatiz[es] her past" (Hunter 477), an act that indelibly involves identification with her mother figures. That there might be limits, however, to the effect of narrative (written and/or oral) as healing trauma, is implied when Lillian takes her life (Bailey 35).

Lillian's history/hysteria is intertwined with her maternal heritage. At the age of fourteen, Lillian learns her mother's and her grandmother's identity. Her godmother, Mary-Alice, a former nun, also tells Lillian that Iris was committed to an asylum prison after having drunkenly come to reclaim her five-year-old daughter (John 193). Iris dies of a broken heart on the night she is imprisoned in 1971. Lillian experiences guilt and grief connected to her mother. Iris's attempt to reunite herself, her body and her heart, with her daughter leads to her being locked away. Iris's hysteria is unacceptable in this colonial society; she is deemed an unfit mother, and thus she is separated from her daughter. Upon learning this news, "Lillian had run away then, from her godmother, not found until the next day, sleeping in her mother's grave, still alive because the edge of the shovel she used on her wrist had not been sharp enough. Within weeks of digging up her mother's grave and attempting suicide, Lillian was put on a plane to America" (John 193). Mirroring her mother's hysteric actions, Lillian attempts to reunite herself with her mother, to metaphorically return to the tomb/womb, thereby restoring her distorted and fragmented matrilineage.

Lillian takes up her quest again nearly three decades later. She convinces her famous African American historian-author friend and former lover, Theodore Morgan (Teddy), to accompany her back to Dominica. Returning for the first time since she left in the 1970s, significantly, Lillian wears gold cufflinks, which feature an African design that in Ghanaian Twi "was called

Hye won Hye"—"that which does not burn" (John 7). While gold cannot be destroyed, even by fire, the precious metal also reminds the reader of the history of slavery, Africa's Gold Coast, and the profits gleaned by European colonial powers. Lillian's desire to return stems not only from the psychological trauma she suffers from having her Caribbean matrilineage excised from her life but also from the rumors surrounding her matronymic. Bailey convincingly argues that "while the corrective capacities of orality are affirmed in the novel, the role of oral stories in inflicting trauma is given substantial prominence" (45). Even the consequences of the maroon village's silence and secrecy (necessary for its survival during the period of slavery) when it comes to Matilda's actions are likewise destructive: "The maroon community's separate oral culture further details how the management of stories and concomitant use of silence inflict and perpetuate trauma in *Unburnable*," writes Bailey (45).

Old and new stories alike do not always guarantee healing, but paradoxically, all Lillian has is stories. Lillian doubts the folktales and the historical record's accuracy, both of which claim that her grandmother was a murderer. Lillian's goal to reconnect with her heritage and to absolve her grandmother of her crimes becomes a means to clear her name and to remap the matrilineage as one not of madness and violence but of racism, sexism, maleficence, and survival. Lillian notes that "the story of Matilda—what the songs said she was, what they say she did—consumed her, obsessed her" (John 17), but she supposes that Matilda "didn't do it" (John 130). The maternal connection in John's novel therefore plays out in several ways but most importantly in Lillian relearning her matrilineage by physically returning to the village, referred to by the locals as "Up There," Matilda's settlement, where her grandmother lived, where her mother was born, and where she will die.[1] Lillian's, Iris's, and Matilda's lives emphasize the maternal defined by both kinship and/as space. For example, that "Iris's navel string was buried" (9) "Up There," emphasizes the maternal bond in this particular place. Inhabited by a small group of African descendants (10), the dwelling, on the plateau of one of the island's highest mountains, functions as a kind of matria. "Up There" "'where Matilda lives' although the latter utterance was left 'unspoken, understood'" (9), sets Matilda and Iris physically and psychically apart from the patriarchal-colonial town of Roseau and the other Dominicans who live beneath them. It also signals that the daughter, protagonist Lillian, has left the place of her birth and, therefore, her mother.

"Up There" did not figure on a map until 1950 (John 9), when it was renamed Noah, which John suggests is already too late, for by this time it had "ceased to exist" (9). The day after Matilda's arrest, "Up There" burns to the ground, and most villagers leap from the high cliffs to their death—echoing that historically, rather than be colonized and dominated, the Caribs "jumped to their deaths from a cliff" (Ashie-Nikoi 25). The village's destruction might also refer to the "unburnable" in John's title. A village that does not figure on any European maps, logically, cannot be burned, but it is this spatial erasure to which the novel draws attention. It is only after the village does burn and Matilda is convicted that it appears on a map. This change in history means that living in a matria, a world apart from and in opposition to the rest of the patriarchal island, is no longer possible. In his postcolonial scholarship, for instance, Huggan claims that "[t]he exemplary role of cartography in the demonstration of colonial discursive practices can be identified in a series of key rhetorical strategies implemented in the production of the map, such as the reinscription, enclosure and hierarchization of space, which provide an analogue for the acquisition, management and reinforcement of colonial power" (21). Although historical and contemporary maps contain neither "Up There" nor Noah, the novel contests traditional Eurocentric definitions of History by calling attention to cartography.

Lillian's quest is to investigate her Afra-Carib history and the location of this seemingly unlocatable past. To reiterate, Lillian travels back to the mother, back to Noah, which through other Dominicans she learns was formerly called Noir (John 268) and "Up There." Lorna Down writes that "Noir/Noah is a village comprised of the remnant of African descendants, saved from the destructive enslavement of Africans in the Caribbean" (235). That the location transitions from being called Noir, the French word for black, to Noah, the name of the final antediluvian patriarch and savior of humankind in the Bible's Book of Genesis, is unmistakable and reinforces the power of patriarchal, colonial naming conventions. As Lennox Honychurch notes: "[T]he planters produced and quoted legal and religious books to justify the power that they had seized in this colonial society.... [T]he Judaic Christian Bible was just as much a tool of colonization and control as were the draconian laws, the land titles, and the maps of appropriation and possession" (*In the Forests* 5). The connected acts of naming and mapmaking mark the genesis of a colonial, Christian, European patriarchy and the fall of a maroon, Obeah, African matriarchy.

Drawing attention to this legacy of trauma, John's paratext includes a factual, late eighteenth-century map of Dominica by English politician and historian Bryan Edwards, Esq. That Edwards was a slave-trade proponent and a plantation owner in Jamaica informs the novel and contextualizes the map. Part of the novel's postcolonial feminist project is to challenge the reliability of maps like Edwards's, including which places get marked, by whom, and for whom. Compare Dionne Brand's statement on maps with Édouard Glissant's comment that history is like "a liquid overflowing its vessel" (Glissant, *Caribbean Discourse* 99): "Paper rarely contains—even its latitudinal and longitudinal lines gesture continuation.... The best cartographer is only trying to hold water" (Brand, *A Map to the Door* 55). Both descriptions distinctly echo Irigaray's notion of the language of the maternal as "fluid," "[a]n indefinite overflowing" (*The Irigaray Reader* 65, 55). In destabilizing colonialism and patriarchy, John's subversive text innovatively fuses maps, history, and the maternal.

Huggan elaborates that "cartographic discourse... is also characterized by the discrepancy between its authoritative status and its approximative function, a discrepancy which marks out the 'recognizable totality' of the map as a manifestation of the desire for control rather than as an authenticating seal of coherence" (23). The same discrepancy can be found in *Unburnable*'s contradictory maps, competing (M)aster narratives, and conflicting gender-race dynamics. Patriarchal-colonial modes of discourse attempt to be "passed off as an accurate, objectively presented and universally applicable copy" faithful to reality (Huggan 23). The problem, as Huggan recognizes, is that the "'reality' represented mimetically by the map not only conforms to a particular version of the world but to a version that is specifically designed to empower its makers," which applies equally to storytellers, historiographers, and even historical novelists (23). In this case, "Up There" where Matilda lives functions as a subversive "blindspot" in the official colonial cartography (Huggan 23).

In conceiving matria, John's postcolonial feminist novel participates in the "geographical and conceptual de/reterritorialization" (Huggan 26) of Dominica, and recognizes the "link between a de/reconstructive reading of maps and a revisioning of the history of European colonialism" (Huggan 26–27). Remapping and retracing her family lineage back to "Up There" is precisely that which Lillian, the Dominican-born and -educated American, seeks to accomplish in the novel. The text therefore deliberately conflates woman with place—a common trope in Caribbean fiction. In this case, Lillian's search for Matilda and "Up There" simultaneously symbolizes the need to revitalize matriarchal African Caribbean traditions and reclaim woman's body. With its focus on "Up There," *Unburnable* once more shows a reconception of maps as conducive to constructing matria through postcolonial feminist rewriting and remapping.

Huggan elaborates:

> The multiple connections/disconnections of the rhizome with the transformative patterns of the map provides a useful . . . working model for the description of postcolonial cultures. . . . Moreover, a number of contemporary women writers . . . have adapted [Gilles] Deleuze and [Félix] Guattari's model to the articulation of a feminist cartography which dissociates itself from the "oversignifying" spaces of patriarchal representation but which, through its "deterritorializing lines of flight," produces an alternative kind of map characterized not by the containment or regimentation of space but by a series of centrifugal displacements. (28–29)

The maroon village of Matilda's "Up There" functions as a rural-matriarchal-anticolonial-Obeah counterspace, intentionally removed from the urban-patriarchal-colonial-urban Christian center—Roseau.

John thus begins via Lillian to provide a backstory for her defiant maroon heroine and her daughter. For instance, we learn that Matilda, in her early life, illegally practices Obeah. Matilda's Obeah is used to heal, however, until Simon the Carib arrives (John 10). Honychurch argues that "so-called obeah laws were a front for a government policy of de-Africanization of the population. Carve a mask or a statue out of wood and you could be charged with the possession of an instrument of obeah" (*In the Forests* 6). That Obeah came to be legally defined by the colonial system instead of its practitioners also proves problematic. Simon, born in 1903, is one of the few remaining Caribs on the island (John 27), and refusing to be confined to the small Carib reserve designated as tribal land, he first comes to Roseau and then to Matilda (38). Together, Simon and Matilda "healed and cured and mended" (39), which, as they note, directly confronts "the few white physicians in Dominica" (38–39). Mimicking the feminist postcolonial revising of maps and place-names in the novel, western European epistemology as superior to African and Indigenous knowledge is rejected.

The couple's scrupulous ways of "documenting, of experimenting, and testing" (39) begin to extend beyond Dominica to the other islands of the Caribbean. Demands are made for not only healing and cures but also concoctions for revenge, maiming, death, and even sex and love (40). Conflicting ethics lead to disagreements between Matilda and Simon over whether or not to take money and whether or not to prescribe sex-enhancing drugs without the woman's consent. After she refuses his methods, Simon cruelly beats Matilda. But, after biding her time, she "dropped a fingernail's worth of powder into his morning tea. He disappeared after that and it was generally understood that Matilda had killed him" (43). This violent exchange between Matilda and Simon might be read allegorically as increased tensions, precipitated by colonialism, between those with Indigenous and African heritage on the island.

Matilda and Simon's success in trading medicines, for instance, isolates them from others and occludes them from taking an interest in their newborn, Iris. As a result of parental neglect, Iris is loved too much by the other villagers. At the end of World War II, however, the village persuades Matilda to send Iris to school—a decision that means Iris will work for food and board with a family in Roseau. Mary-Alice, the American nun at the Catholic convent school, places Iris with a Lebanese Christian family. John's inclusion of the Lebanese community marks a critical addition to Caribbean historical fiction, which often overlooks marginalized immigrants from the Middle East such as Syrians and Palestinians. The inclusion of the Lebanese family adds complexity to the notion of persecution; as John notes, the Lebanese were an "oppressed people who had transplanted themselves among other oppressed people" (69). It is "this closed culture that shut out everyone else" that "Mary-Alice was hoping would save Iris: the fact that they only mated among themselves, for life" (69) would exclude the Afra-Carib woman. This is ironic because, presumably, had Iris continued to live "Up There," another endogamic space, she would have been shielded from Western Christian patriarchal society.

Iris thrives in the Fadoul household, until she meets John Baptiste (79). Having glimpsed the wealthy mixed-race man at a wedding rehearsal the day before, Iris confronts him. John writes:

> John Baptiste could not keep himself from looking back at the half-Carib servant girl with the gleaming skin. As he climbed the steps, he was already

anticipating what he would do to her, the bold little slut who had openly propositioned him, who had stood in front of the whole of Roseau, in front of his mother, to put her hands on her hips and shove herself at him with that smile, a smile that no decent girl would have made in public. She would get what she was asking for. (80)

Iris's body physically intervenes in John Baptiste's wedding to Cecile. She literally comes between the two soon-to-be lovers and mocks the legal institution of marriage. Iris's body is political: with her sexualized gestures, she breaks conservative rules, such as those held by John Baptiste's mother, Mrs. Richard. Presenting her body publicly is taboo, as "the bold little slut" (80) is not the marrying kind, so the townsfolk surmise from her gestures. Her attempts to transgress class, social, and racial boundaries by propositioning John Baptiste are met with resignation and disdain. Unsurprisingly, despite being engaged to Cecile Richard, John Baptiste contentedly establishes Iris as his mistress and houses her in a one-room place by the Roseau River.

Much like other women's genealogies discussed in *Matria Redux*, the mothers and daughters here are not connected by a patronym; the women are almost exclusively referred to by mononyms that bear a striking similarity, for instance the name of flowers. Note that only male characters with social status in the novel have surnames, like John Baptiste. Marie-Elena John's erasure of the maternal line emphasizes a History of colonial-patriarchal violence toward women. The erasure of names is doubly relevant for those with slave ancestry like Iris and Lillian, as slaves were stripped of their own names and given names by their masters, essentially marking them as the property they were conceived to be. Mirroring the fact that historical slaves inherited their status through their mother, Lillian is defined by her relationship to her mother and to her grandmother. There is a distinct possibility that the father refuses to acknowledge his illegitimate daughter, for Lillian is only called by her father's name, Baptiste, thrice in the entire novel (164, 167, 169). When she is referred to as Lillian Baptiste, it is by other villagers, which might signal that the community recognizes her, even if her father, Winston Baptiste, or she herself do not (Iris later has a sexual relationship with John Baptiste's son, Winston, which results in Lillian's birth).

Although Amelia Fadoul and her community claim that John Baptiste has "kidnapped and desecrated an innocent child, a daughter, of their household" (86), they are helpless in bringing Iris, delusional that John will marry her, home. Despite his marriage to Cecile and the birth of their twins, John Baptiste maintains his sexual relationship with Iris. The relationship continues uneventfully until a certain Carnival Monday when Iris, masked and participating in the songs and dances, moves next to John Baptiste and obscenely rubs herself against him and his wife (122). Foreshadowed by her audacious public performance during his wedding rehearsal, it is from this point on that the people agree that Iris has lost her mind:

> They agreed someone should have grabbed her and pulled her out of the band, thrown her to the *bande mauvais* people for them to beat her and stone her. But, they decided in hindsight, they must have been in shock, immobilized by seeing what they had never witnessed before in bright sunlight.... [I]t was the shock of her vulgarity that stopped them from intervening.... She [Iris] had gyrated up to her [Cecile], she had shown Cecile what she did with her husband, demonstrated to her the act of fornication. She had writhed up to her, pelvis rocking back and forth, in an out, first one leg up, then the other, and with both her hands pulled off Cecile's mask and then easily ripped off the man's pajama suit Cecile was wearing. Tore the top off, brassiere and all, and then pulled off the bottoms by the elastic, panties and all, Cecile going down hard on the tarmac as they came off. John—wearing Cecile's white lace-and-voile nightgown, the one she had worn on their first honeymoon night—had beat Cecile to the ground. He had instantly fainted at the sight of his wife's swollen, milk-dripping breasts springing out from between Iris's hands. (122)

Iris's hysteria, her transgressive actions combining raw sexuality with blunt violence, exploit an inherent rebelliousness in the masquerade tradition (Honychurch, *The Dominica Story* 168).

Iris brings to light her illicit acts with John Baptiste. A mistress, however, is supposed to keep silent about her sexual life, thus protecting the adulterous man's but also arguably his wife's reputation. When Iris unmasks Cecile, she breaks this unwritten social code. Her flagrant display of sex—sexing Cecile as if she were Baptiste, a man—further complicates her taboo act. That Cecile is dressed as John Baptiste and vice versa means that Iris metaphorically violently copulates with her lover but also her lover's lactating wife, publicly. Iris's actions highlight not only her refusal to accept John Baptiste's new family but the unfairness of life for mistresses. As a girl who sleeps with a married man, she is relegated to a lower social position and, like all women, she is hostage to a rigid gender hierarchy (prescribed by the Christian white patriarchy) in which women's sexuality both within and outside of marriage is shamed. Iris is deemed crazy because she refuses to submit to the rules. The masquerade is already an intended parody of genders, classes, and races, but Iris performs the arbitrariness of identity and gender through her own parody of the parody. Iris's sexuality emasculates John Baptiste. As per tradition, the masquerade requires first and foremost a mask and then an outfit of the opposite gender (John 136). Wearing his wife's white premarital nightgown, a symbol of virginity, innocence, and moral purity, John Baptiste appears womanly and absurd when the scandal occurs; his cowardice manifests when, instead of reprimanding Iris or rescuing his wife, he faints.

Iris is punished: not by John Baptiste, but by Cecile's mother, Mrs. Richard. Amy K. King argues that Mrs. Richard's violence is sanctioned by patriarchal colonialism because she seeks to uphold social, sexual, and racial hierarchies, rationalized further as a "civilizing mission" by white women (197). The "sexual violence she enacts upon Iris's body further solidifies her role as a maternal guardian of imperialist ideals" (A. King 206). Iris is thus repudiated by the local elites and the colonizers, male and female. Mrs. Richard also appeals to the locals by referencing the African codes that demanded "a bloodletting, a sacrifice" (John 124) for Iris's insolence and her desecration of the social hierarchies. Mrs. Richard, along with her cook and housekeeper, therefore severely beat Iris. Iris, as expected of Caribs, takes "her blows in silence" (126), but after Mrs. Richard takes a bottle from her purse, Iris's screams begin.

John writes:

> In the one-room house, Mrs. Richard found what she needed, Iris's enamel chamber pot. It was a graceful movement, a single, fluid sweep of arm that came from high and went down low to break the bottle near the floor. Her whole body swung down, following her arm, and then she rose up in an easy pivot to align herself with the place where Iris lay on her bride's gift bed, knees pinned down to the sides of her chest. And then it stopped being graceful as Mrs. Richard planted the jagged end of the bottle as far up into Iris as her hand would go. And then again, and then again. Until finally her hand came out empty, covered with blood midway to her elbow. (127)

Sexual assault against women by women is rare in Caribbean historical fiction.[2] In this scene, John defies reader expectations—in which one is more accustomed to violence against women by men, as in Julia Alvarez's *In the Time of the Butterflies* (1994), and violence by women against men, typically in a slave-overseer relationship, such as Kitty murdering her rapist in Andrea Levy's *The Long Song* (2010). In this case, the female violence is predicated on sexual transgressions and social taboo.

After Iris's shocking behavior at the masquerade, Mrs. Richard takes it upon herself to seek justice and revenge. Cracking the glass against the chamber pot reinforces the idea that bodily fluids are not to be made public, and when they are, it is humiliating, as one sees earlier in the novel with Cecile's lactating breasts. In exacting her revenge, Mrs. Richard sets out to degrade Iris, not to mention scar and possibly murder her. Mrs. Richard violently rapes Iris in order to assert her power and to disfigure the alleged hypersexual, vulgar Carib African body that has led to Iris's downfall. Although Amy King argues that Mrs. Richard "is not appropriating a masculine sexuality through her actions against Iris . . . but enforcing what society deems appropriate for male and female roles according to their class" (210), not to mention race, it is still possible to read Mrs. Richard as such because the bottle, a phallic symbol, rapes Iris. The female-to-female penetration with the bottle as penis suggests the superfluous male sex. Like her daughter and son-in-law's swapping of clothes and genders at the masquerade and Iris's sexual encounter with Cecile there, in which she takes on the stereotypical role of the heterosexual male lover, when Mrs. Richard penetrates Iris, she takes on the role of John Baptiste. In contradistinction to her impotent son-in-law, Mrs. Richard asserts her virility. The Coke bottle, a symbol of the American dream, capitalism, leisure, and pleasure, perhaps indicating that American culture is replacing British culture, nevertheless reminds Iris that she overstepped her boundaries. As an insignificant teenage mistress, Iris has aimed too high.

One presumes that Mrs. Richard's leaving the broken bottle inside her victim warns Iris that she is not in America; she is a poor, uneducated Afra-Carib girl who lives as a mistress in a small shack; there is no social mobility, but there are broken chamber pots and bottles—broken dreams—which Iris realizes too late. In violating Iris's vagina, Mrs. Richard attempts to disarm Iris of her power, effectively "unvoic[ing] the victim" (Carole Sweeney, qtd. in A. King 209). With a damaged womb, she will no longer exert power over John Baptiste. More than a physical assault, Iris is punished for trying to break Roseau's social structures, and for this she is "almost destroyed" (Down 237). Adding to the maternal imagery of the scene, Mrs. Richard and her servants leave Iris in a fetal position, meant, ironically, to assist with conception; a position that, after sexual intercourse with John Baptiste, Iris had refused to take.

The novel picks up again on a dark *j'ouvert* morning (John 136), with the presence of the *bandes mauvais* on the roads, signaling the commencement of another year's masquerade. Meanwhile, Matilda has spent the previous twelve months painstakingly caring for her daughter. Although Matilda and "Up There" provide respite from the harsh social codes of Roseau, a patriarchal Christian colonial society, Iris cannot stay in her mother's world/womb. Her spatial movements from "Up There" to Roseau back to "Up There" and then once more to Roseau suggest her shift from the maternal to the paternal, back to the maternal, and then a final return to the paternal realm and the law of the colonial Father, which, like her mother before her, finally kills her. Such traversing between matriarchal and patriarchal worlds leaves Iris without a space of her own; caught between both locations and belonging fully to neither, she remains on the fringes of both worlds—worldless/wordless, she becomes a hysteric.

That masculinity is primarily determined not by the men in the novel but by the women is evident, too, at the next masquerade. John Baptiste's reputation as a womanizer at the heart of a sexual scandal is secured by the *chantuelles*, and it earns him enough respect to run with the Newton *bande mauvais*, a group of masked men and women who threaten and intimidate others. Spectators out on verandas eagerly watch for Baptiste to come down King George V Street (George V ruled Britain from 1910 to 1936). Mrs. Richard views the masquerade as an opportunity for "her coward of a son-in-law" (John 145) to prove his masculinity and redeem himself. Part spectacle and a demonstration of prowess, the masquerade offers John Baptiste a chance to earn back his family's respect. Mrs. Richard takes on a masculine role, a patriarchal role, again, however, when her son-in-law fails to be violent and courageous. John writes, "[I]f he did not prove himself today, act like a man this time, she would go down there and use her own hands to beat him, and then she would go to the bishop, to the pope if necessary, and get the marriage annulled" (145). That Mrs. Richard's definition of marriage rests on such specific gender roles, however, is undermined by her own admission that she will, if necessary, take on the traditional role of her family's patriarch (offering a reversal of the swapped gender roles discussed in chapter 6 in Andrea O'Reilly Herrera's *The Pearl of the Antilles*). Thus, while gender norms and expectations may be constructed, Mrs. Richard's logic suggests that certain constructs, those that clearly attempt to delineate masculinity from femininity, and by default men from women, are preferable.

Both Iris and John Baptiste, if not every character in the novel, to a certain extent disrupt traditional gender norms, which angers Mrs. Richard. Her anger stems from fear, a fear that she, and her family, will lose privilege and power. If norms pertaining to sexuality can change, if young, unmarried half-Carib women with "gleaming skin" can force their bodies into the public domain, a way of staking territory—occupying and taking up space—and putting themselves on the social map, then other identity markers such as race and class are also subject to change. Mrs. Richard's subscription to the dominant European Christian ideology implemented at the time of colonialism is at risk of being toppled by a young, unmarried Black woman's body. This explains why the mother-in-law is desperate for John Baptiste to retain his position and rebalance the sexual-social sphere.

John Baptiste's showboating initially impresses those around him. All seems to be in order until another band is spotted on the street indicating an inevitable "clash." Hearkening back to his fainting spell when Iris attacked Cecile, this time, he urinates and sobs. The ensuing conflict, narrated by two British colonial administrators invited to attend the masquerade by Mrs. Richard, adds to readerly distance. Like the spectators on the balcony, and the British colonialists, there is a strict spatial delineation between those on the street and those literally, many of whom are also socially, above them. Mrs. Richard, accompanied and supported by British colonialism, physically looks down on her son-in-law as the violence erupts. The colonialists explain that there is an unmistakable African warrior feel to this masquerade, with masks, posturing, and gesturing signaling ties to several different African cultures from across the continent (John 140). That it is the British who are the authorities in African ways and cultures is ironic. Thus, the clash is in one sense between Dominicans struggling to maintain strong ties to Africa and their African roots versus those Dominicans striving for British assimilation and modernization. As Mrs. Richard coolly states, "We here in the West Indies, we are not Africans" (145), and it is not lost on the reader that the struggle plays itself out on a street named for a dead British monarch. The struggle is also, however, between maternal and paternal authority.

As one administrator notes, "One variation, an adaptation of significant note . . . is the fact that here [in Dominica], unlike in Africa, women also perform masquerades, even the masks imbued with the most authority and power" (149). The most dangerous participant emerges wearing such a mask:

> [It consisted of] antelope horns . . . [and] warthog tusks sprouting from crocodile jaws that jutted far out. It was a masquerade that only came out to direct strong magic against those who had broken the law, perpetrated a taboo. . . . The thing looked as if it would jump up into the very sky. It raged against the three sets of rope noosed around its head and torso, tethered to the street only by the effort of three struggling masked beings with whips. (147)

The allusion to historical slavery manifests in the ropes and chains as the masked participant struggles to break free. The mask also suggests that the legacy of slavery continues in contemporary Dominica.

Paralyzed by fear and abandoned by his fellow Newton *bande mauvais* members, John Baptiste faces the warrior. Despite competing claims from eyewitnesses, there is a general consensus that

> the masquerade had levitated, then had flown around John Baptiste. . . . [T]he thing that flew three times around John Baptiste, was not a human being, because not only did it fly in a circle at the level of his head, it also clearly had no limbs, no arms, no legs. And it emitted a sound, the high pitch of which would never be made by a human voice. And the statements all agreed, the thing never touched him. (148)

According to the people, the "Flying Masquerade" is Matilda retaliating against Mrs. Richard's rape and beating of Iris and John Baptiste's mistreatment of her daughter. Yet, according to the coroner's report, John Baptiste dies of a heart attack (158). The tensions within Dominican society are expressed in the masquerade. Matilda, the maternal, conflicts with John Baptiste, the paternal. The "clash" is between Obeah and Christianity, between women and men, and between *hystérie* and History.

Matilda's hanging is a result of Mrs. Richard's insistence that John Baptiste was not a coward, thus avoiding bringing further dishonor and shame to her family. Obliging Mrs. Richard, the police chief agrees to investigate Matilda, but the consequences are disastrous. The villagers from "Up There" wage war on the officers, resulting in multiple injuries and deaths on both sides. Furthermore, when the police chief finds human remains, signaling mass murders by poisoning (231), Matilda confesses. Matilda, however, is neither the murderer the authorities claim her to be nor a practitioner of the African religious tradition, "where the sacrifice of a human being to placate an irate god was simply the correct thing to do" (85), as Teddy surmises. Instead, Lillian learns that Matilda presided as a magistrate, judging over and administering justice to her maroon society, including determining the death penalty if necessary, an irony not lost on the reader when Matilda is sentenced to death by Dominica's patriarchal, colonial society.

Lillian's insistence that Matilda's power as her ancestor directly influences her life is one of the reasons that Lillian's sanity is repeatedly questioned by others, including Teddy. When confronting such injustice, however, "[o]ften there is a price to pay, and frequently voicing feminine issues has the potential to destroy subject-hood, sending the author's heroine into an abyss of insanity from which she cannot extract herself" (Orlando 14). One sees such a decline in Lillian: she envisions the grandmother she never knew, shackled like a slave and compelling her to return to Dominica. Lillian must rewrite and re-right the history of her maternal kin, and by extension her island. John states, "It was not unusual or superstitious for her [Lillian] to believe that in death she would be able to speak with her mother and her grandmother: it was more than a fundamental tenet of her faith, it was logical" (297). Lillian thus anticipates her life being turned into song—continuing her female matrilineage, "she wanted her own song, it was her birthright. A *chanté mas* to guarantee her place in history, alongside her grandmother and her mother" (John 298). Exposing the paradoxical aspects of *chanté mas* as revealing a "social scandal" and "a piece of injustice" (Honychurch, *The Dominica Story* 168), Lillian, hearing Iris's and Matilda's voices and feeling their strong ancestral presence, makes her way "Up There," back to her matria.

Unburnable emphasizes that crucial to this counterhistory is the revival of Afra-Caribbean ritual and folklore evident when Lillian becomes a *soucouyant*, which we can read as a typical Freudian castrating figure. In her article "The Woman That Turned into a Ball of Fire and Whipped across the Sky at Night: Recreating History and Memory in the Diaspora," María Alonso Alonso provides important context:

> Mythographically speaking, a *soucouyant* . . . usually represents marginal women as it is commonly considered to be a female who looks like an old person and lives an apparently ordinary life in the outskirts of a city or village. But at nights, this woman turns into a ball of fire and travels across the sky to suck the blood of her victims while they sleep. . . . In diasporic literature, the figure of the *soucouyant* normally emerges in relation to women that carry some kind of cultural or familial burden. This misfortune usually reduces them to being alienated characters, rejected by society and pushed into the background. In many cases, we find examples of this social repudiation under the shape or rumours that work in many cases as the carrier of prejudices against marginal women from generation to generation. (16)

Replicating both the *soucouyant*'s and her Carib ancestors' actions, Lillian flies from the clifftop.

Lillian's *hystérie*, the madwoman's voice, disrupts and contradicts both the patriarchal Afra-Caribbean context (*chanté mas*, oral) and the patriarchal colonial context (official History, written). Lillian embodies that which literary and historiographic traditions have already claimed her and her maternal kin to be. The power in such an undertaking, this shedding of skin, is a "liberating madness" (Cooper 84). As if speaking about herself, Lillian realizes, "My mother wasn't crazy. She was destroyed" (John 261). Preparing for death, Lillian intuits that she is "slipping away back," submerging "into women's territory or, deeper still, back to" the mythic time and space of her maternal ancestors, her matria (205). The daughter's returning to and revising of her Afra-Caribbean past reappropriates the mother-island who has been vilified, hystericized, and silenced; thus, she awakens "the sleeping language of volcanoes" (Cezair-Thompson 26) and remaps the maternal future through the maternal past.

CONCLUSION
Matria Redux

A generation of pan-Caribbean women writers emerged in the 1980s whose work was antipatriarchal and postcolonial. *Matria Redux: Caribbean Women Novelize the Past* demonstrates that these writers returned to the maternal past and depicted similar matria constructs. In identifying and defining matria as a recuperation of mother-daughter bonds in an imaginary motherland, *Matria Redux* provides a new way of reading Caribbean women's historical fiction. Advancing a postcolonial-psychoanalytic feminist framework, the book engages with and expands existent critical conversations and recent interventions in the genre (e.g., Francis, Halloran, Machado Sáez, Praeger, Rody). The woman-authored Caribbean historical novels assessed challenge the predominantly masculinist literary lineage and parameters of the genre as well as narratives of the region and its developments, such as slavery, colonialism, revolution, and imperialism. My close readings of four late twentieth-century and four early twenty-first-century historical novels reveal matria as these works' central conceit.

In part I: Mythologizing Matria, matria manifests as a desire to restore the broken link between enslaved mothers and daughters. The imagining of an Afra-Caribbean past and maternal genealogy critically informs these neo-slavery novels. For Dionne Brand, the Afra-Caribbean mother, Marie Ursule, serves as the literal and metaphorical foundation for not only *At the Full and Change of the Moon* specifically but also the Caribbean historical novel more generally. Brand's novel repurposes arborescent and rhizomatic root theory so that matria mythologizes the Afra-Caribbean mother and radically disrupts patriarchal, colonial conceptions of family and lineage. Andrea Levy, meanwhile, envisions matria through the power of the enslaved woman's voice. July, the enslaved heroine in *The Long Song*, deliberately interrupts, parodies, and rejects (M)aster narratives. The novel's Afra-Caribbean polyphonic voice alerts us to the constructed nature of texts and that the framing of narrative authority, despite being multilayered, remains predominantly defined and confined by masculine parameters.

Part II: Decolonizing Matria captures postcolonial daughters searching for mother-lands and mother-tongues. Updating the classic bildungsroman, these novels, set in the mid-twentieth century, provide insight into the young Caribbean woman's experiences of colonialism and patriarchy. The daughter's break from her colonized mother serves as an allegory for gaining national independence. For example, Jan Lowe Shinebourne's *The Last English Plantation* depicts a critical juncture in the Indo-Chinese protagonist's life: June struggles to forge her own identity while Guyana seeks its independence from Britain. June reappropriates the derogatory term "coolie" as a means to honor her Indo-Chinese maternal past, and she envisions matria in anticolonial, antipatriarchal terms for herself and her nation. In Judith Ortiz Cofer's *The Meaning of Consuelo*, however, the titular heroine rejects the patriarchal, conservative discourses surrounding womanhood and sexuality espoused by her family and her island, Puerto Rico. Guided by the novel's transgressive figures, Consuelo seeks a new language and space in which to express herself: she imagines matria not as returning to Puerto Rico's colonial past but as envisioning a future in which Puerto Rican women and other marginalized people might live their genders and sexualities freely.

These postcolonial narratives of deterritorialization resonate with the narratives of politicization or political awakening found in part III: Revolutionizing Matria. Centralizing women's lives and voices, these works provide powerful counternarratives to romanticized and/or male-dominated accounts of historical events, particularly dictatorships and revolutions. The result is that matria, conceived as an antinationalistic maternal space that brings mothers and daughters together, provides the means to heal from the violence of the past. For example, Edwidge Danticat's novel *The Farming of Bones* relays a Haitian woman fleeing the Dominican Republic during the infamous Parsley Massacre of Rafael Leónidas Trujillo's regime. At the novel's end, Danticat's heroine, Amabelle, rejects patriarchal, anti-Black nationalism and considers the Massacre River, which flows between Haiti and the Dominican Republic, the appropriate maternal site for her rebirth. In *The Pearl of the Antilles*, Andrea O'Reilly Herrera depicts the lead-up to and aftermath of the Cuban Revolution. The novel's matria rejects the incestuous patriarchal family and nation in favor of a matrilineage. Margarita's American daughter Lilly plays a key role in restoring the broken bond between mothers and daughters by relaying her hitherto unknown family herstory. The daughter protagonist's recognition and attempt to reconcile with trauma is a dominant theme throughout *Matria Redux*.

Caribbean women writers' reimagination and reinvention of History is the focus of the final section, part IV: Returning Matria. Matria is distinctly envisioned by authors Paule Marshall and Marie-Elena John as a Caribbean daughter's homecoming. Marshall's *Praisesong for the Widow* deftly takes on the maternal past when her protagonist, Avey, after much denial and repudiation, realizes that to be spiritually whole she must relearn and reconnect with her Afra-Caribbean ancestry. Maternal figures guide Avey on her spiritual journey so that by the novel's end, she willingly becomes a repository of cultural memory for her grandchildren in Tatem, South Carolina. The daughter's search for her maternal ancestors is also taken up in John's *Unburnable*. Lillian's mother and grandmother have been slandered in both Dominica's oral tradition (Afro-Caribbean folk) and written record (white colonizers). John's text sees Lillian attempt to piece together the lives of her foremothers and exonerate them of their alleged crimes and transgressions. In solidarity with the women in her family, Lillian becomes the fierce mythic figure of the *soucouyant* and dies by suicide. In bringing three women's tragic fates together, the novel's matria challenges the racist and sexist discursive practices from which women have little means of escaping.

As an intersection of maternal space and maternal time, matria takes several forms, as the pre- and postmillennium novels' engagement with matrilineage, ancestors, nonhistory, voice(lessness), trauma, revolution, and myth demonstrates. Although women's experiences of violence, migration, and loss are also consistent motifs in each novel, for the most part, premillennium novels conclude cautiously hopeful. Bola stands in the ocean remembering her mother and calling to her children, June sits with her mother watching the lights of Diwali spread across the village, Amabelle swims in the Massacre River at dawn, and Avey repeats the story of the Ibos to her grandchildren. O'Reilly Herrera's novel, meanwhile, usefully serves as an intermediary text because it was published in 2001, and despite the hardships her Cuban foremothers endured, Lilly manages to piece together her Cuban matrilineage and renew her relationship with her mother, Margarita. In the other postmillennium novels, however, optimism toward the Caribbean woman's future dwindles. July's kidnapped daughter remains unknown to her, Consuelo boards a plane departing the island, and Lillian commits suicide. This shift in more recent writing suggests that the twenty-first century has not delivered on its promise to combat the legacy of trauma and slavery, which continues to haunt the region and detrimentally affect women. For although I have suggested that Brand's novel ends with Bola happily engaging with her maternal past and present, her future descendants both in the region and in the diaspora have difficult, troubled lives.

For writers like Brand, Shinebourne, O'Reilly Herrera, and Marshall, the centralizing of a maternal ancestor further necessitates a reckoning with and recognition of the traumas of History, notably slavery. These novels provide daughter figures with a maternal history and matrilineage that has traditionally been either absent or denigrated in historiography and literature. In repositioning the Caribbean foremother, the matrias depicted reconceive antipatriarchal, postcolonial futures for women in the region. While also acknowledging the importance of maternal figures, Levy, Ortiz Cofer, Danticat, and John nevertheless emphasize that the power of patriarchy, colonial History, and nationalism cannot be underestimated. These authors make readers aware of the irreparable violence committed against women while gesturing toward potential subversive paths, however limited. A postcolonial feminist Caribbean space in which mothers and daughters live physically and psychically free from patriarchal-imperial brutality, borders, and prescriptive norms thus defines these matrias. To this extent, matria repeatedly comes to be defined by in-betweenness, an intra-uterine space between island and diaspora, between fact and fiction.

Indebted to pioneering works like Marie Vieux-Chauvet's *Dance on the Volcano* and Sylvia Wynter's *The Hills of Hebron*, Caribbean women writers since the 1980s have radically transformed the historical novel genre. Whether recounting tales of maternal survival (Levy and Danticat), reclaiming repressed maternal ancestors (Shinebourne and Marshall), rewriting maligned foremothers (Brand and John), or relaying maternal loss (O'Reilly Herrera and Ortiz Cofer), these texts strongly suggest that reimagining the future for Caribbean daughters can only be accomplished by returning to their maternal pasts. The historical novel therefore provides the Caribbean woman writer with the ability to define fiction and history differently, so she can "dance out of her own mother's womb" (Lara 57). *Matria Redux*'s reframing of matria as a postcolonial, psychoanalytic strategy therefore envisions, by returning to history—that metaphorical volcano—alternative feminist fictions, futures, and Caribbeans.

NOTES

INTRODUCTION: EX MATRIA

1. A notable exception is scholarship on Jamaica Kincaid's writing.

2. See also Celia Brickman's *Race in Psychoanalysis: Aboriginal Populations in the Mind*.

3. Throughout this work, I often capitalize words like Father, History, and Master to emphasize their symbolic omnipotence in a patriarchal, colonial society and the genre's patriarchal, colonial roots. I deliberately link common phrases from the historical novel lexicon, for example master texts, master discourses, or master narratives, with the legacy of slavery and masters owning slaves.

4. Donette Francis convincingly shows that after the Haitian Revolution, the Black Father held symbolic power in Haiti (2).

5. See Elena Machado Sáez's work *Market Aesthetics* for an extended analysis.

6. Machado Sáez adds: "One distinction from the experience of the Caribbean exile generation is the role that academic and feminist presses of the 1980s played in the incorporation of Caribbean diasporic writing by women into ethnic canons" (9). Her study also examines how, contrary to Vivian Nun Halloran's stance, market demands are compatible with the pedagogical and ethical positions taken by postcolonial, diasporic historical novelists: "Entertainment is one facet of market demands, but there are also academic markets for contextualization. Historical fiction is the product of a complex negotiation between the demands to entertain and to teach, to simplify and to complicate, to make history both palatable and challenging" (26).

7. To be fair, Lukács argues for a fictional middle-of-the-road type, like Scott's protagonist, as preferable to an atypical hero type, but the main backdrop for the action is certainly performed by men of fictional and/or historical importance. Diana Wallace, among others, has since argued for an alternative British genealogy that precedes Scott and privileges women's lives, for instance Sophia Lee's *The Recess; or, A Tale of Other Times* (1783).

8. Nana Wilson-Tagoe traces the historical novel in English; studies of the origins of the twentieth-century historical novel in the Francophone and Hispanophone Caribbean tend to privilege novels by Martinican writer Édouard Glissant and Cuban writer Alejo Carpentier, respectively.

9. Machado Sáez and Francis are responding primarily to David Scott's work on romance and tragedy in *Conscripts of Modernity: The Tragedy of Colonial Enlightenment* (2004).

10. Rody is citing from Kristeva's article "Women's Time."

11. Patricia Hill Collins coined the term "othermothers" to refer specifically to nonbiological Black mothers (329), but the term also recognizes woman-centered kinship, families, and communities, or networks.

12. Unlike some criticism on the Caribbean historical novel, for example Seymour Menton's *Latin America's New Historical Novel* (1993), which considers the Dominican Republic, Puerto Rico, and Cuba "as part of a discussion of the historical novel of Latin America" (Barker 13), I examine novels set across the region. Although concentrating on works written in English, this study also references established novels written in French and Spanish but translated into English, for instance Vieux-Chauvet's *Danse sur la volcan*.

13. These demarcations are not intended to be rigid; some novels, such as Cliff's *No Telephone to Heaven* or Brand's *At the Full and Change of the Moon*, adhere to more than one category.

AFRICA'S DAUGHTERS: THE NEO-SLAVERY NOVEL'S CARIBBEAN MATERNAL GENEALOGY

1. Edgell's heroine transitions from enslavement to slave owner, joining another sub-branch of contemporary women's neo-slavery writing; instead of centralizing the Afra-Caribbean enslaved woman, these texts focus on women as slave owners, for instance Esmeralda Santiago's *Conquistadora* (2011).

2. Vint quotes from A. Timothy Spaulding's *Re-forming the Past: History, the Fantastic, and the Postmodern Slave Narrative*.

CHAPTER 1: MATERNAL GENEALOGIES AND THE LEGACY OF NONHISTORY IN DIONNE BRAND'S *AT THE FULL AND CHANGE OF THE MOON*

1. In other exploratory seminar papers, I have compared *At the Full and Change of the Moon*'s family tree with the matrilineal trees found in Schwarz-Bart's *Pluie et vent sur Télumée Miracle* and Jenny Jaeckel's *House of Rougeaux* (2018).

2. Calling Brand's approach a "tidal poetics," Evans argues that "[w]hereas Glissant and [Antonio] Benítez-Rojo use the concept of fluidity as the basis for an articulation of Caribbean cultural identity, and as a framework for new configurations of community, I propose that in Brand's work the Utopian potential of liquid imagery is overshadowed by the association of water—in a Caribbean context—with deprivation and suffering" (3).

3. Nothing is known of the youngest ancestor except that she is born in 1987 and is "the girl who was flooded in everything" (Brand, *At the Full* n.p.).

4. The notion of country, patria, is embedded in the word "patriarchy," which promotes male privilege, genealogies, and superiority.

5. Kristeva's concept of women's time is in reference to Europe specifically, but its broader arguments resonate beyond Western thinking.

NOTES

CHAPTER 2: VOICE, VIOLENCE, AND MASCULINE SUFFOCATION IN ANDREA LEVY'S *THE LONG SONG*

1. See the video with Levy for the TV Book Club, YouTube, January 29, 2011, https://www.youtube.com/watch?v=7CSRN_qO2jM.

2. This alludes to Walter Scott's acclaimed historical novel *Waverley; or, 'Tis Sixty Years Since* (1814), which for many scholars such as Georg Lukács set the standard of sixty years as the ideal distance between an author's publication of a novel and the novel's historical setting. July's pamphlet is published in 1898.

DISPOSSESSED DAUGHTERS: SEARCHING FOR CARIBBEAN MOTHER-LAND/TONGUE

1. Suriname (Dutch Guiana) remained under Dutch control until its independence in 1975, while French Guiana remains an overseas department of France (Hyles 7).

2. In 1964, Forbes Burnham became prime minister and enacted the National Security Act giving police the power to search, seize, and arrest anyone virtually at will. His political leanings were leftist and pro-African, and he developed strong relations with Cuba and other communist countries. He declared Guyana a cooperative republic, banning imports and taking state ownership over the private sector. Oonya Kempadoo's *Buxton Spice* revisits Guyana's violent postindependence past.

3. Until the late 1960s, Puerto Ricans in the United States wrote mostly in Spanish. Consider Allison Fagan's thoughts on *The Meaning of Consuelo*: "The proliferation of translations on this very first page signals Cofer's (and the narrator's) desire to accommodate English-monolingual readers, to make them 'insiders' even as 'outsiders' are being defined. But even when writers like Cofer work to make their texts linguistically accessible, publishers can amplify that accessibility by appending glossaries to texts that did not originally include them. In the case of *The Meaning of Consuelo*, the Farrar, Straus and Giroux edition, published in 2003, does not contain a glossary, while the Blue Streak series edition published by Beacon Press in 2004 does.... Given that most of the Spanish in Cofer's work is easily understandable in context, or directly translated by the narrator, this added attempt to make the Spanish as clear as possible shows that even when authors believe they are being most accommodating, publishers have a different view" (62).

CHAPTER 4: *MATRIZ*, TRANSGRESSIVE SEXUALITY, AND NATIONAL AMBIGUITY IN JUDITH ORTIZ COFER'S *THE MEANING OF CONSUELO*

1. Moreno is quoting Jorge Duany, *The Puerto Rican Nation on the Move*, 24.

2. In the first in-depth study comparing Puerto Rican women's writing from the island and from the diaspora, Moreno claims that discovering the commonalities and differences between island and diaspora communities is now of interest and that *la gran familia* "continues to inform both," with the latter using it as "a strategy to reclaim its kinship ties to the greater Puerto Rican family" (*Family Matters* 3).

3. Rosamond King is quoting, first, from Yasmin Tambiah, "Creating (Im)moral Citizens: Gender, Sexuality and Lawmaking in Trinidad and Tobago, 1986" (2009), and second, from Susan Harewood, "Transnational Soca Performances: Gendered Re-Narrations of Caribbean Nationalism" (2006).

POLITICIZED MOTHERS: DREAMING THE MATRIA

1. Danticat also narrated the massacre in an earlier short story called "1937."
2. Unlike Lima, who deems Collins's *Angel* and Cliff's *No Telephone to Heaven* bildungsromane, I prefer to read these texts, and others like Alvarez's *In the Time of the Butterflies*, in relation to the military regimes the protagonists experience as adults.
3. Consider Merle Collins's foreword to the 2011 edition of *Angel* (the novel spans Doodsie's and Angel's, mother's and daughter's, experiences of the turbulent years prior to and after Grenada's fight for autonomy from Britain). Collins recalls that following independence in 1974, Grenada's political troubles continued, and after the "October 19th, 1983 collapse of Grenada's attempt at a revolutionary government and the October 25th invasion of the country by the United States of America" (5), she left for the United States. Collins has recently reflected that at the time of writing the novel in the 1980s, she was too close to her subject; the text's voices were "too emotional" and her "own emotions were too involved" (6–7). Collins's foreword proposes that when there is more historical time and distance between the writer and her past, more revolutionary novels will appear.

CHAPTER 5: "MOTHER OF THE RIVERS": MATERNAL TROPES IN EDWIDGE DANTICAT'S *THE FARMING OF BONES*

1. An English translation of Vieux-Chauvet's trilogy *Amour, Colère, Folie* (*Love, Anger, Madness*) was published with an introduction by Danticat in 2009. The political nature of Vieux-Chauvet's work forced her to live in exile.
2. Shemak notes that Alvarez's novel, by focusing on "the white elite[,] . . . ignores class and racial divisions within the nation"—a nation "with a majority mulatto population" (84). See also my work on Fela, the novel's Afra-Dominican servant, spirit medium, and storyteller, in "Unauthorized Storytelling: Reevaluating Racial Politics in Julia Alvarez's *In the Time of the Butterflies*."
3. Shemak quotes from, first, Marilyn Houlberg, "Magique Marasa: The Ritual Cosmos of Twins and Other Sacred Children," and second, VèVè A. Clark, "Developing Diaspora Literacy and *Marasa* Consciousness."
4. The somewhat optimistic ending is at odds with Haiti's political reality at this time. For although Trujillo was assassinated in 1961, Haiti would suffer greatly under the dictators François Duvalier ("Papa Doc") and his son, Jean-Claude Duvalier ("Baby Doc") until the late 1980s, as evidenced in Danticat's novel *Breath, Eyes, Memory*. It is worth mentioning that the United States backed the military dictatorships of the Duvaliers (S. A. J. Alexander, "M/othering the Nation" 378).

CHAPTER 6: REVOLUTIONARY HERSTORY AND MARTIAL/ MARITAL LAW IN ANDREA O'REILLY HERRERA'S *THE PEARL OF THE ANTILLES*

1. O'Reilly Herrera's play *Tres Flores*, based on her novel, appeared in 2015.

ANCESTRAL MOTHERS: THE CARIBBEAN DAUGHTER'S HOMECOMING

1. Rowley contends that "matriarchy" and "matrifocality" are closely related terms, but they are not interchangeable: "'Matriarchy'... transcends notions of kinship, and addresses not only the familial centrality of women, but also a centrality that extends to the ideological and institutional ordering of social organization" (24). Homogeneous images of the "strong Caribbean matriarch" (22) and the "matrifolk (Afro-Caribbean, low-income, single female heads of household)... have traditionally dominated" Caribbean discourses (29).

2. A notable premillennium exception is Cliff's character Clare Savage, who, in *No Telephone to Heaven* (1987), dies fighting for social justice in Jamaica.

3. Guyanese works by Beryl Gilroy and Ryhaan Shah gesture toward a third alternative. In Gilroy's *Gather the Faces* (1996) and Shah's *A Silent Life*, the Guyanese heroine leaves for the mother country, namely Britain, but returns later in life to work toward decolonization and psychic healing in the region.

CHAPTER 8: CARTOGRAPHY, *HYSTÉRIE*, AND MATRILINEAGE IN MARIE-ELENA JOHN'S *UNBURNABLE*

1. From here on I refer to Matilda's settlement as simply "Up There."

2. Two other notable Caribbean women's fictions featuring sexual violence against women by women include Ada Quayle's *The Mistress* and Edwidge Danticat's *Breath, Eyes, Memory*: in both examples, the mother performs a virginity test on her daughter, which for all intents and purposes constitutes rape.

WORKS CITED

Alao, Folashade. "'Will You Come and Follow Me?' Walking Literacy and Paule Marshall's *Praisesong for the Widow*." *Palimpsest: A Journal on Women, Gender, and the Black International*, vol. 1, no. 4, 2015, pp. 51–71.
Alexander, M. Jacqui. *Pedagogies of Crossing: Meditations on Feminism, Sexual Politics, Memory, and the Sacred*. Duke UP, 2005.
Alexander, Robert J., with Eldon M. Parker. *A History of Organized Labor in the English-Speaking West Indies*. Praeger, 2004.
Alexander, Simone A. James. *Mother Imagery in the Novels of Afro-Caribbean Women*. U of Missouri P, 2001.
Alexander, Simone A. James. "M/othering the Nation: Women's Bodies as Nationalist Trope in Edwidge Danticat's *Breath, Eyes, Memory*." *African American Review*, vol. 44, no. 3, Fall 2011, pp. 373–90.
Alexander, Simone A. James. "M/Otherly Guise or Guide? Theorizing Jamaica Kincaid's 'Girl.'" *Feminist and Critical Perspectives on Caribbean Mothering*, edited by Dorsía Smith Silva and Simone A. James Alexander, Africa World Press, 2013, pp. 211–24.
Aljoe, Nicole N. "Caribbean Slave Narratives: Creole in Form and Genre." *Anthurium: A Caribbean Studies Journal*, vol. 2, no. 1, 2004, pp. 1–15.
Allfrey, Phyllis Shand. *The Orchid House*. 1953. Rutgers UP, 1996.
Alonso Alonso, María. "'The Woman That Turned into a Ball of Fire and Whipped across the Sky at Night: Recreating History and Memory in the Diaspora." *Journal of English Studies*, vol. 9, no. 13, May 2011, 13–28.
Alvarez, Julia. *In the Time of the Butterflies*. Plume, 1994.
Alvarez-Borland, Isabel. "Displacements and Autobiography in Cuban-American Fiction." *World Literature Today*, vol. 68, no. 1, Winter 1994, pp. 43–49.
Anderlini-D'Onofrio, Serena. "Is Feminism Realism Possible? A Theory of Labial Eros and Mimesis." *Journal of Gender Studies*, vol. 8, no. 2, 1999, pp. 159–80.
Arnold, Josephine V. "Guyanese Identities." *A History of Literature in the Caribbean*. Vol. 2: *English- and Dutch-Speaking Regions*, edited by A. James Arnold, John Benjamins Publishing, 2001, pp. 97–110.
Ashie-Nikoi, Edwina. *Beating the Pen on the Drum: A Socio-Cultural History of Carriacou, Grenada, 1750–1920*. 2007. New York University, PhD dissertation.

Ashworth, Rebecca. "Writing Gender, Re-Writing Nation: *Wide Sargasso Sea, Annie John, Jane and Louisa Will Soon Come Home,* and *Myal.*" *The Routledge Companion to Anglophone Caribbean Literature,* edited by Michael A. Bucknor and Alison Donnell, Routledge, 2011, pp. 209–17.

Bailey, Carol. "Destabilising Caribbean Critical Orthodoxies: Interrogating Orality in Marie-Elena John's *Unburnable.*" *Caribbean Quarterly,* vol. 59, no. 1, March 2013, pp. 31–49.

Baksh, Anita. "Breaking with Tradition: Hybridity, Identity and Resistance in Indo-Caribbean Women's Writing." *Bindi: The Multifaceted Lives of Indo-Caribbean Women,* edited by Rosanne Kanhai, U of the West Indies P, 2011, pp. 208–24.

Baksh-Soodeen, Rawwida. "Issues of Difference in Contemporary Caribbean Feminism." *Feminist Review,* vol. 59, no. 1, June 1998, pp. 74–85.

Barker, Carrie K. *Genealogy and Decolonization: The Historical Novel of the Twentieth-Century Caribbean.* 2007. New York University, PhD dissertation.

Baxter, Jeannette. "Exquisite Corpse: Un/dressing History in *Fruit of the Lemon / The Long Song.*" *Andrea Levy: Contemporary Critical Perspectives,* edited by Jeannette Baxter and David James, Bloomsbury, 2014, pp. 79–94.

Behind the Name. S.v. "Mary." https://www.behindthename.com/name/mary.

Belgrave, Valerie. *Ti Marie.* 1988. iUniverse, 2007.

Bellamy, Maria Rice. *Bridges to Memory: Postmemory in Contemporary Ethnic American Women's Fiction.* U of Virginia P, 2016.

Benstock, Shari. "Expatriate Modernism: Writing on the Cultural Rim." *Women's Writing in Exile,* edited by Mary Lynn Broe and Angela Ingram, U of North Carolina P, 1989, pp. 19–40.

Bergner, Gwen. "Myths of Masculinity: The Oedipus Complex and Douglass's 1845 Narrative." *The Psychoanalysis of Race,* edited by Christopher Lane, Columbia UP, 1998, pp. 241–60.

Beyer, Charlotte. "'My Mama Had a Story': Mothers and Intergenerational Relations in Andrea Levy's Fiction." *Reading/Speaking/Writing the Mother Text: Essays on Caribbean Women's Writing,* edited by Christina Herrera and Paula Sanmartín, Demeter Press, 2015, pp. 121–42.

Bhabha, Homi K. *The Location of Culture.* Routledge, 2010.

Bhabha, Homi K. "Of Mimicry and Man: The Ambivalence of Colonial Discourse." *October,* vol. 28, Spring 1984, pp. 125–33.

Bhabha, Homi K. "The World and the Home." *Social Text,* nos. 31–32, 1992, pp. 141–53.

Böttcher, Nikolaus. "Neptune's Trident: Trinidad, 1776–1840; From Colonial Backyard to Crown Colony." *Jahrbuch für Geschichte Lateinamerikas,* vol. 44, no. 1, 2007, pp. 157–85.

Boyce Davies, Carole. *Black Women, Writing and Identity: Migrations of the Subject.* Routledge, 2002.

Boyce Davies, Carole. "Some Where in This Great Wide World: My Mother's Sweetness." *Feminist and Critical Perspectives on Caribbean Mothering,* edited by Dorsía Smith Silva and Simone A. James Alexander, Africa World Press, 2013, pp. 25–38.

Boyce Davies, Carole, and Elaine Savory Fido. Introduction. *Out of the Kumbla: Caribbean Women and Literature,* edited by Carole Boyce Davies and Elaine Savory Fido, Africa World Press, 1990, pp. 1–22.

Bragard, Véronique. "Coolie Woman Fictionalizing Political History: Janice Shinebourne's Memories of Violence." *Journal of Caribbean Literatures,* vol. 3, no. 1, Summer 2001, pp. 13–25.

Bragard, Véronique. "Gendered Voyages into Coolitude: The Shaping of the Indo-Caribbean Woman's Literary Consciousness." *Kunapipi*, vol. 20, no. 1, 1998, pp. 99–111.
Brand, Dionne. *At the Full and Change of the Moon*. Vintage Canada, 1999.
Brand, Dionne. *A Map to the Door of No Return: Notes to Belonging*. Vintage Canada, 2001.
Brathwaite, Edward K. *Contradictory Omens: Cultural Diversity and Integration in the Caribbean*. Savacou Publications, 1974.
Brathwaite, Kamau. *ConVERSations with Nathaniel Mackey*. We Press, 1999.
Brereton, Bridget. "Gender and the Historiography of the English-Speaking Caribbean." *Gendered Realities: Essays in Caribbean Feminist Thought*, edited by Patricia Mohammed, U of the West Indies P, 2002, pp. 129–47.
Brereton, Bridget. *An Introduction to the History of Trinidad and Tobago*. Heinemann, 1996.
Brereton, Bridget. "Resistance to Enslavement and Oppression in Trinidad, 1802–1849." *Journal of Caribbean History*, vol. 43, no. 2, 2009, pp. 157–76.
Brickman, Celia. *Race in Psychoanalysis: Aboriginal Populations in the Mind*. Routledge, 2018.
Brodber, Erna. *Myal*. Waveland Press, 2014.
Brontë, Charlotte. *Jane Eyre*. 1847. Penguin, 2008.
Brown, J. Dillon, and Leah Reade Rosenberg. "Introduction: Looking Beyond Windrush." *Beyond Windrush: Rethinking Postwar Anglophone Caribbean Literature*, edited by J. Dillon Brown and Leah Reade Rosenberg, UP of Mississippi, 2015, pp. 3–24.
Bruns, Gerald L. *Maurice Blanchot: The Refusal of Philosophy*. Johns Hopkins UP, 1997.
Buchanan, David. *Acts of Modernity: The Historical Novel and Effective Communication, 1814–1901*. Routledge, 2017.
Butler, Judith. *Gender Trouble: Feminism and the Subversion of Identity*. 1990. Routledge, 2006.
Cámara Betancourt, Madeline. *Cuban Women Writers: Imagining a Matria*. Translated by David Frye, Palgrave Macmillan, 2008.
Campbell, Elaine. "An Expatriate at Home: Dominica's Elma Napier." *Kunapipi*, vol. 4, no. 1, 1982, pp. 82–93.
Carter, Marina, and Khal Torabully. *Coolitude: An Anthology of the Indian Labour Diaspora*. Anthem Press, 2002.
Caruth, Cathy. *Unclaimed Experience: Trauma, Narrative, and History*. Johns Hopkins UP, 1996.
Cezair-Thompson, Margaret. *The True History of Paradise*. Random House, 1999.
Chancy, Myriam J. A. *From Sugar to Revolution: Women's Visions of Haiti, Cuba, and the Dominican Republic*. Wilfrid Laurier UP, 2012.
Christian, Barbara T. "Ritualistic Process and the Structure of Paule Marshall's *Praisesong for the Widow*." *Callaloo*, no. 18, Spring–Summer 1983, pp. 74–84.
Clark, VèVè A. "Developing Diaspora Literacy and *Marasa* Consciousness." *Theatre Survey*, vol. 50, no. 1, May 2009, pp. 9–18.
Cliff, Michelle. *Abeng*. 1984. Plume, 1995.
Cliff, Michelle. "Caliban's Daughter: The Tempest and the Teapot." *Frontiers: A Journal of Women Studies*, vol. 12, no. 2, 1991, pp. 36–51.
Cliff, Michelle. *No Telephone to Heaven*. 1987. Plume, 1996.
Cobb, Lauren. "*The Meaning of Consuelo*: A Handbook for Resisting Narratives of Oppression." *Rituals of Movement in the Writing of Judith Ortiz Cofer*, edited by Lorraine M. López and Molly Crumpton Winter, Caribbean Studies Press, 2012, pp. 133–50.

Cohn, Dorrit. *The Distinction of Fiction*. Johns Hopkins UP, 1999.
Collins, Merle. *Angel*. 1987. Peepal Tree Press, 2011.
Collins, Patricia Hill. "The Meaning of Motherhood in Black Culture and Black Mother/Daughter Relationships." *Toward a New Psychology of Gender: A Reader*, edited by Mary M. Gergen and Sara N. Davis, Routledge, 1997, pp. 325–40.
Condé, Maryse. *I, Tituba, Black Witch of Salem*. Translated by Richard Philcox, U of Virginia P, 1992.
Cooper, Carolyn. "'Something Ancestral Recaptured': Spirit Possession as Trope in Selected Feminist Fictions of the African Diaspora." *Motherlands: Black Women's Writing from Africa, the Caribbean and South Asia*, edited by Susheila Nasta, Rutgers UP, 1992, pp. 64–87.
Crespo-Kebler, Elizabeth. "'The Infamous Crime against Nature': Constructions of Heterosexuality and Lesbian Subversions in Puerto Rico." *The Culture of Gender and Sexuality in the Caribbean*, edited by Linden Lewis, UP of Florida, 2003, pp. 190–212.
Dalleo, Raphael. "Another 'Our America': Rooting a Caribbean Aesthetic in the Work of José Martí, Kamau Brathwaite and Édouard Glissant." *Anthurium: A Caribbean Studies Journal*, vol. 2, no. 2, 2004, pp. 1–11.
Danticat, Edwidge. *Breath, Eyes, Memory*. 1994. Soho Press, 2015.
Danticat, Edwidge. *The Farming of Bones*. Soho Press, 1998.
Danticat, Edwidge. "The Long Legacy of Occupation in Haiti." *New Yorker*, July 28, 2019, n.p.
Danytė, Milda. "National Past/Personal Past: Recent Examples of the Historical Novel by Umberto Eco and Antanas Sileika." *Literatūra*, vol. 49, no. 5, 2007, pp. 34–41.
Dash, Michael. "In Search of the Lost Body: Redefining the Subject in Caribbean Literature." *The Post-Colonial Studies Reader*, edited by Bill Ashcroft, Gareth Griffiths, and Helen Tiffin, Routledge, 1995, pp. 332–35.
Dash, J. Michael. Introduction. *Caribbean Discourse: Selected Essays*, by Édouard Glissant, U of Virginia P, 1999, pp. xi–xlv.
Davidson, J. S. *Grenada: A Study in Politics and the Limits of International Law*. Gower Publishing, 1987.
Davies, Catherine. *A Place in the Sun? Women Writers in Twentieth-Century Cuba*. Zed Books, 1997.
Davis, Andrea. "Women and Healing in Anglophone Caribbean Literature." *The Encyclopedia of Caribbean Religions*, 2 vols., edited by Patrick Taylor and Frederick I. Case, U of Illinois P, 2013, pp. 525–34.
Davis, Angela Y. *Women, Race and Class*. Vintage Books, 1983.
Davis, Kimberly Chabot. "Generational Hauntings: The Family Romance in Contemporary Fictions of Raced History." *Modern Fiction Studies*, vol. 48, no. 3, Fall 2002, pp. 727–36.
Davis, Rocío G. "Back to the Future: Mothers, Languages, and Homes in Cristina García's *Dreaming in Cuban*." *World Literature Today*, vol. 74, no. 1, Winter 2000, pp. 60–68.
Dhar, Nandini. "Trauma, Mourning, and Resistant Melancholia: Dionne Brand's *At the Full and Change of the Moon*." *Come Weep with Me: Loss and Mourning in the Writings of Caribbean Women Writers*, edited by Joyce C. Harte, Cambridge Scholars Publishing, 2007, pp. 27–55.
Donahue, Jennifer. *Taking Flight: Caribbean Women Writing from Abroad*. UP of Mississippi, 2020.
Down, Lorna. "'Flying Inna Massa Face': Woman, Nature, and Sacred Rites/Rights in Marie-Elena John's *Unburnable*." *Experiences of Freedom in Postcolonial Literatures and Cultures*, edited by Annalisa Oboe and Shaul Bassi, Routledge, 2011, pp. 231–41.

Duany, Jorge. *The Puerto Rican Nation on the Move: Identities on the Island and in the United States*. U of North Carolina P, 2002.
Edgell, Zee. *Beka Lamb*. 1982. Waveland Press, 2015.
Edgell, Zee. *Time and the River*. Heinemann, 2007.
Edwards, Whitney Bly. "Psychoanalysis in Caribbean Literature." *The Routledge Companion to Anglophone Caribbean Literature*, edited by Michael A. Bucknor and Alison Donnell, Routledge, 2011, pp. 314–22.
Eller, Anne. *We Dream Together: Dominican Independence, Haiti, and the Fight for Caribbean Freedom*. Duke UP, 2016.
Esnard, Talia. "Towards Matricentric Feminism in the Caribbean: Inroads and Opportunities." *Journal of the Motherhood Initiative*, vol. 10, nos. 1–2, Spring–Fall 2019, pp. 257–72.
Evans, Lucy. "Tidal Poetics in Dionne Brand's *At the Full and Change of the Moon*." *Caribbean Quarterly*, vol. 55, no. 3, September 2009, pp. 1–19.
Fagan, Allison. "Translating in the Margins: Attending to Glossaries in Latina/o Literature." *Journal of Modern Literature*, vol. 39, no. 3, Spring 2016, pp. 57–75.
Fanon, Frantz. *Black Skin, White Masks*. 1952. Translated by Richard Philcox, Grove Press, 2008.
Ferguson, Moira. *A Human Necklace: The African Diaspora and Paule Marshall's Fiction*. State U of New York P, 2013.
Ferly, Odile. *A Poetics of Relation: Caribbean Women Writing at the Millennium*. Palgrave Macmillan, 2012.
Fernández Olmos, Margarite, and Lizabeth Paravisini-Gebert. *Creole Religions of the Caribbean: An Introduction from Vodou and Santería to Obeah and Espiritismo*. New York UP, 2003.
Francis, Donette. *Fictions of Feminine Citizenship: Sexuality and the Nation in Contemporary Caribbean Literature*. Palgrave Macmillan, 2010.
Freud, Sigmund. *Beyond the Pleasure Principle*. 1920. Translated by James Strachey, Dover Publications, 2015.
Freud, Sigmund. *Civilization and Its Discontents*. 1930. Translated by James Strachey, W. W. Norton, 1962.
Freud, Sigmund. "Female Sexuality." *Psychoanalysis and Woman: A Reader*, edited by Shelley Saguaro, Macmillan, 2000, pp. 21–34.
Freud, Sigmund. "Fetishism." *The Standard Edition of the Complete Psychological Works of Sigmund Freud*, vol. 21, Hogarth Press; Institute of Psycho-Analysis, 1961, pp. 147–57.
Freud, Sigmund. "Mourning and Melancholia." *The Standard Edition of the Complete Psychological Works of Sigmund Freud*, vol. 14, Vintage, 2001, pp. 243–58.
Freud, Sigmund. *The Question of Lay Analysis*. 1927. Translated by James Strachey, W. W. Norton, 1969.
Freud, Sigmund. *Totem and Taboo: Resemblances between the Psychic Lives of Savages and Neurotics*. Translated by A. A. Brill, George Routledge and Sons, 1919.
Freud, Sigmund. *The Uncanny*. 1919. Translated by David McLintock, Penguin, 2003.
Freud, Sigmund, and Josef Breuer. *Studies on Hysteria*. 1895. Forgotten Books, 2012.
García, Cristina. *Dreaming in Cuban*. Ballantine, 1992.
Garvey, Johanna X. K. "'The Place She Miss': Exile, Memory, and Resistance in Dionne Brand's Fiction." *Callaloo*, vol. 26, no. 2, Spring 2003, pp. 486–503.
Gatto, Katherine Gyekenyesi. "Mambo, Merengue, Salsa: The Dynamics of Self-Construction in Latina Autobiographical Narrative." *West Virginia University Philological Papers*, vol. 46, 2000, pp. 84–90.

Gikandi, Simon. "Narration in the Post-Colonial Moment: Merle Hodge's *Crick Crack Monkey*." *Past the Last Post: Theorizing Post-Colonialism and Post-Modernism*, edited by Ian Adam and Helen Tiffin, Harvester Wheatsheaf, 1991, pp. 13–22.
Gilbert, Sandra M. "From *Patria* to *Matria*: Elizabeth Barrett Browning's Risorgimento." *PMLA*, vol. 99, no. 2, March 1984, pp. 194–211.
Gilbert, Sandra M., and Susan Gubar. *The Madwoman in the Attic: The Woman Writer and the Nineteenth-Century Literary Imagination*. 2nd ed., Yale UP, 2000.
Glissant, Édouard. *Caribbean Discourse: Selected Essays*. Translated by J. Michael Dash, U of Virginia P, 1999.
Glissant, Édouard. *Faulkner, Mississippi*. Translated by Barbara Lewis and Thomas C. Spear, U of Chicago P, 2000.
Glissant, Édouard. *Poetics of Relation*. U of Michigan P, 1997.
Goldman, Marlene. *DisPossession: Haunting in Canadian Fiction*. McGill-Queen's UP, 2012.
Gordon, Avery F. *Ghostly Matters: Haunting and the Sociological Imagination*. U of Minnesota P, 1997.
Gott, Richard. *Cuba: A New History*. Yale UP, 2005.
Haigh, Samantha. "Between Irigaray and Cardinal: Reinventing Maternal Genealogies." *Modern Language Review*, vol. 89, no. 1, January 1994, pp. 61–70.
Hall, Stuart. "Cultural Identity and Diaspora." *Identity: Community, Culture, Difference*, edited by Jonathan Rutherford, Lawrence and Wishart, 1990, pp. 222–37.
Halloran, Vivian Nun. *Exhibiting Slavery: The Caribbean Postmodern Novel as Museum*. U of Virginia P, 2009.
Harford Vargas, Jennifer. *Forms of Dictatorship: Power, Narrative, and Authoritarianism in the Latina/o Novel*. Oxford University Press, 2018.
Harford Vargas, Jennifer. "Novel Testimony: Alternative Archives in Edwidge Danticat's *The Farming of Bones*." *Callaloo*, vol. 37, no. 5, Fall 2014, pp. 1162–80.
Harris, Joel Chandler. *Uncle Remus and His Legends of the Old Plantation*. David Bogue, 1881.
Hayes, Jarrod. *Queer Roots for the Diaspora: Ghosts in the Family Tree*. U of Michigan P, 2016.
Henderson, Joseph L. *Thresholds of Initiation*. Chiron Publications, 2005.
Henderson, Mae G. "The Stories of O(Dessa): Stories of Complicity and Resistance." *Female Subjects in Black and White: Race, Psychoanalysis, Feminism*, edited by Elizabeth Abel, Barbara Christian, and Helene Moglen, U of California P, 1997, pp. 285–304.
Higman, B. W. *Slave Populations of the British Caribbean, 1807–1834*. Johns Hopkins UP, 1984.
Hirsch, Marianne. *The Mother/Daughter Plot: Narrative, Psychoanalysis, Feminism*. Indiana UP, 1989.
Hochberg, Gil Zehava. "Mother, Memory, History: Maternal Genealogies in Gayl Jones's *Corregidora* and Simone Schwarz-Bart's *Pluie et vent sur Télumée Miracle*." *Research in African Literatures*, vol. 34, no. 2, Summer 2003, pp. 1–12.
Hodge, Merle. *Crick Crack, Monkey*. 1970. Waveland Press, 2013.
Honychurch, Lennox. *The Dominica Story: A History of the Island*. Macmillan, 1995.
Honychurch, Lennox. *In the Forests of Freedom: The Fighting Maroons of Dominica*. UP of Mississippi, 2019.
Houlberg, Marilyn. "Magique Marasa: The Ritual Cosmos of Twins and Other Sacred Children." *Sacred Arts of Haitian Vodou*, edited by Donald J. Cosentino, University of California, Los Angeles, Fowler Museum, 1995, pp. 267–84.

Huggan, Graham. "Decolonizing the Map: Postcolonialism, Poststructuralism and the Cartographic Connection." *Interdisciplinary Measures: Literature and the Future of Postcolonial Studies*, Liverpool UP, 2008, pp. 21–33.
Hunter, Dianne. "Hysteria, Psychoanalysis, and Feminism: The Case of Anna O." *Feminist Studies*, vol. 9, no. 3, Autumn 1983, pp. 465–88.
Hutcheon, Linda. *A Poetics of Postmodernism: History, Theory, Fiction*. Routledge, 1988.
Hyles, Joshua R. *Guiana and the Shadows of Empire: Colonial and Cultural Negotiations at the Edge of the World*. Lexington Books, 2013.
Inter-American Commission on Human Rights. "Report on the Situation of Human Rights in the Dominican Republic." Organization of American States, OEA/Ser. L/V/II, Doc. 45/15, December 31, 2015. http://www.oas.org/en/iachr/reports/pdfs/dominicanrepublic-2015.pdf.
Irigaray, Luce. *The Irigaray Reader*. Edited by Margaret Whitford, Blackwell, 1995.
Irigaray, Luce. *Speculum of the Other Woman*. Translated by Gillian C. Gill, Cornell UP, 1985.
Irigaray, Luce. *This Sex Which Is Not One*. Translated by Catherine Porter, Cornell UP, 1985.
Jamaica Information Service. "The History of Jamaica." 2020. https://jis.gov.jm/information/jamaican-history/.
John, Marie-Elena. *Unburnable*. E-book ed., HarperCollins, 2006.
Johnson, Kelli Lyon. "Both Sides of the Massacre: Collective Memory and Narrative on Hispaniola." *Mosaic: A Journal for the Interdisciplinary Study of Literature*, vol. 36, no. 2, June 2003, pp. 75–91.
Johnson, Kelli Lyon. *Julia Alvarez: Writing a New Place on the Map*. U of New Mexico P, 2005.
Jonte-Pace, Diane. "At Home in the Uncanny: Freudian Representations of Death, Mothers, and the Afterlife." *Journal of the American Academy of Religion*, vol. 64, no. 1, Spring 1996, pp. 61–88.
Josephs, Kelly Baker. *Disturbers of the Peace: Representations of Madness in Anglophone Caribbean Literature*. U of Virginia P, 2013.
Kempadoo, Kamala. "Negotiating Cultures: A 'Dogla' Perspective." *Matikor: The Politics of Identity for Indo-Caribbean Women*, edited by Rosanne Kanhai, U of the West Indies, School of Continuing Studies, 1999, pp. 103–13.
Kempadoo, Kamala. *Sexing the Caribbean: Gender, Race, and Sexual Labor*. Routledge, 2004.
Kempadoo, Oonya. *Buxton Spice*. 1998. Dutton, 1999.
Kevane, Bridget. *Profane & Sacred: Latino/a American Writers Reveal the Interplay of the Secular and the Religious*. Rowman and Littlefield, 2008.
Khanna, Ranjana. *Dark Continents: Psychoanalysis and Colonialism*. Duke UP, 2003.
Kincaid, Jamaica. *Annie John*. E-book ed., Farrar, Straus and Giroux, 2013.
Kincaid, Jamaica. *The Autobiography of My Mother*. HarperCollins Canada, 1996.
King, Amy K. "'She Had Put the Servant in Her Place': Sexual Violence and Generational Social Policing between Women in Marie-Elena John's *Unburnable*." *Reading/Speaking/Writing the Mother Text: Essays on Caribbean Women's Writing*, edited by Christina Herrera and Paula Sanmartín, Demeter Press, 2015, pp. 195–214.
King, Rosamond S. *Island Bodies: Transgressive Sexualities in the Caribbean Imagination*. UP of Florida, 2014.
Kristeva, Julia. "Women's Time." Translated by Alice Jardine and Harry Blake, *Signs*, vol. 7, no. 1, Autumn 1981, pp. 13–35.
Kyiiripuo Kyoore, Paschal B. *The African and Caribbean Historical Novel in French: A Quest for Identity*. Peter Lang, 1999.

La Fountain-Stokes, Lawrence. *Queer Ricans: Cultures and Sexualities in the Diaspora*. U of Minnesota P, 2009.
Lane, Christopher. "The Psychoanalysis of Race: An Introduction." *The Psychoanalysis of Race*, edited by Christopher Lane, Columbia UP, 1998, pp. 1–37.
Lara, Ana-Maurine. *Erzulie's Skirt*. RedBone Press, 2006.
Laramee, Michael. "Maps of Memory and the Sea in Dionne Brand's *At the Full and Change of the Moon*." *Anthurium: A Caribbean Studies Journal*, vol. 6, no. 2, 2008, pp. 1–14.
Levy, Andrea. *Fruit of the Lemon*. 1999. Tinder Press, 2016.
Levy, Andrea. *The Long Song*. 2010. Picador, 2011.
Light, Alison. "'Young Bess': Historical Novels and Growing Up." *Feminist Review*, vol. 33, no. 1, November 1989, pp. 57–71.
Lima, Maria Helena. "Revolutionary Developments: Michelle Cliff's *No Telephone to Heaven* and Merle Collins's *Angel*." *Ariel: A Review of International English Literature*, vol. 24, no. 1, January 1993, pp. 35–56.
Lima, Maria Helena. "A Written Song: Andrea Levy's Neo-Slave Narrative." *EnterText*, vol. 9, 2012, pp. 135–53.
Lionnet, Françoise. *Postcolonial Representations: Women, Literature, Identity*. Cornell UP, 1995.
Llanos-Figueroa, Dahlma. *Daughters of the Stone*. St. Martin's Press, 2009.
López Springfield, Consuelo. "Introduction: Revisiting Caliban; Implications for Caribbean Feminisms." *Daughters of Caliban: Caribbean Women in the Twentieth Century*, edited by Consuelo López Springfield, Indiana UP, 1997, pp. xi–xxi.
Lugo-Lugo, Carmen R. "Getting to the Colonial Status through Sexuality: Lessons on Puerto Rico's Political Predicament from Women Writers." *Centro: Journal of the Center for Puerto Rican Studies*, vol. 30, no. 2, Summer 2018, pp. 234–53.
Lukács, Georg. *The Historical Novel*. Translated by Hannah Mitchell and Stanley Mitchell, U of Nebraska P, 1983.
Machado Sáez, Elena. *Market Aesthetics: The Purchase of the Past in Caribbean Diasporic Fiction*. U of Virginia P, 2015.
Maes-Jelinek, Hena, and Bénédicte Ledent. "The Novel since 1970." *A History of Literature in the Caribbean*. Vol. 2: *English- and Dutch-Speaking Regions*, edited by A. James Arnold, John Benjamins Publishing, 2001, pp. 149–98.
Mahabir, Joy, and Mariam Pirbhai. "Introduction: Tracing an Emerging Tradition." *Critical Perspectives on Indo-Caribbean Women's Literature*, edited by Joy Mahabir and Mariam Pirbhai, Routledge, 2013, pp. 1–24.
Maisier, Véronique. *Violence in Caribbean Literature: Stories of Stones and Blood*. Lexington Books, 2015.
Marshall, Paule. *Praisesong for the Widow*. Plume, 1983.
Martin, W. Todd. "'Naming' Sebastien: Celebrating Men in Edwidge Danticat's *The Farming of Bones*." *Atenea*, vol. 28, no. 1, June 2008, pp. 65–74.
McAuliffe, Samantha L. "Autoethnography and Garcia's *Dreaming in Cuban*." *CLCWeb: Comparative Literature and Culture*, vol. 13, no. 4, 2011, pp. 1–9.
McCallum, Pamela, and Christian Olbey. "'Standing in the Middle of the World Cracking': Class, Cultural Memory, and Collectivity in Dionne Brand's *At the Full and Change of the Moon*." *Beyond the Canebrakes: Caribbean Women Writers in Canada*, edited by Emily Allen Williams, Africa World Press, 2008, pp. 11–35.
McDaniel, Lorna. *The Big Drum Ritual of Carriacou: Praisesongs in Rememory of Flight*. UP of Florida, 1998.

McDonald, Ellie. "'What Is This T'ing t'en about Caribbean Feminisms?' Feminism in the Anglophone Caribbean, circa 1980-2000." *Caribbean Review of Gender Studies*, no. 10, December 2016, pp. 45-68.

Meehan, Kevin. "Rise Up? New Directions in the Caribbean Women's *Bildungsroman*." *Palimpsest: A Journal on Women, Gender, and the Black International*, vol. 7, no. 1, 2018, pp. 11-18.

Mehta, Brinda J. "The Colonial Curriculum and the Construction of 'Coolie-Ness' in Lakshmi Persaud's *Sastra* and *Butterfly in the Wind* (Trinidad) and Jan Shinebourne's *The Last English Plantation* (Guyana)." *Journal of Caribbean Literatures*, vol. 3, no. 1, Summer 2001, pp. 111-28.

Mehta, Brinda. *Diasporic (Dis)locations: Indo-Caribbean Women Writers Negotiate the Kala Pani*. U of the West Indies P, 2004.

Mehta, Brinda. *Notions of Identity, Diaspora, and Gender in Caribbean Women's Writing*. Palgrave Macmillan, 2009.

Méndez, Susan C. "Señora, Niña, o Señorita: The Story of Puerto Rico as Nation, Commonwealth, or Ethno-Nation through Women in Judith Ortiz Cofer's *The Meaning of Consuelo*." *Confluencia: Revista Hispánica de Cultura y Literatura*, vol. 27, no. 1, Fall 2011, pp. 33-44.

Méndez Rodenas, Adriana. "Engendering the Nation: The Mother/Daughter Plot in Cuban American Fiction." *Cuban-American Literature and Art: Negotiating Identities*, edited by Isabel Alvarez Borland and Lynette M. F. Bosch, State U of New York P, 2009, 47-60.

Menton, Seymour. *Latin America's New Historical Novel*. U of Texas P, 1993.

Merkur, Daniel. "The Discharge of Guilt: Psychoanalytic Theories of Ritual." *Journal of Ritual Studies*, vol. 5, no. 2, Summer 1991, pp. 15-32.

Misrahi-Barak, Judith. "Biopolitics and Translation: Edwidge Danticat's Many Tongues." *International Journal of Francophone Studies*, vol. 17, nos. 3-4, November 2014, pp. 349-71.

Misrahi-Barak, Judith. "Looking In, Looking Out: The Chinese-Caribbean Diaspora through Literature—Meiling Jin, Patricia Powell, Jan Lowe Shinebourne." *Journal of Transnational American Studies*, vol. 4, no. 1, 2012, pp. 1-15. http://escholarship.org/uc/item/0pn2w8cs.

Moglen, Helene. "Redeeming History: Toni Morrison's *Beloved*." *Female Subjects in Black and White: Race, Psychoanalysis, Feminism*, edited by Elizabeth Abel, Barbara Christian, and Helene Moglen, U of California P, 1997, pp. 201-20.

Mohammed, Patricia. "Stories in Caribbean Feminism: Reflections on the Twentieth Century." *Caribbean Review of Gender Studies*, no. 9, 2015, pp. 111-42.

Mohammed, Patricia. "Towards Indigenous Feminist Theorizing in the Caribbean." *Feminist Review*, vol. 59, no. 1, Summer 1998, pp. 6-33.

Momsen, Janet. "The Double Paradox." *Gendered Realities: Essays in Caribbean Feminist Thought*, edited by Patricia Mohammed, U of the West Indies P, 2002, pp. 44-55.

Moreno, Marisel C. *Family Matters: Puerto Rican Women Authors on the Island and the Mainland*. U of Virginia P, 2012.

Moreno, Marisel. "Family Matters: Revisiting *La Gran Familia Puertorriqueña* in the Works of Rosario Ferré and Judith Ortíz Cofer." *Centro: Journal of the Center for Puerto Rican Studies*, vol. 22, no. 2, Fall 2010, pp. 75-105.

Morris, Ann R., and Margaret M. Dunn. "'The Bloodstream of Our Inheritance': Female Identity and the Caribbean Mothers'-Land." *Motherlands: Black Women's Writing from*

Africa, the Caribbean and South Asia, edited by Susheila Nasta, Rutgers UP, 1992, pp. 219–37.

Muñoz-Valdivieso, Sofía. "'This Tale Is of My Making': Empowering Voices in Andrea Levy's *The Long Song*." *Journal of Postcolonial Writing*, vol. 52, no. 1, 2016, pp. 38–50. doi: 10.1080/17449855.2015.1125147.

NameDoctor. S.v. "Bola." https://www.name-doctor.com/name-bola-meaning-of-bola-47967.html.

Newman, Judie. "The Untold Story and the Retold Story: Intertextuality in Post-Colonial Women's Fiction." *Motherlands: Black Women's Writing from Africa, the Caribbean and South Asia*, edited by Susheila Nasta, Rutgers UP, 1992, pp. 24–42.

O'Callaghan, Evelyn. *Women Writing the West Indies, 1804–1939: "A Hot Place, Belonging to Us."* Routledge, 2004.

Oliver, Kelly. "Julia Kristeva's Maternal Passions." *Journal of French and Francophone Philosophy/Revue de la Philosophie Française et de Langue Française*, vol. 18, no. 1, 2008–2010, pp. 1–8.

O'Reilly Herrera, Andrea. "Cristina García, *Dreaming in Cuban*." *Reading U.S. Latina Writers: Remapping American Literature*, edited by Alvina E. Quintana, Palgrave Macmillan, 2003, pp. 91–102.

O'Reilly Herrera, Andrea. *The Pearl of the Antilles*. Bilingual Press, 2001.

O'Reilly Herrera, Andrea. "Women and the Revolution in Cristina García's *Dreaming in Cuban*." *Modern Language Studies*, vol. 27, nos. 3–4, Autumn–Winter 1997, pp. 69–91.

Orlando, Valérie. *Of Suffocated Hearts and Tortured Souls: Seeking Subjecthood through Madness in Francophone Women's Writing of Africa and the Caribbean*. Lexington Books, 2003.

Ortiz Cofer, Judith. *The Meaning of Consuelo*. Beacon Press, 2003.

Oxford English Dictionary. S.v. "avatar."

Oxford English Dictionary. S.v. "tar baby."

Paravisini-Gebert, Lizabeth. "Caribbean Literature in Spanish." *The Cambridge History of African and Caribbean Literature*, edited by F. Abiola Irele and Simon Gikandi, Cambridge UP, 2003, pp. 670–710.

Paravisini-Gebert, Lizabeth. "Decolonizing Feminism: The Home-Grown Roots of Caribbean Women's Movements." *Daughters of Caliban: Caribbean Women in the Twentieth Century*, edited by Consuelo López Springfield, Indiana UP, 1997, pp. 3–17.

Patton, Venetria K. *The Grasp That Reaches beyond the Grave: The Ancestral Call in Black Women's Texts*. State U of New York P, 2013.

Perfect, Michael. "'Fold the Paper and Pass It On': Historical Silences and the Contrapuntal in Andrea Levy's Fiction." *Journal of Postcolonial Writing*, vol. 46, no. 1, February 2010, pp. 31–41.

Persaud, Lakshmi. *Butterfly in the Wind*. Peepal Tree Press, 1990.

Pirbhai, Mariam. "Recasting *Jahaji-Bhain*: Plantation History and the Indo-Caribbean Women's Novel in Trinidad, Guyana and Martinique." *Critical Perspectives on Indo-Caribbean Women's Literature*, edited by Joy Mahabir and Mariam Pirbhai, Routledge, 2013, pp. 25–47.

Pollard, Velma. "Cultural Connections in Paule Marshall's *Praise Song for the Widow*." *Caribbean Quarterly*, vol. 34, nos. 1–2, March–June 1988, pp. 58–70.

Pollock, Griselda. "Mother Trouble: The Maternal-Feminine in Phallic and Feminist Theory in Relation to Bracha Ettinger's Elaboration of Matrixial Ethics/Aesthetics." *Studies in the Maternal*, vol. 1, no. 1, January 2009, pp. 1–31.

Praeger, Michèle. *The Imaginary Caribbean and Caribbean Imaginary.* U of Nebraska P, 2003.
Quayle, Ada [Kathleen Louise Woods]. *The Mistress.* 1957. Four Square Books, 1961.
Rahim, Jennifer. "Jones, Marion Patrick." *Encyclopedia of Post-Colonial Literatures in English,* edited by Eugene Benson and L. W. Conolly, 2nd ed., Routledge, 2005, p. 741.
Ramírez, Rafael. "Masculinity and Power in Puerto Rico." *The Culture of Gender and Sexuality in the Caribbean,* edited by Linden Lewis, UP of Florida, 2003, pp. 234–50.
Reyes, Angelita. *Mothering across Cultures: Postcolonial Representations.* U of Minnesota P, 2002.
Rhys, Jean. *Wide Sargasso Sea.* 1966. W. W. Norton, 1992.
Rivero, Eliana. "Writing in Cuban, Living as Other: Cuban American Women Writers Getting It Right." *Cuban-American Literature and Art: Negotiating Identities,* edited by Isabel Alvarez Borland and Lynette M. F. Bosch, State U of New York P, 2009, pp. 109–25.
Rody, Caroline. *The Daughter's Return: African-American and Caribbean Women's Fictions of History.* Oxford UP, 2001.
Rogers, Susan. "Embodying Cultural Memory in Paule Marshall's *Praisesong for the Widow.*" *African American Review,* vol. 34, no. 1, Spring 2000, pp. 77–93.
Rowley, Michelle. "Reconceptualizing Voice: The Role of Matrifocality in Shaping Theories and Caribbean Voices." *Gendered Realities: Essays in Caribbean Feminist Thought,* edited by Patricia Mohammed, U of the West Indies P, 2002, pp. 22–43.
Russell, Heather. *Legba's Crossing: Narratology in the African Atlantic.* U of Georgia P, 2009.
Ryan, Connor. "Defining Diaspora in the Words of Women Writers: A Feminist Reading of Chimamanda Adichie's *The Thing around Your Neck* and Dionne Brand's *At the Full and Change of the Moon.*" *Callaloo,* vol. 37, no. 5, Fall 2014, pp. 1230–44.
Sadowski-Smith, Claudia. "Andrea O'Reilly Herrera, *The Pearl of the Antilles.*" *Reading U.S. Latina Writers: Remapping American Literature,* edited by Alvina E. Quintana, Palgrave Macmillan, 2003, pp. 129–40.
Sandiford, Keith A. "Paule Marshall's *Praisesong for the Widow*: The Reluctant Heiress, or Whose Life Is It Anyway?" *Black American Literature Forum,* vol. 20, no. 4, Winter 1986, pp. 371–92.
Sanmartín, Paula, and Christina Herrera. "Introduction: The Poetics of Motherhood and Maternity in Caribbean Women's Writing." *Reading/Speaking/Writing the Mother Text: Essays on Caribbean Women's Writing,* edited by Christina Herrera and Paula Sanmartín, Demeter Press, 2015, pp. 1–16.
Schwarz-Bart, Simone. *Pluie et vent sur Télumée Miracle.* Éditions du Seuil, 1972.
Scott, David. *Conscripts of Modernity: The Tragedy of Colonial Enlightenment.* Duke UP, 2004.
Scott, Helen. *Caribbean Women Writers and Globalization: Fictions of Independence.* Ashgate Publishing, 2006.
Scott, Walter, Sir. *Waverley; or, 'Tis Sixty Years Since.* 1814. Edited by Claire Lamont, Oxford UP, 2008.
Shah, Ryhaan. *A Silent Life.* Peepal Tree Press, 2005.
Shemak, April. "Re-Membering Hispaniola: Edwidge Danticat's *The Farming of Bones.*" *Modern Fiction Studies,* vol. 48, no. 1, Spring 2002, pp. 83–112.
Shinebourne, Jan Lowe. *The Last English Plantation.* 1988. Peepal Tree Press, 2007.
Shinebourne, Janice. *Timepiece.* Peepal Tree Press, 1986.
Sjoberg, Laura, and Caron E. Gentry. *Mothers, Monsters, Whores: Women's Violence in Global Politics.* Zed Books, 2007.

Smith, Barbara Fletchman. *Transcending the Legacies of Slavery: A Psychoanalytic View.* Karnac Publishing, 2011.

Smith, Carissa Turner. "Women's Spiritual Geographies of the African Diaspora: Paule Marshall's *Praisesong for the Widow*." *African American Review*, vol. 42, nos. 3–4, Fall 2008, pp. 715–29.

Smith Silva, Dorsía, and Simone A. James Alexander. "Introduction: Caribbean Mothering; A Feminist View." *Feminist and Critical Perspectives on Caribbean Mothering*, edited by Dorsía Smith Silva and Simone A. James Alexander, Africa World Press, 2013, pp. vii–xvii.

Socolovsky, Maya. *Troubling Nationhood in U.S. Latina Literature: Explorations of Place and Belonging.* Rutgers UP, 2013.

Sourieau, Marie-Agnès. Introduction. *Reflections of Loko Miwa*, by Lilas Desquiron, translated by Robin Orr Bodkin, U of Virginia P, 1998, pp. vii–xxviii.

Spillers, Hortense J. "Mama's Baby, Papa's Maybe: An American Grammar Book." *Diacritics*, vol. 17, no. 2, Summer 1987, pp. 64–81.

Stone, Katherine. "Ties that Bind in Tanja Dückers's Novel *Himmelskörper*: History, Memory, and Making Sense of Motherhood in Twenty-First-Century Germany." *Motherhood in Literature and Culture: Interdisciplinary Perspectives from Europe*, edited by Gill Rye et al., Routledge, 2017, pp. 124–36.

Sykes, J. B., ed. *The Pocket Oxford Dictionary of Current English.* 6th ed. S.v. "hysteria." Oxford UP, 1978.

Theile, Verena, and Marie Drews. "Introduction: African American and Afro-Caribbean Women Writers; Writing, Remembering, and 'Being Human in the World.'" *Reclaiming Home, Remembering Motherhood, Rewriting History: African American and Afro-Caribbean Women's Literature in the Twentieth Century*, edited by Verena Theile and Marie Drews, Cambridge Scholars Publishing, 2009, pp. vii–xxi.

Thomas, Jennifer R. "Talking the Cross-Talk of Histories in Maryse Condé's *I, Tituba, Black Witch of Salem*." *Emerging Perspectives on Maryse Condé: A Writer of Her Own*, edited by Sarah Barbour and Gerise Herndon, Africa World Press, 2006, pp. 87–104.

Tolan, Fiona. "'I Am the Narrator of This Work': Narrative Authority in Andrea Levy's *The Long Song*." *Andrea Levy: Contemporary Critical Perspectives*, edited by Jeannette Baxter and David James, Bloomsbury, 2014, pp. 95–108.

Torres-Saillant, Silvio. "Dominican Literature and Its Criticism: Anatomy of a Troubled Identity." *A History of Literature in the Caribbean*. Vol. 1: *Hispanic and Francophone Regions*, edited by A. James Arnold, Julio Rodriguez-Luis, and J. Michael Dash, John Benjamins Publishing, 1994, pp. 49–64.

United Nations Economic Commission for Latin America and the Caribbean. "The Caribbean in the Decade of the 1990s." January 31, 2000. https://repositorio.cepal.org/bitstream/handle/11362/27454/LCcarG600_en.pdf?sequence=1&isAllowed=y.

Vieux-Chauvet, Marie. *Dance on the Volcano.* Translated by Salvator Attanasio, William Sloane Associates, 1959.

Vint, Sherryl. "'Only by Experience': Embodiment and the Limitations of Realism in Neo-Slave Narratives." *Science Fiction Studies*, vol. 34, no. 2, July 2007, pp. 241–61.

Von Dirke, Sabine. "Feminist Criticism and the Historical Novel: Elisabeth Plessen's *Kohlhass*." *Seminar*, vol. 34, no. 4, November 1998, pp. 410–27.

Wallace, Diana. *The Woman's Historical Novel: British Women Writers, 1900–2000.* Palgrave Macmillan, 2005.

Watson, Sonja Stephenson. "*Changó, el gran putas*: Contemporary Afro-Hispanic Historical Novel." *Afro-Hispanic Review*, vol. 25, no. 1, Spring 2006, pp. 67–86.

Whitford, Margaret. Introduction to Section I. *The Irigaray Reader*, edited by Margaret Whitford, Blackwell, 1991, pp. 23–29.

Whitford, Margaret. Introduction to Section II. *The Irigaray Reader*, edited by Margaret Whitford, Blackwell, 1991, pp. 71–78.

Wilson-Tagoe, Nana. "The Historical Novel in the Caribbean." *The Oxford History of the Novel in English*. Vol. 11, *The Novel in Africa and the Caribbean since 1950*, edited by Simon Gikandi, Oxford UP, 2016, pp. 285–300.

Wucker, Michele. *Why the Cocks Fight: Dominicans, Haitians, and the Struggle for Hispaniola*. Hill and Wang, 1999.

Wynter, Sylvia. *The Hills of Hebron: A Jamaican Novel*. Simon and Schuster, 1962.

Zimmerman, Tegan. "Unauthorized Storytelling: Reevaluating Racial Politics in Julia Alvarez's *In the Time of the Butterflies*." *MELUS*, vol. 45, no. 1, Spring 2020, pp. 95–116.

Zimra, Clarisse. "Righting the Calabash: Writing History in the Female Francophone Narrative." *Out of the Kumbla: Caribbean Women and Literature*, edited by Carole Boyce Davies and Elaine Savory Fido, Africa World Press, 1990, pp. 143–59.

Zimra, Clarisse. "What's in a Name: Elective Genealogy in Schwarz-Bart's Early Novels." *Studies in Twentieth Century Literature*, vol. 17, no. 1, 1993, pp. 97–118.

INDEX

Africa, 4, 42, 51, 52, 160, 170, 201, 203, 213, 214, 215, 216, 220, 222, 225, 227, 246
Alexander, M. Jacqui, 211–12, 218, 219, 220, 224, 226–27
Alexander, Simone A. James, 4, 163, 178, 206, 221
Aljoe, Nicole N., 66–67, 69, 72, 74
Allfrey, Phyllis Shand, 20, 111; *The Orchid House*, 199, 211, 230
Alvarez, Julia: *In the Name of Salomé*, 12, 151, 204, 209; *In the Time of the Butterflies*, 147, 148, 163–64, 244
ambivalence, 98, 99, 116, 117–18, 130. See also mother: ambivalent
anticolonialism, 6, 15–17, 91, 99, 101, 104, 105, 106, 112, 114, 118, 120, 147, 149, 201, 202, 252
assimilation (cultural), 94, 98, 108, 115, 117, 119, 212

Bailey, Carol, 4, 207, 233–34, 235, 236
Barrett Browning, Elizabeth, 7, 8, 25
Benstock, Shari, 5, 9, 11–12
Bertha (as character), 7–9, 230. See also Brontë, Charlotte; Cliff, Michelle; John, Marie-Elena; Rhys, Jean
Bhabha, Homi, 99, 112, 116–18; mimicry, 99, 116–18; liminality, 156–57, 164
bildungsroman (bildungsromane), 19, 27, 89–101, 126, 151, 252

birth, 8, 23, 38, 42, 47–51, 54, 58, 61, 66, 75, 76, 83, 138, 151, 154, 162, 163, 166, 168–73, 178, 186, 188, 191–94, 219, 224, 236, 241
Boyce Davies, Carole, 4, 17, 99, 200
Bragard, Véronique, 104, 107, 115, 118
Brand, Dionne, 34, 76; *At the Full and Change of the Moon*, 21, 34–42, 43–63; *In Another Place, Not Here*, 34; *A Map to the Door of No Return*, 40, 238
Brathwaite, Kamau, 24, 44, 45
Brereton, Bridget, 20, 35–36, 52–53
Brodber, Erna, 89–90
Brontë, Charlotte, *Jane Eyre*, 7, 8, 229
Butler, Judith, 100, 124–25, 128–29, 134–35. See also sexuality
Butler, Octavia, *Kindred*, 38

Cámara Betancourt, Madeline, 5, 12, 128
capitalism, 40, 115, 140–41, 148, 149, 158, 219, 227, 244
Carib. See Indigenous people
Carnival. See masquerade
cartography, 229, 237–39
Caruth, Cathy, 156, 157
castration, 5, 6, 8, 10, 22, 57, 71, 84, 176, 182. See also Freud, Sigmund
Cezair-Thompson, Margaret, *The True History of Paradise*, 147, 249
Chancy, Myriam J. A., 150, 162, 165
Christian, Barbara T., 205, 215, 216, 220, 225

277

Cliff, Michelle, 10, 11; *Abeng*, 9, 82, 90, 91, 92; as critic, 9, 10, 91; *No Telephone to Heaven*, 9, 147, 204
Collins, Merle, *Angel*, 147, 202, 260nn2–3
colonialism, 3, 4, 8, 9, 11, 17, 22, 24, 27, 29, 39, 44, 47, 89, 90, 97, 98, 100, 118, 127, 140, 204–8, 212, 225, 230–34, 238, 240, 243, 251, 252; British, 103, 110, 116–18, 120, 246; French, 164; Spanish, 164, 180
Condé, Maryse, *Moi Tituba sorcière . . . noire de Salem* (*I, Tituba, Black Witch of Salem*), 23–24, 33, 39, 74
coolitude, 104–7, 118, 120. *See also* Torabully, Khal
Creole: Créolité, 13, 106, 107; language, 67, 69, 74, 108, 217, 221; person, 7, 8, 17, 18, 111, 203, 230
Crespo-Kebler, Elizabeth, 135–36, 137, 140–41
Crossing, the, 205, 211, 213, 219, 220
Cuba, history of, 152–53

Dalleo, Raphael, 47
Danticat, Edwidge, 148; *Breath, Eyes, Memory*, 10–11, 148, 163, 208; *The Farming of Bones*, 19, 148–59, 161–78
Dash, Michael, 10, 23, 25
daughter: mother-daughter duo, 3, 4, 7, 10, 13–17, 22, 24, 28, 33, 41–45, 54–58, 62, 66, 76, 80–82, 90, 99, 100, 101, 117, 131, 148, 149, 156, 158, 179, 180–82, 184, 187, 195, 196, 251; within Oedipus Complex, 5–7, 11, 19, 22, 27, 55, 90, 100, 103, 130, 132, 158, 182, 183, 195, 217, 231; return of, 3, 6, 10, 11, 22, 201, 235, 236, 248, 249, 251, 252, 254, 261n3. *See also* Freud, Sigmund: Oedipus Complex; herstory; voice
decolonization, 3, 15, 17, 91, 92, 97, 99, 100, 105, 115, 211, 231, 261n3
Desquiron, Lilas, *Les chemins de Loco-Miroir* (*Reflections of Loko Miwa*), 176
diaspora, 34, 91, 150, 195–96, 200, 205, 227; writing from, 15–16
dictatorship, 148, 149, 150, 153, 158, 161, 163, 171, 184, 190
Dominica, history of, 202–4
Donahue, Jennifer, 158

dreams, 24, 150, 156, 168, 177, 178, 207, 212, 213, 215–19, 222, 223, 226, 244

Edgell, Zee: *Beka Lamb*, 90, 91; *Time and the River*, 21, 33
editor, 38, 65, 66, 68–72, 74, 83, 86
Edwards, Whitney Bly, 4, 13
empire, 15, 35, 36, 79, 83, 95, 206
Espinet, Ramabai, 104; *The Swinging Bridge*, 204
exile, 9, 11–13, 15, 24, 28, 51, 55, 59, 100, 122, 126, 141, 142, 149, 157, 165, 181, 192–94, 204, 232–34, 257n6, 260n1

Fanon, Frantz, 10, 57, 84, 95
fantastical elements, 16, 38, 66, 75, 80
father/Father: absent, 44, 55; Black, 10, 57, 58, 84, 257n4; in family, 5–7, 10–13, 19, 28, 46, 55–58, 71, 96, 133, 136–39, 149, 167, 171, 179, 181, 184, 186, 188, 189–93, 241; law of/name of/symbolic, 5–7, 10, 12, 19, 27, 55–58, 71, 72, 84, 99, 117, 169, 179, 181, 182, 184–86, 192, 193, 216, 231, 241, 245, 257n3 (*see also* Fanon, Frantz; Freud, Sigmund); master/white, 48, 55–58, 66, 71, 84, 85. *See also* castration; patria
Fatherland. *See* patria
feminism, 3, 4, 20, 61, 101, 104, 106, 124, 139, 140, 157, 234
Ferly, Odile, 45, 47
Fernández Olmos, Margarite, 176, 201
Ferré, Rosario, 123
folklore. *See* oral tradition; *soucouyant*
Francis, Donette, 14, 15, 16, 17, 20, 251, 257n4, 258n9
Freud, Sigmund: feminist criticism of (*see* Butler, Judith; Gilbert, Sandra M.; Irigaray, Luce; Kristeva, Julia); hysteria, 29, 59, 231, 234 (*see also* madness); incest, 134, 157, 183 (*see also* incest); melancholia (and mourning), 11, 58; Oedipus Complex, 5–7, 11, 12, 19, 22, 27, 55, 90, 100, 103, 130, 132, 134, 158, 182, 183, 195, 217, 218, 231 (*see also* castration); pleasure principle, 131–32, 156 (*see also* dreams; uncanny); postcolonial criticism of (*see* Khanna, Ranjana); taboo, 28, 131, 134,

157, 183–84 (*see also under* sexuality). *See also* ambivalence

García, Cristina, *Dreaming in Cuban*, 147, 148, 179, 181, 195
gender. *See* sexuality and gender
ghosts. *See* haunting
Gikandi, Simon, 16, 17, 30, 89, 97
Gilbert, Sandra M., 5, 7–9, 11, 12, 25, 59
Gilroy, Beryl, 104, 261n3
Glissant, Édouard, 4, 13, 21, 22, 44–46, 50, 51, 55, 238, 257n8, 258n2. *See also* nonhistory; root theory
globalization, 9, 15, 53, 97, 206, 223
grandmother, 10, 27, 59, 60, 91–92, 110, 117–19, 128, 154, 169, 172, 190, 192, 204–7, 219, 220, 230, 233, 236, 241, 248
Grenada, history of, 201–2
Guyana, history of, 92–94

Haigh, Samantha, 25, 206
Haiti, history of, 150–52
Hall, Stuart, 10, 11
Halloran, Vivian Nun, 4, 15, 16, 38, 42, 67, 257n6
Harford Vargas, Jennifer, 14, 15, 17, 149, 152, 158, 162
haunting, 11, 21, 34, 40, 41, 43, 50, 59, 60, 90, 157, 161, 166, 175, 176, 218, 219, 254
Hayes, Jarrod, 44–45
Henderson, Joseph L., 212, 215, 217–18
Henderson, Mae G., 38, 41, 66, 69–70
Herrera, Christina, 24
herstory, 3, 19, 21, 148, 149, 158, 179, 180, 187, 190, 195, 253
Hirsch, Marianne, 19, 41, 182, 184–85, 194, 231
historical novel: definition/purpose of, 3, 7, 13, 14–25, 29–30, 33, 34, 39, 42, 68, 97, 98, 110, 155, 157, 166, 199, 204, 205, 208, 211, 220, 251, 254, 255, 257n7, 259n2; early Caribbean, 8, 12, 14, 16, 17–20, 33, 43, 89, 104, 147, 148, 230, 254, 257n8; feminist scholarship on, 12, 14, 18, 19, 38, 98, 158, 257n7 (*see also* Francis, Donette; Halloran, Vivian Nun; Harford Vargas, Jennifer; King, Rosamund S.; Machado Sáez, Elena; Mehta, Brinda; Rody,

Caroline; Wallace, Diana); postmodern, 15, 38, 39, 42, 74, 97; traditional genre scholarship, 14, 16, 18, 66–68, 72, 154, 158, 199, 257n6, 257n7, 258n12 (*see also* Lukács, Georg). *See also* neo-slavery novel
Hodge, Merle, *Crick Crack, Monkey*, 14, 19, 20, 52, 89, 92
home, 8, 11, 12, 15, 16, 29, 52, 78, 90, 94, 108, 122, 125, 127, 138, 140, 154, 165, 174, 182, 206; as homecoming, 29, 57, 200, 201, 207, 223, 224, 253; as homeland, 12, 22, 50, 85, 149, 165, 204; as homesickness, 29, 199, 206. *See also* uncanny
Honychurch, Lennox, 202–4, 237, 242, 248
hysteria. *See hystérie*; madness
hystérie, 29, 207, 229–32, 242, 247, 249

imperialism, 15, 17, 29, 93, 122, 154, 212, 217, 219, 221, 225, 226, 243, 251, 254
imprisonment, 8, 9, 23, 59, 85, 112–13, 121, 149, 190, 230, 235
incest, 57, 134, 157, 179, 180, 182, 183, 186, 189, 192, 193, 253. *See also* Freud, Sigmund
indentured servitude, 11, 15, 92, 93–94, 100, 101, 105–7, 110, 118, 153
Indigenous people, 11, 35, 152, 162, 183, 201, 203, 239–40; Amerindian, 35; Arawak, 201; Carib, 201, 203, 239, 240, 244, 246, 249; Kalinago, 203
Indo-Caribbean: identity, 21, 91–92, 93–94, 97, 105, 107, 108, 114, 118, 120, 121; intersecting with Chinese heritage, 28, 91–94, 100, 101, 103–5, 106, 109, 111, 113–22, 252; women's writing, 89, 93, 104. *See also* Mehta, Brinda; religion: Hinduism
Irigaray, Luce, 4, 6, 9, 11, 13–14, 100, 180, 182–84, 185, 186, 187, 192, 193, 194, 232, 238

Jamaica, history of, 35–37
John, Marie-Elena, 200; *Unburnable*, 19, 29, 199–209, 229–49
Johnson, Kelli Lyon, 4, 5, 12, 152, 162–64, 177, 178
Jonte-Pace, Diane, 166, 167, 176, 177, 178
Josephs, Kelly Baker, 231

Kempadoo, Oonya, 104; *Buxton Spice*, 147, 259n2
Khanna, Ranjana, 3–4, 11, 23
Kincaid, Jamaica: *Annie John*, 10, 91, 92; *The Autobiography of My Mother*, 24
King, Rosamund S., 15, 17, 20, 90, 99, 126, 129
Kristeva, Julia, 4, 5–6, 13, 20, 21, 22, 59, 60–61, 258n10 (intro.), 258n5 (chap. 1)

la gran familia, 96, 123–26, 128, 129, 138, 259n2
language: English, 3, 12–13, 69, 72, 74, 85, 96, 97, 98, 108, 109, 120, 126, 195, 217, 258n12, 259n3; and identity, 12, 96, 139, 142, 195, 213, 252; masculine/of Father, 6, 9, 12, 17, 71, 72, 78, 85, 180; maternal, 12–13, 97, 132, 213, 235, 238, 249 (*see also* mother-tongue). *See also under* Creole
Levy, Andrea, 34; *Fruit of the Lemon*, 204, 208; *The Long Song*, 34–42, 65–86, 244; *Small Island*, 34
Lima, Maria Helena, 67–68, 73, 153, 154, 155, 158, 260n2
Lionnet, Francoise, 96–97
Llanos-Figueroa, Dahlma, *Daughters of the Stone*, 24, 33, 42
Lugo-Lugo, Carmen R., 95, 96, 124, 125, 126, 127, 132, 134
Lukács, Georg, 16, 18, 259n2

Machado Sáez, Elena, 14, 15, 16–17, 148–49, 150, 206, 251, 257n6, 258n9
madness, 8, 29, 100, 207, 229–35, 236, 242, 245, 249; linked to the moon, 61. *See also* Freud, Sigmund: hysteria; *hystérie*
maps. *See* cartography
marasa. *See* twins
maroons, 23, 34, 36, 37, 46, 47, 48, 54, 55, 80, 201, 203–5, 223, 230, 236, 237, 239, 248
marronage. *See* maroons
Marshall, Paule, 199; *Brown Girl, Brownstones*, 200; *The Chosen Place, the Timeless People*, 200; *Praisesong for the Widow*, 19, 199–209, 211–27
masquerade (Carnival), 208, 223, 242–47
(M)aster discourses, critique of, 12, 16, 30, 33, 39, 46, 50, 51, 61, 72, 75, 81, 154, 180, 238, 252

maternal: broken/lost, 7, 11, 85, 122, 142, 157, 195, 206, 220, 233, 234, 235, 236, 254 (*see also* Freud, Sigmund: Oedipus Complex); family tree, 39, 44, 45–47, 52, 56, 58, 59, 63, 258n1 (*see also* root theory); figures, 23, 24, 37, 50, 54, 58, 59, 80, 82, 104, 137, 176, 200, 216, 253, 254; genealogy, 23, 26, 29, 38, 42, 43, 44, 49, 51, 54, 56, 58, 59, 63, 70, 76, 78, 81, 85, 92, 122, 133, 142, 150, 181, 185, 205, 206, 217, 219, 225, 226, 232, 241, 248, 251, 254 (*see also* root theory); as healing, 50, 91, 100, 118, 158, 162, 206 (*see also* grandmother); history/past, 6, 9, 12–15, 19, 23–25, 26, 29, 30, 41, 45, 53, 59, 61, 66, 67, 70, 72, 76, 78, 89, 97, 98, 106, 107, 117, 149, 163, 199, 200, 218, 220, 248, 249, 251, 252, 254, 255; link to water, 23, 24, 25, 158, 162, 164, 166, 174, 178, 238, 249, 253; memory, 7, 12, 23, 60, 62, 63, 76, 78, 166, 189, 204, 208, 215; nonhistory, 23, 46, 49, 50, 59, 61, 63 (*see also* Glissant, Édouard); repressed, 4, 7, 8, 9, 12, 21, 23, 59, 82, 105, 118, 178, 208, 213, 226, 234, 254; spirituality, 204, 205, 218, 220, 226, 253; subjectivity, 19, 42; time, 21–22, 24, 45, 49, 51, 59, 61–63, 220, 249, 253 (*see also* Kristeva, Julia); voice, 39, 62, 66, 72, 75, 76, 81, 86, 173, 194, 195, 204 (*see also* voice). *See also* home; language; matria; mother
matria: definition/purpose of, 3–14, 15, 20, 22–30, 33, 40, 42, 44–51, 52–58, 59–63, 65–69, 72–76, 78, 80, 82, 85–86, 90–92, 94–96, 100, 101, 104–7, 113–16, 118–20, 122–28, 130, 134, 136, 139–43, 147–49, 154, 157–59, 162–66, 174–75, 178, 180–81, 185–88, 194–96, 199–201, 204, 206, 208–211, 215–16, 219–20, 226–31, 234, 236–39, 248–49, 251–55; literary criticism on, 5–14 (*see also* Barrett Browning, Elizabeth; Benstock, Shari; Cámara Betancourt, Madeline; Gilbert, Sandra M.; Johnson, Kelli Lyon). *See also* maternal; mother
matricide. *See* mother: death of
matrifocal, 84, 205, 261n1. *See also* motherhood: scholarship on
matrilineage. *See* maternal: genealogy

INDEX

matrix/*matriz*, 7, 128–29, 130, 132, 135, 143, 187. *See also* womb

Mehta, Brinda, 4, 14, 15, 93, 104, 105–8, 111, 113, 114, 116, 119, 122

melancholia. *See under* Freud, Sigmund

memory, 11, 14, 20, 22–23, 25, 49, 51, 54, 60, 61, 67, 68, 70, 76, 77, 78, 82, 83, 85, 92, 120, 126, 150, 159, 161–62, 164, 177, 195, 199, 200, 207, 214, 215, 227, 231, 253. *See also under* maternal

Middle Eastern heritage and identity, 240

midwifery, 166, 168, 171, 178, 225

migration, 9, 24, 34, 44, 46, 53, 92–100, 125, 126, 142, 165, 200, 206, 211, 219, 231, 253

mimicry, 10, 99, 117, 154, 184, 193. *See also* Bhabha, Homi

Misrahi-Barak, Judith, 93, 105, 117, 119–20, 122, 165, 172, 176

Mohammed, Patricia, 4, 20

Momsen, Janet, 94, 205

Mootoo, Shani, 104

Moreno, Marisel, 15, 95, 96, 123, 126, 259n2 (chap. 4)

Morrison, Toni, 68; *Beloved*, 38; *Tar Baby*, 222

mother: ambivalent, 24, 98–99, 117, 130, 221–22; Black, 10, 46, 47, 50, 57, 62, 69, 77, 78, 81, 84, 95 (*see also* Praeger, Michèle; Fanon, Frantz); death of, 7, 13, 23, 24, 36, 39, 41–42, 47, 62, 75, 82, 117, 137, 167, 169, 176–78, 182, 186, 191, 203, 206, 216, 230, 235, 245; as deity, 52, 162, 178, 220; identity of, 24; mother-in-law, 182–85, 188, 233, 241, 243–46, 248; mythologizing of, 37, 38, 41, 42, 44, 47, 48, 54, 60, 80, 251–52; pre-Oedipal, 6, 7, 11, 12, 22, 158, 195, 196, 218, 235; rejection of, 90, 92, 94, 97, 99–101, 113, 115, 118, 124, 126, 130, 139, 142, 252; repositioning of, 5, 9, 10, 22, 24, 27, 33, 39, 40–42, 43, 44, 45, 47, 50, 63, 82, 85, 86, 105, 106, 114, 119, 120, 128, 251, 254; search for, 6, 11, 12, 41, 42, 60, 85, 162, 168, 190, 200, 258n11; as survivor, 49, 148, 154, 156, 166, 192, 254. *See also* castration; Freud, Sigmund: Oedipus Complex; maternal; slavery: impact on family

mother country. *See* mother-land

motherhood: male instruction in and desire for, 100, 132–33, 137–38, 163, 182, 184, 188, 192; scholarship on, 24, 205, 261n1. *See also* mother

mother-land, 7–13, 19, 23, 25, 27, 28, 42, 52, 61, 85–100, 108, 119, 126, 127, 128, 137, 142, 143, 150, 204, 206, 208, 216, 225, 249

mother-tongue, 12, 13, 27, 69, 89, 97, 98, 99, 126, 142, 143, 252. *See also* language

Muñoz-Valdivieso, Sofía, 4, 37, 65, 68, 82–83

myth. *See* oral tradition

Naipaul, V. S., 16, 49, 89

nation: colonial mother country, 19, 28, 79, 91–95, 99–101, 103–4, 120, 126, 132, 134, 200, 261n3 (*see also* assimilation); female body as symbol of, 9, 10, 19, 84, 85, 90, 92, 124–36, 154, 162–63, 169–76, 186, 226, 252 (*see also* mother-land); identity, 27, 95, 124, 125, 128, 134, 136, 141, 150, 152, 156, 164, 165, 203; independence, 15, 16, 28, 37, 90–95, 98, 101, 103, 110, 120–29, 149, 150–53, 164, 202, 204, 223, 252, 259n1; national consciousness, 16, 27; national myth, 96, 124, 126; nationalist, 17, 98, 126, 127, 129, 135, 149, 158, 162, 163, 164, 170, 178, 253, 254 (*see also* dictatorship)

neo-slavery novel, 23, 26–27, 33, 34, 35, 37–38, 40–42, 55, 65–74, 83, 97, 202, 206, 208, 251, 258n1; compared with slave narratives, 38, 66–71, 72, 74, 76, 85

nonhistory, 3, 13, 22, 23, 44–68, 253. *See also* Glissant, Édouard

Obeah, 207, 237, 239–40, 247

Oedipus Complex. *See under* Freud, Sigmund

oral tradition, 19, 29, 62–74, 120, 199, 201, 206–9, 217, 221, 222, 231, 233–36, 248, 249, 253; chanté mas, 206, 208, 248, 249; song, in relation to mother, 44, 53, 62, 72, 85; song, in relation to slavery, 48, 52, 53, 62, 63, 83, 85–86, 213, 214, 215, 217, 225, 236. *See also* ritual; *soucouyant*; *testimonio*; voice

O'Reilly Herrera, Andrea, 148; as critic, 180, 189; *The Pearl of the Antilles*, 19, 148–59,

179–96; *ReMembering Cuba: Legacy of a Diaspora*, 148

Ortiz Cofer, Judith, 91; *The Meaning of Consuelo*, 89–101, 123–43

Papa Legba, 200, 222–24. *See also* Vodou

Paravisini-Gebert, Lizabeth, 4, 12–13, 176, 201

patria, 5, 7, 9, 12, 59, 149, 172, 175, 187, 204, 258n4

plantation/plantocracy, 8, 18, 28, 34–39, 46–53, 62, 65, 73–84, 93, 94, 101, 103, 108–15, 121, 122, 131, 150, 164, 167, 202, 203, 213, 214, 222, 226, 230, 238

postcolonialism, 13, 16, 41, 98, 104, 156–57, 164, 229, 237 (*see also* Bhabha, Homi; Gikandi, Simon); feminist theory, 3, 4, 6, 7–8, 9, 12, 13, 14, 17, 19, 27–29, 37, 39, 49, 55, 66, 92, 98, 101, 104, 106, 107, 120, 143, 148–49, 157, 159, 204–5, 208, 227, 231, 238, 254–55 (*see also* Bragard, Véronique; Cliff, Michelle: as critic; coolitude; *hystérie*; Mehta, Brinda; Machado Sáez, Elena); literature, 8, 9, 10, 13, 14, 16, 17, 21, 25, 29, 33, 37, 68, 72, 73, 78, 91, 96, 104, 107, 110, 122, 147, 149, 153–55, 161, 201, 209, 229–31, 234, 239, 251, 252; in relation to politics, 15, 16, 17, 20, 59, 93, 116, 118, 124, 150, 204, 205, 225. *See also* matria

Praeger, Michèle, 10, 38, 57, 84, 251

psychoanalysis. *See* Edwards, Whitney Bly; Fanon, Frantz; Freud, Sigmund; Irigaray, Luce; Kristeva, Julia; Praeger, Michèle

Puerto Rico, history of, 95–96. *See also la gran familia*

Quayle, Ada, *The Mistress*, 17–18, 20, 111, 261n2

rape, 38, 40, 55, 56, 66, 73, 74–76, 81–82, 149, 188, 233, 244, 247, 261n2

redux, 25, 39. *See also* daughter: return

religion: African cosmologies and African-derived, 29, 52, 199–201, 202, 204, 205, 209, 211–15, 218–27, 234, 237, 248 (*see also* Alexander, M. Jacqui; Fernández Olmos, Margarite; Obeah; Paravisini-Gebert, Lizabeth; Vodou); Christianity, 35, 52–54, 108, 114, 129–30, 199, 220, 221, 237, 239, 240, 243, 245, 246, 247; Hinduism, 21, 91, 109, 120, 122, 253

revolution, 3, 9, 15, 17, 26, 28, 29, 147–49, 153–55, 159, 178, 190, 201, 232, 251, 252; Communist, 28, 147–49, 158, 190, 193, 259n2; Cuban, 28, 148, 149, 150, 153, 155, 179–81, 189, 190, 192, 193, 253; Grenada, 202, 223, 260n3; Haitian, 53, 147, 150, 202, 257n4

rhizome. *See* root theory

Rhys, Jean, 20, 111, 230; *Wide Sargasso Sea*, 8, 9, 14, 19, 65, 229–30

ritual, 3, 29, 53, 107, 118, 174, 200, 201, 205, 208, 209, 211, 213, 214, 215–17, 219, 221, 223–27, 248. *See also* Freud, Sigmund: ritual; oral tradition

Rody, Caroline, 11, 14–15, 20, 21, 22, 42, 46, 47, 50, 51, 62, 79, 85, 89, 92, 98, 200, 206, 222; on Jean Rhys, 14, 229–30

root theory, 27, 44, 51, 55, 252; arbolic/single root, 27, 44, 45, 47, 50, 54, 55, 61, 63, 186; kinship, 39, 44, 45, 54–55, 150, 236, 259n2; rhizomatic, 23, 27, 39, 44–47, 50, 51, 53, 54, 55, 61, 63, 239, 247, 251. *See also* Glissant, Édouard; maternal: family tree

sacred. *See* religion

Sanmartín, Paula, 24

Santiago, Esmeralda, 123, 258n1

Savory Fido, Elaine, 4, 17

Schwarz-Bart, Simone, *Pluie et vent sur Télumée Miracle* (*The Bridge of Beyond*), 14, 33, 39, 43, 258n1

sexuality and gender, 15, 21, 33, 69, 101, 107, 123–43, 188; agency, 48, 95, 126, 129, 130, 207, 229; autonomy, 16, 93, 94, 95, 122, 128, 149; blindspot, 4, 10, 13, 176, 234; consciousness, 28, 49, 103, 125, 128; equality, 19, 57, 101, 107; homosexuality, 99, 125, 128, 134–36, 140; intersecting with race, 10, 21, 34, 69–71, 73, 93, 103, 112, 114, 176, 221, 233, 238; norms, 92, 96, 99–100, 123, 125, 128, 129, 130, 134–35, 163, 243, 245–47, 252; queer, 124, 126–27, 132; taboos and transgression, 90, 99, 124–25, 127, 129–31, 134–37, 182, 241–44, 252; transgender, 99,

124, 130, 136, 140; virginity, 54, 99, 129–30, 136, 139, 155, 191, 192, 193, 243, 261n2. *See also* Butler, Judith; feminism; Freud, Sigmund; incest; matrix/*matriz*; rape

Shah, Ryhaan, 98, 104; *A Silent Life*, 21

Shemak, April, 4, 162, 169, 170, 171, 172, 174, 175

Shinebourne, Jan Lowe, 91; *The Last English Plantation*, 89–101, 103–22; *Timepiece*, 89, 91, 94, 103

slavery: abolishment, 37, 50, 53, 66, 70, 80, 82, 93, 150–52, 203; criticism of Master narrative (counternarrative), 19, 26–27, 34, 37, 38, 39, 41, 48, 65, 68, 72, 80, 92, 125, 173, 221, 251, 257n3; historical male hero of, 15, 17, 38; history of, 35–37, 93, 105, 150–53, 202–3, 214, 236; impact on family, 24, 27, 38–42, 47, 50, 51, 53, 54–59, 62, 63, 65, 67, 69, 71, 73, 77, 81, 84, 85, 90, 97, 165, 172, 204, 215–16, 225, 227, 231, 234, 247, 254 (*see also* mother: death of; root theory: kinship); Middle Passage, 200, 219, 220, 224, 227; postemancipation (postslavery), 27, 35, 37, 69, 84, 85, 203, 221; in relation to matria, 8; resistance to, 36–37, 48, 49, 50, 52–54, 58, 60, 70, 79, 81, 82, 201–2, 204, 206, 215, 222; women as slaveowners, 8, 51–53, 62, 77, 79, 84, 85, 258n1. *See also* neo-slavery novel; oral tradition: song, in relation to slavery

Smith, Barbara Fletchman, 40, 55, 56, 57, 59

Smith Silva, Dorsía, 24

Socolovsky, Maya, 100, 124, 125–26, 136, 140, 142

soucouyant, 201, 230, 248–49, 253

Sourieau, Marie-Agnès, 176

Spillers, Hortense J., 53, 55–56, 58

spirituality. *See* religion

storytelling. *See* oral tradition

suicide, 8, 29, 34, 48, 51, 62, 79, 207, 220, 229, 230, 235, 237, 253, 254

testimonio, 154, 162

Torabully, Khal, 105–6. *See also* coolitude

trauma, 3, 27, 28, 42, 63, 67, 83, 90, 106, 148, 150, 156–58, 162, 166, 168, 176, 178, 208, 216, 219, 222, 224, 227, 231, 233, 235, 236, 238, 253, 254. *See also* Caruth, Cathy; zombification

Trinidad, history of, 35–36

twins, 154, 168, 170, 171, 173–74, 176, 191, 242; *marasa*, 174, 176

uncanny (unhomely), 28, 157, 164–66, 176–78

Vieux-Chauvet, Marie, 14, 161; *La Danse sur la volcan* (*Dance on the Volcano*), 14, 29, 147, 254, 258n12, 260n1 (chap. 5)

Vint, Sherryl, 37, 59, 67, 71, 74, 208

Vodou, 52, 54, 162, 174, 200, 223. *See also* Papa Legba; twins: *marasa*

voice: countervoice, 45, 76, 119, 159; disorganized speech (pre-Oedipal), 12, 131, 132, 137, 141, 142, 158, 235; double-voiced, 18, 187; polyphonic, 18, 19, 39, 69, 83, 148, 154, 158, 181, 252; restoring speech, 24, 27, 30, 76, 78, 82, 104, 158, 232, 233; silencing of mother, 6, 9, 10, 11, 24, 41, 62, 69, 71–72, 75–76, 78, 80, 81, 99, 108, 121, 155, 163, 184, 221, 232, 234, 249; ventriloquy, 19, 98, 109, 133, 184; voicelessness, 17–18, 71, 234. *See also* Freud, Sigmund: hysteria; madness; maternal: voice; mimicry; mothertongue; oral tradition

Wallace, Diana, 16, 257n7

womb, 7, 21, 130, 142, 158, 162, 166, 168, 171, 174, 177, 178, 185, 187, 190–92, 194, 207, 229, 231, 235, 244, 245, 255. See also *hystérie*; matrix/*matriz*

Wynter, Sylvia, 14, 18, 22; *The Hills of Hebron*, 14, 19, 29, 254

zombification, 176–77

ABOUT THE AUTHOR

Photo by Declan Bird

Dr. Tegan Zimmerman specializes in Caribbean women's writing, with a focus on historical fiction, the maternal, and sexual politics. Her teaching and research interests include Caribbean and postcolonial literature, Canadian literature, and women's and gender studies/feminist theory. Her work has appeared in journals such as *Feminist Theory*, *MELUS*, *Women's Studies: An Inter-Disciplinary Journal*, and the *Journal of Romance Studies*.

www.ingramcontent.com/pod-product-compliance
Lightning Source LLC
Chambersburg PA
CBHW030611230426
43661CB00053B/1932